SPONGES (Plates 10, 11)
porous
encrusting or erect

rubbery-leathery crusts, lumps
tiny zooids in clusters
COMPOUND
ASCIDIANS
(Plate 10)

tiny zooids
with tentacles

lacy, hard
crusts and lumps

CORALS

stony
cups

ENCRUSTING
BRYOZOANS
(Plate 16)

2 siphons

SEA
SQUIRTS
(Plate 17)

(both
Plate 17)

SESSILE
JELLYFISH

GOOSE
BARNACLES

BUSHY
BRYOZOANS
(Plate 15)

tiny zooids
with tentacles

HYDROIDS
(Plates 13, 14)

ACORN
BARNACLES
(Plate 18)

SESSILE ANIMALS
(attached to substratum)

soft
solitary

tiny,
contractile zooids
with 8 tentacles;
OCTOCORALS
(Plates 10, 11)

colonies tough,
leathery

contracted

SEA ANEMONES
(Plate 12)

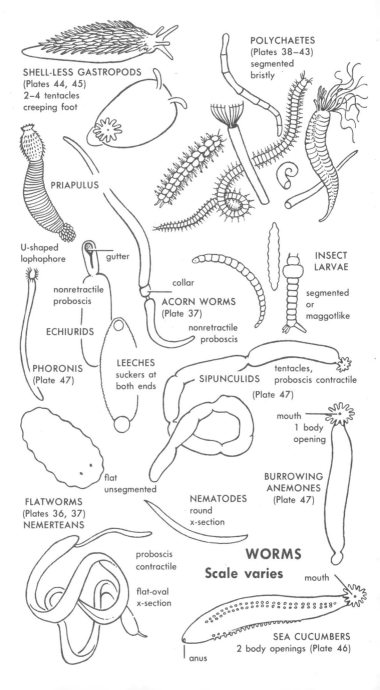

SHELL-LESS GASTROPODS
(Plates 44, 45)
2-4 tentacles
creeping foot

POLYCHAETES
(Plates 38-43)
segmented
bristly

PRIAPULUS

U-shaped
lophophore

gutter

nonretractile
proboscis

collar

ACORN WORMS
(Plate 37)

INSECT
LARVAE

segmented
or
maggotlike

ECHIURIDS

nonretractile
proboscis

PHORONIS
(Plate 47)

LEECHES
suckers at
both ends

SIPUNCULIDS
(Plate 47)

tentacles,
proboscis contractile

mouth
1 body
opening

FLATWORMS
(Plates 36, 37)
NEMERTEANS

flat
unsegmented

NEMATODES
round
x-section

BURROWING
ANEMONES
(Plate 47)

proboscis
contractile

flat-oval
x-section

WORMS
Scale varies

mouth

SEA CUCUMBERS
2 body openings (Plate 46)

anus

A FIELD GUIDE
to the ATLANTIC
SEASHORE

THE PETERSON FIELD GUIDE SERIES

A Field Guide to the

Atlantic Seashore

from the Bay of Fundy to Cape Hatteras

Kenneth L. Gosner

Illustrations by
Kenneth L. Gosner

*Sponsored by the National Audubon Society,
the National Wildlife Federation,
and the Roger Tory Peterson Institute*

HOUGHTON MIFFLIN COMPANY · BOSTON

Library of Congress Cataloging-in-Publication Data

Gosner, Kenneth L., 1925–
A field guide to atlantic seashore.

(The Peterson field guide series; 24)
Bibliography: p.
Includes index.
1. Seashore biology.   2. Marine invertebrates–
Identification.   3. Coastal flora–Identification.
I. Title.
QH95.7.067   1979   574.909'4'6   78-14784
ISBN 0-395-24379-3 (hardbound)
ISBN 0-395-31828-9 (paperbound)

Printed in the United States of America

VB   17   16   15   14   13   12   11   10   9   8

For my father and mother,
who encouraged
independence and curiosity.

Editor's Note

THE BEACHCOMBER tends to be a generalist. If he is ornithologically inclined — a 'birder' — he spots the sandpipers, gulls, and terns and consults his *Field Guide to the Birds*. Those few flowers that invade the dunes or the salt marshes above the line of sea wrack, he will find in *A Field Guide to the Wildflowers*. However, that leaves a great gap — the seaweeds and the many forms of invertebrate life that live along the edge of the sea in wading or snorkeling depths, and also some of the denizens of deeper waters that are often cast ashore by the waves. There is, of course, *A Field Guide to the Shells* by Percy Morris, but aside from a partial overlap in the *Mollusca,* the present *Field Guide* by Kenneth Gosner fills the void, describing and illustrating not only the seaweeds but also 19 major groups or phyla of invertebrates, some of which — sea anemones, sand dollars, crabs, and barnacles — are rather familiar, and others — bryozoans, amphipods, tunicates, medusae, and comb jellies — which are not.

The "Peterson Identification System," which emphasizes distinctions between similar species, pointing to critical 'field marks' or recognition characteristics with little arrows, was developed originally in the bird guides and was later extended to cover the whole spectrum of natural history. It is a visual rather than phylogenetic approach wherein similar but unrelated forms may often be shown on the same plate for ready comparison. This technique is here applied to the identification of intertidal life.

Although this guide is designed primarily to cover the area from the Bay of Fundy in Maritime Canada to Cape Hatteras in North Carolina, many of the forms described — or their counterparts — will be found southward to the West Indies while others may range northward to the Arctic.

Kenneth Gosner is one of those rare biologists who is equally skilled as an artist. In fact, biological illustrators competent to handle certain subjects are even harder to come by than academic specialists in the same field. During my many visits to the editorial offices at Houghton Mifflin to monitor the progress of this and other field guides, I have marvelled at the color plates that Kenneth Gosner submitted. There is no room for "happy accident" in this kind of illustration. It must be highly controlled, and because of the evanescent nature of color and form of some of the marine animals when out of the water it becomes almost an act of legerdemain to translate them to paper.

A good drawing is usually more helpful in identification than a photograph. The latter is a record of a single moment, subject to the vagaries of chance, angle, light, and the limitations of latitude in color film. On the other hand, a drawing is a composite of the artist's past experience, in which he can emphasize the important and edit out the irrelevant if he chooses.

The illustrations and text in this *Field Guide* which depict and describe the incredible variety of treasures to be found in the tide pools and intertidal flats have demanded a staggering amount of field work on the part of Kenneth Gosner. But do not be an armchair marine biologist and be satisfied with merely thumbing through the plates, attractive as they are. Take the book with you to the shore and use it. And do not confine your seaside sorties to the summer beach; there are things to be found at all seasons.

There has been a breakthrough in environmental awareness in recent years. When the first astronaut put his foot on the moon, millions of people became suddenly aware of the uniqueness and isolation of our planet Earth, the only world we will ever have. Ours is a fragile world, whose seas are suffering ecological attrition on a global scale.

The problems of survival of whales, porpoises, and seals are easily dramatized and a number of new conservation organizations have arisen to publicize their plight. But the lesser organisms of the tide pools and the shore are no less important in an evolutionary sense, and they are no less vulnerable. They send out signals when the sea is abused by pollution, exploitation, or some other form of neglect. Inevitably the beachcombing naturalist becomes a monitor of the marine environment.

ROGER TORY PETERSON

Acknowledgments

THIS BOOK is to some degree the product of other people's efforts. My debt begins with the generations of naturalists who have studied and written about the plants and animals of this coast. The zoological part of this literature is cited in some detail in my *Guide to Identification of Marine and Estuarine Invertebrates* published in 1971. I began work on the present book almost immediately afterward, and the earlier volume served as a technical base for this one; therefore the 80-odd specialists who read parts of that book in manuscript, and are acknowledged therein, should be thanked again. More directly I am grateful to the following for critical comments on parts of this guide: the entire botanical section was examined by John M. Kingsbury, Arthur C. Mathieson, Jonathan E. Taylor, Jacques S. Zaneveld, and Robert L. Vadas; the nudibranch parts were read by Larry G. Rivest, Terrance Harris, Alan M. Kuzirian, and Brian R. Rivest, and the echinoderm section by John H. Dearborn. Ann Frame not only strove valiantly with the polychaete material but loaned most of the specimens used in making the drawings of those worms. While these readers have materially improved the guide, they are in no way responsible for the errors I have managed to insert despite their efforts.

For additional loans of specimens I want to thank Henry Roberts and Mike Carpenter (U.S. National Museum), Robert Robertson (The Academy of Natural Sciences, Philadelphia), Rosalie M. Vogel (Virginia Institute of Marine Science), Jerry Thurman, William Old, William K. Emerson, and, especially, Harold Feinberg (The American Museum of Natural History). Clark T. Rogerson gave me free access to herbarium materials at The New York Botanical Garden.

Requests for information on systematics, distribution, and other matters were generously responded to by Frederick M. Bayer, E. L. Bousfield, Louise Bush, Maureen E. Downey, Clay Gifford, Don Kunkle, Robert E. Knowlton, Frank Maturo, Byron Morris, Patrick Purcell, John B. Pearce and colleagues, Kenneth R. H. Read, Emery F. Swan, Lowell P. Thomas, Henry Tyler, Pierre Trudel, Dana E. Wallace, Marvin L. Wass, Austin Williams, David L. Pawson, and Harold H. Plough.

I owe a special debt to the commercial fishermen of the Atlantic and Gulf coasts who have taken me to sea with them, given me the pleasure of their company, sometimes fed me, and allowed me to pick over their vastly miscellaneous catches. Without this privilege I would never have seen many of the invertebrate inhabitants of this coast in other than a wizened, pickled state. Specifically I want to thank Bert Maxon, the Schnoor brothers, Norman Sickles (Jr. and Sr.), Barry Irwin, George Boyce, Jack Slater, Richard Robbins, Howard Bogan, and others whose names I have lost or never knew at Belford, Shark River, and Point Pleasant, New Jersey; Thomas Lou Hallock, Eldon Willing, Eugene Wheatley, and Alfred Biddlecomb of Virginia and Maryland; Caroll Willis and others at Beaufort and Atlantic, North Carolina; Gabe, Andrew, Charlie, and Mike Gargano of Long Island Sound; Alexander Lindall and additional hardy seamen at Cundy's Harbor, Maine; Morrison (Captain Motto) Gisclair and other shrimpers at Golden Meadow and Grand Isle, Louisiana. I am also grateful to the following for putting me in touch with some of the above men or in other ways aiding my field work: Tan Estay, W. Herke, David W. Frame, Robert B. Chapoton, C. M. Cubbage, Harold Haskins, Fred Hersom, as well as Roy Rafter of the Maryland Tidewater Police. The officers and crews of the Coast Guard buoy tenders "Arbutus," "Red Beach," and "Firebush" made me welcome on their vessels, and I thank them.

In a very different way the librarians of the American Museum of Natural History, and especially Mildred Bobrovich, have been enormously helpful in aiding me to make full use of that magnificent collection of books and periodicals.

My own personal librarian and wife, Pamela, has sustained a long and frequently grueling schedule of homework and has been the best of field companions on innumerable trips up and down the coast in the "Libbie H. Hyman." We both wish to thank, with much affection, the friends who have fed and sheltered us on some of these excursions: Marian and Sam Halperin, Bibbo and Burt Whitman, Petey and Ken Spoor, Nancy and Kent Mountford, John and Anna Deming, Susan Ford, Don Kunkle, and, also, Woody Hartman, who allowed us to "crash at his pad" in Crystal River, Florida. We are grateful to Charles Huntington for visits to Kent Island, New Brunswick, and Tan Estay made my stay on Bayou La Fourche both professionally rewarding and an exceeding pleasure.

Most of the manuscript was typed by Dorothy Witte. And finally my thanks are due to several members of the staff of Houghton Mifflin Company for their efforts in putting the book together: Morton H. Baker, Virginia Ehrlich, Carol Goldenberg, Richard McAdoo, Austin Olney, Stephen Pekich, James Thompson, and Richard Tonachel. I want especially to thank Lisa Gray Fisher for her patience and tact during the final editing and for seeing the book through the press.

Contents

Illustrations

A FIELD GUIDE
to the ATLANTIC
SEASHORE

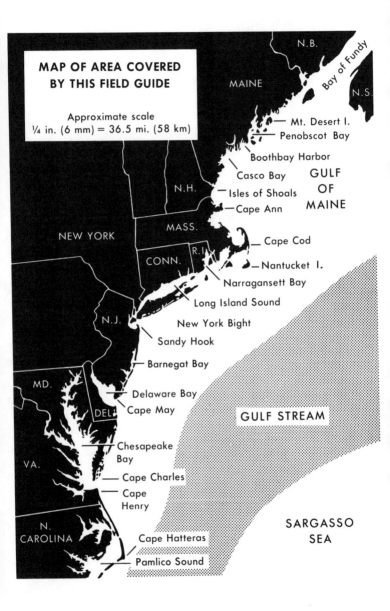

**MAP OF AREA COVERED
BY THIS FIELD GUIDE**

Approximate scale
¼ in. (6 mm) = 36.5 mi. (58 km)

N.B.

Bay of Fundy

MAINE

N.S.

— Mt. Desert I.
— Penobscot Bay

— Boothbay Harbor

Casco Bay   GULF

— Isles of Shoals   OF

— Cape Ann   MAINE

N.H.

MASS.

NEW YORK

— Cape Cod

CONN.   R.I.

— Nantucket I.

Narragansett Bay

Long Island Sound

New York Bight

N.J.

Sandy Hook

— Barnegat Bay

MD.

— Delaware Bay

DEL.   Cape May   GULF STREAM

— Chesapeake
Bay

VA.

— Cape Charles

— Cape
Henry

N.
CAROLINA   Cape Hatteras   SARGASSO
SEA

— Pamlico Sound

How to Use this Book

THIS is an informal book for identifying saltwater plants and invertebrate animals. In writing it I have tried to emphasize a practical rather than a rigidly scientific approach. Wherever possible I have substituted plain language for technical jargon. Also, the arrangement of plates and the descriptive comparisons are intended to serve the untrained eye of the amateur rather than the dictates of formal systematics.

The book is also quite literally a *field* guide. This restriction effectively eliminates a substantial number of organisms that have to be studied with a microscope. These, in any event, are mainly of interest to specialists. The majority of amphipod crustaceans, nematode worms, and hydroid cnidarians are in this category; we shall only sample such groups and skip entirely microscopic algae, ostracods, rotifers, gastrotrichs, kinorhynchs, tardigrades, protists, and the like. Most of these also require special collecting techniques and special preparation for study. (Omitting these forms also has the thoroughly practical benefit of bringing the book within reasonable size for publication.) I am also taking the *shore* part of the title to mean, quite literally, only those plants and animals that live along the edge of the sea or in wading or snorkeling depths, plus a few that are frequently cast ashore from deeper water. Geographically our nominal limits are the Bay of Fundy and Cape Hatteras, but actually the book should be useful considerably farther north and south (see p. 14).

Keep in mind that identification is the beginning and not the end of the game. Splendid as the details of form and color may be, they touch only the surface of the subject. So study the *living* forms in their own habitats and going about their daily rounds.

General Organization: Species identification is mainly a matter of narrowing down the possibilities by comparing and contrasting similar and potentially confusable plants and animals. As a first step give some attention to the endpapers, which are intended to help sort out the major groups of invertebrate animals and distinguish the few that might be taken for plants. These pictorial presentations should be used in conjunction with phylum, class, and other taxon accounts under centered headings in the text.

Some animal forms are so familiar that you may not feel obliged to key them out with the endpapers — crabs and sea stars (starfish), for example. In this case turn directly to the plates at the center of the book. Scanning the plates and their legend pages, placed

1

opposite, should suggest a probable identification, or at least lead you in the right direction. Turn then to the appropriate text account. Each account is divided into several sections.

Identification: A selection of key traits or field marks rather than a full description is the goal here. Sometimes a distinctive feature, habitat preference, or geographic range is emphasized when it helps distinguish the species from another for which it might be mistaken.

Similar Species: This section serves two purposes. First, all species listed share one or more traits with the species discussed in the main entry, and here the key differences are explained. The second purpose is to increase species coverage by a special shorthand device. Thus, there are really two categories of similar species. (1) Those in the first category have their own separate accounts and are simply cross-referenced here for comparison. They are cited only by common name and the plate where they are illustrated; the legend page opposite the plate gives the text page where such species appear as main entries. (2) Species in the second category are not described elsewhere; hence their coverage here includes all the elements of a separate account in abbreviated form. This system saves considerable space and more than doubles the number of species covered. Note one special device: When the *range* of similar species is not given, the reader may assume it is the same as that of the main species. Many of these additional species are also illustrated, and the accounts under which they appear are indicated on the plate legend-page.

Finally, I should emphasize that similar species are not always closely related; key similarities are often quite superficial and have little to do with the characteristics used in scientific classification.

Season: When species occur only, or much more abundantly, during a particular season(s), I have given that information here. If no pronounced seasonality is associated with the species, this section has been omitted.

Where Found: A brief statement of geographic range is given here. Readers may note an inconsistency in that ranges are sometimes given as "south to . . ." and other times as "north to . . ." Much of the coast covered by this guide is transitional biogeographically, and many species have their centers of abundance or main distribution north or south of our limits. This subject is dealt with in more detail in the chapter *Distribution and Habitats* (p. 14). Note also that the boundaries given here represent limits within which the species are definitely known to occur; they may not in every case be the absolute limits of the species' range.

This section also provides some indication of vertical range and habitat, although these subjects may be discussed or enlarged upon in the concluding **Remarks.** Since this is a guide to the seashore, we are mainly concerned with distributions in shallow water and the intertidal zone; therefore maximum subtidal depth limits are not always given. When the vertical range of a species is given simply as "subtidal," its upper or shore limit is just below the low tide line. "Subtidal to shallow depths" means from the tide line down to about 30 ft. (9 m).

The words "inshore" and "offshore" are frequently used in range descriptions; the definition of these terms is somewhat arbitrary and subjective. "Inshore" is intended to mean within easy reach of the land, close enough for a small boat to travel in safety. The "offshore" area requires a boat with greater sea-keeping ability. Animals that are cited as living offshore are much less likely to come to the readers' attention than ones found inshore. Another term used in some range descriptions is "oceanic"; in this context it refers to animals living in the open sea beyond the continental shelf.

Remarks: Additional details deemed likely to be of special interest are included here, mainly such matters as habits and behavior, distribution and habitat, economic or ecological importance, or gustatory appeal.

Illustrations: 64 plates are grouped together at the center of the book; additional drawings are placed on some legend pages and at intervals throughout the text. Pointers are used to draw attention to pertinent details, but are omitted when the general appearance of the subject is distinctive enough.

The organization of the plates may offend some systematic purists. Their arrangement is based on the Peterson principle of grouping forms according to *visual* similarities. The varied array of worms illustrates this approach. Nearly every phylum has evolved species to exploit the advantages of a wormlike existence, and animals widely different in basic structure and relationship may be very similar in superficial appearance. The visual approach brings these animals together for comparison regardless of how distantly they are related biologically.

The sequence of plates starts off with plants (Plates 1–9) and moves on to animals that are plantlike to the extent of being attached to a substratum (Plates 10–18); some of these, such as the hydroids and bushy bryozoans, resemble plants quite closely. The shelled mollusks, an easily recognized group, appear on Plates 19–28. Swimming and planktonic animals follow them (Plates 29–35), and then the various worms (Plates 36–47). Most jointed-leg animals, or arthropods (Plates 48–61), can be recognized as such, and the main groups of spiny-skinned animals, or echinoderms (Plates 62–64), are also familiar. An arrangement of this sort, unorthodox as it is, reflects the preferences of the compiler and cannot expect universal acclaim. With practice the reader will find it useful. The plates are cross-referenced on the legend pages to the text accounts, which follow a systematic sequence acceptable to most scientists.

All species in the text are shown on a plate (or in a text or legend-page drawing) unless I have specifically indicated that they are not.

Measurements: Because the metric system is coming into use in the United States, metric equivalents have been included in parentheses throughout this guide. An inch/millimeter scale is shown below and stamped on the fore edge of the back cover. Because the original measurements are necessarily approximate, the metric equivalents have been rounded off as follows: 25 millimeters (mm) for an inch; 0.3 meter (m) for a foot. Dimensions are given in millimeters up to 1000, then in meters. Spicule sizes for sponges are given in microns (μ), with 1 micron equal to 0.001 millimeter or 1/25,000 inch.

CENTIMETERS (1 CM.= 10 MM.)

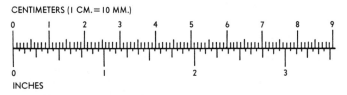

INCHES

Comparison of millimeter and inch scales.

The dimensions of most invertebrates and seaweeds do not have the same significance for identification that the reader may have encountered elsewhere. Many invertebrates are soft-bodied and in life can change their proportions drastically; when pickled in strong preservatives they often become extremely contracted or unnaturally distorted. Therefore the "normal" size of the animal can be difficult to measure accurately. Invertebrate zoologists are usually more interested in the relative proportions of structural details than in the size of the whole animal, and they are often rather casual about recording total sizes. Also, the growth patterns of marine animals and plants are often affected by different habitats or seasons, and these variations have not been thoroughly studied in most groups. Nevertheless, for field identification it is more than just convenient to have some idea of how big or small the subject is likely to be. Dimensions given in this guide are intended to fill this need, but they should not be interpreted as having the same precision as equivalent data on birds or mammals.

Color: As an identification trait, color is more useful in some groups than others; hence this detail is not always given. Many invertebrates can change color — squids as quickly as one might wash over them with a paintbrush, others more slowly, some not at all. Certain species change to match their habitat or vary between daylight and dark, or have special breeding "plumages." Many species have been studied only as pickled specimens, and their living colors have not been recorded. In life even the lowly worm may be exquisitely pigmented or show brilliant hues of structural color; all this, or most of it, disappears in preservative. Another reason to study animals alive!

Definition of Terms: Although scientific terms have been avoided as much as possible, a certain number of them are necessary and useful. These are defined in the introductory sections under centered headings throughout the text and/or in the *Glossary* (p. 279).

Nomenclature: Species names, whether common or scientific, always pose a problem. With regard to common, or vernacular, names, horticultural writers somehow have managed the no-nonsense approach of often not providing any. Thus we accept without a qualm geranium, philodendron, coleus, and others, all of which are scientific *and* common names. Zoologists, more timid perhaps, have not accomplished this, and laymen are generally assumed to regard scientific animal names with suspicion or as an affectation of the learned. In accordance with the Peterson Field Guide Series policy, the publisher therefore requested common names for this guide. With occasional exceptions, I have supplied one for each species appearing as a main entry; for those listed only as similar species I usually have not given common names. Only a few marine invertebrates have vernacular names in common use, and the most interesting of these are indecent, having been applied by fishermen and other plain-seeing folk. At least 90% of my names have had to be invented, and for the results I beg understanding. The simplest approach is to translate classical names into plain English, but this often results in names that are at best meaningless and frequently ludicrous. I have tried to make my common names useful; however, in some cases the reader may choose to ignore them. (For clues to pronunciation and translation see Jaeger's *A Source Book of Biological Names and Terms,* C. C. Thomas, 1972.)

The scientific name of an individual species always has two parts, since it includes the genus name as well. The generic name comes first, with its first letter capitalized; the specific name follows, entirely in lower-case letters. A species name (such as *americana*) may be used over and over but never for another organism within the same genus. The scientific classification of plants and animals is a filing system in which individual kinds of organisms, *species,* are grouped in progressively more inclusive categories for easy reference. Thus species are grouped in *genera,* genera in *families,* families in *orders,* orders in *classes,* and classes in *phyla.*

(The plant and animal *kingdoms* are not so absolutely separate as one might think, since some lowly organisms are claimed by both zoologists and botanists.) It is impractical and would not even be especially useful to present a complete classification in this *Field Guide.* Some of the larger groups, the class Crustacea, for one, have so many species that it has been necessary to invent various supra, infra, and other subdivisions of the main categories. A few phyla are so small that zoologists have not bothered to fill-in the whole hierarchy.

Scientific names are supposed to have the advantage of universal application and understanding; their origins can be traced through the technical literature. Unfortunately, these names are unstable in groups of plants and animals that are not thoroughly understood. This includes many marine invertebrates. As species definitions and relationships are refined, the names may change, and this is exasperating to everyone but the systematists involved. Also, systematics is more a matter of individual opinion than of divine enlightenment. For higher animals such as birds, reptiles, or amphibians, there are enough students to exert a majority opinion on name selections; but in marine invertebrate zoology there often are only a few experts per group, and they must cope with a proportionately larger assortment of animals that are difficult to sample and study.

The scientific names used here are as up-to-date as I can reasonably make them, human error (my own) aside; the results in any event are bound to be transitory and imperfect. Before publication, lists of current names for most invertebrate groups were submitted to specialists for revision, as were the plant names. For groups that appear to be nomenclaturally stable I have used the same names as in my *Guide to Identification of Marine and Estuarine Invertebrates* (1971). Some recently obsolete or alternate names are listed in the *Index* and cross-referenced there to the current or preferred name.

Collecting and Preserving Specimens

IF THERE isn't enough time to study specimens thoroughly in the field, then take them with you. When you do this, however, respect both the organisms and their environment. Only collect if there is a real purpose to it; otherwise, resist the impulse. Collecting can be a mindless activity resulting only in bucketfuls of evil-smelling refuse or forgotten, ill-labeled jars of desiccated "specimens." These hardly resemble the living things they once were and are useless and wasted. If collecting is necessary, take only what you need, which is often less than you might estimate. You will find that to be true especially at the end of a long day in the field when it is time to process specimens. This is a chore, but must be done if what has been collected is to be saved.

Where and How to Collect: No matter how often you visit the shore, the variety of life and the changing moods of the sea's edge are such that you can hardly fail to turn up something new or something familiar in a new light. Collecting techniques vary with the kind of shoreline, but in any case variety and abundance increase as one descends through the intertidal zone. Field work therefore should be geared to the tidal cycle and particularly to take advantage of spring tides, when the lowest, richest levels are exposed (see **Tides,** p. 18).

On rocky shores collecting is mainly a matter of handpicking, with some help from a knife or cold chisel and hammer to dislodge attached organisms. Seaweeds are a major element of rocky shore habitats in providing shelter and an attachment base for the animals that live there and for smaller, epiphytic algae. Take your time looking around and turning plants to expose normally hidden surfaces. Masses of seaweed, particularly of such tangled or minutely branching forms as *Spongomorpha* and the finer red weeds, should be transferred to a white enameled tray or washbasin for careful examination; or a bucketful can be taken away for later study. Such weeds often teem with small invertebrates.

Pay particular attention to shaded or sheltered places, turning rocks where there are loose ones and searching beneath overhangs and in crevices. Tide pools, gullies and basins that hold water between tides, are prime collecting grounds and often contain organisms that normally live farther down the shore or are subtidal. These are fascinating miniature cosmoses with resident

7

populations and an unpredictable bonus of transients trapped by the falling tide. Pools lowest in the intertidal zone have greater variety, but ones high on the shore are of interest because of their limited biota adapted to withstand extreme changes of salinity and temperature.

Docks, jetties, and neglected boat bottoms attract plants and animals that need a base for attachment. Because they usually stand in quieter waters, these surfaces often have inhabitants not found on the more turbulent open coast. Southward, where natural rock habitats are scarce, man-made structures provide the principal or only hard-surface attachments to be found. Mussel or oyster shoals are also good bases.

On sandy and muddy shores digging, dredging, and seining are the main collecting methods. Here intertidal levels may be bare of plant life. Most of the animals are burrowers — mainly worms, bivalve mollusks, and specialized members of other phyla. Burrow openings give clues of where to dig. Often the burrowers are much deeper than you might expect or wish, and it is hard to get some of the more fragile worms out in one piece. A good collecting technique is to wash diggings through one or more sieves made of fine screening, of decreasing mesh sizes, nailed to the bottom of shallow wooden frames. The texture of the substratum — whether clayey, peaty, soft and muddy, or hard and sandy — determines what animals are present. Intertidal zonation (see Fig. 2, p. 21), though less obvious, is found here as well as on rocky shores.

Vast areas of soft-ground shoreline are covered by marshes. These have their own special biota consisting of forms that crawl over or fasten themselves to the plants and others that burrow among the plant bases. Search also under the boards and other junk that usually litter the upper shore of our much abused marshlands. Subtidally, beds of Eelgrass and Widgeon Grass are especially rich collecting places. The technique is to gather a quantity of grass or bottom seaweeds and sort through it in a tray or wooden trough (culling board). The plants can be gathered by hand in shallow water, but it is often more profitable to dredge up material from deeper water or collect it with a bait seine. Weedy bottoms are richer than clean sandy or gravelly ones for dredging and seining unless you have a dredge or rake that actually digs into the bottom.

Night collecting is an interesting technique applicable to almost any type of shoreline. The secretive animals that lie hidden in daytime may then be exposed and active. Many are attracted to a light suspended over or just below the water surface. A headlamp is most practical for stalking, since it frees both hands. It is a good safety practice to carry a spare light of some sort, and a lighted lantern left ashore at your starting point is a reassuring and often helpful beacon when it is time to start home from far out on tideflats or intertidal rocks.

Precautionary Measures: Aside from a few fish that bite, crabs that pinch, and jellyfish that sting, there are not many harmful inhabitants along our coast and none that are potentially lethal under normal circumstances. Still, reasonable care and common sense are basic necessities around any aquatic habitat. Intertidal rocks can be very slippery. This is obvious enough at lower levels, where thick seaweed growths give about as much traction as a layer of wet noodles; higher levels covered by thin algal films can also be treacherous, partly because they look safer. Discretion at the expense of dignity may decree going on all fours in such places. The other peril on intertidal rocks is getting out too far in some areas — such as the Bay of Fundy — where the intertidal zone is very wide. The flood tide comes in with alarming insistence; so always keep a practical escape route in mind.

Field Equipment: The most important tools for collecting specimens are eyes and hands. Vision is often substantially improved by polaroid sunglasses, which reduce water-surface reflections and glare. A good hand lens (preferably one of the triplet type with about 5–20X) is required for the smaller animals covered by this guide. Microscopes, though hardly field equipment, open up a vast new world; however, they should be selected with care. Some of the cheaper ones are almost worse than useless, provoking only frustration and disappointment. Good ones are expensive.

Gloves are necessary to avoid getting sore hands from salt-soaked barnacle cuts and other inevitable scrapes. Cheap cotton work gloves will do, or get the heavier rubberized ones used by commercial fishermen. A longshoreman's baling hook is handy for turning rocks (be sure to turn them back the way you found them).

Feet also need protection. Over the years I have accumulated an assortment of boots that always seem to be a little shorter than the water depth I stray into. Armpit-high waders are the ultimate protection; though bulky and often hot when you are out of water, they offer the great advantage of protecting the wearer's seat when squatting in cold tide pools. Sneakers or tennis shoes and bathing suit are fine for warm water. If you can't see the bottom, bare feet are risky — just as they are where broken glass, spiky boards, and such hazards are likely to occur (which is often the case along our littered shoreline).

Small plastic buckets are cheap and almost indispensable. Also, the assortment of light plastic bags available in any supermarket are a boon to the field collector and nearly eliminate the need for bulkier bottles and jars. Live specimens can breathe through the plastic; however, alcohol also seems to leak through them, and they are hazardous to use for formalin collections. Double or triple bagging is safer for preserved specimens; be sure to keep them well away from live collections. Heavier-stock plastic bags are available from biological supply houses (see p. 10).

For removing attached animals and seaweeds, a knife or short flat-bladed spatula is handy, and on rocky shores a cold chisel with about a $1\frac{1}{2}$-in. (38 mm) blade may be needed, along with some sort of hammer (the one I have is steel, with a nail-lifting claw at one end and a light double-headed hammer at the other).

On sandy or muddy shores, digging equipment is necessary. The selection of shovels, pitchforks, or clamrakes is mainly dictated by portability, price, and personal preference; a garden trowel is a simple and often very useful tool. Nets also come in a variety of shapes and sizes. Crabnets are not useful for much more than their intended purpose, although an unmounted net bag, available without frame or handle, is handy for carrying things when beachcombing. Dipnets and even small aquarium nets are needed for more elusive prey. Dipnets should have long handles or handle extenders. Bait seines catch invertebrates as well as fish; the important point in handling them is to keep the lower edge as close to the sea bottom as possible, using it like a bulldozer to push and ultimately entrap the quarry. Plankton nets can be improvised from hosiery stock; proper bolting-cloth (silk) nets are relatively expensive but will last a long time if well cared for — thoroughly wash and dry them after each use. These nets and other specialized collecting equipment are available from biological supply houses such as Carolina Biological Supply Co., Burlington, N.C., and Ward's Natural Science Establishment, P.O. Box 24, Beechwood Station, Rochester, N.Y. Two publications listing other and more specialized suppliers are: *Guide to Scientific Instruments,* published by the American Association for the Advancement of Science, and *Sources of Limnological and Oceanographic Apparatus and Supplies,* published by the American Society of Limnology and Oceanography. Locate the most recent editions through your local library.

Supply houses also have various dredges and nets for sampling subtidal levels. A rowboat is sufficient for light dredging and for towing small plankton nets. In shallow water, carry or throw the dredge out into the water and tow it in with a line. More elaborate "grabs" and sampling devices are expensive and require rather complex construction, but some at least can be improvised from generally available materials. In any case they should be sturdily built and carefully washed after use in salt water.

Care of Live Material: Many marine animals can be kept alive in aquariums, and a tank with a few, varied, mutually tolerant inhabitants is a constant source of discovery. The first problem is to get the material home in good condition. Temperature and oxygen supply are the key factors. *Don't crowd your specimens.* You will fare better by taking just a few carefully selected animals than by collecting indiscriminately with the intention of sorting out aquarium candidates many hours later. Crowding aggravates the shock of moving an animal from the wide ocean to a small container.

In the field keep your collection cool and well-protected from the sun. Specimens in plastic sandwich bags can be placed in a baitfish trap and anchored in a safe shady place or immersed in a quiet pool until you are ready to leave the shore. Then transport them in an ice chest with enough ice to keep the temperature low but not frigid. Give the collection a change of water before starting home; on extended trips along the coast replace the water once or twice a day en route. Take an aerator, hose, and air stones (all available at pet shops) with you and use them whenever possible, such as when you are camping or staying in a motel overnight. Battery-powered equipment is available. Watch out for casualties and remove them promptly — and of course separate potential predators and prey.

It is helpful to have a saltwater aquarium ready and waiting when you reach home. Aquariums should be all glass or plastic and have adequate filtration and aeration. Avoid sudden and extreme changes of temperature when transferring specimens; leave material in plastic bags and immerse both in the established tank for a half-hour or so to allow temperatures to equalize.

Some animals adjust better than others to aquarium life. These will settle down to a long residence; others may live for only a few days or weeks, and some will not survive the trip home. New animals may appear spontaneously even in long-established tanks as subtle changes in water chemistry bring resting stages to life or allow the development of undetected larvae. Your aquarium will never be balanced in the sense of being a stable, self-sustaining system. It is too small a cosmos to support a real plankton community, which is the base of most marine food pyramids. Indirect light is preferable to avoid excess proliferation of algal scums. Seaweed cultivation is a special project in itself and probably not practical on a long-term basis in small aquariums.

Vigorous predators such as large crabs require solitary confinement, but less ferocious ones add interest to the activity of a tank. Small crabs, hermit crabs, anemones, sea stars, and such will eat bits of baitfish cut from a frozen supply. Fishes, such as killies (mummichogs), pipefish, small flatfish, and other tolerant estuarine forms easily caught with bait seines or traps, make interesting aquarium companions for invertebrates. A balanced dried fish food will supply them with sustenance, and the fragments missed by larger fishes may be sufficient for detritus- and filter-feeding invertebrates. Many invertebrates can be kept for days, weeks, or even months without food and suffer no apparent hardship. Overfeeding is a more serious problem. Uneaten food or a defunct organism can quickly foul a tank, rendering it uninhabitable; remove such contamination without delay.

Finally, pay attention to salt concentration. Many estuarine animals are good candidates for aquarium life because they can survive in a fairly wide salinity range and are otherwise tolerant of environmental variables. Sudden changes, however, should be avoided. Salt concentration increases by evaporation; the dissolved salts do not evaporate, only the water. Check salinity with a hydrometer, thermometer, and the table on p. 17, or simply mark the level of a tank freshly supplied with seawater. Then keep the level up with pond- or rain-water or tap water that has been allowed to stand for about 2 weeks. Do not add more seawater.

Additional sources of information include *Culture Methods for Invertebrate Animals* by Paul S. Galtsoff et al., Dover Publications, New York, 1959; *Marine Aquarium Keeping* by Stephen Spotte, John Wiley and Sons, New York, 1973; and *The Salt Water Aquarium in the Home* by Robert P. L. Straughan, A. S. Barnes and Co., New York, 1970.

Preservation: Seaweeds and certain kinds of animals (shelled mollusks, bryozoans, corals, and some echinoderms) are kept mainly as dry specimens, but wet preservation is best for most others. The two convenient and readily available preservatives for permanent collections are formaldehyde and alcohol. Chemical supply houses sell commercial formalin (a 40% solution of formaldehyde) and 95% isopropyl alcohol, which is an acceptable substitute for the prohibitively expensive ethyl alcohol. Emergency supplies can sometimes be found in drugstores at greater expense; rubbing alcohol is usually 70% isopropyl or other denatured alcohol, which is the standard strength used for preserving specimens. In formalin solutions, dilute 1 part formalin with about 8–10 parts of water (preferably seawater).

Both preservatives have disadvantages and cannot be used for all material. Formalin is obnoxious to work with; its vapor is irritating to eyes and nose. Wear rubber gloves to protect your skin, or rinse your hands frequently. Also, formalin is corrosive to organisms with a calcium carbonate skeleton; these include crustaceans, corals, bryozoans, mollusks, and echinoderms. Its acidity can be neutralized temporarily by adding 1 tablespoon (15 ml) of borax per quart (liter) of solution, and this is a desirable procedure to follow for all material. One pound (454 g) of hexamine added to a gallon (4.5 l) of formalin solution is a more permanent buffer. Most animals seem to preserve better if fixed for a few days in formalin; then transfer them to a 70% alcohol solution. Alcohol does not penetrate as well and specimens preserved without formalin-fixing may become flabby and soft. Seaweeds should be left permanently in formalin; some people also prefer it for noncalcareous animals. To guard against desiccation, add about 1 part glycerin to 20 parts of preservative; then if the alcohol or formalin evaporates, the glycerin will usually keep the specimens wet and the preservative can be renewed.

Certain types of animals require special treatment. *Never put sponges in formalin, even temporarily.* Fix them in 95% alcohol. Most comb jellies are totally and quickly destroyed by formalin.

One part glacial acetic acid in 20 parts of 1% chromic acid solution is a fixing agent for them; after about 20 minutes transfer to fresh seawater for 15 minutes and add alcohol gradually to reach a 70% solution. Specialists often evolve particular formulas for fixing and preserving their material, especially when microscopic sections are planned. For reference see J. W. Knudsen's *Biological Techniques,* Harper and Row, New York, 1966, or my *Guide to Identification of Marine and Estuarine Invertebrates,* John Wiley and Sons, New York, 1971. E. Yale Dawson gives complete instructions for making seaweed collections in his *Marine Botany: An Introduction,* Holt, Rinehart, and Winston, New York, 1966. Most seaweeds are mounted on herbarium paper available from biological supply houses.

Narcotization is a necessary but tedious preliminary step for preserving some animals if prime specimens are to be obtained (see the above references for techniques). Not surprisingly, many live animals react to being placed directly in formalin or alcohol solutions by contracting or becoming grossly distorted; soft-bodied forms may be rendered quite useless, and worms often fragment themselves. The object of narcotization is to suppress these reactions. The effort is not always successful, and in any event requires experimentation. Sometimes chilling will sufficiently dull an individual to allow pickling with a minimum of distortion, and certain material will expire in a relaxed, expanded condition if deprived of oxygen.

Labeling: Preserved collections have little value without proper record-keeping. The minimum information to be recorded is the date and place of capture. Be as specific as possible about the location; for example, "Manasquan, New Jersey; ocean beach $\frac{1}{4}$ mile north of inlet." More complete records show the depth or tide level, type of habitat, temperature, salinity, time of day, and any other observation of interest. Since this might become a rather wordy label, keep the details in a journal or other record book and a condensed version with the specimen; correlate the two with a catalog number. Use *waterproof paper and ink* for labels to go in preservative. Biological supply houses (see p. 10) or stationery dealers can provide appropriate material. Ink on labels will often smear or run when placed in alcohol, even though it appears to be dry; to avoid this, rinse the dry label in water and place it while still wet in the specimen jar.

From the preceding description it should be apparent that making and maintaining a pickled collection requires considerable effort. It is an essential process if a permanent record or demonstration collection is needed; also, systematic and other special studies require preserved specimens. Otherwise, your time might be more profitably and enjoyably spent at the beach observing the *live* organisms.

Distribution and Habits

Geographical Distribution: The coast covered by this book can be divided biogeographically into northern and southern sections with Cape Cod as the dividing point; our nominal limits are the Bay of Fundy and Cape Hatteras. Actually, the *American Atlantic Boreal Region* extends northward from Cape Cod to Labrador. The biota (all plants and animals in a given region) becomes noticeably more arctic in species composition northward, and some biologists divide the region into subregions or provinces, with a break on the coast of Newfoundland. Many of our Boreal species (up to 80% in some taxonomic groups) are also found on the northern parts of the European coast and our northwestern Pacific. Compared to the region south of Cape Cod, the Gulf of Maine enjoys considerable climatic stability. At Mt. Desert the extreme annual range in water temperature is about 20 Fahrenheit degrees (11 Centigrade degrees), whereas at New York it is about 48 Fahrenheit degrees (27 Centigrade degrees).

The *American Atlantic Temperate Region* extends from Cape Cod south to Texas. This whole part of the coast becomes virtually subtropical in summer. The Atlantic and Gulf of Mexico coastal areas are separated by an intrusion of the Caribbean biota in southern Florida. Cape Hatteras is a natural boundary, dividing the Atlantic section into Virginian and Carolinian Provinces. Many of the common shore forms of the Carolinian Province will be found in this book; parts of the Texas and Florida coast, however, have a considerable admixture of tropical plants and animals, and in these areas particularly, the guide will be less complete.

Biogeographical boundaries in the sea are not absolute but in effect are filters. The Virginian Province has very few *endemic species* (native or confined to a particular region) and is really a transitional province with an impoverished southern biota plus an even weaker Boreal component. Thus only about 30% of the species of decapod crustaceans found in the Carolinian Province pass through the Cape Hatteras filter; these, however, make up about 80% of the northern province's decapod population. Most of these species range all the way to Cape Cod and a few straggle even farther north — the Blue Crab, for example.

The effectiveness of such barriers varies seasonally. Temperature is the main controlling influence. Cape Hatteras is a very weak barrier in summer, when the surface water becomes stratified and warmed all along the coast north to Cape Cod. Even northward in Massachusetts Bay and in shallow bays along the coast of

Maine, water temperatures rise enough to allow some human swimmers to immerse themselves at least briefly.

The survival of larvae of southern species carried northward at this season depends on how well they tolerate the subsequent chill of winter. At that time a constant procession of cyclonic storms stirs and cools the water north of Cape Hatteras. The change in water temperature at that cape in winter is rather abrupt and inhibits any tendency for Boreal species to move farther south. Cape Cod is hardly any barrier at all in winter when the cod themselves migrate southward to be caught in profitable quantities off New Jersey and Maryland. In summer the water north of Cape Cod is substantially cooler than southward.

Water temperature also decreases with depth. As a result, many northern cold-water species are found southward in progressively deeper water. The Green Sea Urchin, for example, is at home in Gulf of Maine tide pools but ranges south of Cape Cod only subtidally. Off the New Jersey coast it is rarely found in less than 80–100 ft. (24–30 m). Similarly, both the northern Jonah Crab and the northern lobster are found off the Carolinas only in cold, deep water.

Animal distributions change with time. The Common Oyster and the Hard-shelled Clam, or Quahog, both have populations on the northern New England coast that increase or diminish, presumably in response to cyclic trends in water temperature. The so-called Magdalen Pocket in the area of Prince Edward Island on the Gulf of St. Lawrence has many warm-water species, possibly because of a period in the remote past when a warming trend allowed southern species to expand their ranges northward. Locally favorable conditions permit these relics to survive far beyond their normal range. Ocean currents are constantly transporting larval forms into new areas and when conditions are even temporarily favorable, immigrant colonies may become established.

Salinity: While temperature is most important in setting broad patterns of distribution, salinity is crucial where fresh- and salt-water habitats intermingle. The proportion of different chemicals in seawater is amazingly constant in all the world's seas, but the total quantity of dissolved salt varies. Salinity is measured in parts per thousand, (‰), and the usual concentration in the open sea is about 35‰. This means that there are about 35 grams of dissolved solids per 1000 grams of water. (The amount of solutes even in "hard" fresh water is relatively much smaller and is measured in parts per million.)

Inshore along this coast salinity averages closer to 32‰. The dilution from 35 to 32‰ does not sound like much, but it is more than some organisms can stand. Hence in the sea there are *oceanic* animals that are only found well offshore beyond the continental shelf, and *neritic* animals that live chiefly in the shallower waters over the shelf and do not mind the vicissitudes of the inshore environment. Around the mouths of our larger rivers salinity may drop at times to as low as 19–22‰.

There is a fairly regular seasonal variation in salinity inshore. The minimum is usually in spring, when the upland snows are melting and filling the rivers with their peak load of runoff water. Hurricanes with their enormous output of rainfall can also cause sudden and drastic reductions in salinity; the effects of such episodes on populations of oysters, clams, and other organisms can be catastrophic. Most estuarine and neritic organisms can stand considerable fluctuation in salinity, but you will find a nicely balanced sequence of biotic communities as you travel from strictly freshwater localities to more densely salty ones. "Brackish" is a general term for transitional waters. At salinities of 7–10‰ the number of resident species reaches a minimum, because this range is too salty for most freshwater organisms and too fresh for marine varieties. A few species, however, are endemic in such waters.

Most of the methods for measuring salinity require a more elaborate effort than nonprofessionals may wish to undertake. However, a simple hydrometer and thermometer (available for a few dollars from a laboratory supply house) used with the table in Fig. 1 will provide a good approximation of salinity changes in estuarine situations. Float the hydrometer in a container of the water being tested; also check the water temperature and match the readings as closely as you can.

Currents: The most conspicuous hydrographic feature off this coast is the northeast-flowing Gulf Stream with its relatively high temperature and salinity. The landward boundary of this famous "ocean river" is actually visible as a change in water color and transparency — from blue and clear offshore to greenish and murky inshore. Usually the line is also marked by drifting streamers of Gulfweed. In late winter when the water temperature off Chesapeake Bay is around 45°F (7°C), the Gulf Stream far offshore is in the mid to upper 70s°F (21°C and above). Similarly the salinity inshore may average as low in some months as 27‰, whereas that of the Gulf Stream is much more consistently about 36.5‰. The boundaries and configuration of the Gulf Stream vary, and there are shifting eddies within it and along its edges. Its landward boundary, in any event, lies beyond the edge of the continental shelf, and its chief interest for us is that strange and fascinating biota associated with the Sargasso Sea. Elements of this flora and fauna are caught up in the Gulf Stream off the West Indies and eventually may be blown ashore along the Carolinas coast, along the southern shore of Martha's Vineyard and Nantucket, and less frequently along the middle coast in between. Whenever you find Gulfweed washed ashore there is a good chance

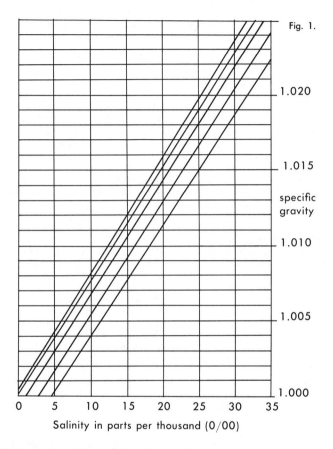

Fig. 1.

Table for determining salinity with a small, inexpensive hydrometer (specific gravity range 1.000–1.030 or wider). Most such instruments are calibrated for use at 60°F (16°C); at a higher or lower water temperature a correction must be made. Heavy diagonal lines are (left to right) for 50°F (10°C), 60°F (16°C), 70°F (21°C), and 80°F (26°C). To use table, measure specific gravity and water temperature; then find appropriate intersection of horizontal and diagonal lines and read down to find equivalent salinity. Intermediate values can be estimated.

of finding other visitors from the deep sea. These include the Portuguese man-of-war, Purple Jellyfish, bits of driftwood with goose barnacles, and the host of epiphytic algae, bryozoans, hydroids, and other small animals that live on or among the drifting fronds of the weed itself.

South of Cape Cod the water between the shore and the Gulf Stream has a slow and rather vague flow southward. This is evidenced by the tendency for most inlets and capes to drift in that direction. There is, in fact, a general southward trend in water movement all along the coast. Cold water moves down around Nova Scotia into the Gulf of Maine and, drifting counterclockwise along the shore, eventually flows around Cape Cod and on southward. Only occasionally is there much leakage of warm Gulf Stream water northward into the Gulf of Maine.

Because of prevailing westerly winds, our coastal waters are strongly affected by weather coming from the interior of the continent. The shore climate is softened by the proximity of the sea, but we do not have a maritime climate in the sense that western Europe does. Our sea climate extends but a short distance inland.

Tides: The terms *low water* and *high water* refer to the tides, their levels (or extremes) at ebb and flood. Many of the plants and animals in this guide live in the *intertidal zone* — the part of the seashore between high and low water; awareness of the timing of the tides is therefore a first consideration. The tidal cycle is *semidiurnal,* meaning there are two, more or less equal, highs and lows each day. Today's highs and lows will be about an hour *later* than yesterday's. The range of tidal extremes also varies. The best tides for shore collectors are around the time of full or new moon. These are the *spring tides,* when the sea both rises higher and falls lower; *neap tides* are the opposite and occur about halfway through the lunar cycle. Tides are mainly controlled by the pull of the sun and moon, but weather conditions also affect them, especially in shallow bays and sounds. Onshore winds counteract the normal fall of low tides and enhance the highs; offshore winds have the opposite effect.

Tidal range varies greatly in different places, depending mainly on the width of the continental shelf. It averages about 3–4 ft. (0.9–1.2 m) along most of the open coast between Cape Hatteras and Cape Cod but departs from this in estuaries in accordance with their size and shape. Large lagoons with small entrances, such as Barnegat Bay, New Jersey, and Pamlico Sound, North Carolina, have practically no astronomical tide, but there the water level is greatly affected by the wind. Conversely, Long Island Sound has only a 2-ft. (0.6 m) range at Montauk Point but a 7 ft. (2.1 m) range at its western end. North of Cape Cod the tidal range is generally 9 ft. (2.7 m) or more and increases "Down East"; the Minas Basin of the Bay of Fundy has one of the greatest tides in the world — almost 45 ft. (13.5 m) at spring tides. Unfortunately, the Basin is muddy and a somewhat disappointing collecting ground; around the mouth of the Bay the interval is about 20 ft. (6 m) and the water not muddy.

Professional watermen often refer to *tidal currents* as "tides." These are not of great concern to the beachcomber, but in a rowboat or weakly powered outboard they may carry you away from where you want to go. Choose periods of slack water between peak ebbs and floods. The timing of tidal currents in relation to the tide itself varies locally, and current strength is influenced by wind and the lunar cycle.

Local newspapers usually give tidal listings for one or more local stations plus anticipated departures from the average. Also, shore-related businesses often distribute local tables as a courtesy to their customers. The most complete tables are published annually in book form by the U.S. Department of Commerce and especially helpful in listing correction factors for a multitude of local stations. Tidal Current Tables are also available. Tables for the East Coast cover the coast from Greenland to Argentina.

Biomes: The broad community of living organisms that characterizes a major habitat is called a *biome.* Tropical forest, tundra, and grassland are terrestrial examples of such habitats. Three marine biomes exist on this coast: (1) Pelagic, (2) Balanoid-Thallophyte, and (3) Pelecypod-Annelid. The first is composed of plants and animals that either float or drift free as part of the *plankton,* or are strong swimmers called *nekton.* Many invertebrates are planktonic; only a few, such as squids, qualify as nekton. Members of the other two marine biomes are *benthic;* they creep, crawl, burrow, or attach themselves to the bottom or to each other. Benthic *plants* are confined to shallow water, since the depth of their habitat is controlled by light penetration.

(1) The *Pelagic Biome* contains microscopic plants called *phytoplankton,* which are the basis of food chains in the sea. Herbivorous *zooplankters,* mostly copepod crustaceans, feed on the plants and in turn are eaten by larger predators. *Detritus,* consisting in part of dead phytoplankters and fragments of seaweeds and grasses, are also a major food source, particularly in salt marshes.

The composition of the plankton changes seasonally. There is usually a spring "bloom" starting on the southern part of this coast as early as January. Plants large enough to be caught by plankton nets (mostly diatoms) then reach numbers on the order of 40 million cells per cubic meter. Minute plant cells, too small to be caught by even the finest plankton nets, may be 100–1000 times more numerous. As the zooplankters that feed on these plants begin to multiply, invertebrates and fishes prey on them. The zooplankton is usually most abundant and varied in summer, and many of its members are easily seen with a hand lens; even the larger jellyfish qualify as plankton. A second phytoplankton bloom often takes place in the fall.

"Red tides" usually occur in warm weather on this coast. They are caused by blooms of certain pinkish dinoflagellates that are toxic to fishes and other organisms. Phytoplankton blooms depend partly on an accumulation of nutrients in the water, and it is just possible that inadequately treated sewage is one source of such overfertilization.

(2) The *Balanoid–Thallophyte Biome* is typical of rocky coasts, since its dominant members need something to attach themselves to. This biome is best developed on the traditionally rockbound New England coast, and intertidal zonation is its most conspicuous feature. Zonation appears as a succession of colored bands, like bathtub rings. The biome's name comes from the balanoid barnacles and thallophyte seaweeds that characterize several of these bands. Typically, the topmost zone consists of brightly colored lichens and a few other terrestrial plants and animals that do not mind an occasional misting of salt spray. Below them in a *littoral fringe* the surface is often darkened by films of microscopic blue-green algae — very slippery when wet. This is also the main periwinkle zone. The littoral fringe is only wetted by spring tides and spray, so it may extend far above actual sea level. Barnacles mark the top of the *mid-littoral zone;* they form a noticeable whitish band, although sometimes they must compete with blue-black patches of young Blue Mussels. Next are the seaweeds, which often separate into olive-green to bronzy-red subzones dominated by one or a few plant species. Rockweeds and Knotted Wrack predominate in the upper seaweed levels; in the lowest part of the mid-littoral various red seaweeds are important, though north of Long Island Sound this is a kelp zone.

(*Note:* The term *littoral,* though frequently used as a synonym for *intertidal,* actually refers to the whole shore area within reach of the ocean's water; thus it includes the spray zone or littoral fringe. In quiet water without much splash or spray and without great wave amplitude *littoral* is nearly equivalent to *intertidal.* However, on exposed coasts the subzones are broadened. In the West Indies where the intertidal range may be less than 1 ft., 0.3 m, the top of the littoral fringe may be 40 ft., 12 m, or more up the face of a cliff.)

Obviously, intertidal zonation is caused in some measure by variations in exposure to air and water due to tidal rise and fall as well as splash and spray, but the relationship is not a simple one and has provoked considerable argument among ecologists. Differences in light exposure and competition between the resident species also affect the pattern. There are infinite variations in detail.

The seaweeds of the Balanoid–Thallophyte Biome shelter a host of invertebrates and some fishes. In dark grottoes and other places where light is insufficient for plant growth, the hard surfaces

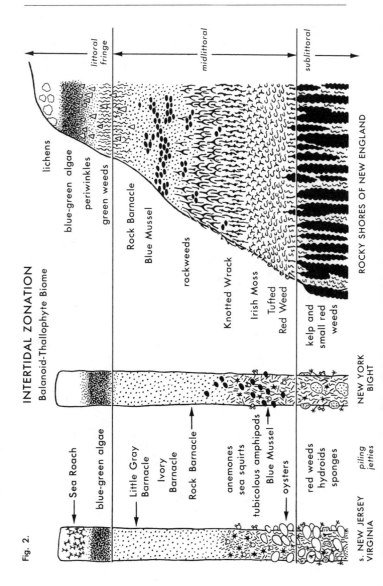

Fig. 2.

INTERTIDAL ZONATION
Balanoid-Thallophyte Biome

littoral fringe — midlittoral — sublittoral

ROCKY SHORES OF NEW ENGLAND

lichens
blue-green algae
periwinkles
green weeds
Rock Barnacle
Blue Mussel
rockweeds
Knotted Wrack
Irish Moss
Tufted Red Weed
kelp and small red weeds

NEW YORK BIGHT

S. NEW JERSEY VIRGINIA

Sea Roach
blue-green algae
Little Gray Barnacle
Ivory Barnacle
Rock Barnacle
anemones
sea squirts
tubicolous amphipods
Blue Mussel
oysters
red weeds
hydroids
sponges

piling
jetties

of the lower mid-littoral and sub-littoral are usually covered by sponges, encrusting hydroids, and bryozoans, or tube-making amphipods and small worms. South of Delaware Bay oysters often take over part of this zone. On sandy shores the Balanoid–Thallophyte Biome is developed on docks and jetties — anywhere a hard substratum presents itself.

(3) The *Pelecypod–Annelid Biome* occupies unconsolidated sediments, and its characteristic members are bivalve mollusks and polychaete worms (annelids). South of Cape Cod the outer coast consists mainly of a line of barrier islands broken by shifting inlets and the mouths of great sounds and estuaries. The outer shore is sandy. Offshore the bottom slopes gently away in a broad sandy

COMMON WHELK   Fig. 3.

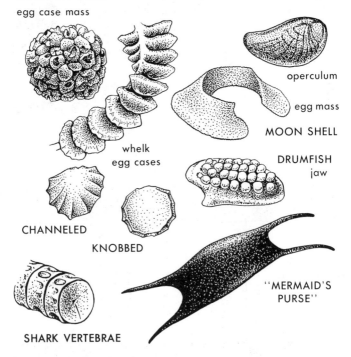

egg case mass

operculum

egg mass

MOON SHELL

whelk
egg cases

DRUMFISH
jaw

CHANNELED

KNOBBED

"MERMAID'S
PURSE"

SHARK VERTEBRAE

Beach Drift. Each high tide, particularly if it is a storm tide, brings something ashore. Some items may have drifted many hundreds of miles; others come from shallow depths off the coast or have been dislodged from somewhere close by. A few common objects, not shown elsewhere, are illustrated here.

plain, the continental shelf, which quickly widens from about 20 miles (32 km) off Cape Hatteras to 70–100 miles (113–161 km) off New Jersey and Cape Cod.

The texture of the bottom largely determines the distribution of individual species. Soft grounds are classified into a number of categories according to varying combinations of silt, clay, and sand, which are defined quite precisely by their particle sizes.

Intertidal zonation is found on soft grounds as well as hard, but often is inconspicuous because the inhabitants are burrowers. On ocean beaches these are mainly small to microscopic creatures that live in the water between sand grains (called *interstitial fauna*); here animal life consists of various amphipods, minute flatworms, and little-known microscopic forms such as gastrotrichs and tardigrades. The conspicuous animals on the more turbulent ocean beaches usually have been cast there from farther offshore, but a few larger animals actually prefer surf-swept habitats. All are migratory in that they move up and down the beaches with the tide. Mole Crabs and Coquina Clams are mainly aquatic, while Ghost Crabs and beach fleas are terrestrial visitors to the swash zone of broken waves.

Fig. 4.

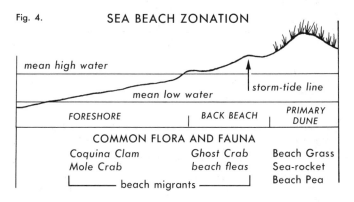

SEA BEACH ZONATION

In protected places the quality of the bottom varies from semi-liquid mud to hard-packed sand and clay, each with its characteristic fauna. Bay, lagoon, and river habitats are frequently dominated by plants. Subtidally Eelgrass and Widgeon Grass compete with Sea Lettuce and various red seaweeds, together blanketing the bottom of whole bays and estuaries where they are not swept clean by tidal currents. The grasses in particular provide a home for a great variety of invertebrates and a nursery for young fishes. At higher levels, but often separated by a bare strip in the lower intertidal zone, salt marshes take over. At the lowest level Tall

Cordgrass (*Spartina alterniflora*) often forms a solid marginal wall. It gives way at higher levels to more diverse salt-marsh plant associations that grow in patchworks or mosaics, reflecting subtle differences in elevation and drainage. These levels are wetted by high tides, though some only by the greatest spring tides. Higher still the marshes merge with terrestrial habitats; those of the barrier islands are especially interesting in their adaptation to the ever-present threat of inundation by storm tides and salt spray.

Each of these communities also has its own fauna. The roots of Tall Cordgrass often intermingle with half-buried Ribbed and Blue Mussels, to which are attached a wide variety of benthic invertebrates and smaller plants. The soil is full of burrowers, notably fiddler crabs, worms, and small clams; other animals climb or cling to the grasses or hide among the debris washed ashore at the drift line.

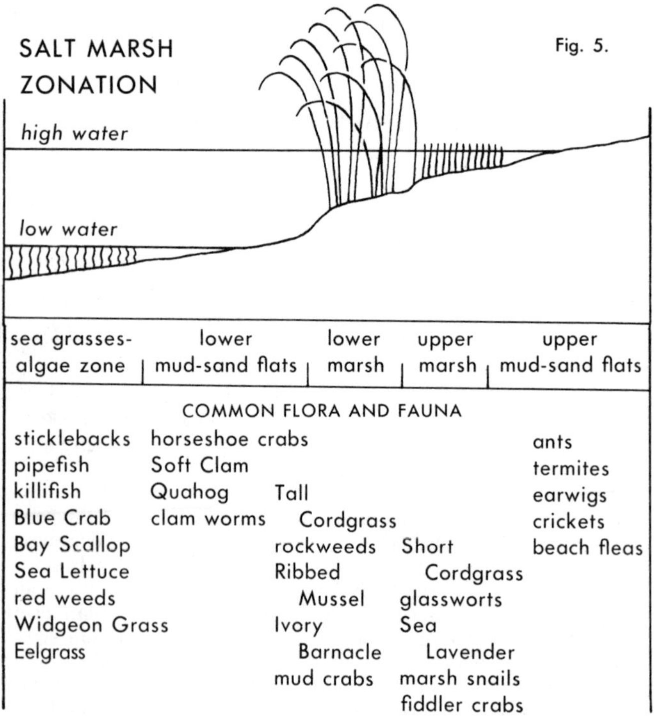

SALT MARSH ZONATION

Fig. 5.

high water

low water

sea grasses-algae zone	lower mud-sand flats	lower marsh	upper marsh	upper mud-sand flats

COMMON FLORA AND FAUNA

sea grasses-algae zone	lower mud-sand flats	lower marsh	upper marsh	upper mud-sand flats
sticklebacks	horseshoe crabs			ants
pipefish	Soft Clam			termites
killifish	Quahog	Tall		earwigs
Blue Crab	clam worms	Cordgrass		crickets
Bay Scallop		rockweeds	Short	beach fleas
Sea Lettuce		Ribbed	Cordgrass	
red weeds		Mussel	glassworts	
Widgeon Grass		Ivory	Sea	
Eelgrass		Barnacle	Lavender	
		mud crabs	marsh snails	
			fiddler crabs	

Plants

THE PREDOMINANT vegetation on land consists of seed plants or spermatophytes. Some of these can stand a dousing with salt spray or grow with their feet wet in salt marshes, but few of them live fully *submerged* in saline water. On this coast there are only 2 marine species of these flowering plants (p. 52). Some classes of plants, such as ferns, mosses, and club mosses, are entirely absent in salt water, although lichens are common in the spray zone, and at least 1 lichen species ranges down into the intertidal zone. Marine fungi are important pathogens (disease-causing organisms) infecting seaweeds, fishes, oysters, sponges, crustaceans, and presumably other invertebrates. They are essential, too, in affecting the decay of submerged wood and cordage. Some are visible without magnification as spots or other discolorations, but most are essentially microscopic.

Algae are the dominant aquatic flora in marine habitats. They form an assemblage of separate phyla for which there is no simple all-inclusive definition. Many have complex reproductive cycles, but they are usually simpler in structure than higher plants. Some algal groups are microscopic or nearly so, notably the *diatoms, chrysophytes,* and *dinoflagellates,* whose teeming billions of planktonic cells are the most important marine vegetation in total productivity. The last 2 groups are unicellular, but many diatoms form chains or branching aggregations of linked cells. Some of these are benthic, rather than planktonic, and are visible as fine whiskery or fuzzy coatings on almost any substratum available.

Three phyla contain what most people call seaweeds. Early botanists grouped such plants according to color, and this system, with refinements, is still used. Thus, there are the Chlorophyta (green), Phaeophyta (brown), and Rhodophyta (red). All 3 contain green photosynthetic pigments (chlorophylls) and usually yellowish xanthophylls or carotenes as well. The Phaeophyta and Rhodophyta have additional brown or red pigments that give them their principal colors or combine with the greens and yellows to produce such hues as olive or purplish green. In general, color distinctions are an effective identification aid, but they are not infallible; some care and scrutiny are called for, since color may vary according to habitat and the well-being of the plant. Dead or dying weeds may fade to white or yellowish, or turn green or black, completely losing their original color. In body form some seaweeds approach higher plants, but instead of roots have *holdfasts.* The algal *stipe* is approximately equivalent to the stem of other plants, and the leaf of leafy forms is called a *blade* or *frond*. The whole plant is called a *thallus* (plural *thalli*). Except for some of the kelps, seaweeds generally lack the elaborate water-conductive tissues of higher vascular plants, and the holdfast, lacking the more complex function of true roots, is simply for attachment.

Many seaweeds are seasonal in occurrence. A few develop quickly, mature, and are gone within periods as short as a month. Others are present through whole seasons or almost year-round. Many, especially the smaller species, are annuals. Others are perennials; some of these die back at the end of a growth season to a persistent holdfast, and some are present year-round as whole plants.

Fig. 6.

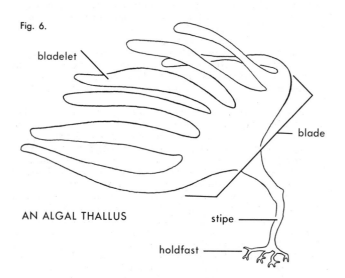

bladelet

blade

AN ALGAL THALLUS

stipe

holdfast

Green Seaweeds:
Phylum Chlorophyta

Thalli are usually grass-green when alive and healthy, sometimes tinged with yellow, blue, or black, but not with brown or red. For filamentous and crustose species see p. 48. Greens need plenty of light and are most common at higher intertidal levels or subtidally in shallow water.

HOLLOW GREEN WEEDS *Enteromorpha* species   **Pl. 1**
     Identification: *Tubular,* branched or not and sometimes flattened. *Grass-green.* Hollow structure in larger specimens is easily determined by the presence of air bubbles *within* the thallus. Ranges in width from $\frac{1}{16}$ in. (1.6 mm) or less to 1 in. (25 mm) or more, and 1 ft. (300 mm) or more long.

     Numerous species; 2 are minute and inconspicuous. *E. linza* (not shown) resembles Sea Lettuce (see Plate 1 and next account). Identification of the remaining species is difficult; they fall into 2 groups: those with unbranched thalli and those with branches. *E. intestinalis,* the most common *unbranched* species, reaches the maximum dimensions given above. Most of the *branched* species are slender, $\frac{1}{8}$ in. (3 mm) or less wide, and less than 1 ft. (300 mm) long. *E. compressa* and *E. prolifera* (neither shown) are sparsely branched, the first with branches near the *base,* the second with *scattered* branches; they are $\frac{5}{8}$-1 in. (16-25 mm) wide and about 1 ft. (300 mm) long.
     Similar species: The more slender forms could be mistaken for filamentous green seaweeds (p. 50); *Enteromorpha* species are usually coarser but individual cells are *not visible* even with a hand lens.
     Season: *E. linza,* winter-spring only. *E. intestinalis,* year-round. Most others are spring-summer annuals.
     Where found: Several species, including *E. intestinalis,* range from the Arctic south to the Carolinas; the others south only to n. New England, Cape Cod, or n. N.J.
     Remarks: These species occur in a variety of habitats. Common on rocks, dead shells, or wood in lower intertidal zone, on mud flats, drifting free, or even as epiphytes. Several grow at higher levels in tide pools or places kept wet by freshwater seepage; some have a wide tolerance for varying and greatly reduced salinity and penetrate deep into estuaries. *E. compressa* is a good candidate for seawater aquariums.
     Family: Ulvaceae.

SEA LETTUCE *Ulva lactuca*   **Pl. 1**

Identification: Thallus a translucent *bright green sheet,* often lobed or ruffled at edges. Initially attached by a short marginal stalk but later drifting free. To 3 ft. (900 mm).

Similar species: (1) *Monostroma* species (not shown) are very similar, but can possibly be distinguished from Sea Lettuce by using the following 2 field tests: *Ulva* has consistency of *wax paper* and fingerprints are *indistinctly* visible through it; *Monostroma* is thinner, more like *tissue paper,* and fingerprints are *clearly* visible. Several species and varieties; microscopic study required to distinguish between them. To 1 ft. (300 mm). Often epiphytic, also in pools or on rocks in shallow, brackish to salt water. Annuals: early spring–summer. 4 of the 5 species in our area range from L.I. Sound or N.J. to n. Mass. or subarctic; *M. oxyspermum* south to Fla. (2) *Enteromorpha linza* (preceding account) is very similar in thickness and form to young elongated Sea Lettuce, but is usually attached by a *tubular tapering* stipe and basal disk to *upper* intertidal rocks; to 1 ft. (300 mm) long by 1¼ in. (31 mm) wide; late spring–summer; Carolinas to Gulf of St. Lawrence.

Season: Holdfast perennial; blade annual.

Where found: Subarctic to tropics.

Remarks: Sea Lettuce is one of the most familiar shallow-water seaweeds. It grows in a variety of places ranging from exposed rocks to quiet, semistagnant, brackish pools, where huge detached sheets carpet the muddy bottoms. Tolerant of or actually thriving in moderate pollution. Edible; see the *Field Guide to Edible Wild Plants of Eastern and Central North America.*

Family: Ulvaceae, including *Monostroma.*

GREEN FLEECE *Codium fragile*   **Pl. 1**

Identification: Coarsely bushy, often branching in regular Y-shaped forks; branches *thick* — to ¾ in. (19 mm) — ropelike or *spongy.* Dark green, bleaching to yellowish. To 3 ft. (900 mm).

Season: Variously described as perennial, biennial, or "pseudoperennial"; in any event often living for several years.

Where found: Accidentally introduced from Europe or North Pacific about 1957. Now found from Orient Point, Long Island, to Chatham, Cape Cod, and south to Barnegat Bay; a separate population in Boothbay Harbor.

Remarks: This distinctive plant lives in shallow water of sounds and bays but often washes ashore in heavy, ropy masses, dragging along its mooring of pebbles and shells. A serious pest where common because of its choking effects on shellfish. Other *Codium* species are tropical.

Family: Codiaceae.

GREEN SEA FERN *Bryopsis plumosa*   **Pl. 1**
  Identification: Delicately bushy, branching *regularly;* grows in *fernlike* tufts. Light green. Collapses out of water. To 4 in. (100 mm).
  Similar species: (1) *B. hypnoides* (not shown) branches *irregularly* and is dark green. N.J. to Nova Scotia in lower intertidal zone. (2) See filamentous seaweeds (p. 50) and especially *Spongomorpha* species (Plate 1) which form conspicuous ropy tufts and tangles on intertidal rocks north of L.I. Sound.
  Season: Perennial in South; annual northward.
  Where found: Fla. to Cape Cod and less commonly north at least to Nova Scotia. In tide pools and on wood in fairly quiet water at shallow depths.
  Family: Bryopsidaceae.

Brown Seaweeds:
Phylum Phaeophyta

Healthy weeds vary in color from light to dark brown; some are almost black, or yellowish to golden brown, and when tinged with green they usually appear a shade of olive. These are the conspicuous algae of rocky shores in the mid to lower intertidal zone; north of New York the large kelp species dominate the lowest levels exposed by the tides and extend down into the subtidal. A few browns are crustose or filamentous, p. 48, but most are medium to large seaweeds.

BOTTLEBRUSH *Cladostephus verticillatus*   **Pl. 4**
  Identification: Unlike any other brown weed; bushy with thickish — $\frac{1}{16}$ in. (1.6 mm) — branches composed of a somewhat stiff central core and whorls of tiny curving branchlets. Resembles a very fine bottlebrush or pipe cleaner. Whole plant to 10 in. (250 mm).
  Season: Perennial; dies back and sheds branchlets in winter.
  Where found: N.Y. to Cape Cod, rarely northward. Subtidal at moderate depths in exposed places; washes ashore.
  Family: Sphacelariaceae.

BLACK WHIP WEED *Chordaria flagelliformis*   **Pl. 4**
  Identification: Bushy; *upper branches* whiplike and *longer* than main axis; has *few* secondary branches. Texture firm, leathery but slippery. Dark brown or black. Often covered with epiphytes by late summer. To 2 ft. (600 mm) or more, axis and branches $\frac{1}{16}$ in. (1.6 mm) thick.

Similar species: Black Whip Weed can easily be confused with several other brown weeds. (1) *Acrothrix novae-angliae* (Plate 4) is a lighter olive-brown, more delicate weed with *more profuse* secondary branching; it also has some branches longer than axis but distinction between axis and branches is more subtle. Whole plant spreading to 12–18 in. (300–450 mm); axis and branches less than $\frac{1}{16}$ in. (1.6 mm) thick. Matures late spring–early summer; epiphytic or subtidal in quiet places. L.I. Sound to Cape Cod; unknown before 1928 and possibly derived from a European relative. Family Acrothricaceae. (2) North of Cape Cod, Black Whip Weed is most easily confused with the sour weeds, *Desmarestia* and *Dictyosiphon* species (Plate 4).
Season: Perennial.
Where found: Formerly (and rarely) from New York harbor to Arctic; now chiefly north of L.I. Sound. On rocks or wood from lower intertidal zone to subtidal, in fairly exposed places.
Family: Chordariaceae.

BROWN SLIME WEEDS *Eudesme* species   Pl. 5

Identification: Slender and stringy; texture soft and *gelatinous* with hardly more substance than thickish egg white. A colorless core can be seen with hand lens if base of specimen is pressed between thin glass plates. Light brown, drying on paper to little more than a yellowish or greenish stain.

2 species. (1) *E. virescens* is a coarsely branching form with main parts to $\frac{3}{8}$ in. (9 mm) thick, whole plant to 14 in. (350 mm). (2) *E. zosterae* (not shown) is more delicate, sparsely branched; to $\frac{1}{8}$ in. (3 mm) thick by 4–6 in. (100–150 mm) long.
Similar species: Red Slime Weed, *Nemalion multifidum* (Plate 5) is similar both in its slimy texture and cored structure but is *rusty to dark red.* To 10 in. (250 mm). On exposed intertidal rocks. Slippery. Maturing in midsummer. Long Island to Nova Scotia. Phylum Rhodophyta, Family Helminthocladiaceae.
Season: (1) *E. virescens* matures spring–early summer. (2) *E. zosterae,* summer–fall.
Where found: (1) *E. virescens,* Long Island to subarctic. Epiphytic on Eelgrass and larger seaweeds, also on pebbles subtidally. (2) *E. zosterae,* Gulf of St. Lawrence south to tropics; chiefly epiphytic on Eelgrass.
Family: Chordariaceae.

SEA POTATO *Leathesia difformis*   Pl. 5

Identification: Grows in lumpy, often hollow, saclike masses. Rubbery in texture, yellow-brown in color. Epiphytic on larger seaweeds or on rocks in lower littoral zone. Suggests a compact sponge but lacks porous structure of sponges; more like partly dried grapes. To 3–4 in. (75–100 mm) across.
Season: Summer.

Where found: Newfoundland south to L.I. Sound and locally to N.C. Initially epiphytic on Irish Moss, Coral Weed, and other plants, but sometimes choking out its host and spreading over rocks.

Family: Chordariaceae.

SLIPPERY TANGLE WEED   Pl. 5
Sphaerotrichia divaricata

Identification: A slender bushy weed, finely branched with ultimate branchlets *wide-angled;* texture *soft* and *slimy.* Largest branches less than $\frac{1}{16}$ in. (1.6 mm) thick, plant spreading to 20 in. (500 mm).

Similar species: Rough Tangle Weed, *Stilophora rhizodes* (Plate 5) is coarser, somewhat *stiff* and *brittle, finely roughened* with bumps. Pale- to yellowish-brown. Thickest branches to $\frac{1}{8}$ in. (3 mm); whole plant to 1 ft. (300 mm). Summer; N.C. to Cape Cod and Prince Edward I. Epiphytic or drifting free in quiet shallow water. Family Stilophoraceae.

Season: Summer.

Where found: N.J. to Labrador; epiphytic.

Remarks: Slippery Tangle Weed from protected and somewhat polluted coves is stiffer, less slimy than average.

Family: Chordariaceae.

SPINY SOUR WEED *Desmarestia aculeata*   Pl. 4

Identification: Bushy; branches somewhat stiff, alternating on main axis and often partly *flattened.* Seasonally variable: has tufts of fine brownish hairs in spring; summer form *bristly* with short, spiky branchlets. Dark brown fading to yellow-brown, often bleaching white or yellowish at tips when exposed by low tides. Usually to 18 in. (450 mm), axis $\frac{1}{16}$–$\frac{1}{8}$ in. (1.6–3 mm) thick.

Similar species: See next account.

Season: Annual, spring and summer only.

Where found: L.I. Sound to Arctic. On rocks or wood from lower intertidal to subtidal at shallow depths in fairly protected places.

Family: Desmarestiaceae.

SOFT SOUR WEED *Desmarestia viridis*   Pl. 4

Identification: Bushy; main branches *opposite* and regularly spaced, with abundant fine, terminal branchlets, and covered in spring with fine hairs. Pale brownish but fading rapidly out of water to yellowish olive. *Sour smelling* especially when out of water for any length of time. Usually to 2 ft. (600 mm), main axis $\frac{1}{16}$–$\frac{1}{8}$ in. (1.6–3 mm).

Similar species: (1) False Sour Weed, *Dictyosiphon foeniculaceus* (Plate 4) is more delicate-looking, though it is stiffer than

Soft Sour Weed. It lacks sour smell, is chiefly *epiphytic,* and more *randomly* and often sparsely branched. Light brown when alive, dries dark. To 2 ft. (600 mm) but main axis usually *less than* $\frac{1}{16}$ in. (1.6 mm). Perennial; L.I. Sound to Cape Cod, less common northward to Arctic; often in rock pools. Family Dictyosiphonaceae. (2) See Plate 4 for other similar species. **Season:** Annual. Winter in Barnegat Bay, but spring and summer from L.I. Sound northward.

Where found: N.J. to Arctic. On rocks and wood from lower intertidal zone to subtidal.

Remarks: The peculiar acrid smell due to acidic cell sap is distinctive and symptomatic of this weed's delicate constitution. *Do not* store collected specimens with other algae; it self-destructs when picked, and in crowded buckets is destructive to other weeds. Specimen mounts should be made as quickly as possible.

Family: Desmarestiaceae.

RIBBON WEEDS *Punctaria* species   Pl. 6

Identification: Ribbon- or oar-shaped, broad to narrow, veinless and undivided. Holdfast a small *pad.* Color light to dark brown sometimes tinged yellowish or olive.

2 species, readily distinguished from each other but not always from several related species in other genera. (1) Delicate Ribbon Weed, *P. latifolia,* tapers *abruptly* to a basal stalk, is lighter, yellowish or olive-brown, and filmy *thin.* (2) Coarse Ribbon Weed, *P. plantaginea,* tapers *gradually* to a short stalk, is *dark* brown and relatively thick and leathery. Both species usually up to 1 ft. (300 mm) but sometimes nearly twice that. **Similar species:** Ribbon weeds and both of the following differ from young kelp (Plate 3) in having a small padlike holdfast; kelp has a branching holdfast and a stipe $\frac{1}{4}$ in. (6 mm) or longer. (1) *Petalonia fascia* (not shown) is easily distinguished *microscopically* but varies in form, resembling *both* ribbon weed species. When abruptly tapered basally (*latifolia*-like), basal parts are usually *asymmetrical.* When tapered gradually (*plantaginea*-like) stalk is usually longer and round; olive- to dark-brown; to 18 in. (450 mm) long. On rocks or wood in *upper* littoral. Sometimes perennial, best from winter–spring; through summer in Chesapeake Bay. Fla. to subarctic. (2) *Desmotrichum undulatum* (not shown), a *paper-thin, light-brown* epiphyte on Eelgrass and algae, has narrowly tapered base; usually less than 3 in. (75 mm) but sometimes much longer. Best in early summer. Southern N.J. to Prince Edward I.

Season: Winter–spring; decays in summer in some areas but flourishes elsewhere — for example, in lower Chesapeake Bay and south shore of Cape Cod.

Where found: (1) *P. latifolia* from s. N.J. to Gulf of St. Law-

rence; mainly *epiphytic* on Eelgrass and larger weeds. (2) *P. plantaginea,* Chesapeake Bay to Arctic; sometimes epiphytic but usually found on stones in pools or shallow water.
Family: Punctariaceae, including *Petalonia* and *Desmotrichum.*

SAUSAGE WEED *Scytosiphon lomentaria*   **Pl. 5**
Identification: Slender, *hollow,* unbranching thalli typically, but not invariably, *constricted* and twisted at intervals to resemble a chain of sausages. Usually in clumps. Golden brown to olive. To 2 ft. (600 mm).
Similar species: Young or variant individuals with few or no constrictions may resemble the following species. (1) Rough Hollow Weed, *Asperococcus echinatus* (Plate 5) is also hollow-bladed, varies greatly in width, and is sometimes twisted but lacks definite constrictions; surface rough, like *fine sandpaper.* To 20 in. (500 mm). In clumps, epiphytic or on stones or wood; lower intertidal in somewhat protected places. Annual, early spring. Del. to Arctic. (2) Smooth Cord Weed (Plate 4) is whiplike; lacks gritty surface. (3) *Halosaccion ramentaceum* (Plate 5) is a hollow-bladed *red* weed that often fades to rusty- or golden-brown; to 1 ft. (300 mm). Extremely variable; some variants resemble Dumont's Red Weed (Plate 6) but others approach Smooth Cord Weed, Rough Hollow Weed, or Sausage Weed. *Halosaccion* lacks gritty surface and sharp constrictions, and usually has at least a few lateral *branchlets.* Phylum Rhodophyta, Family Rhodymeniaceae.
Season: Annual, winter–spring, usually gone by midsummer.
Where found: Subarctic to Fla. Intertidal on rocks and ocean jetties in exposed places; also in quiet bays.
Family: Punctariaceae, including *Asperococcus.*

SMOOTH CORD WEED *Chorda filum*   **Pl. 4**
Identification: A slender, *whiplike,* brown weed without branches. Young plants have a coating of very fine, *colorless* hairs, which are subsequently shed. Hollow-cored; buoyant in water. To 15 ft. (4.5 m) or more long but hardly more than $\frac{1}{4}$ in. (6 mm) thick.
Similar species: *C. tomentosa* (not shown) has a *persistent* coating of fine, *dark* hairs $\frac{1}{4}$–$\frac{3}{4}$ in. (6–19 mm) long. To 3 ft. (900 mm) or longer by $\frac{3}{16}$ in. (5 mm) thick. Winter–spring.
Season: Annual; maturing in late summer.
Where found: From L.I. Sound to Arctic, attached to shells or stones from lower intertidal zone to subtidal.
Family: Laminariaceae.

EDIBLE KELP *Alaria* species   **Pl. 3**
Identification: Long-bladed with *midrib;* usually much frayed. Stalk solid with *lateral bladelets* below main blade;

these have a reproductive function and are shed annually leaving *bumps* as a vestige. Dark brown. To 10 ft. (3 m).

5 species have been named; 2 are considered questionable. Traits are not well developed in young plants. (1) *A. esculenta* has edges of midrib well defined laterally. (2) *A. pylaii* and *A. grandifolia* (neither shown) have midrib edges feathered into the blade, the 1st species with short stalk (usually less than twice width of blade), 2nd with longer stalk.

Season: Perennial.

Where found: Arctic to Cape Cod and *A. esculenta* sparingly to L.I. Sound. Like most kelps, primarily subtidal, but sometimes the dominant seaweed at lowest level of the intertidal zone on exposed rocks or in low pools.

Remarks: The species name *esculenta* refers to this kelp's edibility. See *Field Guide to Edible Wild Plants of Eastern and Central North America* and Euell Gibbons' *Stalking the Blue-Eyed Scallop* for a detailed account of this plant's food uses.

Family: Laminariaceae.

SEA COLANDER *Agarum cribrosum* **Pl. 3**

Identification: This kelp is easily recognized by its *midrib* and *perforated blade*. Dark brown. To 6 ft. (1.8 m), sometimes twice that.

Season: Perennial.

Where found: Cape Cod to Arctic. Chiefly subtidal but can be found washed ashore.

Family: Laminariaceae.

HORSETAIL KELP *Laminaria digitata* **Pl. 3**

Identification: Mature plants have a wide blade split into 6–30 or more straplike "fingers"; young thalli have fewer divisions. Stalk *stiff*, woody, and flattened above; in cross section shows concentric growth rings. To $3\frac{1}{2}$ ft. (1.1 m).

2 forms (not shown), previously considered separate species, are probably only ecological variants. (1) *L. stenophylla* has a weak *flexible* stalk *without* growth rings. Annual; on exposed rocks in lower intertidal zone, Gulf of Mexico to Newfoundland. (2) *L. intermedia* also has a weak stalk, *with* growth rings in older plants; blade sparsely or not at all divided, typically with no more than 3 or 4 "fingers." Annual, subtidal. L.I. Sound to New Hampshire.

Season: Perennial.

Where found: L.I. Sound to Arctic. On exposed rocks in extreme lower intertidal zone, or in pools in e. Maine; subtidal southward.

Family: Laminariaceae.

COMMON SOUTHERN KELP *Laminaria agardhii* **Pl. 3**

Identification: Long-bladed, *without* midrib; stalk *solid,* with branching holdfast. Winter growth is thick-bladed, straplike; summer growth thinner, with ruffled edges. These variations appear in the following species as well. Dark brown. To 10 ft. (3 m).

Similar species: (1) Hollow-stemmed Kelp, *L. longicruris* (Plate 3) has a long stalk that is solid below but expanded and *hollow* above, then pinched at base of blade. Usually to 15 ft. (4.5 m) but to 36 ft. (10.8 m) in deep water. Perennial; subtidal but washes ashore Arctic to Cape Cod, locally to L.I. Sound. (2) *L. saccharina* (not shown) is a problematic species distinguishable only by microscopic section; some authorities consider *L. agardhii* a form of this species. In tide pools and subtidal. A *northern* species, n. Mass. to Arctic. (3) *Saccorhiza dermatodea* (not shown) has a *cuplike* holdfast. In tide pools and subtidal, n. Mass. to Arctic. (4) Ribbon weeds (Plate 6) distinguishable from young kelp by small *padlike* holdfast.

Season: Perennial.

Where found: L.I. Sound and off New York harbor to Gulf of Maine; locally to Arctic.

Remarks: This is the only common long-bladed kelp south of Cape Cod. It may be found washed ashore from deep water but also establishes a *laminarian zone* at the low tide line at Point Judith, R.I., and elsewhere. The species name *saccharina* refers to the sugary, sweet-tasting powder that forms on dry blades of this and other kelp.

Family: Laminariaceae, including *Saccorhiza*.

KNOTTED WRACK *Ascophyllum nodosum*   **Pl. 2**

Identification: Long fronds of this olive-colored weed cover intertidal rocks below the upper band of rockweeds. "Knots" are air bladders placed along narrow *ribless* branches that also bear 1–2-in. (25–50 mm), rabbit-eared branchlets at intervals. Commonly to 2 ft. (600 mm), sometimes much longer. Knotted Wrack is highly variable. Early spring plants have *short*, contrastingly yellow *receptacles*, which are stalked, warty, fruiting structures that release motile sex cells, then fall off. A form that is called "scorpioides" (Plate 2) usually lacks bladders, has weak branchlets, and grows mainly in salt marshes.

Similar species: (1) *A. mackaii* (Plate 2) is also a marsh plant, has slender branches, small air bladders, and *long* podlike receptacles in late winter–early spring. To 8 in. (200 mm). L.I. Sound to Newfoundland. (2) Rockweeds (Plate 2) are ribbed.

Season: Perennial.

Where found: Arctic to L.I. Sound, but see below for variations in normal range.

Remarks: Consider that you are in effect walking over a thick bed of wet noodles concealing sharp rocks, deep crevices, and other pitfalls, and use appropriate care when exploring any expanse of rock covered by this slippery weed.

Knotted Wrack sometimes goes adrift as an oceanic plankter, washing ashore with Gulfweed far south of its normal range. It is also used as packing material for bait worms, lobsters, and the like, so may be found discarded far from home. Drift specimens resemble the typical form but may be golden or yellow-brown and may have oceanic hitchhikers such as goose barnacles attached. Benthic weeds also carry epiphytes, notably some of the tubed weeds (Plate 9), and *Pylaiella littoralis* (p. 50) among others.

Family: Fucaceae.

ROCKWEEDS *Fucus* species   **Pl. 2**

Identification: Blades usually broad and flat with a strong *midrib;* dividing dichotomously (in more or less equal, Y-shaped forks). To 3 ft. (900 mm).

6 species, 5 shown; easiest to distinguish when "in fruit." (1) *F. vesiculosus,* the most common and widespread species, is the only one that has paired, pea-shaped *air bladders* placed at intervals *within* the blade; they pop when you step on them. This is a variable species not always distinguishable from the following. (2) *F. spiralis* is similar but has twisted blades and lacks air bladders. (*Note:* A common variant of *vesiculosus* has even more distinctly *spiraled* blades than *spiralis,* and when found in quiet habitats — borders of bays, marsh ditches, and the like — it sometimes has fewer air bladders than the typical form.) When *spiralis* and *vesiculosus* occur together, the former is usually zoned at a higher level. (3) *F. serratus* (not shown) has blades with saw-toothed edges; note range (below). (4) *F. evanescens,* (5) *F. edentatus,* and (6) *F. filiformis* may be indistinguishable from variant *vesiculosus* and bladderless *spiralis* unless "in fruit." In any event, these 3 species are regarded by some botanists as merely ecological variants of *F. distichus* (not shown), a species reported from Newfoundland.

Season: Perennial.

Where found: (1) *F. vesiculosus,* N.C. to Arctic, mid- to lower-littoral (see p. 20); ecologically versatile with several named salt-marsh varieties. (2) *F. spiralis,* L.I. Sound to Newfoundland in *upper* mid-littoral. (3) *F. serratus,* Nova Scotia to Gaspé Peninsula in *lower* mid-littoral. (4) *F. evanescens,* L.I. Sound (sparingly) to Arctic, usually at the lowest intertidal level and subtidally in quiet places but sometimes on the exposed coast, too. (5) *F. edentatus,* L.I. Sound (sparingly) to Newfoundland, mid- to lower-littoral in places exposed to heavy surf. (6) *F. filiformis,* n. Mass. to subarctic, chiefly in *high* tide pools.

Remarks: The weed-covered appearance of intertidal rocks, usually olive-colored but varying in tint from golden-yellow to deep green, is chiefly due to the rockweeds and Knotted Wrack. These plants also festoon pilings, grow around the bases of

salt-marsh grasses, and float free in ditches and pools. A host of epiphytes and epizoans grow on them. When the tide is out the sun may parch the surface layer of rockweeds but the underside remains cool and wet, sheltering a great variety of smaller plants and animals.
Family: Fucaceae.

GULFWEED *Sargassum* species   **Pl. 2**
  Identification: Bushy; narrow blades have toothed edges, a midrib, and small — $\frac{1}{4}$ in. (6 mm) or less — pealike air bladders on short stalks. Golden-brown when fresh, drying dark brown. To 2 ft. (600 mm) or more.
  3 species in our area, 1 benthic (attached), the other 2 pelagic (free-floating); 2 species shown. (1) *S. filipendula,* like other benthic *Sargassum* species, has small dark *spots* scattered over the leaves; these are scarce or absent in the following. (2) *S. natans* and (3) *S. fluitans* (not shown) are both pelagic. *S. natans* has, and *fluitans* lacks, a short spike on top of each air bladder.
  Season: Perennial, the benthic form dying back in winter in the North.
  Where found: (1) *S. filipendula* occurs locally from Cape Cod to the tropics; abundant at Beaufort, N.C. (just south of Cape Hatteras) and on parts of the south shore of Cape Cod, forming a distinct zone on rocks or rock jetties at or just below the low tide line. Also reported in L.I. Sound a century ago, but now absent from New York harbor, Chesapeake and Delaware bays, and ocean jetties elsewhere along our coast. (2) *S. natans* and (3) *S. fluitans* are strictly pelagic but are washed ashore, particularly in N.C. and the open coast of Martha's Vineyard and Nantucket; *S. natans* is the more common species.
  Remarks: Benthic *Sargassum* species reproduce sexually as well as asexually, while the pelagic species are strictly asexual.
  A fascinating natural community centers on the drifting masses of pelagic *Sargassum,* famed as the principal weed of the Sargasso Sea. Epiphytic algae and a wide variety of encrusting hydroids, bryozoans, and tube worms live attached to the thalli. Shrimps, crabs, and other invertebrates, and several kinds of fish cling to or hide among the floating weeds. Most are peculiar to this community and are not found elsewhere. When pelagic *Sargassum* is found ashore, a search of the tangled plants and associated flotsam will often produce other exotics from far offshore. *Sargassum* has numerous benthic species in the West Indies, where it forms distinct plant associations intertidally as the rockweeds do on our coast.
  Family: Fucaceae.

Red Seaweeds: Phylum Rhodophyta

These weeds are less consistent in color than the greens or browns. Usually the red shows through at least as a modifying tint in shades ranging from pink to purple; a few species, however, are almost black, others brownish, and some strongly tinged with green or yellow. Though usually smaller in size than brown weeds, the reds are greater in variety. For crustose and filamentous species see p. 48. In general, reds need less light than other weeds and are the most common species at lower intertidal levels.

LAVER *Porphyra* species   **Pl. 7**
Identification: Plants soft, paper-thin, and nearly transparent, in ribless, narrow to broad, ruffled blades or sheets. Color brown to purplish or reddish.

3 species, not readily distinguishable but differ somewhat in habitat; typical form shown. (1) *P. umbilicalis* grows on intertidal rocks or wood and becomes dry and waxy-looking between tides; to 1 ft. (300 mm) or more. (2) *P. leucosticta* is smaller — to 6 in. (150 mm) — and often *epiphytic* on intertidal seaweeds. (3) *P. miniata* is twice as thick (2 cells instead of 1) and *rosy* rather than drab-red as the others are; to 1 ft. (300 mm) or more; also epiphytic, but on weeds growing at *lower* littoral or laminarian levels (see p. 34).
Similar species: (1) For other broad-bladed, *veinless* red weeds see Dulse, p. 44. (2) Sea Lettuce (Plate 1) is similar but green and thicker. (3) See also ribbon weeds (Plate 6).
Season: (1) *P. umbilicalis,* best in late winter–early spring in Va., later northward and generally dormant or absent in midwinter. (2) *P. leucosticta,* winter–spring and usually gone by June, or July–August in n. New England. (3) *P. miniata,* midspring–fall in Maine; sometimes year-round southward.
Where found: (1) *P. umbilicalis* and (2) *P. leucosticta,* Fla. to Newfoundland and Maine, respectively. (3) *P. miniata,* n. Mass. to Arctic, mainly in upper intertidal zone.
Remarks: For those inclined to try eating seaweeds, Laver has been recommended above all other species in our area; it may be used to make a clear soup or wrapped around a hamburger-based stuffing. Laver is cultivated in Japan and China. See also the *Field Guide to Edible Wild Plants of Eastern and Central North America.*
Family: Bangiaceae.

DUMONT'S RED WEED *Dumontia incrassata*   **Pl. 6**
Identification: Thallus consists of a main axis sparsely branched along its whole length; branches often *longer* and

thicker than axis. Axis and branches similar in form, $^3/_{16}$ in. (5 mm) wide, solid and *tapering* below, hollow and *twisted* above, tubular parts inflated or collapsed. Usually solitary. Dull red or bleached yellowish especially toward decaying ends. To 1 ft. (300 mm) tall.

Similar species: (1) *Halosaccion ramentaceum* (Plate 5) is a highly variable, hollow-bladed red weed, sometimes indistinguishable even microscopically. *Halosaccion* is usually firmer, less slimy, rarely spiraled, and usually grows in extensive patches in more exposed places than Dumont's Red Weed. Perennial in tide pools and lower intertidal zone. N. Mass. to Arctic. See also Sausage Weed, p. 33. Family Rhodymeniaceae. (2) Additional hollow-bladed coarse algae are either green (*Enteromorpha* species, Plate 1) or brown (Smooth Cord Weed, Plate 4, and Sausage Weed, Plate 5).

Season: Appears in early spring, decaying by July in South; winter–spring most abundant in North.

Where found: New York harbor (formerly?) and L.I. Sound to Nova Scotia; common in n. Europe but unknown here before 1913. In shallow water, usually in sheltered estuaries and salt-marsh ditches.

Family: Dumontiaceae.

CORAL WEED *Corallina officinalis*   **Fig. 34 opp. Pl. 7**
Identification: The fan-shaped tufts of this odd weed are unmistakable; thalli consist of *hard,* jointed, opposite-branching segments. On exposed rocks Coral Weed often forms an inch-deep turf of tightly packed plants; in the undergrowth of larger algae or other protected situations growth is more open and feathery. Pinkish white to deep purple; white when dead. To $1\frac{1}{2}$ in. (38 mm) tall, but varying according to habitat.
Season: Perennial.
Where found: L.I. Sound to Newfoundland; common from lower intertidal zone to subtidal in deep water.
Remarks: Coral Weed, along with *Lithothamnium* (p. 49) and a few other species of seaweeds, precipitates calcium and magnesium carbonate as a hard surface crust on the living thallus. This habit is more common in warm tropical waters where broken fragments of such plants make a substantial contribution to the sediments of lime-sand beaches.
Family: Corallinaceae.

LACY RED WEED *Euthora cristata*   **Pl. 7**
Identification: This elegant rosy pink to red weed, much sought after for decorative dry mounts, grows in broad lacy fans 2 in. (50 mm) high.
Similar species: (1) Ribbed lace weeds, *Membranoptera* species (Plate 6) are sometimes as delicate but have a distinct

midrib that divides with the branches; see under Sea Oak, p. 46. (2) Red Fern (Plate 9) is another decorative red weed, quite different in form.

Season: Perennial.

Where found: Arctic to Cape Cod, in tide pools or extreme lower intertidal zone, less common and in deeper water south to New York harbor. This and the red weeds mentioned above are common epiphytes on coarse seaweeds such as kelp (p. 34), and are often washed ashore.

Family: Kallymeniaceae.

AGARDH'S RED WEED *Agardhiella tenera*   **Pl. 8**

Identification: A coarsely bushy red weed; both axis — $3/16$ in. (5 mm) thick — and branches *round,* tapering at ends *and base.* Texture fleshy and usually deep reddish. Variable; a more delicate and profusely branching form lives in quiet, somewhat brackish places, and another variant has axis and branches covered with short branchlets. To 1 ft. (300 mm).

Similar species: Individual plants of bushy, filamentous red weeds, such as tubed weeds, Banded Weed, and others (Plate 9), may equal coarser species *in mass* but axis and main branches are usually finer — no more than $1/16$ in. (1.6 mm) thick — and have a distinct structure visible with a hand lens. Agardh's Red Weed is more likely to be confused with the following species. (1) Brushy Red Weed (Plate 8) and (2) *Gloiosiphonia capillaris* (not shown) appear delicate by comparison due to their finer, more numerous end branches; see p. 41. (3) In *Gracilaria* species (Plate 8 and next account) branches do *not* taper basally; color is usually tinged *yellowish,* particularly in *G. verrucosa.* Axis and branches are at least partially flattened in *G. foliifera,* and fruiting bodies are more protuberant (see Fig. 35 opp. Plate 8). (4) *Lomentaria baileyana* (not shown) is a small and delicate weed with main axis less than $1/16$ in. (1.6 mm) thick. Branches strongly tapered at base, hollow, and usually *curving* in gentle arcs; the smaller branches often mainly on one side of their supporting branch. Pink to dull reddish, drying brighter. To 3 in. (75 mm). Subtidal in shallow protected waters from Maine to the tropics. Family Champiaceae.

Season: Perennial in most of its northern range.

Where found: Cape Cod south to tropics, and locally north to cen. Maine.

Remarks: This, along with species of *Gracilaria,* is one of the most characteristic plants of warm bays and sounds south of Cape Cod, where it grows attached to shells and stones or is found drifting free.

Family: Solieriaceae.

GRACEFUL RED WEED *Gracilaria foliifera*   **Pl. 8**

Identification: Coarsely bushy with at least some parts of axis and branches *flattened.* Fleshy, reddish or purple but frequently bleached yellowish. Form varies in different habitats, becoming less distinctive in quiet, brackish water. To 1 ft. (300 mm); axis sometimes to $\frac{1}{2}$ in. (12 mm) or more wide.

Similar species: (1) False Agardhiella, *G. verrucosa* (Plate 8) is equally variable in color and form but has *round* axis and branches that do *not* taper basally. To 1 ft. (300 mm). A perennial with distribution similar to Graceful Red Weed and north in warm bays to Prince Edward I.; often abundant, drifting free over muddy bottoms. Not always distinguishable from Graceful Red Weed and lumped with it by some botanists. Graceful Red Weed is more common than False Agardhiella north of Cape Cod and tolerates more brackish water; southward False Agardhiella is the commoner form. (2) For comparison with other bushy red weeds see preceding account.

Season: Usually perennial.

Where found: Common in shallow bays and sounds south of Cape Cod and locally north to cen. Maine. Ranges to tropics.

Family: Gracilariaceae.

BRUSHY RED WEED *Cystoclonium purpureum*   **Pl. 8**
Identification: Bushy, with main axis $\frac{1}{8}$ in. (3 mm) in diameter; larger branches sparsely divided but *fine branches abundant* in outer parts of plant. Variable; usually dark purplish or brownish red but bleaching to yellowish green, often with reproductive bodies remaining as *reddish bumps.* A distinct pigtail-like variant has tightly coiled end branchlets, and is less tufted than the typical form shown on Plate 8. To 2 ft. (600 mm).

Similar species: (1) *Gloiosiphonia capillaris* (not shown) has a pale and partly hollow axis, $\frac{1}{8}$–$\frac{3}{16}$ in. (3–5 mm) in diameter, with *much* smaller main branches and numerous end branches; branching in Brushy Red Weed is from large to small *gradually.* To 1 ft. (300 mm). In tide pools or subtidal; usually perennial, dying back in winter in some places. L.I. Sound to Newfoundland. Family Gloiosiphoniaceae. (2) For comparison with other bushy red weeds, see Agardh's Red Weed, p. 40.

Season: Perennial.

Where found: An abundant red weed from L.I. Sound to Newfoundland, mainly subtidal on sandy or shelly bottoms in both protected and exposed localities.

Family: Rhodophyllidaceae.

HOOKED WEED *Hypnea musciformis*   **Pl. 8**
Identification: A delicate, mosslike, sparsely bushy weed with numerous *short, spiky branchlets* in addition to longer branches with swollen *hooks.* Variable; usually bleached purplish-yellow to white, but may be green or reddish green, and the distinctive hooks may be scarce or absent. To 18 in. (450 mm).

Similar species: *Asparagopsis hamifera* (not shown) bears even more distinct hooks; larger branches are more numerous, and more densely covered with short branchlets, giving them a fir- or spruce-like appearance. Purplish to rosy red. To 4 in. (100 mm). L.I. Sound to Cape Cod; naturalized from Europe. Subtidal but often found ashore in dense tangles or entwined with other weeds. Family Bonnemaisoniaceae.

Season: Usually perennial.

Where found: Abundant south of Cape Hatteras in shallow water of bays and sounds, local in warm coves north to Cape Cod. Subtidal.

Family: Hypneaceae.

WIRE WEED *Ahnfeltia plicata*   **Pl. 7**

Identification: *Resembles coarse steel wool.* Dark purplish or almost black when fresh, but bleaches white. To 8 in. (200 mm); branches less than $\frac{1}{16}$ in. (1.6 mm) thick and about equal width throughout.

Similar species: (1) Twig Weed, *Polyides caprinus* (Plate 7) has more *regular* Y-shaped branching, is somewhat *less stiff* and more robust — branches $\frac{1}{16}$ in. (1.6 mm) thick; whole plant to 8 in. (200 mm). In cold tide pools in e. Maine but chiefly subtidal in deep water southward; washes ashore from Long Island to subarctic. Family Rhizophyllidaceae. (2) *Polysiphonia lanosa* (not shown) is a dark, tough epiphyte, growing in tufts to 2 in. (50 mm) on Knotted Wrack (Plate 2) and sharing its range; easily distinguished by its *polysiphonous* structure, which is visible with strong hand lens; see tubed weeds (p. 47). Family Rhodomelaceae. (3) *Gelidium crinale* (not shown) is wiry or threadlike — less than $\frac{1}{32}$ in. (0.78 mm) thick — and grows in 2-in. (50 mm) tufts; terminal branchlets short, pinnate, and flattened. Intertidal, particularly on steep rock faces. Cape Cod south to tropics; a summer form north of Cape Hatteras. Family Gelidiaceae.

Season: Perennial.

Where found: New York harbor (formerly?) north to Arctic. Mainly subtidal from Cape Cod south but also in low tide pools and crevices northward. Often washed ashore in twiggy tangles.

Family: Phyllophoraceae.

LEAF WEEDS *Phyllophora* species   **Pl. 7**

Identification: Plants distinctly *2-parted* with a sparsely branching stalk and ribless, wedge-shaped or broadly forking blades. Dark red or purple. 4–6 in. (100–150 mm).

2 common species, variable and often indistinguishable. (1) *P. brodiaei* has somewhat *flattened* stalk and gradually expanded blades; upper *margin* of fruiting blades with tiny globular projections. (2) *P. membranifolia* (not shown) has *rounded* stalk and abruptly expanded blades; fruiting bodies on *face* of blades.

Similar species: (1) Tattered pieces of Irish Moss (Plate 7) approach this form but are nearly *stalkless*. (2) Fragments of Sea Oak (Plate 6) might suggest leaf weeds but are *ribbed*.
Season: Perennial.
Where found: Del. to subarctic. Chiefly subtidal.
Family: Phyllophoraceae.

IRISH MOSS *Chondrus crispus*   **Pl. 7**
Identification: Variable in form and color. The *flattened* blades expand from a short stalk, forking broadly and repeatedly. Sometimes minutely divided into broad fans with somewhat overlapping bladelets; at other times sparsely branching with few and *narrow* blades. Color deep purplish red, often with bright bluish iridescence *underwater;* also brown or green; bleaches to yellowish or white. To 7 in. (175 mm) on exposed rocks; to 10 in. (250 mm) in quieter places.
Similar species: See Tufted Red Weed and leaf weeds (both Plate 7).
Season: Perennial.
Where found: L.I. Sound to Labrador. Lower intertidal zone, with a wider range vertically and in habitat than the next species.
Remarks: This is an important zone-forming plant; see **Remarks** under next species. Irish Moss has long been a popular food plant, used particularly in the preparation of blancmange. The commercial product *carrageenin,* which is made from Irish Moss, has had wide application as a gel in industry, pharmacy, and particularly in nutrition as a thickener in soups and dairy products. See *Field Guide to Edible Wild Plants of Eastern and Central North America.*
Family: Gigartinaceae.

TUFTED RED WEED *Gigartina stellata*   **Pl. 7**
Identification: This crisp, close-growing, dark brown or purplish weed has expanded blades, sometimes *curled* at the edges and covered with *short bumps* like Turkish toweling or terry cloth. To 3 in. (75 mm).
Similar species: Plants without bumps resemble variant Irish Moss (Plate 7) but stipe is usually curled.
Season: Perennial.
Where found: R.I. to Newfoundland. Pool edges and wave-beaten rocks in lower intertidal zone.
Remarks: This weed, with Irish Moss, often forms a definite zone between the rockweeds, which grow at higher levels, and the kelp and Coral Weed that fringe the lowest intertidal levels. Growing in a close turf, it provides safe footing and a welcome relief from the treacherously slippery tangles of rockweeds and Knotted Wrack on the upper shore.
Family: Gigartinaceae.

DULSE *Rhodymenia palmata* **Pl. 7**

Identification: Broad-bladed, *ribless,* and with a *small,* usually tapered stalk; forking above, and often with marginal leaflets. Tough and rubbery; *nearly opaque* in life, translucent and papery when dried. Deep purplish red. Dulse has an internal layer of large cells visible with a hand lens against the light. To 1 ft. (300 mm).

Similar species: (1) Laver (Plate 7) is more filmy and grows from a holdfast placed well *within* the margin. (2) Frayed Weed, *Rhodophyllis dichotoma* (Plate 6) also grows in ribless, purple-red, forked blades but is smaller — to 3 in. (75 mm) — and more fragile; typically with slender leaflets *all along* the margin. Intertidal or washed ashore; n. Mass. to Arctic. Family Rhodophyllidaceae.

Season: Perennial.

Where found: L.I. Sound to Arctic; a common plant from lower mid-littoral to deep water.

Remarks: Dulse, one of the edible seaweeds, is still harvested in the Canadian Maritimes and the Bay of Fundy, and packets of dull-red dried weed may be found in specialty stores. The texture of fresh dulse has been compared to salted rubberbands but improves on drying. See also the *Field Guide to Edible Wild Plants of Eastern and Central North America.*

Family: Rhodymeniaceae.

BARREL WEED *Champia parvula* **Pl. 9**

Identification: Bushy, with axis and branches coarsely *segmented;* segments as broad or broader than long, $\frac{1}{16}$-$\frac{1}{8}$ in. (1.6–3 mm) thick in main parts. Color variable but usually pale, reddish or pink to yellowish or greenish. Whole plant to 3 in. (75 mm) tall.

Similar species: Barrel Weed is not filamentous as defined on p. 50, since its segments are microscopically multicellular. Divisions are much coarser than any truly filamentous weeds except Pink Bead (Plate 9), which has a more regularly forking growth and differently shaped segments.

Season: Mainly summer–early fall, but year-round southward.

Where found: Cape Cod to tropics, chiefly subtidal in quiet water, often epiphytic; washes ashore.

Family: Champiaceae.

BANDED WEEDS *Ceramium* species **Pl. 9**

Identification: Bushy plants with axes and branches *banded* at regular intervals; tips of youngest branches with *pincers;* both details usually visible without hand lens. Banding sometimes partly obscured by multiplication of microscopic surface cells, and pincers sometimes missing from older plants. Color extremely variable, usually in shades of red, but bleaching to yellowish, greenish, or white. Soft and collapsing out of water. Main axes seldom more than $\frac{1}{32}$ in. (0.78 mm) thick — in most species about as thick as light sewing thread ($\#40$); whole plants 4–16 in. (100–400 mm).

9 species, varying in size and form; require microscope for positive identification. Even the most widespread species, *C. rubrum,* is extremely variable and not always conspicuously banded.

Similar species: Other coarsely filamentous or delicately bushy genera found with the banded weeds are really quite different if examined closely. See tubed weeds (Plate 9) and filamentous seaweeds, p. 50.

Season: *C. rubrum* is perennial; other species best in summer–early fall.

Where found: Whole coast. Often epiphytic or attached to various substrata from lower intertidal zone to subtidal in shallow water. Together with the tubed weeds (see p. 47), these are important zone-forming plants.

Family: Ceramiaceae.

PINK BEAD *Griffithsia globulifera* Pl. 9

Identification: Bushy, with axis and branches *segmented;* segments varying in shape in different parts from clublike to egg-shaped or spherical. In male plants segments become *larger* at tips but in females and spore-bearing plants, branchlets *taper* at the end. Segments are actually individual cells. Bright pink to nearly transparent. Fragile, collapsing completely when dried. Main parts to $\frac{1}{16}$ in. (1.6 mm) thick, whole plant to $2\frac{1}{2}$ in. (62 mm) or exceptionally to 8 in. (200 mm).

Similar species: (1) See Barrel Weed (Plate 9 and p. 44). (2) *G. tenuis* (not shown) is similar but segments are cylindrical, 3–6 times *longer* than wide and only $\frac{1}{64}$ in. (0.39 mm) thick. Branching is alternate and branches grow out from *middle* of supporting segment, whereas *G. globulifera* has regularly forked branches that grow from *end* of supporting segment. Summer; subtidal in quiet coves. Va. to Cape Cod. (3) Compare this species with other filamentous algae, p. 50, and banded weeds (Plate 9).

Season: Summer.

Where found: Cape Cod to tropics. Subtidal in quiet water, commonly washed ashore.

Family: Ceramiaceae.

RED FERN *Ptilota serrata* Pl. 9

Identification: Bushy, with main branches *flat* and fernlike. Use hand lens to see distinct branching system; branches are consistently *opposite* but one branch of each pair is well developed while its opposite is much smaller; in the next pair the relationship is reversed, so that fully developed branchlets *alternate*. This system is usually carried through to the smallest branchlets. Dark red or brownish red fading to bright red. Whole plant to 6 in. (150 mm).

Similar species: *Plumaria elegans* (not shown) is very similar but branching is *less regular* and whole plant is more delicate; terminal branchlets *filamentous* under hand lens (see p. 50). Habits and distribution similar to Red Fern though it only ranges north to Gulf of St. Lawrence. To 8 in. (200 mm).

Season: Perennial.

Where found: Arctic to Cape Cod; rarely and in deeper water south to L.I. Sound. Subtidal, about bases of kelp, or occasionally epiphytic on coarse seaweeds. Commonly washed ashore.

Family: Ceramiaceae, including *Plumaria*.

GRINNELL'S PINK LEAF *Grinnellia americana*   **Pl. 6**

Identification: Thallus a thin *undivided* leaf with a weak *midrib*. Translucent pinkish with darker spots — females have round spots; spore-bearing thalli, elongate spots; males unspotted. Female and spore-bearing thalli to 2 ft. (600 mm); males to 1 in. (25 mm).

Similar species: A delicately beautiful weed not likely to be confused with any other, but see Sea Oak (next account) for other *ribbed* red weeds.

Season: In North appears and disappears abruptly sometime during the summer, persisting little more than a month; season longer in South.

Where found: N. Mass. south at least to the Carolinas; subtidal.

Family: Delesseriaceae.

SEA OAK *Phycodrys rubens*   **Pl. 6**

Identification: As the name implies, leafy, deeply lobed, with midrib and *lateral* ribs. Deep red, fading to pink. To 6 in. (150 mm).

Similar species: Other pink to red or purplish algae *with midrib* include the following. (1) Ribbed lace weeds, *Membranoptera* species (Plate 6), have finely divided *lacy* thalli; lateral ribs absent in *M. alata,* microscopic in *M. denticulata.* To 8 in. (200 mm) tall. Arctic southward — *M. alata* to n. Mass. and *M. denticulata* to L.I. Sound. Usually subtidal but may be washed ashore. (2) Grinnell's Pink Leaf (Plate 6) is undivided (without lobes) and has only a *weak* midrib. (3) *Caloglossa leprieurii* (not shown) is a more southern red weed with Y-forked, *narrow* thalli, and midrib only. To 2 in. (50 mm) tall. Conn. south to tropics; brackish to fresh water. (4) Tattered fragments of Sea Oak could be mistaken for leaf weeds (Plate 7), but Sea Oak is translucent, leaf weeds are not.

Season: Perennial or biennial.
Where found: Arctic south to Cape Cod, less commonly to New York harbor. In tide pools or extreme lower intertidal zone northward; subtidal in deep water southward but often washed ashore. A common epiphyte on coarse seaweeds such as kelp.
Family: Delesseriaceae, including *Membranoptera* and *Caloglossa.*

CHENILLE WEED *Dasya pedicellata*   **Pl. 8**
Identification: The *furry* strands of this graceful summer weed are unmistakable. Few to many branches; light to deep red or purplish. To 2 ft. (600 mm) or more.
Season: Annual; blooms briefly sometime between midsummer and late fall in North; season longer in South.
Where found: Maine or Nova Scotia to tropics. Subtidal, but often in the wash of quiet water in bays and inlets.
Family: Dasyaceae.

POD WEEDS *Chondria* species   **Pl. 9**
Identification: Bushy, with rounded, alternate branches; end branchlets *short* — $\frac{3}{16}$ in. (5 mm) or less — and club- to spindle-shaped, *tapering at base;* general shape of thallus pyramidal. Color usually faded, purplish or brownish purple to straw-colored. Main branches no more than $\frac{1}{8}$ in. (3 mm) thick; whole plants 4–10 in. (100–250 mm) tall.

4 species, often difficult to distinguish; typical form shown on Plate 9. The 2 most common species, *C. tenuissima* and *C. baileyana,* collapse out of water; in *tenuissima,* branchlets *taper* at outer end while *baileyana* has *blunt-ended* branchlets. *C. baileyana* is usually epiphytic on rockweeds, Eelgrass, and the like; *tenuissima* seldom is. Compared side by side, *baileyana* is more delicate. The less common species, *C. sedifolia* and *C. dasyphylla,* do not collapse out of water; in *dasyphylla,* branchlets *taper* at outer end, whereas *sedifolia* has *blunt-ended* branchlets.
Season: Summer.
Where found: Nova Scotia to tropics; from lower intertidal zone to subtidal with banded and tubed weeds (Plate 9) on rocks or wood. Sometimes drifting free.
Family: Rhodomelaceae.

TUBED WEEDS *Polysiphonia* species   **Pl. 9**
Identification: Bushy plants with main axis and branches *polysiphonous.* (This construction may be visualized roughly as consisting of bundles of filamentous fibers or tubes bound together. Usually visible with a hand lens, particularly in younger parts of plant, and appearing as in the **detail** on Plate 9 with *fine* cross and lengthwise marks.) Light brown or yellowish brown,

pink to reddish, to almost black. Main axes seldom more than $\frac{1}{32}$–$\frac{1}{16}$ in. (0.78–1.6 mm) thick and usually less, but whole plants may be to 16 in. (400 mm) tall.

Numerous species, varying in size and form; microscopic study usually required to distinguish between them. *P. harveyi* and *P. denudata* shown. Another species, *P. lanosa* (not shown) is easily identified by its association with Knotted Wrack, on which it grows as an epiphyte; see Wire Weed (p. 42) for this species.

Similar species: (1) *Rhodomela* is a similar and frequently indistinguishable genus, and the genera *Seirospora, Callithamnion,* and *Pleonosporium,* although technically not polysiphonous, *appear* to be so in part. Altogether these represent about a dozen additional species; none shown. (2) *Spyridia filamentosa* (Plate 9) is coarser — main axis to slightly more than $\frac{1}{16}$ in. (1.6 mm) — with distinctive cellular structure *just* visible with 20X hand lens; covered with tiny branchlets that appear *banded* but lack pincers (see banded weeds, Plate 9); to 1 ft. (300 mm); brown or reddish when alive, bleaching to yellowish. Chiefly summer; Cape Cod to tropics in warm, quiet coves. Family Ceramiaceae for all species listed above except *Rhodomela*.
Season: Some species perennial, others summer annuals.
Where found: Whole coast. Some epiphytic; several, with banded weeds, are important zone-forming plants on rocks and wood in lower intertidal zone south of Cape Cod. May also be found drifting free.
Family: Rhodomelaceae, including *Rhodomela*.

Additional Species Pl. 1

Two types of algal growth that are often conspicuous on the seashore require microscopic study for positive identification. The following accounts are only guidelines indicating general characteristics that will aid the reader in distinguishing some of the common forms. *Note:* Because of the large number of species discussed here, those that *are shown* are indicated rather than those that are not.

CRUSTOSE ALGAE: The encrusting algae that produce such vivid colors and "tar spots" in tide pools and on wave-washed rocks range in structure from feltlike, obviously organic forms to enamel-like coatings that might be mistaken for minerals or even paint. To identify, examine material under water; if obviously *filamentous* rather than crustose see that section below. The plants are grouped according to color.

Olive-Brown to Blackish: (1) *Calothrix* (Phylum Cyanophyta) is the commonest of several blue-green genera that form stainlike coatings in the upper spray zone. Caution: very slippery when wet. Whole coast. (2) Maritime lichens, *Verrucaria* species, form tarlike crusts at this same level. Mainly north of N.Y. (3) *Ralfsia* species (Phylum Phaeophyta) occur in crusts up to ⅛ in. (3 mm) thick by several inches wide; texture varies from firm and tarlike to brittle and crumbly. In pools or on *lower* intertidal rocks. N.J. to Arctic.

Blackish Green: Several species (all Phylum Chlorophyta) are common on rocks in spray zone or upper intertidal: (1) *Prasiola stipitata* scrapes off in ¼ in. (6 mm) *flakes*. Found on rocks with liberal spattering of bird droppings. Cape Cod to Newfoundland. (2) *Codiolum* species form velvety or furry patches of erect *club-shaped,* unicellular filaments easily visible under hand lens. Patches are ⅛-¼ in. (3-6 mm) thick. Maine to Newfoundland.

Fig. 7.

CODIOLUM
GREGARIUM

Dull Green: *Vaucheria* species (Phylum Xanthophyta) form thick films or mats (actually filamentous in structure) on intertidal *sand or mud flats.* Va. to Bay of Fundy.

White to Rose or Purple: Encrusting Corallinaceae (Phylum Rhodophyta) form *chalky* to *stony* crusts, ranging from thin and enamel-like to massive, knobby, or branching; infiltrated with calcium carbonate — hence will fizz with a drop or so of hydrochloric or other strong acid. *Lithothamnium* and *Phymatolithon* form heavy crusts usually on rock; *Melobesia, Lithophyllum,* and *Fosliella* form more fragile patches on Eelgrass and larger seaweeds. Whole coast.

Bright Red, Sometimes Tinted with Orange, Brown, Purple, or Black: All belong to Phylum Rhodophyta. (1) *Petrocelis middendorfii,* forms thin, *gelatinous,* and *slippery* patches less than ½ in. (12 mm) wide on rocks in *low* pools and subtidally. N. New England. (2) Various Squamariaceae: *Hildenbrandtia prototypus* is found in thin but tough *noncalcareous* films, and is common and conspicuous in pools and on intertidal rocks and shells. Whole coast. *Peyssonnelia rosen-vingii* is similar but has a *calcareous* basal layer. N. New England. Other *Peyssonnelia* species and those of *Rhododermis* and *Cruoriopsis* are mainly epiphytic or epizoic, although the latter genus is also abundant subtidally on rocks. *Peyssonnelia* has tropical and northern species; other 2 genera are northern only.

FILAMENTOUS SEAWEEDS: As used here, "filamentous" means a thallus consisting of a *chain of individual cells* attached end to end; see *Chaetomorpha melagonium* (Plate 1). The plants are threadlike, single-stranded or branching, and range in thickness from that of an individual fiber of absorbent cotton — about $\frac{1}{2500}$ in. (0.01 mm) — to that of ordinary paper-clip wire — about $\frac{1}{32}$ in. (0.78 mm). Despite their delicacy some of these plants form conspicuous growths. Cells of the coarser species are visible with a hand lens or even the naked eye. Slender but nonfilamentous weeds with branches $\frac{1}{32}$-$\frac{1}{16}$ in. (0.78 - 1.6 mm) thick are shown on Plates 7, 8, and 9; in these the cellular structure is not visible with a hand lens, or they are distinctive in other respects. Study of the complex life cycles of algae reveals that some filamentous forms are actually reproductive phases of quite different algae; for example, alternate generations of *Spongomorpha* (Plate 1) and *Codiolum* (p. 49) may occur in the same life history. The plants are grouped according to color.

Brown, Tinted with Yellow, Olive, or Rust: All belong to Phylum Phaeophyta. Usually epiphytic and no thicker than a human hair. (1) *Ectocarpus, Pylaiella,* and related genera have *unbranched* filaments; form soft beards on larger plants or other firm substrata; to 2 ft. (600 mm) long. Whole coast. (2) *Elachistea* and related genera grow in short — $\frac{5}{8}$ in. (16 mm) or less — tufts from a hard hatpin-sized *knob;* strictly epiphytic. Summer–fall. N.J. to Arctic. (3) *Sphacelaria* species occur in *stiff* tufts that do not collapse out of water; also form turf- or felt-like mats on larger plants, stones, and so forth. *Polysiphonous* structure is visible microscopically (see tubed weeds, p. 47). Whole coast.

Green, Sometimes Tinted with Yellow or Blue but usually not brownish or olive and usually not epiphytic: Various Chlorophyta in 3 groups.

(A) Filaments *unbranched,* cells *not visible* with hand lens; spring–summer only. (1) *Ulothrix* species have filaments about as thick as cotton fiber; to 1 in. (25 mm) long. *Attached* to rocks or wood in upper intertidal. Va. to Arctic. (2) *Rhizoclonium* species range up to as thick as cotton fiber. Floating *free* in mats or soft tangles in pools or shallow water or on the peaty banks of salt marshes. Whole coast.

(B) Filaments *unbranched,* cells *visible* with hand lens or

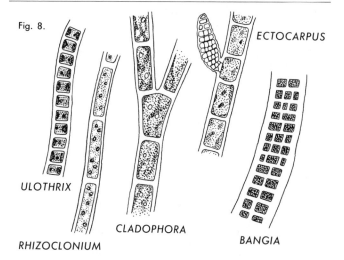

Fig. 8.

ULOTHRIX

RHIZOCLONIUM

CLADOPHORA

ECTOCARPUS

BANGIA

COMMON GENERA OF FILAMENTOUS SEAWEEDS

naked eye; coarse and wiry, or beadlike. (1) *Chaetomorpha* species: *C. melagonium* (Plate 1) is about as thick as paper-clip wire; cells $\frac{1}{8}$ in. (3 mm) or more long, whole plant to 1 ft. (300 mm) or more; blue-green. Attached in pools or on *lower* intertidal rocks. Arctic south to Cape Cod; uncommon beyond. *C. aerea* is similar but more slender; whole coast. *C. linum,* also a delicate form, is found in *drifting* tangles; whole coast. (2) *Urospora* species: usually at least as thick as human hair, with filaments tapering. To 8 in. (200 mm) long. Attached intertidally; N.J. to Arctic.

(C) Filaments *branched,* cells *not visible* with hand lens. Thickness ranges from hairlike to about that of light sewing thread (#40); sometimes epiphytic. (1) *Spongomorpha* species (Plate 1) have filaments united by hooks (rhizoids) in ropelike, 6-in. (150 mm) tangles (often teeming with minute invertebrates). Early spring–fall. N.Y. to Arctic. (2) *Cladophora* species *lack* hooklets; to 2 ft. (600 mm) long. Attached intertidally, and subtidally at shallow depths, or floating free as a greenish mist. Abundant; whole coast.

Dark Red, Tinted Purple, Brown, or Black: *Bangia fuscopurpurea* (Phylum Rhodophyta) is about as thick as horsehair and up to 8 in. (200 mm) long, but cells *not visible* with hand lens; *unbranched.* In slippery patches *above* barnacle zone on rocks or wood. Fades on drying to yellow-brown. Winter–late spring, waning in summer; whole coast.

Pink to Red: All belong to Phylum Rhodophyta. (1) *Rhodochorton purpureum* is as thick as cotton fiber; to almost 1 in. (25 mm) tall. Forms mounds or turf in shallow water. Long Island to Arctic. (2) *Antithamnion* and related genera are usually *thicker,* to width of #40 sewing thread or more; cells barely or not visible with hand lens. Epiphytic or on rocks in *lower* intertidal pools or shallow water. Whole coast. Thicker parts of *Seirospora, Callithamnion,* and *Pleonosporium* have a structure similar to tubed weeds (see Plate 9).

Seed Plants:
Phylum Spermatophyta

The two aquatic marine seed plants found on this coast are related to the pondweeds and are variously placed with them in the family Zosteraceae, Potamogetonaceae, or Najadaceae.

EELGRASS *Zostera marina*   **Fig. 9**
  Identification: Leaves $\frac{1}{4}$–$\frac{1}{2}$ in. (6–12 mm) wide, up to 3 ft. (900 mm) long. Grows from a creeping runner that sends up leafy stems at intervals. Flowers and fruit inconspicuous in 2 rows on a 1-sided spike.
  Season: Perennial; requires several years to mature. Older leaves die off, turn black, and are washed ashore in windrows. Flowers in late spring to early summer.
  Where found: S.C. to Arctic. Also Pacific Coast.
  Remarks: An ecologically important plant. At full growth Eelgrass may cover acres of shallow bottom in bays and sounds, stabilizing soft sediments and often playing a role in the successional development of coastal marshes. It is a principal winter food of the Brant, a small sea goose, and it supports and gives shelter to a host of small animals. Numerous invertebrates and epiphytic algae grow on the plant; others creep or burrow about the roots, and the floating leaves make a hiding place for sticklebacks and other small fish and swimming invertebrates. Dried Eelgrass was once important as mattress and upholstery stuffing.

  Periodically Eelgrass is stricken by a blight whose causes are still only partly understood. The last such episode began in the 1930s and recovery is still incomplete in some places. Among the side effects of this ecological disaster was a tremendous decline in Brant, as well as Bay Scallops, whose young cling to Eelgrass to avoid suffocation in bottom muck.

Fig. 9.

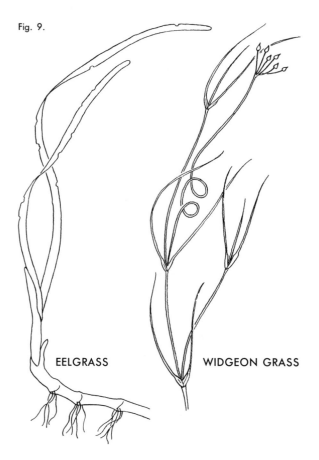

EELGRASS WIDGEON GRASS

WIDGEON or DITCH GRASS Fig. 9
Ruppia maritima
Identification: Leaves narrow, needle-like, 2 in. (50 mm) long, growing from a slender stem. Flowers and fruit small, in clusters of 2–4 on a slender stalk.
Season: Perennial.
Where found: Whole coast to Texas, in brackish bays; also widely distributed *inland* west of the Mississippi R. in alkaline waters.

Animals

WELL OVER 90% of the animal species (roughly a million altogether) are invertebrates — animals without backbones — classified in 25 major groups; 19 of these phyla are represented in this guide. The others are excluded because their members are either internal parasites (Mesozoa and Acanthocephala), completely microscopic or nearly so (Protozoa, Tardigrada, and Gnathostomulida), or found only in deep water (Pogonophora).

Form and Function: The arrangement of animals in a scientific classification is one of increasing structural and functional complexity. Thus the simplest animals, protozoans, are usually thought of as *unicellular,* single cells carrying on all basic life activities. All other animals are *multicellular.* They exhibit a progressively more elaborate organization of body parts, first in having some cells specialized for particular functions and then in having them arranged in tissues and organs whose activities are clearly defined and limited.

Animals are often spoken of as "higher" or "lower" on an evolutionary scale. This progression is obvious — up to a point. Sponges have little structural organization and have been described as being mere aggregations of cells. They cannot move and have no sensory apparatus, and so lack two attributes usually associated with animals. Comb jellies and cnidarians are far more elaborately constructed, and the basic body plan of the latter allows for much diversity in form and habits. Nevertheless, both phyla show only the rudiments of organ systems. They form a low branch of the family tree, set apart in being *radially symmetrical* — with parts arranged like the spokes of a wheel. Most higher animals are *bilaterally symmetrical;* they can be divided down the middle with each half a mirror image of the other. (Many echinoderms have reverted to radial symmetry, but their ancestors presumably were bilateral.)

Further progress includes the perfection of organ systems. The need for this will be more apparent if we consider an animal that *has not* evolved that far. Much of the body space of a cnidarian, such as a sea anemone, is taken up by a gastrovascular cavity with a mouth opening to the outside. When food is ingested this cavity becomes, in effect, a soup bowl from which the body cells (in 2 thin, surrounding layers) can absorb what they need. These layers are also in close contact with the environment and so can absorb oxygen easily. Wastes are exchanged in the same way. But as an animal gets bulkier or thicker, most of its cells are far removed

from the environment and food tract. The development of organ
systems is necessary for greater efficiency in various life functions,
and it also allows animals to grow to larger sizes.

Progress in these matters varies. There has been a great deal of
evolutionary experimentation. Certain groups of animals have
perfected some systems more than others, becoming experts in one
way of life in preference to another. Tunicates and bivalves, for
example, have evolved very efficient and specialized feeding apparatus but are not good at locomotion. Crustaceans have perfected
crawling and swimming techniques and the sensory apparatus
needed by active animals but are generally less specialized feeders.
The result of such divergence is that once a certain level of organization has been reached, it is no longer easy to say that one
evolutionary branch is higher than another. How does one decide,
for example, between a squid and a shrimp?

In the following section, animals are grouped according to their
form and function. Each category covers a diversity of taxonomic
classifications. See the endpapers (front and back) for correspond-
ing illustrations. Also note that one large category is being excluded from discussion here: Arthropods, including all the crustaceans (right back endpaper), which have a wide variety of very
distinctive forms, are treated in detail in the introduction to that
section; see pp. 205–211.

(1) SESSILE OR PLANTLIKE FORMS (*left front endpaper*): Sessile
means "affixed, not free-moving." Many such animals attach
themselves firmly to other objects and remain permanently fixed
in one spot or move about with prodigious slowness. Others are
colonial; tiny individual animals are united in branching, encrusting, or more massive shapes. These colonies may also be attached
to some object — a rock or wharf piling — or they may simply lie
about on soft ground.

Some of the larger *solitary* sessile animals have hard shells or
protective covering plates. Lamp shells and such bivalve mollusks
as oysters and jingle shells have 2 shells permanently fixed by a
stalk or have 1 shell glued down. Limpetlike gastropod mollusks
and chitons can and do move about but are often found firmly
clamped to a substratum; limpets have a single, uncoiled, conical
or caplike shell; chitons have 8 separate plates in a row. Acorn
barnacles also have more or less conical shells, but they are made
of separate plates with a central trapdoor. Goose barnacles appear
at first glance to be quite different from the acorn species, mainly
because they are flattened and mounted on a rubbery stalk; the
animal inside is similar. Sessile jellyfish and a few specialized sea
squirts, are stalked, too, but have no hard parts. Sea anemones
and the more typical sea squirts are also soft-bodied, solitary
animals. Anemones have a circlet of retractile tentacles, sea
squirts a pair of protruding, pipelike siphons. Even though some of

these solitary animals may be found bunched together, there is no structural continuity between individuals as there is between true colonial forms.

Most *colonial* invertebrates are sessile, although a few, the siphonophores for example, are pelagic. Many pose problems in identification because the shape and color of the colony varies depending on where and how it is growing. Some have hard "skeletal" parts; others are soft. They range in form from bushy, twiggy, or plantlike, to encrusting or lumpy.

One of the simplest designs for colonial organization consists of a vinelike stolon with individuals animals at intervals along the way. Some species of bryozoans, entoprocts, and hydroids take this form, as do some of the calcareous sponges. Other hydroid and bryozoan colonies may form luxuriantly bushy growths that are easily mistaken for fine seaweeds. However, the activities of the tiny polyps or zooids — popping in and out of their chambers or miraculously expanding and contracting flowerlike whorls of tentacles — quickly set them apart from plants. Individual species are distinguished by differences in colony form or fine details of the animals themselves. Creeping Ascidian, one of the colonial tunicates, also lives in finely branching colonies but is distinctive in having a pair of sea squirt-like siphons.

Though many bryozoan colonies are bushy, others grow as hard crusts; each nearly microscopic animal (zooid) lives in its own chamber with a calcareous shell. Colonies range from thin and lacy to thick and nodular. The individual animals are only $\frac{1}{50}$ in. (0.5 mm) or less long. Coral polyps are considerably larger — to $\frac{3}{16}$ in. (5 mm) in diameter in our few species.

Some colonial invertebrates that lack a protective outer shell have an internal "skeleton" of limy or glassy spicules; this may not be apparent without dissection, but often such forms have a tough or gritty structure. To study in detail, cut out a small block of the colony — $\frac{1}{8}$ x $\frac{1}{4}$ in. (3 x 6 mm) — place on a glass slide, and dissolve away the soft parts with Clorox. Then examine the residue with a microscope.

Sponges are considered colonial animals by some authorities, solitary individuals by others. Positive identification of many species requires study of their microscopic spicules. Only a few of our sponges have calcareous spicules; the others have glassy ones (insoluble in dilute acids). Sponges are perhaps most likely to be confused with certain octocorals, colonial tunicates, or bryozoans, which are rather blobby or lumpy in shape. They are definitely colonial, with individual animals sunk in a common matrix. Octocorals and some colonial tunicates have distinctive, imbedded, calcareous spicules; bryozoans do not. Live colonies are easily distinguished. When submerged in water the individual polyplike animals of octocoral or bryozoan colonies emerge and identify themselves: all octocoral polyps have 8 pinnate tentacles; bryozoans usually have more numerous filamentous tentacles. Individual colonial tunicates are tiny saclike animals, often grouped in clusters.

(2) WORMLIKE FORMS (*right front endpaper*): No shape is more practical for burrowing or wriggling into narrow spaces than that of the worm. Nearly all phyla have evolved wormlike forms and telling them apart can be difficult.

Some worms are *annulated* — distinctly and regularly segmented or ringed. (Don't be misled by irregular folds or wrinkles.) Annelid worms usually have lateral appendages on some or most segments; these include fine bristles and in many cases an assortment of lobed "feet." These feet are especially characteristic of the annelid polychaetes, a major and highly varied group of marine worms with many species. Often the polychaete body is divided into regions with different kinds of appendages in each; the head end may have a complex arrangement of tentacles, gills, and other structures, some or all of which may be contractile.

Another annelid division, the earthworms or oligochaetes, is less conspicuous around salt water; its species are small, very thin, and have only fine bristles as appendages. A few wormlike larval insects occur in salt water; usually they only have appendages on segments at the head and rear. Priapulus, an aschelminthean worm, has 30–40 warty rings, a cluster of short, thick appendages at the rear, and a large contractile proboscis and spiny mouth region. Some nematodes are also ringed, but most of these are tiny (almost microscopic) worms.

Other wormlike forms may have folds or wrinkles, especially when contracted, but the whole body is not regularly annulated. The simplest are soft, smooth, and either flat or oval to round in cross section with little or no differentiation of body regions. Flatworms are among these; they have no appendages at all except (in some species) tiny "horns" or "earflaps," and one genus has a sucker at the tail end; the mouth is at midbody, underneath. Nemertean or ribbon worms are thicker and usually more elongate but also smooth and soft; the mouth, near the front end, has a completely retractile tubular proboscis; sometimes they have a short curved tail. Certain ribbon worms resemble leeches but they are not parasitic, although *Malacobdella grossa,* a commensal species in bivalve mollusks, has a sucker at the rear. True marine leeches, found mostly as parasites on fish, have a sucker at both ends. Acorn worms have distinct body regions including a proboscis, collar, and long trunk. Shallow-water echiurids are sausage-shaped with a noncontractile grooved proboscis. All of these soft-bodied worms must be handled very gently and should be studied live.

Several unrelated groups of shell-less gastropods are basically sluglike with a creeping foot; many have a quite elaborate ornamentation of sensory and respiratory appendages.

A very miscellaneous assortment of unsegmented worms has a circlet of tentacles at the front end; often these can be completely contracted. Allow such worms a bit of quiet in subdued light in a bucket of seawater and the tentacles will probably expand nicely. The tentacular loop is U-shaped in Phoronis, a delicate but common subtidal worm. Sipunculids, are small, more than usually secretive worms that burrow in shells or soft bottoms; compare them with the species above; there are only a few.

Sea cucumbers and burrowing sea anemones, though completely unrelated, are also wormlike. Some are translucently delicate; others have more substance and may even be fairly tough-skinned. Anemones have only one body opening, a "mouth" at the center of the tentacular disk. Sea cucumbers have a double-ended digestive tract; most have minute spicules imbedded in their skin, and the more conspicuous species have tube feet.

(3) OTHER FORMS (*left back endpaper*): This is a miscellany of animal forms that do not conveniently fit into either of the previous sections.

The first group of animals to be considered here are shell-less and most are softly transparent or translucent swimmers and plankters. Some are quite familiar animal types, such as squids and jellyfish; the latter group includes a few medium to large species several inches or more across, plus a host of much smaller and more delicate hydromedusae. Comb jellies are usually mistaken for jellyfish, but they are globular, saclike, or lobed in shape rather than umbrella- or bell-like. They move with the aid of 8 rows of comblike cilia instead of jetlike pulses.

The cnidarian class Hydrozoa contains several highly specialized forms, the most familiar being the Portuguese man-of-war with its easily recognized balloonlike float. Related chondrophores and siphonophores are oceanic or tropical plankters not often found along this coast. Siphonophores are usually found (if at all) in dismembered, almost unidentifiable fragments.

At times the water swarms with delicately gelatinous, barrel-shaped animals that have hooplike muscle bands. These are pelagic tunicates called salps and doliolids. They have quite complex life histories, and at certain stages are joined together in chains.

Most shelled animals belong to the phylum Mollusca and are readily divided into bivalves with 2 shells and gastropods with a single, usually coiled shell. In addition there are bivalved lamp shells, Phylum Brachiopoda; our only shallow-water species is attached to the substratum by a rubbery stalk. Other animals with a single calcareous shell include some annelid worms (Family Serpulidae). The shells of a small pelagic squid called Spirula are coiled in a flat plane but are distinctly chambered. Many worms live in papery or leathery tubes or in ones made of sand grains, shells, or other debris glued together, but these are not likely to be interpreted as shells. Some amphipod crustaceans are also tube makers.

Tusk shells, also mollusks, resemble miniature elephant tusks; they are mainly found in deep water. A few other snails have simple uncoiled shells. Those of the caecums are tubular or cucumber-shaped and very small, $\frac{3}{16}$ in. (5 mm) long at most; limpets have cap-shaped shells.

Echinoderms make up one of the most unusual animal phyla. The main types are familiar and easily recognized shore animals. Echinoids have a hard calcareous test (outer shell or covering) that may be more familiar to beachcombers than the live animal. Those of sea urchins are globular and covered in life with large spines, while sand dollars and keyhole urchin tests are flat. Sea stars (or starfish) have tube feet in grooves on the underside of their arms, and the arms merge imperceptibly with the central disk. The tube feet of brittle stars are set obscurely in tiny pores, and the arms emerge from a clearly separate central disk.

Invertebrate Life Histories: The present diversity of animal life presumably has come about through a continuous process of evolution that *could* be traced back through time and countless slowly changing generations *if* the record were complete. It isn't. Nearly all invertebrate phyla were in existence by Cambrian time which began about 600 million years ago and is the 1st geological period for which there is a good fossil record. There are many missing links in charting these relationships. One line of evidence bearing on this problem has to do with how animals develop from egg to adult.

Many invertebrates have distinctive larval forms that are totally unlike the adult animal. They undergo a *metamorphosis,* often passing through several stages as different as tadpole and frog, or more so. These larval forms are very small, mostly microscopic; many of them are pelagic and are found in plankton tows. They are also important as food items for larger invertebrates and fishes, and play a vital role in the dispersal of animals that have little ability to travel far as adults.

The stages in an animal's development often seem to *recapitulate* its presumed evolutionary history; this principle has been much overworked and can only be applied in a very general way. But sometimes the young of one species do resemble adults of another that is lower on the evolutionary scale. This happens among comb jellies and poses a problem in identifying juvenile individuals.

Another reason young animals are often hard to identify is that species descriptions are traditionally based on mature animals, and no one has bothered to learn how to tell immature ones apart. Often the young of related species are much more nearly alike than the adults. One of the problems lies in determining whether

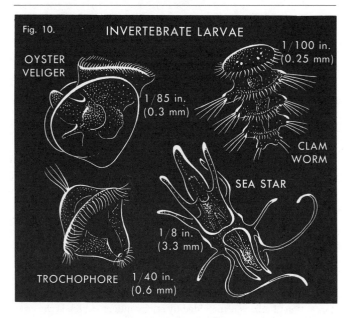

Fig. 10.   INVERTEBRATE LARVAE

OYSTER VELIGER — 1/85 in. (0.3 mm)

1/100 in. (0.25 mm)

CLAM WORM

SEA STAR — 1/8 in. (3.3 mm)

TROCHOPHORE   1/40 in. (0.6 mm)

an individual is mature — a point that is not always obvious.

Echinoderms have distinctive larval types that set them apart from nearly all other phyla. These larvae have been related to a somewhat hypothetical form called a *dipleurula,* a minute planktonic creature with a U-shaped gut and a band of *cilia* (fine, hairlike cell growths) that passes around the body between mouth and anus. Three main lines of larval development stem from this beginning. The ciliary ring may break up into secondary rings or lobes, or undergo other modifications; one line of development leads to sea stars, another to sea cucumbers, and a third to brittle stars and echinoids. Though very different when mature, the latter 2 groups remain quite similar through their early stages.

With various modifications (and some imaginative theorizing), the larvae of most other invertebrates can be related to a basic form called a *trochophore.* This is also a minute planktonic stage, top-shaped, with a tuft of cilia at the upper end, a band of cilia around the middle, and a smaller ring of cilia around the anus at the bottom. A few primitive species are trochophores at the hatchling stage, but most pass through this phase quickly, even before hatching. Subsequent development leads to such divergent forms as mollusks and annelid worms.

The life histories of cnidarians have a bearing on problems of species identification and are discussed in some detail on p. 70. Those of crustaceans are similarly important; see p. 209. For a more extended and very readable account of invertebrate larval development, see Sir Alister Hardy's *The Open Sea*.

Feeding Habits: Ultimately life in the sea as on land depends upon plants. With only the aid of their photosynthetic pigments, sunlight, small amounts of dissolved minerals, carbon dioxide, and water, plants grow and multiply. Animals cannot synthesize food in this way but must feed on other organisms. The microscopic free-floating plants called *phytoplankton* are at the base of marine food pyramids. The larger seaweeds add but little to total production.

Marine invertebrates have evolved many and varied techniques for feeding on small particles of phytoplankton, as well as on bacteria, fine bits of decaying organic matter (detritus), and small zooplankton. Most do this with the aid of cilia, which create currents to carry particles along to the mouth. The flow of water in and out of sponges is maintained in this way, and the tentacles and mouth area of anemones have a conveyor belt of cilia; so do sand dollars. Brachiopods, bryozoans, and sea squirts combine ciliary currents with various filtering devices, and the strange little appendicularian, Oikopleura, has evolved the most extraordinary technique for trapping the smallest phytoplankton (see p. 274). The action of cilia is often aided by sticky mucus, which is the case with sedentary worms that use their tentacles to sweep food particles from the surface. Thick strings or pellets of mucus with entrapped food items are conveyed by cilia in the feeding structures of parchment worms, boat snails, and most bivalves. Crustaceans do not have cilia, but some amphipods, most mysid and euphausiid shrimps, cumaceans, barnacles, and a few decapods, such as certain hermit crabs and mud shrimps, do filter small particles with nets and sweeps of hairlike *setae*.

Many bottom animals are *deposit feeders* that unselectively ingest organic materials along with sand and mud. The Lugworm is a good example, as are most sea cucumbers and some burrowing brittle stars. Other animals browse by means of rasping mouthparts; chitons and many snails and shell-less gastropods feed this way. Gribbles (isopods) and shipworms, which are bivalve mollusks, burrow into wood with rasping mouthparts or shell edges; gribbles feed mainly on wood-attacking fungi, but shipworms actually derive nourishment from the wood itself.

Ctenophores and most cnidarians are carnivorous. The latter capture prey by holding and stinging them with tentacles and sting cells; the ctenophores entrap animals with their tentacles and feeding lobes, aided again by cilia. Nemertean worms and some annelids snag their quarry by shooting out a proboscis armed with teeth or spines. Crustaceans, arrow worms, sea stars, and echinoids have jawed mouthparts for biting and chewing plants and animals that are either caught alive or found dead. Finally, a few invertebrates have sucking mouthparts for drawing out plant or animal juices; certain shell-less gastropods, parasitic copepods, and sea spiders are examples. By one means or another invertebrates utilize almost every available resource in the sea, occupy every habitat, and have fitted themselves into every available ecological niche.

Sponges: Phylum Porifera

Plant or animal? The earliest naturalists were unsure. There is still some question about whether an individual sponge is one animal or a colony. Sponges are the most primitive or simply organized of multicellular animals and lack organs or organ systems. Their cells, however, are specialized for different functions.

The body is porous with 2 types of surface openings; water currents flow *in* through minute (or microscopic) *ostia* and *out* through *oscula* (singular: ostium and osculum). Oscula may also be very small but in some cases are $\frac{1}{4}$ in. (6 mm) or more in diameter. Currents, generated by special cells lining the internal cavities, bring in oxygen and planktonic or detritic food and carry away wastes. Sponges grow asexually, but sexual reproduction also occurs. The details are obscure; sexes are not distinguishable and most individuals presumably are hermaphroditic.

Identification on the basis of color and body form of the whole sponge is not always reliable. Almost all sponges have a skeleton of glassy or limy *spicules* whose form and arrangement are diagnostic features; unfortunately, a microscope is needed. To aid those so equipped, spicule types and sizes are given in species accounts. Sizes are in *microns;* 1 micron (μ) equals 0.001 mm or roughly $\frac{1}{25,000}$ in. The smaller spicules, called *microscleres,* are often only 10–20 μ long; a 12-μ spicule is about $\frac{1}{30}$th the diameter of the visual field when a 10X eyepiece and 43X objective are used on the microscope. To prepare a spicule sample, cut a $\frac{1}{8}$-in. (3 mm) block from the sponge, place it on a glass microscope slide,

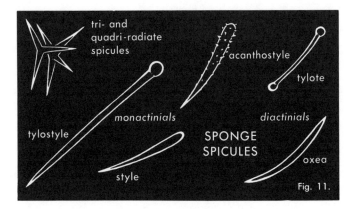

tri- and quadri-radiate spicules

acanthostyle

tylote

monactinials

diactinials

tylostyle

style

SPONGE SPICULES

oxea

Fig. 11.

dissolve away soft parts with Clorox, add a drop of water and cover slip; examine at about 100X or higher.

Sponges live in all seas, from the lower intertidal zone to great depths. Marine forms range into brackish waters with a minimum of about 10‰, a few into almost fresh water; freshwater sponges (Family Spongillidae) may penetrate estuaries but little is known about them there.

There are 3 classes: (1) Hexactinella or glass sponges live only in very deep water and have distinctive, 6-rayed, glassy (siliceous) spicules; (2) Calcarea have limy (calcareous) spicules; (3) Desmospongiae also have glassy spicules but not of hexactine type, or they have horny fibers, or both; most shallow-water sponges belong to this class.

ORGAN-PIPE SPONGES *Leucosolenia* species   Pl. 10

Identification: Colonies consist of clusters of *tubular* or vaselike, usually *branching* sponges. White or pale yellowish. To $\frac{3}{8}$ in. (9 mm) tall; tubes to $\frac{1}{16}$ in. (1.6 mm) thick. Spicules are 3- or 4-pronged stars; *calcareous* (fizz in dilute hydrochloric acid). Typical form shown.

Similar species: Vase sponges, *Scypha* species (typical form shown on Plate 10) have thicker — to $\frac{1}{8}$ in. (3 mm) — *unbranched* vases, to $\frac{1}{2}$ in. (12 mm) tall; osculum surrounded by fringe of spicules. Whitish. Also with tri- or quadri-radiate calcareous spicules. R.I. to Arctic; lower intertidal zone on rocks and pilings. Family Heterocoelidae. Note: *Scypha* species were long mistaken for *Grantia* species.

Where found: South side of Cape Cod to Gulf of St. Lawrence, on rocks, pilings, seaweeds, in tide pools; from lower intertidal zone to subtidal down to several hundred feet.

Family: Homocoelidae (Class Calcarea).

FINGER SPONGE *Haliclona oculata*   Pl. 11

Identification: *Erect* and *branching* from a short stalk. Branches vary from numerous, slender, and round (especially south of Cape Cod) to few, thick, and somewhat flattened. Color yellowish to grayish brown, sometimes tinted purplish. (A red-orange, palmate variant occurs off Cape Cod.) Oscula conspicuous, scattered, inspiring an alternate name, Eyed Sponge. To 18 in. (450 mm) tall; branches to $\frac{1}{2}$ in. (12 mm) thick. Spicules are *oxeas* less than 170 µ long.

Similar species: Palmate sponges, *Isodictya* species (Plate 11) have a broader base and branches. Color yellowish to dark red. 2 species: *I. palmata,* larger spicules mostly *oxeas* about 210 µ, a few *styles;* Nova Scotia to Bay of Fundy; *I. deichmannae,* mostly *styles* about 180 µ, a few *oxeas;* Newfoundland to R.I. Both are found subtidally in 20 feet (6 m) or more but may wash ashore. Family Desmacidonidae.

Where found: Labrador to L.I. Sound, rarely to Cape Lookout, N.C. In lower intertidal zone northward but mostly subtidal from shallow water to more than 400 ft. (120 m). Often washed ashore.

Family: Haliclonidae.

LOOSANOFF'S HALICLONA   Pl. 10
Haliclona loosanoffi

Identification: Dark tan to gold, less often pinkish. Cushion-like white specks called *gemmules* appear at base in late summer. Encrusting, with oscula to $\frac{1}{8}$ in. (3 mm) on *chimneys* up to 1 in. (25 mm) or more tall, sometimes branching and interconnected. Spreading to 2 – 3 in. (50 – 75 mm). Spicules include *oxeas* no longer than 185 µ and averaging 85 – 150 µ.

Similar species: (1) *H. canaliculata* (not shown) forms thin crusts *without* chimneyed oscula, no gemmules; spreading to 4 in. (100 mm) but less than $\frac{1}{2}$ in. (12 mm) thick. L.I. Sound to Bay of Fundy, under rocks. (2) See Bowerbank's Halichondria (Plate 10) for other tan or yellowish encrusting sponges south of Cape Cod. (3) Crumb of Bread Sponge (Plate 10) has similar form but *larger oxeas* and probably little or no overlap in range.

Where found: Cape Cod south probably to Cape Hatteras or beyond, certainly to Chesapeake Bay, where it ranges into brackish water north to the Patuxent R., Md. Common under rocks in lower intertidal zone, on pilings, oyster shells, Eelgrass, and such.

Family: Haliclonidae.

PURPLE SPONGE *Haliclona permollis*   Pl. 11

Identification: *Lavender or pinkish purple;* encrusting, with oscula — largest $\frac{3}{16}$ in. (5 mm) — on raised tubes. Sometimes with raised, interconnected branches spreading to 4 in. (100 mm) or more, with tallest parts 1 in. (25 mm) or more. Spicules include oxeas, the largest 100–200 µ.

Similar species: There *may* be more than one species of this type in our range and perhaps more than one genus; Loosanoff's Haliclona (Plate 10) is structurally similar but less commonly purple.

Where found: Reportedly cosmopolitan. Locally common in Maine tide pools and shallow water; also abundant in lower Chesapeake Bay. Similar sponges at Beaufort, N.C., may or may not be the same species.

Family: Haliclonidae.

EGG SPONGE *Mycalecarmia ovulum*   Pl. 10

Identification: This little sponge forms an *egg-shaped* "knot" on stems of small seaweeds, hydroids, bushy bryozoans. Light creamy to darker yellow. Surface finely shaggy. To $\frac{5}{8}$ in. (16 mm). Spicules include curved *styles* 165–300 µ long.

Where found: Arctic south at least to Isles of Shoals, lower intertidal zone down to subtidal in deep water.
Family: Mycalidae.

CRUMB OF BREAD SPONGE   Pl. 10
Halichondria panicea
Identification: The common greenish sponge encrusting rock walls in partly shaded tide pools and crevices north of Cape Cod; colonies may extend over several feet of surface. Vernacular name refers to texture. Oscula *prominent* on low chimneys. Color variable, green to yellow, or shades of orange or brown. Spicules include *oxeas* as long as 380 μ, average 250 μ.
Similar species: (1) Young or atypical colonies could be mistaken for the closely related Bowerbank's Halichondria (Plate 10) though their ranges are not definitely known to overlap. (2) *Myxilla incrustans* (not shown), may resemble yellow or yellow-orange variants in which case a spicule preparation is needed; *M. incrustans* has several types of double-ended spicules but no oxeas; also it has *spiny,* single-ended *acanthostyles* 200–400 μ long. Form and surface texture vary; often encrusts bivalves or other shelled invertebrates. Arctic south at least to Isles of Shoals; subtidal in shallow water. Family Myxillidae. (3) *Pellina sitiens* (not shown), reported from Maine north to Arctic, has irregular, raised fingers several inches tall; yellow or yellow-orange; has *oxeas* more than 600 μ long. Subtidal in 40 ft. (12 m) or more. (4) See Loosanoff's Haliclona (Plate 10).
Where found: Arctic south to Cape Cod, rarely beyond; from lower intertidal to subtidal down to over 200 ft. (60 m).
Remarks: Green color is attributed to microscopic algae called *zoochlorellae* that live as symbionts in sponge colonies. Green and yellow colonies may be found side by side.
Family: Halichondridae, including *Pellina.*

BOWERBANK'S HALICHONDRIA   Pl. 10
Halichondria bowerbanki
Identification: Colony begins as thin crust, becomes thicker and raised in irregular branches, interconnected leaves or fingers. Texture similar to preceding species. Color varies, often yellow or gold but also tending to shades of brown, cinnamon, or olive. Oscula numerous, variable in size and location; usually less than $\frac{1}{8}$ in. (3 mm), sometimes but not regularly on low chimneys. Colonies to 2–3 in. (50–75 mm) high, spreading to 5–6 in. (125–150 mm). Spicules include *oxeas* at least 250 μ long.
Similar species: Several common fouling species that can be easily confused are often some shade of yellow or tan. (1) Crumb of Bread Sponge (Plate 10) is similar in some variants but seldom as profusely branching; Bowerbank's Halichondria doesn't regularly form chimneyed crusts. *Ranges doubtfully*

overlapping. (2) *Lissodendoryx isodictyalis* (not shown) is called Stinking Sponge, but Bowerbank's Halichondria may also be evil smelling (*Haliclona* species, p. 66, less so). Color sometimes yellow but more often grayish or white, tinted olive or bluish. Spreading to 4 in. (100 mm) or more. Spicules include single-ended *styles* and double-ended *tylotes,* both averaging 150 μ or more. Tropics north to Cape Cod in lower intertidal zone; estuarine. Family Tedaniidae. (3) *Mycale fibrexilis* (not shown) usually in *thin* crusts but sometimes massive; color varies; spreading to 2 in. (50 mm); spicules are single-ended *tylostyles* and *microscleres* (see p. 64) of several types. Cape Cod south. Family Mycalidae. (4) *Prosuberites* species (not shown) also in thin crusts, usually on rocks, shells, or algae; also with *tylostyles* but *no microscleres;* Cape Cod southward. Family Suberitidae. (5) See also Loosanoff's Haliclona (Plate 10). **Where found:** Bay of Fundy south to Cape Cod and Cape Hatteras, from lower intertidal zone to subtidal at shallow depths, and in brackish water. A common fouling sponge on pilings, rocks, and seaweeds.
Family: Halichondridae.

RED BEARD SPONGE *Microciona prolifera* **Pl. 11**
Identification: Color varies but is almost always some shade of red or orange; dries brown. Form also varies; at first encrusting, then with raised lobes or cups, finally (mostly subtidally) in fans or intricately branched. Oscula small, scattered, *inconspicuous.* To 8 in. (200 mm) or more tall subtidally, shorter but spreading widely in shallow water in lower intertidal zone. Spicules single-ended, include *spiny-headed* styles (*acanthostyles*) 500 μ long.
Similar species: Palmate sponges, *Isodictya* species (Plate 11) may be reddish but oscula are *conspicuous.* To 18 in. (450 mm). Largest spicules are mostly either *smooth styles* or *oxeas* 175–200 μ long. See also Finger Sponge, p. 65. Family Desmacidonidae.
Where found: Whole coast. Prince Edward I. to Texas. Lower intertidal to subtidal at shallow to moderate depths. In salinities as low as 15‰.
Remarks: This is one of the more common and easily recognized sponges south of Cape Cod. It grows subtidally in shallow water on pilings and piers in protected, even polluted, water; also in deeper water on oyster beds, wrecks, and other hard surfaces.
Family: Microcionidae.

FIG SPONGE *Suberites ficus* **Pl. 11**
Identification: A compact, massive or lobed sponge with a *smooth, liverlike* surface; oscula few or inconspicuous. Yellow-

ish. To 14 in. (350 mm) wide, more than 1 in. (25 mm) thick. Spicules include *tylostyles* and *styles,* largest 300–400 μ.
Where found: Arctic south to R.I. and possibly to Va. Subtidal in 50 ft. (15 m) or more; usually growing on one of the larger bivalves. Sometimes washed ashore.
Family: Suberitidae.

BORING SPONGES *Cliona* species   **Pl. 10**
Identification: These yellow sponges riddle mollusk shells, particularly oysters, boring within and surfacing as pock marks $\frac{1}{16}$–$\frac{3}{16}$ in. (1.6–5 mm) wide. *C. celata* sometimes overgrows host shell or, after dissolving it completely, lives independently.
    Several species: *C. celata* sulfur yellow, largest pores $\frac{3}{16}$ in. (5 mm). Other species (not shown) paler; differentiated mainly by microscleres. To $\frac{1}{16}$ in. (1.6 mm).
Where found: Gulf of Mexico north to L.I. Sound and *C. celata* and *C. vastifica* locally to Gulf of St. Lawrence and Bay of Fundy respectively; subtidal to 100 ft. (30 m) or more. Salinity tolerances vary: *C. celata* mostly above 15‰; *C. truitti* as low as 3‰.
Remarks: A pest on oyster beds. Not actually parasitic but weakens shell and in severe cases may exhaust and even kill its host.
Family: Clionidae.

Polyps and Medusae: Phylum Cnidaria

Most cnidarians are marine- or brackish-water animals. Exceptions include the freshwater hydras plus a few hydroids and small, rarely encountered jellyfish.

The range of body form is so wide that a brief and tidy definition of the phylum is not easy. Cnidarians are usually *radially symmetrical* — with parts arranged around the center like the spokes of a wheel. They lack complex organs and usually have a single *gastrovascular cavity* where absorption and digestion of food take place. This cavity may be a simple vaselike tube, but in many cases pockets extend out from the sides, or the cavity is partitioned. There is only one opening, the mouth.

Two basic body plans have evolved in Cnidaria. One, the *polyp,* is typified by sea anemones; jellyfish are examples of the other form, called a *medusa.* Polyps are usually cylindrical and attached at the base to a firm support; the mouth is at the opposite end and is surrounded by a ring of tentacles. Most medusae are umbrella-,

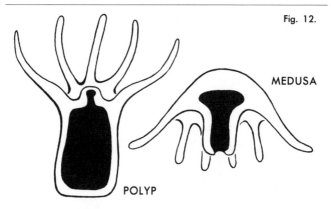

Fig. 12.

MEDUSA

POLYP

bell-, or saucer-shaped with tentacles around the edge; they swim
with the mouth at the center, below. Medusae move by means of
slow-motion jet propulsion. When the umbrellalike bell contracts
or closes, water is forced out, pushing the jellyfish in the opposite
direction. While most cnidarians can be referred without much
trouble to one or the other of these body plans, considerable
variation in detail does occur.

There is also a further complication. Many cnidarians have
alternating polyp and medusa generations. Here is how this cycle
works in hydrozoans: In the medusoid generation the jellyfishlike
animals are either male or female and reproduce sexually through
a union of eggs and sperm. The eggs hatch into microscopic larvae
called *planulae*. The individual *planula* swims about for a time,
then settles down and metamorphoses into a polyp. Most hydrozoans are colonial in this generation, and the first polyp becomes
the parent of the colony by budding additional polyps. This is an
example of *asexual reproduction*. Eventually some of the buds of
the polypoid colony produce and release free-swimming medusae.
And so on. Variations on this straightforward scheme complicate
many hydrozoan life histories (see p. 72), and cnidarians in other
classes do not always conform.

Nematocysts ("thread bladders") are unique to Cnidaria. They
function defensively to protect the cnidarian and are also a means
of trapping food. Nematocysts cause the stings of jellyfish. All
cnidarians have them, but in most cases they are not powerful
enough to make any impression on human skin. Nematocysts are
microscopic, more or less egg-shaped capsules imbedded in special
cells, each with a triggerlike bristle projecting from its surface.
Inside the nematocyst a long tube lies neatly coiled. When the
trigger is disturbed, the tube suddenly flies out and becomes im-

bedded in whatever caused the disturbance — a fish or hand brushing too close — and a minute amount of poison is injected.

Nematocysts actually vary considerably in form; some are not poisonous but work like lassos to snare tiny projections on prey animals. Others are sticky, like flypaper. Nematocysts have been sorted into 17 types; the classification of anemones is based to an important extent on the kinds of nematocysts found in each species.

While only cnidarians produce their own nematocysts a few flatworms and shell-less gastropods manage to feed on cnidarians without disturbing their nematocysts; they then incorporate the nematocysts into their own body armor and use them defensively.

The phylum is divided into 3 classes: Hydrozoa (below), Scyphozoa (p. 87), and Anthozoa (p. 92).

Hydrozoans: Class Hydrozoa

Hydrozoans form a very large class with 7 orders, numerous families and genera, and about 250 species on this coast. Most typical hydrozoans (hydroids and hydromedusae) are recognizably polypoid or medusoid in form or have alternating generations of each phase. The orders Siphonophora and Chondrophora, however, contain specialized planktonic animals that are variously regarded as either highly modified medusae or polyps *or* colonies with both types of structure (p. 86).

Hydroids and Hydromedusae

This is a difficult group. There are many species and most are small and delicate. Also they have confusing life histories involving both polyp and medusa stages (see p. 69); the animals are called, respectively, hydroids and hydromedusae.

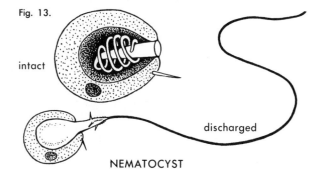

Fig. 13.

intact

discharged

NEMATOCYST

Two of the 5 orders considered here are exclusively medusoid; they have no polyp phase. About $\frac{1}{3}$ of the hydrozoans exist as *both* hydroids and hydromedusae; others are exclusively hydroid. The 1st scientists to research hydrozoan species usually had no easy means of matching polyp and medusa stages of individual species. Indeed, without carefully rearing medusae from hydroid colonies there is, at best, only circumstantial evidence to link them. As a result 2 relatively independent classifications developed, one for hydroids, the other for hydromedusae. For example, *Clytia* is a common hydroid genus, and numerous species are listed from this coast. Before anyone recognized their relationship, hydromedusae from *Clytia* colonies were described, given totally different species names, and placed in a separate genus called *Phialidium.* This error has not yet been fully corrected. The common genus *Obelia* is a case wherein fairly easily distinguishable hydroids produce hydromedusae that are unidentifiable as individual species and are simply listed as "*Obelia* species." Even more confusing situations exist. Some hydromedusae are so different that they have been put in different *families,* yet their polyp stages are very much alike. Specialists are gradually unraveling such problems; meanwhile we must bear with a classification system that has discrepancies and inconsistencies.

Fig. 14.

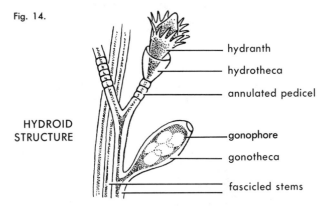

HYDROID
STRUCTURE

- hydranth
- hydrotheca
- annulated pedicel
- gonophore
- gonotheca
- fascicled stems

The hydroid or polyp stage: Individual hydroid animals or *zooids* consist of a stem or *pedicel* and a flowerlike *hydranth* usually with a central mouth and ring of tentacles. The whole zooid may be only $\frac{3}{16}$ in. (5 mm) tall; some are smaller, a few larger. Most hydroids are armored with a tough, chitinous *periderm* that covers the stem and may extend up around the hydranth as a cuplike *hydrotheca* into which the hydranth can withdraw for protection. Sometimes the hydrotheca has a hinged lid or *operculum.* The stem is often ringed or *annulated,* and sometimes the stems of individual zooids or branching parts of a colony are bound together or *fascicled.*

A very few hydroids are solitary and arise from a rootlike *holdfast.* Others grow from a creeping vinelike *stolon* or network of stolons, and a few develop from a hard crust. Some colonies are very small and consist of a few tiny zooids growing singly from a threadlike stolon. At the other extreme are large bushy or plant-like colonies several feet tall.

Usually the zooids of a colony are all more or less alike in appearance, but in some species clearly differentiated zooid types occur. Also, the *gonophores* or sexual buds are usually distinct in size and shape; in a few cases male and female gonophores are quite different in appearance. Usually colonies only produce one or the other, not both. They are only produced seasonally. The gonophores may be encapsuled in a *gonotheca.*

The hydromedusa or medusoid stage: The sexual buds of some hydrozoans are released as free-swimming jellyfish — the hydro-medusae. These little medusae vary in size from less than $\frac{3}{16}$ in. (5 mm) to 1 in. (25 mm) across; a few species reach twice that diameter. Their structure is usually simpler than that of typical jellyfish. The hollow underside of the bell in all but *Obelia* species has a shelf or *velum* around the edge. Internally a system of spokelike *radial canals* extend from the stomach to the edge of the bell. All except a few degenerate hydromedusae have marginal tentacles, and additional structures such as *cirri* (tentaclelike but smaller, more slender) and several types of sense organs are also placed along the rim; these include light-sensitive *ocelli* and balancing organs called *statocysts.* Variations in mouth structure are also used for identification. In simplest form the mouth is a round opening at the end of a short tube suspended below the stomach; in some species this tube is lengthened into a clapperlike *manubrium.* Tentacles are sometimes attached to the tube above the

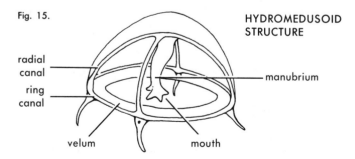

Fig. 15.

HYDROMEDUSOID STRUCTURE

radial canal

ring canal

manubrium

velum

mouth

mouth. The mouth may be 4-lipped, sometimes with the lips drawn out as tentacles.

Two hydrozoan orders, Trachymedusae and Narcomedusae, have no polyp stage; a 3rd, Limnomedusae, is separated from them on minor technical grounds. These 3 orders are small, with few species; the first 3 species accounts below deal with them. The orders Athecata and Thecata contain most typical hydrozoans. Thecata has hydroids with hydrothecae and gonothecae; Athecata has hydroids with unprotected hydranths and gonophores. Athecate hydromedusae are usually taller, with ocelli but no statocysts; gonads are placed on the mouth tube. Thecate hydromedusae are flatter, usually have statocysts; with gonophores on the radial canals.

Identification of hydromedusae may prove difficult partly because of their small size but also because some of them change substantially as they grow, particularly in bell shape and tentacle complement. Unless stated otherwise, the seasons indicated in the species accounts are for hydromedusae.

SPLENDID HYDROMEDUSA   Pl. 30
Aglantha digitale

Identification: POLYP: None. HYDROMEDUSA: $1\frac{1}{2}$–2 times taller than wide with 8 radial canals. Up to 100 tentacles, which are brittle and usually break off in netted hydromedusae. To $1\frac{1}{8}$ in. (28 mm), smaller in South.

Where found: Arctic south to Chesapeake Bay. Mainly subtidal at depths of 45 ft. (13.5 m) or more, but also found at surface inshore. Year-round in Gulf of Maine; winter–spring southward.

Remarks: The most common representative of Trachymedusae, a small order; another species, *Liriope tetraphylla,* is discussed under Clapper Hydroid (p. 76).

Family: Rhopalonematidae (Order Trachymedusae).

CRADLE HYDROMEDUSA *Cunina octonaria*   Pl. 29

Identification: POLYP: None. HYDROMEDUSA: Easily identified by 8 stiff tentacles emerging *halfway up* the side of the bell. No radial canals. To $\frac{1}{4}$ in. (6 mm).

Where found: Tropical, oceanic, but sometimes common inshore north to N.J. Fall.

Remarks: Our only example of the small order Narcomedusae. Larvae parasitic in hydromedusae of Tower Hydromedusa (Plate 29) at which stage they bud additional larvae.

Family: Cuninidae (Order Narcomedusae).

ANGLED HYDROMEDUSA   Pl. 30
Gonionemus vertens

Identification: POLYP: Unknown. HYDROMEDUSA: Bell a flattish dome with 4 radial canals and up to 80 tentacles, each with a *sharp bend* near outer end, and a microscopic sucker at the angle. To $\frac{3}{4}$ in. (19 mm).

Where found: Circumboreal along the coast in northern waters but distribution is localized. Once a well-known experimental animal at Woods Hole (Cape Cod) but erratic since Eelgrass blight, (see p. 52). Not reported from Delaware or Chesapeake bays.

Family: Olindiidae (Order Limnomedusae).

TUBULARIAN HYDROIDS *Tubularia*   Pl. 13

and related genera

Identification: POLYPS: Long-stemmed, flowerlike hydroids, mostly unbranched. Whorl of longer filiform tentacles *at base* of hydranth and 1 or more whorls of shorter filiform tentacles on the hydranth. Unbranched polyps to 6 in. (150 mm).

Several species of *Tubularia,* plus *Ectopleura dumortieri,* several *Hybocodon* species, and other, little-known genera are all difficult to distinguish without microscope; often impossible if immature.

HYDROMEDUSAE: *Tubularia* none; gonophores in berrylike clusters on hydranth *above* basal whorl. *E. dumortieri* (not shown) has tiny — $\frac{1}{8}$ in. (3 mm) — free hydromedusae with 4 radial canals, 4 tentacles, *8 rows of wartlike nematocysts;* gonophores medusalike. For *Hybocodon* species see next account.

Where found: Whole coast. *T. crocea* is the common species south of Cape Cod, plus *E. dumortieri* in *brackish* waters (salinity 5–18‰).

Remarks: Tubularian hydroids, particularly *T. crocea,* form dense pinkish growths on pilings, buoys, jetties from lower intertidal zone to subtidal at shallow depths south of Cape Cod. Tangled knots of battered stems, often without hydranths, wash ashore on ocean and bay beaches.

Family: Tubulariidae, including *Ectopleura* and *Hybocodon.*

ONE-ARMED HYDROMEDUSAE   Pl. 29

Hybocodon species

Identification: POLYPS (not shown): *Tubularia*-like but *solitary with rootlike base:* (1) *H. prolifer,* a tide-pool species, has base of hydranth *ringed.* To 2 in. (50 mm). (2) *H. pendula,* found in deeper water, has simple hydranth. To 4 in. (100 mm). HYDROMEDUSAE: (1) *H. prolifer* (not shown) has *cluster* of 1–4 tentacles. (2) *H. pendula* has only 1 tentacle. Both are small, $\frac{3}{16}$ in. (5 mm) or less.

Similar species: POLYPS: See tubularian hydroids (Plate 13). HYDROMEDUSAE: *Euphysa aurata* (not shown) also has 1 tentacle. *Hybocodon* species have bells roughened by *5 radial* *rows of nematocysts: E. aurata* does not. To $\frac{1}{2}$ in. (12 mm). Chiefly Boreal. Polyp unknown. Family Corymorphiidae.

Where found: Both species chiefly Boreal but hydromedusae of *H. pendula* reported south to Cape Cod and *H. prolifer* to lower Chesapeake Bay. Hydromedusae winter–spring.

Remarks: Both species best known as hydromedusae. Polyp of *H. pendula,* also classified as *Corymorpha pendula,* often is placed in a separate family, Corymorphiidae.

Family: Tubulariidae.

CLAPPER HYDROID   *Sarsia tubulosa*   **Pls. 13, 29**
AND HYDROMEDUSA

Identification: POLYP (Plate 13): Identification somewhat problematic. Solitary or sparsely branched stems rise from a stolon; hydranth is spindle-shaped with 10–20 *scattered, capitate* (knobbed) tentacles. To $\frac{3}{4}$ in. (19 mm) tall. HYDROMEDUSA (Plate 29): A *pendulous manubrium* extends below bell; mouth simple, tubular. 4 roughened tentacles. To $\frac{1}{4}$ in. (6 mm).

Similar species: POLYPS (not shown): Related genera also have *capitate* tentacles. *Dipurena* and *Zanclea* species (Family Zancleidae) are minute, but *Linvillea agassizi* reaches $\frac{3}{4}$ in. (19 mm), has 30 tentacles on a swollen hydranth, and is unbranched. Cape Cod south; a common summer hydroid in lower Chesapeake Bay. HYDROMEDUSAE: Others with *pendulous manubrium:* (1) *Dipurena strangulata* (not shown) is smaller, to $\frac{1}{8}$ in. (3 mm), has 4 *knobbed* tentacles. Cape Cod south, summer–fall. (2) *Liriope tetraphylla* (not shown) has 4 radial canals, *lobed* mouth, *smooth* bell margin; 4 primary tentacles and 4 short, hairlike ones. To $1\frac{1}{8}$ in. (28 mm). Cape Cod south, mainly oceanic. No polyp stage. Family Geryonidae (Order Trachymedusae). (3) Note Elegant Hydromedusa (Plate 30).

Where found: Arctic south to Chesapeake Bay. A common and easily recognized winter–spring hydromedusa.

Family: Corynidae, including *Dipurena* and *Linvillea.*

FEATHER HYDROID *Pennaria tiarella*   **Pl. 13**

Identification: POLYP: Colonies branching; to 6 in. (150 mm). Stems annulated; hydranths have both *capitate* (knobbed) tentacles in 4–5 whorls and a basal whorl of *filiform* tentacles. HYDROMEDUSA (not shown): Degenerate, minute — less than $\frac{1}{16}$ in. (1.6 mm) — with no tentacles but only bumps at base of 4 radial canals.

Where found: Maine south to West Indies; summer–early fall.

Remarks: A common hydroid on Eelgrass, pilings, and other substrata; the tiny hydromedusa also abundant.

Family: Pennariidae.

CLUB HYDROID *Clava leptostyla*   **Pl. 13**

Identification: POLYP: For its small size — $\frac{3}{8}$ in. (9 mm) — a conspicuous and pretty little hydroid; in pinkish clumps and patches on rockweeds and Knotted Wrack. Stems *unbranched;* hydranth clublike with 20–30 *scattered, filiform* tentacles.

HYDROMEDUSA: None; gonophores in berrylike cluster *on hydranth.*

Similar species: POLYPS: (1) Freshwater Hydroid, *Cordylophora caspia* (Plate 13) has *branching, annulated* stems, similar hydranth. To $2\frac{3}{8}$ in. (59 mm). Whole coast in *brackish* estuaries, salinity 5‰ or less; on rocks, shells, pilings. No hydromedusa. (2) *Rhizogeton* and *Tubiclava* (neither shown) are related genera of tiny, unbranched polyps with similar hydranths. *R. fusiformis* has 12 tentacles and a soft stem; *T. cornucopiae,* a slender, vaselike stem with *distinct periderm.* Both $\frac{1}{4}$ in. (6 mm) tall, growing from a creeping stolon; gonophores *on stolon.* Whole coast in shallow water. No hydromedusae. (3) Note Tower Hydromedusa (next account), the only clavid with a free medusa.

Where found: L.I. Sound to Labrador; intertidal to subtidal at shallow depths.

Family: Claviidae, including *Cordylophora, Rhizogeton,* and *Tubiclava.*

TOWER HYDROMEDUSA Pl. 29
Turritopsis nutricola

Identification: POLYP (not shown): Rarely seen. Unbranched or sparsely branching with a thick periderm; hydranth has *scattered,* filiform tentacles. To $\frac{3}{16}$ in. (5 mm). HYDROMEDUSA: Thimble-shaped with 4 radial canals, 4-lipped mouth, and *abundant tentacles,* up to 85 on a $\frac{1}{8}$ in. (3 mm) bell. To $\frac{3}{16}$ in. (5 mm).

Similar species: POLYPS: (1) Several related species (not shown) have minute polyps with scattered, filiform tentacles. (2) See Club Hydroid (Plate 13). HYDROMEDUSAE: Other small hydromedusae with as many tentacles have more than 4 radial canals.

Where found: Cape Cod to West Indies; polyps reported on shallow-water sponges; hydromedusae common in estuaries, summer–fall.

Family: Claviidae.

SNAIL FUR *Hydractinia echinata* Fig. 16

Identification: POLYP: Colonies encrust snail shells containing hermit crabs; expanded polyps form a pinkish fuzz. Polyps of various shapes and sizes (*polymorphic*) emerge from a brownish crust with short, erect, flattish spines. To $\frac{3}{16}$ in. (5 mm), sometimes much taller. HYDROMEDUSA: None.

Similar species: Related and problematic hydractiniids (not shown) have uniform polyps (not polymorphic) rising from a

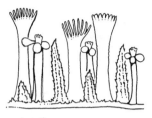 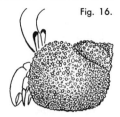

Fig. 16.

detail

whole colony on
hermit crab
shell

SNAIL FUR

stolon network, which may be covered by a hard crust: polyps usually 1 in. (25 mm) or less, but up to $1\frac{1}{2}$ in. (38 mm) tall, with 10–20 tentacles in a single or double whorl. Some forms have a free medusoid stage but hydromedusae are minute and/or lack tentacles. Whole coast.

Where found: Labrador to Gulf of Mexico. Common in shallow water, usually on shells occupied by Long-clawed and Flat-clawed Hermit Crabs (Plate 57), but sometimes on other substrata.

Family: Hydractiniidae.

BOUGAINVILLIA HYDROIDS AND HYDROMEDUSAE   Pls. 13, 29

Bougainvillia and related genera

Identification: POLYPS (Plate 13): In branching colonies, some quite large (sizes given in table below). Periderm *thick,* often wrinkled and expanded as a cuplike *pseudohydrotheca* at base of hydranth. Stems often wrinkled, annulated, or *fascicled.* 6–20 filiform tentacles in 1–3 close whorls.

Numerous species in shallow water; require microscopic examination to distinguish. For *Bougainvillia* and *Garveia* species, see table below. Polyps of *Nemopsis* unknown.

HYDROMEDUSAE (Plate 29): *Garveia* species do *not* have free medusae; *Bougainvillia* and *Nemopsis* species do. Bells small — $\frac{1}{2}$ in. (12 mm) or less — with 4 radial canals; tentacles in 4 *clusters* (4 pairs at hatching); mouth with *branching tentacles.* (1) *B. carolinensis* has 7–9 tentacles per cluster; mouth tentacles usually *forked;* less than $\frac{3}{16}$ in. (5 mm). (2) *B. superciliaris* (not shown) has 11–15 tentacles per cluster; mouth tentacles divided 4–7 times; to $\frac{3}{8}$ in. (9 mm). (3) *B. rugosa* (not shown) has 3 tentacles per cluster; undivided mouth tentacles; less than $\frac{1}{8}$ in. (3 mm). (4) *N. bachei* (not shown) has 14–16 undivided tentacles per cluster *plus* a pair of short clublike ones. To $\frac{1}{2}$ in. (12 mm).

Similar species: POLYPS: See stick hydroids (Plate 13 and

Polyps of *Bougainvillia, Garveia,* and *Eudendrium* species

	fascicled stems	annulated stems	number of tentacles	with pseudohydrothecae	with free medusae	colony size
B. carolinensis	yes	yes	10–12	yes	yes	12 in. (300 mm)
B. superciliaris	no	yes	15–20	yes	yes	2 in. (50 mm)
B. rugosa	yes	no	8–10	yes	yes	10 in. (250 mm)
Garveia species	no	yes	8–12	yes	no	3 in. (75 mm)
Eudendrium species	some yes, some no	some yes, some no	20–30	no	no	6 in. (150 mm)

table above). HYDROMEDUSAE: *Rathkea octopunctata* (Plate 29) has 4 radial canals and *8 clusters* of 3–5 tentacles. To $\frac{3}{16}$ in. (5 mm). Arctic south to Chesapeake Bay, winter–spring. Polyp unknown. Family Rathkeidae.
Where found: Polyps from lower intertidal to subtidal at shallow depths on pilings and the like. (1) *B. carolinensis,* Boothbay Harbor to Fla., summer–fall. (2) *B. superciliaris,* Arctic south to Cape Cod; hydromedusa in spring, through summer northward. (3) *B. rugosa,* Chesapeake Bay south; late spring through fall. (4) *N. bachei,* whole coast, year-round except fall and early spring. (5) *Garveia* species, whole coast.
Family: Bougainvilliidae.

STICK HYDROIDS *Eudendrium* species   **Pl. 13**
Identification: POLYPS: In branching colonies. Similar to preceding but *without* cuplike pseudohydrothecae; hydranths with trumpet-shaped (rather than cone-shaped) mouth region. Tentacles 20–30, filiform in a single whorl (sizes given in table, p. 80).

At least 10 species, differing in number of tentacles, sexual structures, colony form, extent of annulation (all but one have branches with at least a basal ring); larger species have *fascicled* stems. 2 conspicuous species are: (1) *E. carneum* with *bright red* hydranths; branches with gonophores have vestigial hydranths. To 5 in. (125 mm). (2) *E. ramosum* is white to pinkish green; branches with gonophores have normal hydranths. To 6 in. (150 mm).

HYDROMEDUSAE: None. Gonophores sexually dimorphic (sexes easily distinguished), which is useful for species identification.

Similar species: (1) See bougainvillia hydroids (Plate 13 and table, p. 79). (2) Additional hydroids with simple, branching colonies, ringed stems, and without distinct hydrothecae are shown on Plate 13; note differences in *tentacles* and *gonophores* particularly. (3) Halecium hydroids (Plate 14) have stems and branches divided in *nodes;* simple, tubular or *flared* hydrothecae; different gonophores.

Where found: Whole coast, subtidal in shallow water on a wide variety of hard substrata.

Family: Eudendriidae.

CAMPANULARIAN HYDROIDS AND HYDROMEDUSAE   Pls. 14, 29, 30

Campanularia and related genera

Identification: POLYPS (Plate 14): Hydrothecae *cup-shaped with smooth or toothed rim.* Colonies range from minute creeping forms with unbranched stems to erect bushy growths 1 ft. (300 mm) or more tall; some have *fascicled* stems.

Identification of individual species may be impossible unless gonothecae are present. *Gonothyraea* (3 species) and *Campanularia* (13 species) do *not* produce free hydromedusae; *Obelia* (8 species) and *Clytia* (9 species) do. The table (below) compares some of the more conspicuous species; see also Fig. 17. A typical form is shown on Plate 14.

HYDROMEDUSAE: *Obelia* species (Plate 29) are nearly flat, have *no visible velum,* 4 radial canals and numerous short tentacles. To $\frac{1}{4}$ in. (6 mm). Individual species indistinguishable;

Campanularian Hydroids

	Teeth	Stems	Size
1. *Gonothyraea loveni*	10–12	simple	$1\frac{1}{4}$ in. (32 mm)
2. *Obelia bicuspidata*	14–20, bicuspid	fascicled	1 in. (25 mm)
3. *Campanularia flexuosa*	none	few branches, flexuous	$1\frac{1}{4}$ in. (32 mm)
4. *Campanularia gelatinosa*	10, bicuspid	fascicled	10 in. (250 mm)
5. *Obelia commissuralis*	none	flexuous	8 in. (200 mm)
6. *Campanularia verticillata*	16	simple	14 in. (350 mm)
7. *Clytia edwardsi*	12–14	simple	1 in. (25 mm)
8. *Campanularia calceolifera*	none	geniculate	$1\frac{1}{4}$ in. (32 mm)

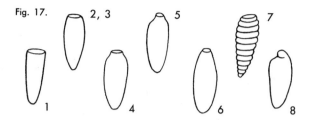

Fig. 17.

CAMPANULARIAN GONOTHECAE

typical form shown. The hydromedusae of *Clytia* hydroids are known under the generic name *Phialidium* (Plate 30) and have not been matched with polypoid phases (see p. 72). They are more nearly hemispherical, with typical velum; up to 32 rather short tentacles alternating with bulbs or vesicles. Mouth 4-lipped. Most species $\frac{1}{4}$ in. (6 mm) or less; *P. languidum* to $\frac{3}{4}$ in. (19 mm). Typical form shown.

Similar species: POLYPS: Note lovenellid hydroids (Plate 14). HYDROMEDUSAE: None.

Where found: POLYPS: (See table, opp.) Whole coast, except *Campanularia verticillata* and *Campanularia flexuosa,* which are mainly Boreal; *Clytia edwardsi* and *Gonothyraea loveni* are found from Chesapeake Bay north. From lower intertidal to subtidal at shallow depths. Some of these hydroids form conspicuous colonies on rocks, shells, pilings; smaller species often grow on larger hydroids and seaweeds. HYDROMEDUSAE: Whole coast; late spring–early fall.

Family: Campanulariidae.

MANY-ARMED HYDROMEDUSA   Not shown
Laodicae undulata

   Identification: POLYP: Unknown; thought to be *Cuspidella*-like. HYDROMEDUSA: Up to several hundred tentacles when mature, tips often coiled, *plus* coiled cirri and club-shaped vesicles between. Bell saucer-shaped; 4 radial canals. To $1\frac{3}{8}$ in. (34 mm).

   Where found: West Indies north to Boston harbor; summer–early winter in our area.

   Family: Uncertain. Hydromedusae put in Laodiceidae.

LOVENELLID HYDROIDS   Pl. 14
Lovenella and related genera

   Identification: POLYPS: Hydrothecae on stalks (sometimes very short ones), cup- or spindle-shaped, closed by a *cone- or* *wedge-like operculum.* Colonies vary, creeping to erect, branching or not.

4 genera in shallow water (at least 9 species); others deeper. *Opercularella* and *Lovenella* species have erect stalks, branched or unbranched; stalks annulated in *Lovenella,* wrinkled in *Opercularella.* ⅝–2 in. (16–50 mm). *Calycella* and *Cuspidella* species (none shown) are minute creeping forms with hydrothecae on short stalks.

HYDROMEDUSAE (none shown): *Calycella* and *Opercularella* do not have free hydromedusae; *Cuspidella* presumably does but they are unknown. *Lovenella gracilis* hydromedusae are less than ⅛ in. (3 mm); superficially *Phialidium*-like (Plate 30). Also, at least 7 genera of hydromedusae (in at least 5 families) have been described as having *Cuspidella-, Campanulina-,* or *Lovenella*-like polyps, but actual polyps are unknown or dubious. These genera epitomize the difficulty of correlating polypoid and medusoid forms and defining family groups. See accounts of Black-Eyed and Branchlet Hydromedusae, following. **Where found:** Whole coast but distribution uncertain; some subtidal in shallow water, others only in deep.

Family: The genera discussed have been allocated to different families by various authorities. Family names include Lovenellidae and Campanulinidae, among others.

BLACK-EYED HYDROMEDUSA   Pl. 30
Tiaropsis multicirrata

Identification: POLYP (not shown): Minute; poorly known. HYDROMEDUSA: Look for 8 tiny *black spots* along margin in gaps between groups of tentacles. 4 radial canals; tentacles numerous, usually 24 on a 1/16 in. (1.6 mm) bell, to 200 when mature — 1⅛ in. (28 mm).

Similar species: HYDROMEDUSAE: (1) *Blackfordia* species (not shown) have numerous tentacles (70–80 when mature) alternating with 1–3 tiny vesicles. Also, though not visible without microscope, each tentacle has 2 minute, nipplelike, upward projections at the base. To ½ in. (12 mm). 2 species, doubtfully distinct. Delaware and Chesapeake bays, in fall. Polyps unknown. Usually put in Family Lovenellidae. (2) *Phialidium* species (Plate 30) somewhat resemble young *Blackfordia* or *Tiaropsis* but lack details indicated. (3) See also Tower Hydromedusa (Plate 29). (4) Related but not visually similar hydromedusae have *Cuspidella*-like polyps.

Where found: Arctic south to Cape Cod (occasionally along south shore). Common in shallow water in spring.

Family: Uncertain; usually put in Mitrocomidae.

BRANCHLET HYDROMEDUSA   Pl. 29
Eucheilota ventricularis

Identification: POLYP: Unknown; thought to be *Lovenella-*

like. HYDROMEDUSA: Tentacles (about 20) with 1–3 *branchlets or cirri* emerging from base, plus 8–12 marginal vesicles. 4 radial canals. To $\frac{1}{2}$ in. (12 mm).

Where found: Arctic to Fla.; late summer–fall in our area.
Family: Lovenellidae.

MANY-RIBBED HYDROMEDUSAE   Pl. 30
Aequorea species

Identification: POLYPS: Unknown. HYDROMEDUSAE: Radial canals *very numerous,* 24–100 when mature with about $1\frac{1}{2}$–3 times as many tentacles and even more numerous marginal vesicles. Number of radial canals and tentacles increases with age. Bell hemispherical to saucer-shaped. To 7 in. (175 mm). Species variable and not well known; number of species uncertain. Typical form shown.

Similar species: HYDROMEDUSAE: (1) *Rhacostoma atlanticum* (not shown) is very similar but has *rows of tiny bumps* on *underside* of bell between radial canals. Pinkish. To $4\frac{1}{2}$ in. (112 mm). Whole coast; *oceanic,* summer–fall. North of Cape Cod colorless and even larger — to 1 ft. (300 mm). Polyp unknown. (2) *Halopsis ocellata* (not shown) has 12–16 radial canals in *4 clusters*. To $2\frac{3}{4}$ in. (69 mm). Gulf of Maine; summer–fall. Rare. Polyp unknown; thought to be *Cuspidella*-like. Usually put in Family Mitrocomidae.

Where found: Nearly worldwide, chiefly oceanic. Occasionally inshore summer–fall.

Family: Uncertain. Hydromedusae of *Aequorea* and *Rhacostoma* usually placed in Aequoreidae.

WHITE CROSS HYDROMEDUSA   Not shown
Staurophora mertensi

Identification: POLYP: Unknown; thought to be *Cuspidella*-like. HYDROMEDUSA: 2 traits easily identify this *large* hydromedusa: 4 frilly-edged radial canals form a milky white cross; slit-like mouth extends as *open groove* along underside of each radial canal. Tentacles *numerous,* more than 4000 when mature. Bell broad, low; to 9 in. (225 mm).

Where found: Arctic south to Cape Cod, less often to R.I. Spring–early summer southward; spring–early fall northward. Larger bells at surface at night, at depths of 3 ft. (900 mm) or more in daylight.

Family: Uncertain. Hydromedusa usually put in Laodiceidae.

EIGHT-RIBBED HYDROMEDUSA   Pl. 30
Melicertum octocostatum

Identification: POLYP (not shown): Questionably identified. HYDROMEDUSA: Bell-shaped with *8 radial* canals and 64–72 tentacles when mature. $\frac{3}{16}$-in. (5 mm) young have 8 canals, 4 of them very fine, and 32 tentacles. To $\frac{1}{2}$ in. (12 mm).

Similar species: HYDROMEDUSAE: (1) Note Splendid Hydromedusa (Plate 30). (2) Other hydromedusae with 8 radial canals are oceanic and rarely seen inshore.
Where found: Arctic or subarctic south to Cape Cod; late spring through summer along shore.
Family: Melicertidae.

ELEGANT HYDROMEDUSA *Tima formosa*   **Pl. 30**
    Identification: POLYP (not shown): Minute. HYDROMEDUSA: Easily recognized *when mature;* manubrium long, *clapperlike;* mouth has 4 long frilly lips; 4 radial canals and 32 tentacles (16 short, 8 medium, 8 long). This large hydromedusa reaches a width of 4 in. (100 mm). Young — $1\frac{1}{2}$ in. (38 mm) wide — have 16 tentacles; mouth does not extend beyond velum.
    Similar species: HYDROMEDUSAE: (1) *Eutima mira* (not shown) has pendulous manubrium and frilly lips, also, but only 4 tentacles; *bell margin finely scalloped* with warts and vesicles. To $1\frac{1}{4}$ in. (31 mm). A southern species, common south of Cape Hatteras, erratically north to Cape Cod in summer. (2) See Plate 29 for small hydromedusae with clapperlike manubrium.
    Where found: Massachusetts Bay to R.I., *chiefly* fall–winter north of Cape Cod, spring southward, but known to occur year-round.
    Family: Eutimidae, including *Eutima.*

HALECIUM HYDROIDS *Halecium* species   **Pl. 14**
    Identification: POLYPS: Hydrothecae reduced to a *flared rim* with *trumpetlike* opening. Mostly in branching colonies with stems and branches divided by *nodes;* usually not annulated. To 3 in. (75 mm). HYDROMEDUSAE: None. Gonothecae saclike, with or without a spout.
    Numerous species, mostly Boreal and subtidal at depths of 40 ft. (12 m) or more. Shallow-water species, *H. tenellum, H. beani,* and *H. gracile,* have different gonothecae. *H. tenellum* is sparsely branched, lacks nodes, has annulations; reaches $\frac{5}{8}$ in. (15 mm). *H. beani* and *H. gracile* have fascicled stems and are larger, to $1\frac{1}{2}$–2 in. (38–50 mm).
    Similar species: Compare with polyps of bougainvillia hydroids (Plate 13).
    Where found: *H. beani* is mainly Boreal; *H. tenellum* and *H. gracile* range the whole coast, with *H. gracile* the most frequently reported species south of Cape Cod. All from lower intertidal zone to subtidal at great depths; *H. gracile* into brackish water.
    Family: Halecidae.

GARLAND HYDROIDS *Sertularia*   **Pl. 14**
and related genera
    Identification: POLYPS; Hydrothecae emerge as short, tubular,

macaroni-like or vase-shaped segments *on opposite sides* of branches or unbranched main stem; colonies sometimes large and bushy, to 1 ft. (300 mm) or more.

Numerous species in 7 genera, much in need of revision; commonly reported ones given here. (1) *Abietinaria* species have bottle-shaped hydrothecae, alternate to nearly opposite, in pinnately branching colonies up to 1 ft. (300 mm). Usually *subtidal.* (2) *Sertularia argentea* has *alternate* hydrothecae in branching, tufted colonies to 1 ft. (300 mm); chiefly a winter species. (3) *Sertularia cornicina* has hydrothecae in *opposite pairs;* colony small; usually unbranched. To ½ in. (12 mm), exceptionally to 2 in. (50 mm). (4) *Sertularia pumila* and (5) *Diphasia* species resemble *S. cornicina* but are larger; *S. pumila* to 2 in. (50 mm); *Diphasia* species to 4 in. (100 mm). Note gonothecae.

HYDROMEDUSAE: None. Gonothecae of several types; important in species identification. See Plate 14.

Similar species: POLYPS: Compare with halecium hydroids (Plate 14).

Where found: (1) *Abietinaria* species, Arctic to Cape Cod. (2) *S. argentea,* Arctic to Cape Hatteras. (3) *S. cornicina,* Cape Cod to Fla. (4) *S. pumila,* Labrador to L.I. Sound. (5) *Diphasia* species, Arctic to R.I. Additional species Boreal or in deeper waters only; others on Gulfweed. Those discussed are common on seaweeds, rocks, pilings from lower intertidal zone to subtidal at considerable depths.

Family: Sertularidae.

PLUMED HYDROID *Schizotricha tenella* **Pl. 14**
Identification: POLYP: Hydrothecae are *stemless cups* attached along *one edge* of main stem or branches; also with tiny, modified polyps called *nematophores.* Colonies feathery, with zigzag branching; to 4 in. (100 mm). HYDROMEDUSA: None; gonothecae horn-shaped.

Similar species: POLYPS: (1) *Plumularia* species (not shown) are very similar but only occur in our area on drifting Gulfweed. To ½ in. (12 mm). (2) *Aglaophenia* species (Plate 14), also found on Gulfweed, have distinctive, toothed hydrothecae. Commonly to ½ in. (12 mm), but sometimes much larger; typical form shown. (3) Additional plumularid genera in deep water.

Where found: Casco Bay to Caribbean. On pilings, seaweeds, and other substrata to shallow depths.

Family: Plumularidae, including *Plumularia* and *Aglaophenia.*

Additional Hydromedusae **Pls. 29, 30**

Proboscidactyla ornata. POLYP (not shown): Minute, with only 2 tentacles or none; grow on sabellid worm tubes. HYDRO-

MEDUSA (Plate 29): Easily identified by its 4 *branching* radial canals; up to 20 tentacles when mature. To $\frac{3}{16}$ in. (5 mm). Cape Cod to Caribbean, summer–fall. Family Proboscidactylidae (Order Limnomedusae). *Niobia dendrotentaculata* (not shown), an equally small, tropical species reported on this coast only as a stray, has 2 branching radial canals, 2 unbranched ones. Family Pandeidae.

Catablema vesicarium. POLYP: Unknown. HYDROMEDUSA (Plate 30): Has a large *apical process* (projection on top of bell); 4 radial canals and 4 tentacles initially, increasing to 32. To 1 in. (25 mm). Arctic south to Cape Cod, summer. Family Pandeidae. Additional members of this family may be found, with generic and species nomenclature tangled. *Amphinema* species (not shown) also have distinct apical process but only 2 tentacles. To $\frac{1}{4}$ in. (6 mm). Cape Cod to Fla., summer. Polyps minute.

Siphonophores and Chondrophores

Most of these extraordinary hydrozoans are oceanic plankters that only occasionally drift inshore. They are variously regarded as colonies of polyp- or medusa-like individuals called *persons* or as highly modified single animals. Different types of persons are specialized for catching and ingesting food, flotation, propulsion, defense, and reproduction. They occur in aggregations called *cormidia,* and colonies often consist of a number of such groups arranged in a series. In some species these chains reach lengths of 65 ft. (19.5 m). Persons arise from *planula* larva (see p. 70) by varied and rather devious budding processes. Colonies are hermaphroditic, and many species release male or female medusoids whose offspring are planulae.

The 4 species accounts below represent the main groups into which these hydrozoans are now classified; 3 are suborders of Siphonophora; the 4th belongs to Chondrophora, previously also placed within Siphonophora. Possible strays include at least 20–30 species, mostly from the Gulf Stream, but don't expect to find them intact in water more dilute than 30‰.

DIPHYES DISPAR   Pl. 33
Identification: Colony consist of 2 powerful swimming bells, the larger one to $\frac{3}{4}$ in. (19 mm) long, and a trailing stem with simple *cormidia,* each with 3 types of persons. Individual cormidia may be released as free-swimming units in which case one of the sexual persons becomes modified as a swimming bell. (See above for definition of terms.)
Where found: Whole coast. One of the more likely examples of its suborder to be found inshore.
Family: Diphyidae (Order Siphonophora).

BY THE WIND SAILOR *Velella velella* Pl. 31

Identification: Float is plasticlike, flat, translucent amber or brownish; *oval* with a triangular *sail* and suspended persons below (see introduction, p. 86). To 4 in. (100 mm) long.

Similar species: *Porpita porpita* (not shown) is *round* and has no sail; to 1 in. (25 mm). Like By The Wind Sailor, tropical and oceanic. Family Porpitidae.

Where found: A cosmopolitan, warm-water drifter sometimes blown ashore from the Gulf Stream.

Family: Velellidae (Order Chondrophora).

PORTUGUESE MAN-OF-WAR Pl. 31
Physalia physalia

Identification: The balloonlike float, brilliantly blue to pink or purple, with a deflatable, sail-like ridge above, is unmistakable. Float grows to more than 1 ft. (300 mm) long, extended tentacles to 40–50 *feet* (12–15 m).

Where found: A tropical, oceanic species regularly cast ashore with Gulf Stream flotsam. North to Cape Cod. Rarely drifting into Gulf of Maine but sometimes carried as far as w. Europe. 1 worldwide species.

Remarks: This famous wanderer is a powerful stinger (see p. 70), but human fatalities have *not* been verified. Exercise care in handling beached specimens; tentacles retain their stinging power for a long time and even dried stings may revive when wet. Sea turtles and the fish *Nomeus* feed on them, a peppery diet indeed!

Family: Physaliidae (Order Siphonophora).

STEPHANOMIA CARA Pl. 33

Identification: Colony has 3 parts: (1) a tiny, $\frac{1}{16}$-in. (1.6 mm) float; (2) 4 pairs of jet propulsive *nectophores* strung along the stemlike axis; (3) a series of similar but complex *cormidia* each with 4 main types of persons and their accessory parts (see introduction, p. 86). The whole colony extends to 3 in. (75 mm) or more. Unfortunately, these siphonophores are usually fragmented when found inshore.

Where found: Whole coast, summer especially. This is the only siphonophore that occurs with some regularity between Chesapeake Bay and Nova Scotia, but it is still not a very familiar object inshore.

Family: Agalmidae (Order Siphonophora).

Jellyfish: Class Scyphozoa

This is the smallest of the 3 cnidarian classes but important because it contains the larger, more conspicuous jellyfish. The medusoid generation (see p. 73) is the main one in Scyphozoa; some species skip the polypoid generation almost entirely, and in others it is an inconspicuous stage. The scyphozoan polyp, called a **scyphistoma,** is only $\frac{3}{16}$–$\frac{5}{8}$ in. (5–16 mm) tall when mature (Fig. 18). Scyphistomae are found attached to seaweeds, Eelgrass, or other supports in shallow water. The medusa buds develop at the top of the columnar body with somewhat the appearance of a stack of saucers. Young jellyfish are called **ephyrae** (Plate 34) and hardly resemble adult medusae; they are 8-armed and measure at most $\frac{3}{16}$ in. (5 mm) across. Ephyrae tend to be secretive and stay near the bottom as they gradually metamorphose into the adult form.

There are 5 scyphozoan orders; members of 4 are quite recognizably jellyfishlike (Plate 31). The 5th order, Stauromedusae, has highly specialized members that are not obviously medusoid (p. 91 and Plate 17).

Typical Jellyfish

Four orders are represented here. The order Semaeostomeae contains our most familiar species; members of the other 3 orders (first 3 species accounts below) are less often seen along this coast. The notorious Sea Wasps, Order Cubomedusae, are mainly warm-water species, as are members of the order Rhizostomeae, and occur here as strays. Jellyfish of the order Coronatae live in deep water, usually far offshore.

The 8-part symmetry of the juvenile *ephyra* (see Plate 34 and the general account, preceding) is preserved in adult jellyfish, which usually have structural parts arranged in 8 primary lobes or *octants.* Species identification is usually not difficult except during young, developmental stages. See also Hydromedusae, p. 73.

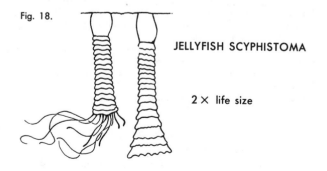

Fig. 18.

JELLYFISH SCYPHISTOMA

2 × life size

SEA WASP *Tamoya haplonema* **Pl. 30**
   Identification: 4 distinctive 2-part tentacles, each with a paddlelike base and strong filament. Bell strong and rigid, taller than wide. To $3\frac{1}{2}$ in. (88 mm).
   Where found: Tropical Atlantic but straggling north to L.I. Sound; summer–fall. Rare.
   Remarks: These strong, fast-swimming jellyfish tend to stay near the bottom. They are notorious stingers; the Australian Sea Wasp, *Chironex fleckeri,* is widely known to be dangerous to humans. Treat with care.
   Family: Carybdeidae (Order Cubomedusae).

CROWN JELLY *Nausithoe punctata* **Pl. 29**
   Identification: Umbrella flatter than a hemisphere, divided by a *horizontal groove* into a cap and wider margin of deeply scalloped lappets. 8 tentacles, 16 lappets. To $\frac{5}{8}$ in. (16 mm).
   Similar species: Additional crowned (coronate) medusae may be carried inshore *very rarely;* umbrella similarly divided by groove, but *taller* than broad; up to 12 tentacles; to 2–6 in. (50–150 mm). Normally in deep water at or below 500 ft. (150 m).
   Where found: Regarded primarily as a warm-water form, but a similar (possibly the same) species occurs in the Arctic; a rare stray from offshore.
   Family: Nausithoidae (Order Coronatae).

MUSHROOM CAP *Rhopilema verrilli* **Pl. 31**
   Identification: Umbrella thick, *without* tentacles; margin with *8 lappets* per octant; creamy-colored, with dark brown or yellow marks on mouth-arms. To more than 1 ft. (300 mm) across.
   Similar species: *Stomolophus meleagris* (not shown) is smaller, to $7\frac{1}{2}$ in. (188 mm) across; margin with *16 lappets* per octant; yellowish with a wide brown margin. A tropical jellyfish, found north of Cape Hatteras as a stray only. Family Stomolophidae.
   Where found: Often regarded as a rare jellyfish but appearing regularly in Pamlico Sound, N.C., and occasionally in bays and sounds north to L.I. Sound. Like other southern strays, it is most likely to occur in late summer–fall.
   Remarks: The Mushroon Cap obtains food through numerous small openings on its strongly developed mouth-arms.
   Family: Rhizostomatidae (Order Rhizostomeae).

LION'S MANE or RED JELLY **Pl. 31**
Cyanea capillata
   Identification: A large jellyfish with broad, flattish bell, and numerous mouth-arms and tentacles below. Umbrella has 8 primary lobes with up to 32 lappets; tentacles in 8 *clusters* on

underside. Color and average size vary geographically: pinkish and to 5 in. (125 mm) south of Cape Hatteras; yellow or orange-brown and to 8 in. (200 mm) from Cape Hatteras to Cape Cod; darker brown or red and to 18 in. (450 mm) northward. Maximum size much larger — to at least 8 ft. (2.4 m) (Gulf of Maine).
Season: Appears initially in swarms, winter–spring in south, spring–summer northward; maturing in May along the mid coastal region. Scattered larger individuals until fall.
Where found: Whole coast, in bays and sounds and on the open sea. Probably a single North Atlantic species; a similar jellyfish occurs in the North Pacific and another in the southern hemisphere.
Remarks: This is the largest jellyfish in the world but giants — larger than 3 ft. (1 m) across — are rare; the tentacles of an 8-ft. (2.4 m) specimen might extend 200 ft. (60 m). Young fish, haddock and butterfish especially, often huddle beneath the bells and wander with them.
Family: Cyanidae.

SEA NETTLE *Chrysaora quinquecirrha*   Pl. 31
Identification: Tentacles emerge from marginal *clefts;* upper surface smoothish or with fine pimples. Brackish and saltwater forms differ. Marine form is larger, to $7\frac{1}{2}$ in. (188 mm) across; pinkish, with 16 radiating, reddish bars, and up to 40 tentacles. Estuarine form to 4 in. (100 mm); milky white, with up to 24 tentacles.
Similar species: Purple Jellyfish, *Pelagia noctiluca* (Plate 31) has *no more than* 8 tentacles; umbrella surface *warty;* brownish or purplish; to 2 in. (50 mm). An oceanic species sometimes drifting ashore from Gulf Stream. Has luminescent spots and streaks. Without a scyphistoma (polyp) stage.
Season: Summer–fall; appearing in Chesapeake Bay in May or June, persisting until Oct. or Nov.
Where found: Cape Cod south at least to West Indies; relationship to other Atlantic species of *Chrysaora* uncertain. Primarily an estuarine jellyfish extending into water as dilute as 3‰.
Remarks: Especially common in Chesapeake Bay, where its sharp stings (see p. 70) often drive swimmers from the water as far north as Sandy Point State Park, Md.; northern limit depends on salinity.
Family: Pelagidae, including *Pelagia*.

MOON JELLY *Aurelia aurita*   Pl. 31
Identification: Has 4 conspicuous, *horseshoe-shaped* gonads. Tentacles marginal, *fringelike* and very numerous, to 30 or more per octant. Translucent whitish or tawny, gonads opaque white or pinkish. To 10 in. (250 mm) across.
Season: Spring–summer; ephyrae appear with spring thaw in

Cape Cod bays and mature there by July, or by Sept. in Maine. Persist to Oct.

Where found: Greenland to West Indies. Irregular south of Cape Cod. There is probably a single cosmopolitan species. To salinities of 16‰.

Remarks: Reportedly less venomous than other jellyfish in our area. Adults feed on small plankters caught on sticky mucous bands on umbrella and licked off the margin by the mouth-arms.

Family: Ulmaridae.

Sessile Jellyfish

These little animals do not at all resemble typical jellyfish (Plate 31). They are stalked and customarily rest with mouth upper-most; the bell is flower- or trumpet-shaped and divided into 8 lobes. Tentacles are clublike and clumped at the end of each lobe. Some species are permanently attached; others move about with the aid of adhesive *anchors* located in notches between lobes. Order Stauromedusae.

STALKED JELLYFISH *Haliclystus auricula* **Pl. 17**
Identification: Seen from above with bell expanded, lobes are *paired;* 100–120 tentacles per cluster. Anchors present. To 1¼ in. (31 mm).

Similar species: See Fig. 19, below. (1) *Craterolophus convolvulus* has stalk *much shorter* than extended bell. Does *not* have anchors. To 1 in. (25 mm). Family Cleistocarpidae. (2) *Lucernaria quadricornis* has stalk somewhat *longer* than bell; does *not* have anchors. Said to reach 2¾ in. (69 mm). (3)

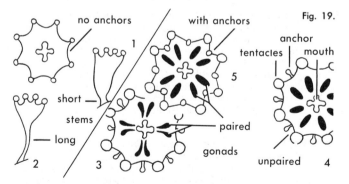

Sessile Jellyfish. (1) *Craterolophus convolvulus,* (2) *Lucernaria quadricornis,* (3) *Thaumatoscyphus atlanticus,* (4) *Haliclystus salpinx,* (5) *Haliclystus auricula.*

Thaumatoscyphus atlanticus has anchors and paired lobes. About 30 tentacles per cluster. Gonads (seen from above through body wall) form a Maltese cross; those of Stalked Jellyfish are paired but more widely (evenly) spaced. To 1 in. (25 mm). Family Cleistocarpidae. (4) *Haliclystus salpinx* has unpaired lobes and gonads. To ⅜ in. (9 mm).

Where found: Boreal, and locally on south shore of Cape Cod; lower intertidal zone to subtidal at shallow depths.

Remarks: Look for these interesting jellyfish in quiet runoff basins and tide pools, attached to seaweeds, rocks, even live periwinkles. For their size they catch quite large annelid worms and other shore animals. Mature in one season and disappear by fall.

Family: Eleutherocarpidae, including *Lucernaria*.

Anthozoans: Class Anthozoa

The polypoid generation (see p. 69) predominates in this class; there are no medusoid forms. Anthozoan polyps are structurally more complex than hydrozoan polyps (p. 72); in particular the gastrovascular cavity is divided by partitions called *mesenteries*.

Most anthozoans — anemones are an exception — are colonial; colony form varies greatly. Anthozoans reproduce sexually and have the usual planula larvae, or asexually by budding or dividing (fission).

There are 3 subclasses and 7 orders distinguished by differences in internal structure.

Octocorals

Colonial anthozoans, individuals anemonelike in structure *with 8 pinnately branching tentacles;* polyps retractile in a flexible but tough, fleshy, or rubbery matrix, which forms the common mass of the colony and is imbedded with *calcareous* spicules ¹⁄₂₅₀-¹⁄₂₅ in. (0.1-1 mm) long. Colony form varies from coarsely feathery or whiplike to massive and rubbery. Common in tropics but only a few shallow-water species on this coast; others deeper.

Octocorals form a separate subclass, Octocorallia, with 4 orders; only one of these, Alcyonacea, occurs in shallow water on this coast.

DEAD MAN'S FINGERS *Alcyonium digitatum*   **Pl. 10**
 Identification: Grows in fleshy to tough lobes and fingers attached to stones, shells, pilings, or suspended from walls and ceiling of quiet, shaded rock pools. White to pink or pale orange. 4-8 in. (100-200 mm), smaller inshore. Spicules are slender, bumpy, cucumber-shaped rods ¹⁄₁₀₀ in. (0.25 mm) long; see p. 64.

Where found: Gulf of St. Lawrence south to R.I.; subtidal in shallow water in Bay of Fundy or e. Maine, but in 25 ft. (7.5 m) or more off Cape Cod.
Family: Alcyoniidae.

SEA WHIP *Leptogorgia virgulata*   **Pl. 11**
Identification: Stem and *branches* slender, whiplike; with a tough outer rind and horny core. Color varies locally, purple to orange-yellow, tan, or even red. To 3 feet (900 mm).
Similar species: *L. setacea* (not shown) is similar but *unbranched;* less common than *virgulata*. Northward in Chesapeake Bay to mouth of Patuxent R., Md.
Where found: N.J. to Gulf of Mexico; lower intertidal to subtidal at shallow depths, on jetties, pilings, and rocks. Sea Whips have been found off Hereford Inlet (Cape May), N.J., and Indian R., Del., but are more common south of Cape Hatteras.
Family: Gorgoniidae.

SEA PANSY *Renilla reniformis*   **Fig. 36 opp. Pl. 11**
Identification: Colony *shaped like a lily pad* but thick and leathery with polyps scattered on upper surface; a thick stem below. Pinkish to violet, the polyps lighter. To $2\frac{3}{5}$ in. (65 mm).
Similar species: Sea Pen, *Pennatula aculeata* (Fig. 36 opp. Plate 11) has a long stem; polyps are on plumelike upperpart. To 4 in. (100 mm). Carolinas northward in deep water — 360 ft. (108 m) or more — but sometimes brought in by fishermen because of its curious form. Family Pennatulidae.
Where found: N.C. to Fla. and e. South America; subtidal in shallow water on sandy bottoms. These pretty little flowerlike octocorals are common on the N.C. coast off Cape Lookout and have been reported north to Cape Hatteras.
Family: Renillidae.

Stony Corals

Colonial anthozoans, individuals anemonelike in structure with a calcareous *external* skeleton. Individual polyps more or less retractile in stony cups or tubes (*corallites*) with thin internal partitions radiating from the center. Colonies consist of a crust or solid mass joining or surrounding individual corallites. Shallow-water corals are colored by symbiotic algae (zooxanthellae), and reef-building corals (Fla. southward) depend on them, as well as on year-round warm water.

Stony corals form a distinct order, Scleractinia, placed in the subclass Zoantharia along with sea anemones and the tropical and deepwater zoanthids.

STAR CORAL *Astrangia danae*   **Fig. 20**
Identification: Colonies consist of low, cuplike corallites, $\frac{3}{16}-\frac{1}{4}$ in. (5–6 mm) in diameter, united by a thin crust, or sometimes

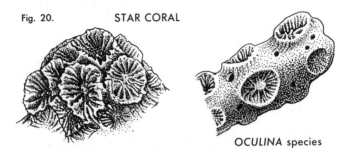

Fig. 20.   **STAR CORAL**

OCULINA species

forming low, branching groups several inches across. With up to 30 individuals per colony. Polyps colorless to pinkish when in deep shade, translucent greenish in light.

Similar species: *Oculina* species (Fig. 20) found in strong branching colonies $\frac{1}{4}$–$\frac{3}{8}$ in. (6–9 mm) thick, with $\frac{1}{8}$-in. (3 mm) raised corallites; washed ashore from Cape Hatteras south to West Indies. Family Oculinidae.

Where found: Cape Cod to Fla.; common from w. L.I. Sound to Cape Cod, locally southward. Subtidal from shallow depths to 120 ft. (36 m).

Remarks: Our only shallow-water northern coral is found on pilings, rocks, and shells. Limited tolerance for brackish water and turbidity, plus lack of suitable attachments inshore, may account for scarcity along most of the coast. Dead specimens, usually much worn, are found in beach drift.

Family: Astrangiidae.

Sea Anemones

Solitary, soft-bodied anthozoans with unbranched tentacles. Typical anemones are columnar with an adherent *pedal disk* at the base and an *oral disk* with 1 or more rings or *cycles* of tentacles circling the mouth. Ability to retract tentacles and contract column varies, but most anemones shrink down to a soft blob when touched. *Acontia* are threadlike structures that may be protruded through the mouth or pores in the column when the animal is severely disturbed; these are heavily armed with nematocysts and presumably function defensively. However, none of our species has a sting poisonous to humans.

Despite a seemingly sedentary disposition, anemones can glide about freely on their pedal disks. They feed on live or dead animals ranging from small plankters to fish. Burrowing anemones are elongate and wormlike, and somewhat resemble sea cucumbers (see Plate 46 and p. 253).

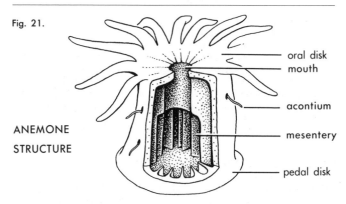

Fig. 21.

oral disk
mouth
acontium
ANEMONE
STRUCTURE
mesentery
pedal disk

Anemones reproduce sexually or in some cases asexually by budding new individuals from the base of their column, or by dividing (a process called transverse or longitudinal fission); the offspring separate from the parent.

Anemones can be hard to identify, and our species are in need of expert attention. Positive identification in difficult cases requires a study of the arrangement of mesenteries, types of nematocysts (pp. 70–71), and other details of internal anatomy.

Cerantharian anemones resemble burrowing anemones but are classified separately (Order Ceriantharia, Subclass Ceriantipatharia) on the basis of internal anatomy. Typical anemones, including burrowing species, form Order Actiniaria, Subclass Zoantharia; corals make up a 2nd order in this subclass.

ATHENARIAN BURROWING ANEMONES Pl. 47
Edwardsia and related genera

Identification: Elongate, wormlike; bottom-end rounded, tapered, or formed into an inflatable digging organ (*physa*) instead of a clasping pedal disk. Oral disk has *single whorl* of 12–20 tentacles.

3 genera and species. (1) *Nematostella vectensis* is smooth, transparent; lacks physa and collar. To $\frac{3}{4}$ in. (19 mm). (Compare with synaptas, p. 255). (2) *Edwardsia elegans* has *3-part column* including a smooth collar, a rough, warty, deeply grooved middle section, and a distinct physa: about 16 slender tentacles; to $1\frac{3}{8}$ in. (34 mm). (*E. leidyi* — not shown — is about same size, pink, and young are found as parasites in Leidy's Comb Jelly, p. 100). (3) *Haloclava producta* has a distinct physa, column with about 20 rows of coarse warts, and 20 blunt, *knobbed* tentacles. To 6 in. (150 mm).

Similar species: (1) See Thenarian and Ceriantharian anemones (Plate 47). (2) Additional, little-known, burrowing anemones have been found in deep water off our coast.

Where found: (1) *N. vectensis,* whole coast; in brackish water with salinity of about 18‰ or less. (2) *E. elegans,* whole coast south at least to Chesapeake Bay; subtidal from shallow water to more than 300 ft. (90 m), and into moderately brackish water. (3) *H. producta,* Cape Cod southward, on sand flats intertidally and subtidal in shallow water.

Families: Edwardsiidae, *Nematostella* and *Edwardsia;* Haloclavidae, *Haloclava.*

THENARIAN BURROWING ANEMONES   Pl. 47
Actinothoe species

Identification: Elongate and wormlike, but with typical anemonelike oral and *pedal disks. Acontia* present. Tentacles numerous, 48–64 or more in several cycles. The taxonomy and identification of individual species are unsettled. (1) *A. modesta* has a pale, whitish or pink column that is smooth or nearly so. To 2½ in. (62 mm) long; 64 tentacles. (2) *A. gracillima* (not shown) is similar but less than 1 in. (25 mm) long; has no more than 48 tentacles. (3) *A. eruptaurantia* (not shown) has 10–11 vertical rows of red warts on column, grows to 1 in. (25 mm) long, and has 64 or more tentacles.

Similar species: (1) *Paranthus rapiformis* (not shown) has a small pedal disk, finely grooved column up to 3 in. (75 mm) long, 144 or more tentacles, and *lacks acontia.* Common at mouth of Chesapeake Bay. Family Actinostolidae. (2) See Athenarian and Ceriantharian burrowing anemones (Plate 47).

Where found: (1) *A. modesta* and (2) *A. gracillima,* Cape Cod south presumably at least as far as Cape Hatteras. (3) *A. eruptaurantia* is southern; north to lower Chesapeake Bay.

Remarks: Look for daisylike oral disks lying flush with sandy bottom; column extends vertically down to pedal disk adhering to pebble or shell. Pops out of sight when disturbed. Sometimes found partly buried under rocks or other debris.

Family: Sagartidae.

NORTHERN RED ANEMONE *Tealia felina*   Pl. 12
Identification: A variable, wide-ranging, Boreal anemone with several named varieties. Column smooth, deep wine-red to chestnut or purplish, often streaked or variegated with green. Adheres strongly to substratum and is completely contractile. Tentacles short, thick, blunt; usually with 1–2 dark rings but color varies; red-green varieties often complexly ringed as shown in Plate 12. Height about half width, which is 2–3 in. (50–75 mm) intertidally, to 5 in. (125 mm) in deeper water. To 160 tentacles in 5 cycles.

Similar species: Compare with Silver-spotted and Frilled Anemones (both Plate 12) which commonly live in the same places.
Where found: Common intertidally from Casco Bay north to subarctic; rarely and only subtidally to south shore of Cape Cod. Other varieties on shores of North Pacific and n. Europe.
Family: Actinidae.

SILVER-SPOTTED ANEMONE *Bunodactis stella*   **Pl. 12**
Identification: Column translucent, pale olive to bluish green (sometimes pinkish) with *rows of sticky bumps* to which bits of shell and pebbles adhere. Tentacles same color, slender, with pale ring about midway; often with an opaque silvery white spot at base. Oral disk may have radial white stripes. To $1\frac{3}{8}$ in. (34 mm) tall, 2 in. (50 mm) wide. Tentacles 48–96 in 4 or 5 cycles.
Similar species: Northern Red Anemone (Plate 12) has smooth column; usually dark-ringed tentacles, and is more completely contractile. Both *lack* acontia. Note also young Frilled Anemone (Plate 12).
Where found: Boreal but limits uncertain; locally common in shallow water from Maine (south to Casco Bay?) north at least to Nova Scotia. Adheres firmly to rocks; often found buried up to its oral disk in crevices and pools where sand collects.
Family: Actinidae.

FRILLED ANEMONE *Metridium senile*   **Pl. 12**
Identification: Compared to other species, specimens of equivalent size have *many more* and finer tentacles, up to about 1000 on large anemones. Oral disk lobed. Column smooth, orange or yellow-brown, even-colored, less often pink or whitish, streaked or mottled. Tentacles *not* ringed. To 4 in. (100 mm) tall by 3 in. (75 mm) wide subtidally, smaller along shore.
Similar species: May be found with *any* species on Plate 12. Distinguish from Silver-spotted and Northern Red Anemones by coloration; also, Frilled Anemone has *acontia;* others do not. Southward, small ones occur intertidally with Striped and Ghost Anemones (which have acontia); Frilled Anemone can be distinguished by color, more numerous tentacles.
Where found: Arctic south to Delaware Bay, intertidal to subtidal down 500 ft. (150 m). Our commonest and largest anemone; on wharf pilings, in rock crevices, and pools.
Family: Metridiidae.

STRIPED ANEMONE *Haliplanella luciae*   **Pl. 12**
Identification: Column dark green with blood-red to dull yellow or whitish *stripes.* To $\frac{3}{4}$ in. (19 mm) tall by $\frac{1}{4}$ in. (6 mm) wide. About 50 tentacles.

Similar species: Pale individuals with buff-colored stripes might be mistaken for Ghost Anemone (Plate 12) whose mesenteries show through skin as thin silvery-white stripes. Striped Anemone usually more opaque.

Where found: Whole coast; an immigrant (presumably from Japan but also occurs in Europe), first found at New Haven, Conn., in 1892, but now abundant, south at least to Chesapeake Bay and north to Maine; on rocks and pilings intertidally, in estuaries and other protected waters. Also reported in Texas.

Family: Aiptasiomorphidae.

GHOST ANEMONE *Diadumene leucolena*   **Pl. 12**

Identification: A rather nondescript little anemone. Pale, very *translucent;* whitish, tinted pink to olive. Column appears smooth, but viewed closely, small, scattered, darker bumps can be seen. To 1½ in. (38 mm) tall by ½ in. (12 mm) wide. Tentacles 40–60.

Similar species: Compare with Striped and young Frilled Anemones (Plate 12) which are found in the same places.

Where found: Mainly south of Cape Cod, although reported north at least to Mt. Desert I. Common fouling species on pilings intertidally and *under* rocks in protected shallow water of bays and harbors.

Family: Diadumenidae.

CERIANTHARIAN ANEMONES   **Pl. 47**
Cerianthus and *Ceriantheopsis* species

Identification: Similar to burrowing anemones (pp. 95–96) but with *2 distinct whorls of tentacles,* inner ones short, outer ones longer. Bottom of column rounded, without pedal disk. Brownish.

2 species. (1) *Cerianthus borealis* (not shown) is a northern, deepwater form with tentacles in outer whorl *varying* in size. To at least 18 in. (450 mm) tall with 9-in. (225 mm) tentacle span. (2) *Ceriantheopsis americanus* has marginal tentacles of equal length; column to 8 in. (200 mm).

Similar species: Athenarian and thenarian burrowing anemones (both Plate 47) have either a single whorl of at most 20 tentacles or more numerous ones in multiple but vaguely defined cycles.

Where found: (1) *Cerianthus borealis,* Cape Cod northward, subtidal at depths of 40 ft. (12 m) or more. (2) *Ceriantheopsis americanus,* Cape Cod south, mainly subtidal but usually in less than 100 ft. (30 m); has been reported in lower intertidal zone on silty-clay bottoms.

Family: Cerianthidae.

Comb Jellies: Phylum Ctenophora

Often mistaken for jellyfish but differ as follows: They do *not* sting; common forms have 8 rows of comblike ciliary plates; structural plan is biradial (combines radial and bilateral symmetry), with 2 tentacles or 2 lobes, or with the body saclike and flattened. Large individuals frequently tinted with pinkish or brownish; otherwise colorless and almost invisible in water. Comb jellies develop directly; they do not have distinctive larval and sessile stages as most jellyfish do. Our species are easily identified *when mature;* young may be more difficult.

Like jellyfish, comb jellies are gelatinous and fragile. Out of water, most species are reduced nearly to amorphous blobs. Catch them by gently scooping with a cupped hand or a bucket. Do not fix comb jellies in formalin; use a solution of 20 parts chromic acid (1%) in 1 part glacial acetic acid; fix for $\frac{1}{2}$ hour, then wash in water for 15 minutes. Store in 70% alcohol.

Comb jellies are voracious predators. They are cannibals and have also been reported eating such prickly fish as young sculpins. Like many plankters they often occur in swarms; although common inshore and in estuaries, they keep to deeper levels when water is rough. Exclusively marine.

SEA GOOSEBERRY *Pleurobrachia pileus*　　　　　　　**Pl. 32**
Identification: Body spherical, egg- or walnut-shaped, with *2 long tentacles* contractile into sheaths. Usually $\frac{3}{4}$–$1\frac{1}{8}$ in. (19–28 mm) in Bay of Fundy, smaller southward.
Similar species: (1) *Mertensia ovum* (not shown), an Arctic form; occurs rarely in Massachusetts Bay but swarming sometimes in e. Maine; reaches 2 in. (50 mm); also tentacled but pear-shaped and *flattened* when mature; young, which may be carried south of Cape Cod in winter, nearly indistinguishable from Sea Gooseberry but are said to have orange combs. (2) Common Northern Comb Jelly and (3) Leidy's Comb Jelly (both Plate 32) pass through a tentacled, lobeless, larval stage; Common Northern Comb Jelly is lobed at $\frac{3}{8}$ in. (9 mm), Leidy's Comb Jelly at $\frac{1}{4}$ in. (6 mm).
Season: Year-round from Maine to N.C. In Gulf of Maine confined to inshore waters in winter; probably reaches peak abundance in summer–early fall, when it ranges farther offshore. South of Cape Cod a winter–spring swarmer; gone from coastal waters by April or May at Cape Cod and L.I. Sound but reported offshore in summer–fall, usually at depths of 30 ft. (9 m) or more.
Where found: Whole coast but seldom in estuaries; less common southward.
Remarks: Ecologically important as a predator on fish eggs and

larvae, particularly cod and haddock. The tentacles catch prey by adhesion. Henry B. Bigelow, writing about the Gulf of Maine, said, "Wherever these ctenophores swarm they sweep the water so clean and they are so voracious that hardly any smaller creatures can coexist with them." They are in turn eaten by mackerel, spiny dogfish, and other fishes.

Family: Pleurobrachiidae, including *Mertensia*.

COMMON NORTHERN COMB JELLY   Pl. 32
Bolinopsis infundibulum

Identification: Body oval, somewhat flattened, with lobes *shorter* than body. To 6 in. (150 mm).

Similar species: (1) Leidy's Comb Jelly (Plate 32) most similar, but almost no range overlap: lobes shorter. (2) See also larval stage discussed in Sea Gooseberry (preceding account).

Season: Chiefly in summer; Gulf of Maine, April–Sept.

Where found: From Cape Cod (rarely on south shore) to Arctic.

Remarks: Most common comb jelly in shallow water on New England coast in summer.

Family: Bolinopsidae.

LEIDY'S COMB JELLY *Mnemiopsis leidyi*   Pl. 32

Identification: Body oval, somewhat flattened with lobes *exceeding* body length. Brilliantly luminescent. To 4 in. (100 mm).

Similar species: (1) See Common Northern Comb Jelly (Plate 32) for adults and (2) Sea Gooseberry for larval stage (p. 99).

Season: Year-round, but usually most abundant late summer–early fall; sometimes swarms in midwinter.

Where found: From Cape Cod Bay south; irregular north of N.J., although reported to Boothbay Harbor. Penetrates the nearly freshwater parts of estuaries; found in Chesapeake Bay, for example, at least as far up as Middle R. north of Baltimore, Md.

Remarks: Most common ctenophore south of Cape Cod. Bright green luminescent flashes along combs when animal is disturbed. Young of a burrowing anemone, *Edwardsia leidyi* (p. 95), are parasitic in gut of comb jellies including this species; they resemble pinkish, tentacled worms.

Family: Mnemiidae.

BEROE'S COMB JELLIES *Beroe* species   Pl. 32

Identification: Body flattened and saclike; no lobes or tentacles at *any* stage of development. Mature specimens pinkish or rusty brown; color visible at a distance. To 4½ in. (112 mm).

B. cucumis and *B. ovata* distinguishable only when mature and not always then. Beneath each comb row there is a meridi-

onal canal with lateral branches; in mature *ovata,* branches
from opposing canals fuse; in *cucumis* they do not. Note ranges.
Season: Mainly summer–fall.
Where found: *B. ovata* abundant as far north as Chesapeake
Bay, regularly in Delaware Bay; swarms in Sandy Hook Bay but
occurrence there and north to Cape Cod more erratic. *B.
cucumis* common in Gulf of Maine and rarely to south shore of
Cape Cod.
Remarks: Beroë was one of the sea nymphs, a daughter of
Oceanus.
Family: Beroidae.

VENUS GIRDLE *Cestum veneris*   **Pl. 32**
Identification: *Ribbonlike* body divided into 2 lobes with double row of combs along upper margin of each lobe; other 4 combs
rudimentary. Reaches length of 5 ft. (1.5 m) but usually much
smaller.
Where found: Tropical and oceanic; a Gulf Stream species
rarely encountered inshore but most likely in late summer–early
fall.
Family: Cestidae.

Flatworms: Phylum Platyhelminthes

These little worms resemble flying carpets as they skim in soft
undulations above the bottom. Flatworms are structurally simple,
without appendages or segmentation. The gut, which shows
through the translucent body, may have numerous branches or
diverticulae but has only one opening, near midbody or somewhat
farther forward. Tiny eyespots, in clusters or bands, are useful in
identification.

Most flatworms are carnivorous, often scavenging on dead animals. Some species live in close relation with particular animals
and are described as *commensals* — nonparasitic associates. Marine flatworms do not have the extraordinary regenerative powers
that have made freshwater worms so useful in biology classes. A
very few species, however, reproduce asexually by fission. In others, parthenogenesis (reproduction by all-female populations
through development of the eggs without fertilization) occurs.
Among the species that reproduce sexually, some have direct
development; others undergo a metamorphosis from a trochophore-like larva (see p. 61).

Order Polycladida contains larger, free-living flatworms. Only 1
member of Order Tricladida is included here; the others, plus
members of 3 other orders, are mostly minute and require special
study. Various freshwater and terrestrial species also belong to the

same phylum as flatworms, as do internally parasitic tapeworms and flukes (Classes Cestoda and Trematoda).

LIMULUS LEECH *Bdelloura candida* **Pl. 36**

Identification: Look for these flatworms on book gills of Atlantic Horseshoe Crabs. Easily identified by *sucker at rear end*. Gut extends backward in 2 branches that *do not* join at rear. To $\frac{5}{8}$ in. (16 mm).

Similar species: (1) *B. propinqua* (not shown) reaches half the size of Limulus Leech; requires microscopic study. (2) *Syncoelidium pellucidum* (not shown), to $\frac{1}{8}$ in. (3 mm); branches of gut *join at rear*. Both species found with Limulus Leech on horseshoe crabs. (3) For true leeches see p. 164.

Where found: Whole coast; range same as that of host.

Family: Bdellouridae, including *Syncoelidium* (Order Tricladida).

OYSTER FLATWORM *Stylochus ellipticus* **Pl. 36**

Identification: A pale, cream-colored flatworm with a band of eye specks along $\frac{1}{3}$ *or more of front margin* plus a scattering of eyes on head. *Pair of tiny tentacles* best seen from side. To 1 in. (25 mm) but usually smaller.

Similar species: All with a marginal band of eyespots: (1) Zebra Stylochus, *S. zebra* (Plate 36) has dark and light crossbands. To $1\frac{1}{2}$ in. (38 mm). Found in shells with Flat-clawed Hermit Crab; south of Cape Cod. (2) Additional *Stylochus* species (not shown) with eyes *all around* margin reported on oysters, but evidently less common. (3) *Coronadena mutabilis* (Plate 36) has marginal eyespots around *front half* plus *4 clusters* of eyespots on head; to $\frac{3}{4}$ in. (19 mm). A southern, estuarine species reportedly common in Chesapeake Bay, rare at Cape Cod. Family Discocelidae.

Where found: Whole coast north to Casco Bay. Feeds on oysters but also reported on barnacles and under rocks in tide pools and shallow water.

Family: Stylochidae.

SLENDER FLATWORM *Euplana gracilis* **Pl. 36**

Identification: Has 4–5 eyespots in a row on each side of head plus 2 more farther back; no tentacles or marginal eyespots. Yellowish to gray-brown. To $\frac{3}{8}$ in. (9 mm).

Where found: Whole coast. On Eelgrass and pilings among sponges and hydroids.

Family: Leptoplanidae.

SPECKLED FLATWORM *Notoplana atomata* **Pl. 36**

Identification: Probably the most common New England flatworm. *Eyes in 4 clusters, none along margin;* no tentacles.

Brownish above, variably marked with fine flecks. To 1 in. (25 mm).

Similar species: (1) *Acerotisa* species (not shown) also have 4 eye clusters but front pair reach margin. *A. baiae,* ⅛ in. (3 mm), is found inshore south of Cape Cod; *A. notulata,* is a minute Gulfweed species. Family Euryleptidae. (2) *Coronadena mutabilis* (Plate 36) has 4 clusters *plus* marginal eyespots; see also Oyster Flatworm account, p. 102.

Where found: New England coast and probably northward as well, since it occurs in n. Europe. Questionably reported from Delaware Bay, but not common inshore south of Cape Cod. Under rocks from lower intertidal to subtidal in deep water.

Family: Leptoplanidae.

GULFWEED FLATWORM *Gnesioceros sargassicola*   **Pl. 36**
Identification: The common flatworm *on drifting Gulfweed* has 2 small tentacles covered with eyespots and a cluster of eyespots on head in front of each tentacle. No marginal tentacles. Brownish, spotted. To ⅜ in. (9 mm).

Similar species: *G. floridana* (not shown) is similar but is found inshore on Eelgrass. To ⁵⁄₁₆ in. (8 mm). Cape Cod south.

Where found: Oceanic but washed ashore from Cape Cod south.

Family: Planoceridae.

HORNED FLATWORM *Prosthecereaus maculosus*   **Pl. 36**
Identification: A slender flatworm with 2 eye-covered tentacles on the front margin and 2 eye clusters on the head. To ½ in. (12 mm).

Where found: South shore of Cape Cod; estuarine, on pilings.

Family: Euryleptidae.

Nemertean Worms:
Phylum Rhynchocoela

Soft and leechlike. Nemerteans are much more complex structurally than flatworms (see p. 101), though, like them, they are unsegmented and have no appendages. Gut has both a mouth opening and anus, the latter inconspicuous. Some species have eyespots or *ocelli* and various types of sensory grooves (often obscure) on the head. In front of the mouth is a tiny pore through which a completely retractile (*eversible*) *proboscis* is thrust to impale prey; structural details are important systematically but not really useful in the field. Proboscis is *not* used to impale

human fingers. Handle nemerteans gently, as they break into
pieces at the slightest provocation.

Sexes are usually separate, although some nemerteans reproduce
asexually by fission. Certain species bear live young; others lay
eggs that either develop directly into worms or produce planktonic
larvae derived from a trochophore type (see p. 61).

Study nemerteans alive. Color is important for identification
and disappears in pickled worms (which are not very attractive
anyway). Most are highly contractile and are constantly changing
proportions; *length and width* are given for extended worms.

A few terrestrial and freshwater species known, only 1 of the
latter in North America.

KEELED NEMERTEAN   Not shown
Carinoma tremaphoros

Identification: With *neither* ocelli nor grooves, though head
has a row of fine pits down middle. Body flattened in mid
region. Whitish towards head; yellowish, reddish, or pale brown
behind. To 6 x $\frac{3}{16}$ in. (150 x 5 mm).

Where found: Cape Cod south at least to Chesapeake Bay.
Common in protected bays and estuaries in silty clay; shallow
water.

Family: Carinomidae.

LINED NEMERTEANS *Lineus* species   Pl. 37

Identification: Body rounded to threadlike, somewhat flattened in middle; tail end *without* a cirrus. Head *grooved lengthwise;* ocelli present.

4 species, distinguished mainly by color. (1) Striped Lineus,
L. bicolor, is green with a light median stripe; to 2 x $\frac{1}{16}$ in.
(50 x 1.6 mm). (2) Sandy Lineus, *L. arenicola,* is rosy; to
4 x $\frac{1}{16}$ in. (100 x 1.6 mm). (3) Social Lineus, *L. socialis,* resembles next species but contracts in coils rather than by shortening
and thickening; very slender when extended. Sometimes with
lighter rings. Often found with many tangled together in a
mass — hence the name. (4) Red Lineus, *L. ruber,* actually
varies from dark red to green or brownish green; head light-
edged; to 6 x $\frac{1}{8}$ in. (150 x 3 mm).

Similar species: (1) *Micrura affinis* (not shown) resembles red
or brown variants of Red Lineus but has larger ocelli and a
cirrus (though it is sometimes broken off). To 6 x $\frac{1}{8}$ in.
(150 x 3 mm). A Boreal and usually subtidal nemertean but
can be found under stones in lower intertidal zone in Bay of
Fundy. (2) Milky Ribbon Worm and (3) micruran nemerteans
(both Plate 37) have similar head grooves but lack ocelli; have
cirrus unless damaged.

Where found: (1) Striped Lineus is mainly subtidal in 6 ft.
(1.8 m) or more; Cape Cod south (rarely north to cen. Maine

coast). (2) Sandy Lineus, locally from Gulf of St. Lawrence to Chesapeake Bay. (3) Social Lineus, Bay of Fundy to Chesapeake Bay. (4) Red Lineus, the commonest species, Arctic south to Cape Cod and e. L.I. Sound. The latter 3 species are found intertidally, burrowing in mud or sand and among pebbles and debris.

Family: Lineidae, including *Micrura.*

SHARP-HEADED NEMERTEAN   Pl. 37
Zygeupolia rubens

Identification: Distinguished from other nemertean worms by its *long, pointed head* (when extended); no ocelli or head grooves. Tail with cirrus. Young are white, turning rosy when older; head white. To $3 \times \frac{3}{16}$ in. (75 x 5 mm).

Where found: Cape Cod south at least to Chesapeake Bay.

Family: Lineidae.

MICRURAN NEMERTEANS *Micrura* species   Pl. 37

Identification: Body thin, rounded to flattish in part; tail-end *with a cirrus* but easily broken off. Head *grooved lengthwise;* intertidal species *without ocelli.* Mouth (on underside) small, round.

2 species. (1) Blind Micruran, *M. caeca* (not shown) and (2) Leidy's Micruran, *M. leidyi,* are both reddish but *caeca* is paler, *leidyi* is darker with light-bordered head. Blind Micruran to $4\frac{3}{4} \times \frac{1}{8}$ in. (119 x 3 mm); Leidy's Micruran to $12 \times \frac{1}{4}$ in. (300 x 6 mm).

Similar species: See lined nemerteans (Plate 37). These have ocelli; *M. affinis,* mainly a subtidal species, does, too, and is discussed with them (p. 104).

Where found: (1) Blind Micruran, L.I. Sound to south shore of Cape Cod. (2) Leidy's Micruran, Bay of Fundy south to Fla. Both are burrowers in sand and under rocks intertidally. Other species subtidal in deep water.

Family: Lineidae.

MILKY RIBBON WORM *Cerebratulus lacteus*   Pl. 37

Identification: A thickish ribbonlike worm. Usually milky or creamy white, or tinted pinkish; strongly colored when breeding — males bright red, females browner. Head grooved lengthwise; mouth (on underside) a small *slot; no ocelli.* Intact worms have a short cirrus. Our largest nemertean, often 3–4 ft. (0.9–1.2 m) long by $\frac{1}{2}$–$\frac{5}{8}$ in. (12–16 mm) wide.

Similar species: (1) *C. marginatus* (not shown) is similar in form and size but is grayish, olive, or brownish with light margins. Arctic south to Cape Cod and R.I. Intertidal in Maine but usually subtidal southward. (2) *Parapolia aurantiaca* (not shown) is also similar in form but lacks head grooves and feathered margin of Milky Ribbon Worm. Bright orange; to 10 x $\frac{3}{8}$ in. (250 x 9 mm). S. Maine south at least to Chesapeake Bay, in sandy mud in lower intertidal zone. (3) See lined and micruran nemerteans (both Plate 37).

Where found: Whole coast. Common intertidally under stones and in sandy mud on bay shores and other places.

Family: Lineidae, including *Parapolia*.

MANY-EYED NEMERTEANS   Pl. 36
Amphiporus and *Zygonemertes* species

Identification: Head with *numerous ocelli;* transverse grooves, often obliquely angled, but may be obscure or seemingly absent.

Numerous species, the following most common inshore. (1) *A. angulatus* is dark purplish or brownish; has ocelli in *4 groups* and has a *light chevron* behind head. To 6 x $\frac{3}{8}$ in. (150 x 9 mm); a common nemertean among rocks and seaweeds in northern tide pools. (2) *A cruentatus* (not shown) is pale yellow or rosy with *fine red lines lengthwise;* ocelli in a *single row.* To $1\frac{1}{2}$ x $\frac{3}{16}$ in. (38 x 5 mm). (3) *A ocraceus* and (4) *A. griseus* (not shown) are both yellow and have numerous ocelli scattered *irregularly* along each side of head; *griseus* exudes a *thick slime* when handled, *ocraceus* doesn't. Both to $1\frac{1}{4}$ x $\frac{1}{16}$ in. (31 x 1.6 mm). (5) *Z. virescens* (not shown) is *greenish* and has ocelli extending back beyond head onto body. To $1\frac{1}{2}$ x $\frac{1}{16}$ in. (38 x 1.6 mm).

Where found: (1) *A. angulatus,* Arctic south to Cape Cod and beyond in deep water. (2) *A. cruentatus,* Fla. north locally at least to Cape Cod; uncommon. (3) *A. ocraceus* and (4) *A. griseus* both range from Fla. north to Cape Cod, and *ocraceus* extends on, locally at least, well up the Maine coast. (5) *Z. virescens,* Bay of Fundy south at least to Chesapeake Bay. All occur among seaweeds and fouling organisms on rocks, pilings, Eelgrass, and the like; intertidal to subtidal in shallow water.

Family: Amphiporidae.

FOUR-EYED NEMERTEANS *Tetrastemma* species   Pl. 36

Identification: 2 traits distinguish these small, roundish nemerteans: (1) The *4 ocelli* are usually quite distinct, and form a square; (2) head grooves transverse or obliquely angled but *hardly detectable.*

At least 6 species, 2 of them *striped.* (1) *T. elegans* and (2) *T. vittatum* (not shown) are *striped. T. elegans* is yellowish with brown stripes, while *vittatum* is usually greenish with 6 light stripes on head and 1–2 on body. *T. elegans* is *slender,* to $\frac{3}{4}$ x $\frac{1}{16}$ in. (19 x 1.6 mm); *vittatum* is *stout,* to $1\frac{3}{16}$ x $\frac{3}{16}$ in. (30 x 5 mm) or sometimes twice that. Other species *uniformly* colored: (3) *T. jeani* (not shown) is dark brown; (4) *T. wilsoni* (not shown) whitish; (5) *T. candidum,* greenish, and (6) *T.*

vermiculus (not shown) yellowish to rosy, often flecked with brown. All are small, $\frac{1}{2}$-$\frac{3}{4}$ in. x $\frac{1}{32}$-$\frac{1}{16}$ in. (2-9 x 0.78-1.6 mm), although *T. candidum* may reach about twice that size. **Similar species:** *Oerstedia dorsalis* (not shown) also has 4 eyes; extremely variable in color but usually somewhat cross-banded; to $\frac{3}{4}$ x $\frac{1}{16}$ in. (19 x 1.6 mm) at most. Whole coast; on Eelgrass and among fouling organisms on pilings and rocks, from lower intertidal to subtidal at moderate depths. Family Prosorhochmidae.

Where found: (1) *T. elegans,* Cape Cod south at least to Chesapeake Bay. (2) *T. vittatum,* Bay of Fundy south to L.I. Sound, especially in muddy protected places. (3) *T. jeani,* York R., lower Chesapeake Bay. (4) *T. wilsoni,* south shore of Cape Cod. (5) *T. candidum,* Labrador to Fla. (6) *T. vermiculus,* Bay of Fundy to Fla. All are shallow-water worms, found among fouling organisms on rocks, pilings, and on shelly Eelgrass bottoms. **Family:** Tetrastemmatidae.

Additional Nemertean Species Plate 36

First 2 are blind and grooveless; last 2 semiparasitic on crabs or bivalves.

Thread Nemertean, *Procephalothrix spiralis* (not shown) is threadlike and coils in *tight spirals;* white, tinged with rose, yellow, or green. Mouth quite far back from front end. To 4 by less than $\frac{1}{32}$ in. (100 x 0.78 mm). Nova Scotia south to L.I. Sound, intertidal in sand, under stones. Family Cephalothricidae.

Tube Nemertean, *Tubulanus pellucidus* (not shown) is found in frail, skinlike tubes among bryozoans and colonial tunicates. Whitish, sometimes with pale yellow or orange line; a dark band in throat region of pickled worms. To 1 by less than $\frac{1}{32}$ in. (25 x 0.78 mm). Cape Cod south, intertidal. Family Tubulanidae.

Crab Nemertean, *Carcinonemertes carcinophila* (not shown) is found on gills and eggs of Blue Crab and other swimming crabs. Has 2 comma-shaped eyes. Pale rosy or yellowish to brick-red. Females to $1\frac{9}{16}$ in. (39 mm), males to 1 in. (25 mm). Whole coast. Family Carcinonemertidae.

Leech Nemertean, *Malacobdella grossa* (Plate 36) is leechlike with a small sucker at rear end; short, broad, pale but variably tinted. To $1\frac{9}{16}$ x $\frac{1}{2}$ in. (39 x 12 mm). Whole coast, in a wide variety of bivalves. Family Malacobdellidae.

Aschelminthean Worms:
Phylum Aschelminthes

A somewhat miscellaneous collection of *6 classes* of worms with no obvious unifying trait useful to field naturalists. They are, in fact, rather loosely allied even on technical grounds and some biologists elevate individual classes to phylum status.

Three classes (none shown) are essentially microscopic: (1) Rotifera. Numerous species but more important in fresh water than salt; some so-called marine rotifers are merely freshwater forms with a broad salinity tolerance. Most are smaller than $\frac{1}{50}$ in. (0.5 mm). Varied in habits and habitat, they include attached, bottom-crawling, and planktonic species. (2) Gastrotricha. A few of these transparent worms reach $\frac{1}{16}$ in. (1.6 m); most are less than half that. Many live in watery spaces between intertidal and subtidal sand grains; also occur in fresh water. Studied very little until recently. About 30 species known in 1969. (3) Kinorhyncha. Several species along this coast; biggest about $\frac{1}{32}$ in. (0.78 mm); superficially segmented. Special collecting and sorting techniques needed to even find them. Marine only.

A 4th class, Nematoda or Roundworms (Fig. 22, below), contains slender, spindle- or thread-like whitish worms; often nearly featureless without a microscope. Many coil in simple arcs, loops, or spirals. They may well be the most numerous marine invertebrates; a half-million *kinds* are estimated to exist; calculated density in a square yard (0.9 m²) of mud off the Dutch coast — $4\frac{1}{2}$ million worms. They are literally *everywhere,* parasitic and free-living, in salt water, fresh water, and on land. Mostly smaller than $\frac{1}{16}$ in. (1.6 mm) but some to 1 in. (25 mm) or more.

A 5th class, Nematomorpha or Hairworms (Fig. 22, below), has only 1 marine species, *Nectonema agile.* It is threadlike, pale,

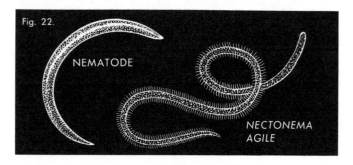

Fig. 22. NEMATODE — NECTONEMA AGILE

108

translucent, whitish or grayish yellow, with grayish bristles all along the body except on the short tail and longer head. Young are parasitic in crabs; adults free-living, attracted to lights on moonless nights, July–October. Less than $\frac{1}{16}$ in. (1.6 mm) thick, but 2–8 in. (50–200 mm) long. So far known only from south shore of Cape Cod and from Narragansett Bay. Hairworms are more common in fresh water and on land.

A 6th class, Priapulida, exclusively marine, has only 1 species in our area (see following account). Priapulids were formerly allied with sipunculan and echiurid worms (pp. 197–99) in a polyphyletic class, Gephyrea, of the phylum Annelida.

PRIAPULUS *Priapulus caudatus* **Fig. 23**
Identification: Stout and wormlike, with a 2-part body. 1st part, called the *prosoma,* consists of 3 sections: a bulbous proboscis, a short collar, and a mouth armed with short hooks and spines. Entire prosoma retractile within a thickish, warty *trunk* that is superficially segmented with 30–40 rings and terminated by a cluster of short, thick appendages. Proboscis whitish; trunk peach color to brownish with yellow appendages. To 3 in. (75 mm).
Where found: Massachusetts Bay north to Arctic. Subtidal at depths of 30 ft. (9 m) or more in e. Maine, deeper southward; at trawling depths off Isles of Shoals.
Family: None designated (only 3 species in the whole class).

Entoprocts: Phylum Entoprocta

These tiny animals are usually overlooked except by specialists. Superficially similar to hydroids (Plates 13, 14) but with a far more complex internal anatomy. Free-swimming larvae are microscopic, trochophore-like; metamorphose directly into the adult

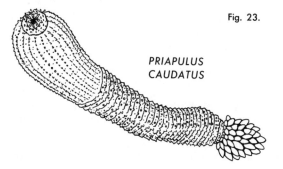

Fig. 23.

PRIAPULUS
CAUDATUS

form. Adults attach themselves to a variety of substrata. Formerly classified as bryozoans (below). Freshwater and marine.

ENTOPROCTS *Barentsia* and *Pedicellina* species   **Pl. 13**
   Identification: Small unbranched *zooids,* consisting of a stalk and calyx with a *circlet* of tentacles, rise from a creeping stolon.
   2 genera. (1) *P. cernua* has a simple stalk usually covered with *spines;* less than ¼ in. (6 mm) tall. (2) *B. major* has a *stiff,* thick-walled stalk, to ⅜ in. (9 mm); (3) *B. laxa* has a *flexible,* thin-walled stalk, less than ¼ in. (6 mm). In both *Barentsia* species base of stalk is distinctly *swollen.*
   Where found: (1) *P. cernua,* whole coast in shallow water including estuaries to minimum salinity of 15‰; (2) *B. major,* Arctic to s. New England, subtidal in 15 ft. (4.5 m) or more; (3) *B. laxa* chiefly south of Cape Cod in shallow water. Additional, nearly microscopic species of *Barentsia* found along whole coast. Distributions and relative abundance uncertain.
   Family: Pedicellinidae.

Bryozoans: Phylum Bryozoa

Bryozoans are sessile, colonial animals. Some colonies are almost microscopic and grow along a creeping vinelike *stolon* (see Fig. 72, p. 269). Others form crusts that range from flat and delicately lacy to thick and irregular (Plate 16). Still others are erect and leafy, or branching and bushy, and may be mistaken for seaweeds or hydroids (Plate 15). A few are rubbery or gelatinous, suggesting colonial tunicates or sponges (Plate 10). Colony size is omitted from most individual accounts. Where conditions are favorable to bryozoan growth, encrusting colonies may cover several square inches or more, and it is difficult to tell where one colony ends and the adjacent one begins. In less favorable places colonies grow in patches with a few to dozens of individual zooids covering less than a square inch.

Colonies are made up of individual *zooecia* variously joined together; each zooecium consists of the animal or *zooid* and its *exoskeleton.* This is calcified in some species, not in others. Calcareous exoskeletons may be glassy and colorless but more often are white, yellow, orange, red, or brown. Uncalcified colonies are horn-colored, yellowish brown. Individual zooecia are boxlike, tubular, or vase-shaped with an opening or orifice through which the zooid extends itself to snare passing planktonic or detrital food.

Individual zooids are minute, about $\frac{1}{50}$ in. (0.5 mm). Each has a circlet of tentacles in the form of a lophophore (see Fig. 39 opp. Plate 24) and somewhat resembles a hydroid polyp; bryozoans,

Fig. 24.

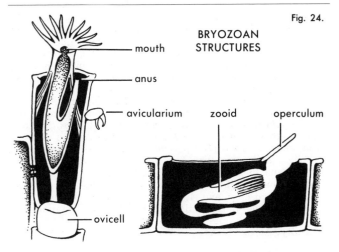

BRYOZOAN
STRUCTURES

mouth

anus

avicularium   zooid   operculum

ovicell

however, are much more complex anatomically than hydroids (see p. 72).

Most zooecia in a colony are nearly identical, but additional structures may be present. *Avicularia* are modified zooecia sometimes recognizable as such but more often much reduced in size and highly specialized in form. Presumably they help fend off fouling organisms that might settle on the colony. However, many bryozoan species do not have them, nor do all zooecia in a colony.

Most bryozoans brood their young, and some have conspicuous external brood chambers called *ovicells* or *ooecia.* These are helpful in identification but are not always present; examples are shown on Plate 16. Bryozoan larvae are microscopic and pelagic. Some live a long time in the plankton, and thus many bryozoan species have wide or even cosmopolitan distributions. After a time the larvae settle down, metamorphose into polyplike zooids, and begin budding individuals to form a colony. Most species are thought to be hermaphroditic, but rather little is known about bryozoan sex lives.

Entoprocts (p. 109) were formerly lumped with this group; bryozoans are often called *ectoprocts* and the phylum has been called Ectoprocta by some specialists. There are a few freshwater species. Nomenclature is particularly troublesome in this phylum.

RUBBERY BRYOZOANS *Alcyonidium* species   **Pl. 10**
  Identification: Colonies *rubbery* or *gelatinous;* encrusting to erect, with branches round to flattish or antler-like. Dull yel-

lowish to brown; encrusting forms sometimes bright red. *Not calcified.* Colonies may extend from several inches to 1 ft. (300 mm) or more; branches ³⁄₁₆–³⁄₈ in. (5–9 mm) thick.

1st encounter may provoke query, "Animal, vegetable, or mineral?" In life and underwater, expanding and contracting zooids identify these animals as bryozoans; pickled, look for regularly *puckered* surface with hand lens.

5 species, difficult to distinguish in the field; only *A. verrilli* shown. (1) *A. parasiticum* and (2) *A. polyoum* are encrusting. (3) *A. gelatinosum,* (4) *A. hirsutum,* and (5) *A. verrilli* become erect as they develop. *A. hirsutum* has surface covered with tiny cone-shaped bumps (1–2 per zooid); other species do not. *A. gelatinosum* is softer than *A. verrilli,* has more widely scattered zooids, and 15–17 tentacles; *verrilli* has 10.

Where found: All species whole coast, except *A. verrilli* south of Cape Cod only, and *A. gelatinosum* mainly Boreal. From lower intertidal to subtidal at shallow depths. Estuarine, with *A. verrilli* to salinities as low as 13‰.

Family: Alcyonidiidae.

BRISTLY BRYOZOAN *Flustrellidra hispida*   **Pl. 15**
Identification: Colonies rather thick — ¹⁄₁₆ in. (1.6 mm) or more — and spongy, forming a *whiskery brownish coating* around stems of rockweeds, Knotted Wrack, and other seaweeds; may extend several inches. With hand lens, note short, *slender, brown spines* that obscure zooecia. Seen alive, expanded zooids immediately identify these as bryozoans; no hydroid has this form.

Where found: Arctic south to L.I. Sound, intertidal to subtidal at shallow depths. Very common.

Family: Flustrellidridae.

LEAFY BRYOZOAN *Flustra foliacea*   **Pl. 15**
Identification: Colonies form erect, leafy, *broad-lobed fronds,* plantlike at 1st glance but easily recognized with hand lens as bryozoan. Creamy to pale brown. Crisp and brittle when dry; calcified. To 4 in. (100 mm) or more.

Where found: An Arctic species, unknown before 1960 on this coast, but abundant in upper Bay of Fundy (Minas Basin) and on outer Nova Scotia coast. Subtidal, attached to rocks, seaweeds, and the like; commonly washed ashore.

Family: Flustridae.

AMBIGUOUS BRYOZOAN *Anguinella palmata*   **Fig. 25**
Identification: Colonies soft (not calcified), *densely bushy.* Zooecia are tubular, with opening at end; ¹⁄₁₆ in. long and a tenth as thick (1.6 x 0.16 mm); growing in somewhat palmate, branching tufts. Mud-colored. Colonies to at least 2½ in. (62 mm), smaller northward.

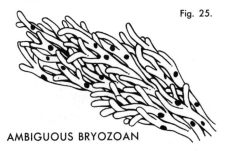

Fig. 25.

AMBIGUOUS BRYOZOAN

Dead specimens may be very puzzling indeed. Unless tentacles are visible, this species does not at all resemble other bryozoans even under magnification.

Where found: Cape Cod to Brazil; rare at its northern limit but abundant at least from Delaware Bay south. In lower intertidal zone on jetties, pilings, shells and stones; in estuaries to 13‰ minimum salinity.

Family: Nolellidae.

CREEPING BRYOZOAN   Fig. 72, p. 269
Bowerbankia gracilis

Identification: Zooecia vase-shaped, growing from a creeping *vinelike stolon.* Minute, up to $\frac{1}{32}$ in. (0.78 mm) tall.

Where found: Caribbean north to Mt. Desert I. and reported north to Arctic. Common on all types of substrata, from lower intertidal to subtidal at shallow depths and in estuaries to 10‰ minimum salinity.

Family: Vesiculariidae.

SPIRAL BRYOZOANS *Amathia* species   Pl. 15

Identification: Bushy, with zooecia in double file *winding spirally* along stem and branches. Horn-colored; not calcified. Easily recognized, even without magnification, since the 2 files of zooecia are darker and look like knots — short wiggly segments — on lighter stems.

2 species. (1) *A. convoluta* has zooecia extending *almost the entire distance* between nodes; to 6 in. (150 mm). (2) *A. vidovici* has zooecia extending *less than* $\frac{1}{2}$ the distance between nodes; to 2 in. (50 mm).

Where found: (1) *A. convoluta,* Md. or Va. (ocean side of Assateague I.) south to Brazil; to minimum salinity of 22‰. (2) *A. vidovici,* Cape Cod to West Indies; ocean salinity to as low as 11‰.

Remarks: These are common, rather sparsely-branched bryozoans often found washed ashore or attached to a variety of substrata in shallow water.

Family: Vesiculariidae.

PINNATE BRYOZOANS *Aeverrillia* species **Pl. 15**

Identification: Colonies erect, bushy; easily recognized by paired zooecia on *short stalks* arranged opposite each other on slender branches. *Horny,* not calcified. To several inches.

2 species. (1) *A. setigera* has a *tiny hook* at base of each zooecium. (2) *A. armata* does not.

Where found: Mainly south of Cape Cod, although *A. armata* reported north to Casco Bay. From lower intertidal zone to subtidal at shallow depths on pilings, seaweeds; *A. armata* estuarine, to 12‰ salinity.

Family: Walkeriidae.

JOINTED-TUBE BRYOZOANS *Crisia* species **Pl. 15**

Identification: Colonies erect, calcified, in *twiggy tufts.* Zooecia *tubular,* opening at top; joined laterally in bundles of 2 or more and in vertical series *separated by horny nodes.* To ³/₄ in. (19 mm).

2 species in shallow water. (1) *C. eburnea* has 5–7 zooecia between each node; (2) *C. cribraria* (not shown) has 18–20.

Similar species: Compare with Panpipe Bryozoans (Plate 15).

Where found: (1) *C. eburnea,* Arctic to Cape Hatteras; abundant, extending into estuarine waters above 18‰ salinity. (2) *C. cribraria,* less common and not found south of Cape Cod.

Family: Crisiidae.

PANPIPE BRYOZOANS *Tubulipora* **Pl. 15**
and related genera

Identification: Zooecia tubular, *opening at end,* and some or all of them partly to wholly *fused* along most of their length. Colonies encrusting or becoming erect and branching, rather antler-like.

(1) *Tubulipora* species (Fig. 26, opp.) form fanlike to nodular *crusts* with individual zooecia *projecting* from the common crust; ³/₈–¹/₂ in. (9–12 mm). Species distinguished by brood chambers: *T. flabellaris* has brood chamber openings small and slitlike; *T. liliacea* openings are as large as those of zooecia but turned to side. (2) *Oncousoecia* species (not shown) form thin, lobed crusts; zooecia openings barely project above surface. To ³/₃ in. (19 mm). (3) *Idmonea atlantica* has erect, antler-like colonies; to 1 in. (25 mm) or more.

Similar species: See Jointed-tube Bryozoan (Plate 15).

Where found: All species Arctic south to Cape Cod, and *T. liliacea* along south shore to Buzzards Bay; subtidal at shallow depths. Generally uncommon.

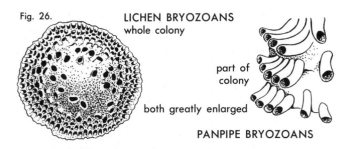

Fig. 26.

LICHEN BRYOZOANS
whole colony

part of
colony

both greatly enlarged

PANPIPE BRYOZOANS

Families: Tubuliporidae, *Tubulipora* and *Idmonea;* Oncouso-eciidae, *Oncousoecia.*

LICHEN BRYOZOANS   Fig. 26
Lichenopora species
   Identification: Round or oval crusts with more or less radial series of short, projecting tubes or rounded openings. Colony *minute,* $\frac{1}{8}$ in. (3 mm) or less.
   2 species. (1) *L. verrucaria* openings have a projecting *spur;* center of colony without zooids. (2) *L. hispida* lacks spur; center with zooids.
   Similar species: *Oncousoecia* species (preceding) in *thin* crusts with scattered, round openings, the rims barely if at all raised. To $\frac{3}{4}$ in. (19 mm). Boreal, shallow water. Family Oncousoeciidae.
   Where found: (1) *L. verrucaria,* mainly Arctic and Boreal. (2) *L. hispida,* whole coast. Both from lower intertidal zone to subtidal at great depths.
   Family: Lichenoporidae.

SHELLED BRYOZOAN *Eucratea loricata*   Pl. 15
   Identification: Colonies calcified, short and stiff to more luxuriantly bushy. Zooecia in double file, joined *back to back;* an oval opening in front without spines or ornamentation. To 10 in. (250 mm).
   Where found: Arctic south to Cape Cod; common subtidally from shallow to great depths.
   Family: Scrupariidae.

LACY CRUSTS *Membranipora*   Pl. 16
and related genera
   Identification: Colonies are *lacy* crusts, usually white. Zooecia boxlike or coffin-shaped with a mostly *membranous frontal*

wall. Colonies spread widely, often covering several inches of surface.

A very difficult and tangled assemblage with several dozen species within or near our range. The following are common and representative shallow-water forms considered in *3 groups.*

(A) 3 species usually *without* spines projecting across opening and *without* avicularia or ovicells (see p. 111): (1) *Membranipora tenuis* has front *partly walled over;* sometimes with rounded knobs at corners. (2) *Membranipora tuberculata,* a common bryozoan on drifting Gulfweed, has 2 strong knobs at *upper* corners of each zooecium. (3) *Conopeum truitti* has an erect *chitinous tube* (yellow-brown) at each *lower* corner.

(B) 2 species *with* spines across opening but no avicularia or ovicells: (4) *Electra pilosa* has lower part of front covered by a *porous wall* (gymnocyst); spines vary in number and length, but usually middle one below is longer than others. (5) *Electra crustulenta* has less well-developed gymnocyst.

(C) 2 species, usually *with* spines, avicularia, and ovicells: (6) *Tegella unicornis* has 2–4 spines (usually 2), sometimes unequal in size; zooecium has *transverse* rib. (7) *Callopora craticula* has 12–14 forward-pointing spines.

Where found: (1) *Membranipora tenuis,* Cape Cod to Brazil; abundant in shallow water and in estuaries to minimum salinity of 6‰. (2) *Membranipora tuberculata,* straying into our area on Gulfweed. (3) *Conopeum truitti,* an estuarine form chiefly known from Chesapeake Bay, in salinities as low as 11‰. (4) *Electra pilosa,* whole coast, to minimum salinity of 11‰. (5) *Electra crustulenta,* Arctic to N.C., to minimum salinity of 2‰. (6) *Tegella unicornis,* Arctic south to Cape Cod (including south shore); subtidal from shallow to deep water. (7) *Callopora craticula,* Arctic south to L.I. Sound; subtidal from shallow to deep water.

Remarks: Lacy crusts are common everywhere — on rocks, wood, seaweeds and sea grasses, and on just about any other substratum available except sand or mud. Attempting to identify the numerous, variable species is often a depressing endeavor, even with the help of a microscope and all the literature at hand. Nomenclature is incredibly jumbled, and species, genera, and families are juggled about with capricious ease.

Family: All genera may be lumped in Membraniporidae or scattered among 4 or 5, *or more,* families.

BUSHY BUGULA *Bugula turrita* Pl. 15

Identification: Colonies yellow-orange to orange-brown, fading to whitish. Bushy, *thickly tufted;* branches in spirals, zooecia in *double* row at least on branches. Illustration shows anchorlike projections sometimes found in this species. Lightly calcified. Usually to 3 in. (75 mm), but exceptionally to 1 ft. (300 mm).
Similar species: (1) *Bicellariella ciliata* (Plate 15) is

smaller — to 1 in. (25 mm) — whitish, feathery; zooecia also in double row, each with *4–8 long slender spines* (visible with a good hand lens). Nova Scotia (Cape Sable) south at least to south shore of Cape Cod; shallow water, on pilings and other supports; not common. Family Bicellariellidae. (2) Other bugulids (see next account) have zooecia in 3–12 rows. (3) *Caberea ellisii* (Plate 15) is a branching form with zooecia in 2–4 rows, some with *whiplike* projections called *vibraculae.* Cape Cod northward to Arctic, usually offshore on pebbles and shells. Family Scrupocellariidae.

Where found: Bay of Fundy south at least to Fla.; from lower intertidal to subtidal at shallow depths and in estuaries to minimum salinity of 20‰. Common on a variety of substrata — pilings, Eelgrass, larger seaweeds, shelled invertebrates — and often washed ashore.

Family: Bugulidae.

FAN BUGULA *Bugula simplex*   **Not shown**

Identification: Zooecia similar to preceding but in rows of *3–6;* colonies are thick *fan-shaped* tufts and whorls. Lightly calcified. To 1 in. (25 mm).

Similar species: (1) *Dendrobeania murrayana* (Plate 15) colonies are leafy; in narrow to broad fronds or ribbons. Zooecia similar to Fan Bugula but opening is protected by *short spines.* Also has *large, crab-claw shaped* avicularia broader than and nearly as long as zooecia (Fan Bugula's avicularia are tiny). To 1½ in. (38 mm). (2) Note Leafy Bryozoan (Plate 15) with quite different zooecia.

Where found: South shore of Cape Cod to coast of Maine; shallow water.

Family: Bugulidae, including *Dendrobeania.*

SHIELDED BRYOZOAN *Scrupocellaria scabra*   **Pl. 15**

Identification: Erect, calcified; colonies are twiggy or narrow-fronded. Zooecia in double file, in groups of 5–12 separated by *horny nodes;* opening in front protected by a flat shield. To ⅝ in. (16 mm).

Similar species: (1) *Tricellaria ternata* (Plate 15) is similar but has more elongate zooecia, usually with *smaller shields,* growing in less crowded groups of 3. (Variety *gracilis,* sometimes listed as a separate species, has up to 10 or 11 zooecia per group.) Shielded Bryozoan has an *antler-shaped* raised area on each shield; *T. ternata* does not. (2) *Tricellaria peachii* (not shown) zooecia lack shields.

Where found: Arctic south to Cape Cod; chiefly subtidal on hard bottoms; sometimes washed ashore attached to larger bryozoans, hydroids, and the like.

Family: Scrupocellariidae, including *Tricellaria.*

GLASSY HIPPOTHOA *Hippothoa hyalina* **Pl. 16**

Identification: Colonies encrusting, *glassy* when young, more opaque but *shiny* when older. Zooecia vase-shaped, partly raised, and somewhat separated, *without pores;* opening circular or oval with a broad, *rounded notch below.* Colonies often minute — $\frac{1}{8}$ in. (3 mm) — but sometimes much larger.

Similar species: *Cylindroporella tubulosa* (not shown) has somewhat similar *tubular zooecia* but riddled with *tiny star-shaped holes;* colonies whitish. $\frac{1}{4}$ in. (6 mm). Arctic south to Cape Cod; in shallow water northward but deeper southward. Family Gigantoporidae.

Where found: Whole coast and common throughout; an extraordinarily wide-ranging species. From lower intertidal to subtidal at great depths; on various substrata but especially on seaweeds in shallow water.

Family: Hippothoidae.

RED CRUSTS *Cryptosula, Schizoporella* **Pl. 16**
and related genera

Identification: Colonies are hard crusts varying from thin and flat to thick, irregular, or ruffled. Front wall of zooecium often riddled with holes. Commonly (but not invariably) orange to red, brown, or purple.

Several species. (1) *Cryptosula pallasiana,* opening *horseshoe-* or *miter-shaped,* pinched-in near bottom corners by a tiny tooth on each side; usually orange to red.

Remaining species have a *round* or *oval* opening with small *notch below.* Variable; zooecia often distorted with much secondary calcification. Crusts often thick, lumpy, or ruffled. Species have proven troublesome to identify, even for experts.

2 species common *north* of Cape Cod: (2) *Stomachetosella sinuosa* lacks avicularia; usually reddish brown. (3) *Schizomavella auriculata* has an avicularium *on midline* just below opening of each zooecium; color variable, glassy or colorless to yellowish or red.

Species common *south* of Cape Cod: (4) *Schizoporella unicornis,* avicularia *pointed,* position varies, sometimes scarce; usually orange to red. (5) *Stephanosella* species, avicularia *oval,* usually on one or both sides of opening; whitish to pink or red. Species difficult to distinguish.

Where found: (1) *Cryptosula pallasiana,* Fla. north to Cape Cod, less commonly to Nova Scotia; in bays and sounds, from lower intertidal to subtidal at shallow depths (apparently absent from Chesapeake Bay). (2) *Stomachetosella sinuosa* and (3) *Schizomavella auriculata,* Arctic south to Cape Cod, common in shallow water northward, deeper near southern limit. (4) *Schizoporella unicornis,* Fla. north to Cape Cod, one of our commonest encrusting bryozoans; reported north to Arctic; from lower intertidal to subtidal at shallow depths and in estuaries to minimum salinity of 18‰. (5) *Stephanosella* species, whole coast but species ranges uncertain: *S. cornuta,* Fla. to Cape Cod, common; *S. biaperta,* Cape Cod to Arctic. These 2 species sometimes regarded as identical.

Families: Cheiloporinidae, *Cryptosula.* Schizoporellidae, including *Schizoporella, Schizomavella, Stephanosella, Stomachetosella,* but the last sometimes placed in its own family or, conversely, all 3 genera often lumped in *Schizoporella.* Bryozoan taxonomy has many problems like this — and worse.

MICROPORE CRUST *Microporella ciliata*   **Pl. 16**
   Identification: Semicircular or archlike opening and *pore below* are fairly constant features; otherwise quite variable. Encrusting, white or silvery; thin and smooth to thick and rough; usually porous.
   Where found: An extremely wide-ranging species, Labrador to Brazil. From lower intertidal to subtidal at great depths, and in estuaries to 20‰ salinity.
   Family: Microporellidae.

BEAKED CRUSTS *Umbonula, Cribrilina,*   **Pl. 16**
and *Escharella* genera
   Identification: Genera unrelated but similar. Have a beak or tooth projecting over lower border of opening. Colonies usually whitish to gray; often with confusing secondary calcification.
   3 genera, several species. (1) *Cribrilina punctata* often has avicularia flanking orifice; pores are *scattered;* usually has 4 short spines above opening. Colonies form large patches. A 2nd, uncommon species, *C. annulata* (not shown), lacks avicularia, has strong *crosswise ribs* and *pores;* red to brown. (2) *Umbonula arctica* usually has *marginal* pores and avicularia on each side of opening. (3) *Escharella* species lack avicularia, have *marginal* pores; opening has a tooth somewhat hidden by the beak on lower border. *E. immersa* often with spines above opening; *E. ventricosa* (not shown) without spines.
   Similar species: Compare with smittinid crusts (Plate 16).
   Where found: (1) *Cribrilina punctata* and *annulata,* whole coast; in lower intertidal zone along coast of Maine, deeper southward. (2) *Umbonula arctica,* Arctic to Cape Cod; subtidal from shallow water to deep. (3) *Escharella* species, Arctic to Cape Cod (*ventricosa*) or L.I. Sound (*immersa*); the latter species common along shore northward, *ventricosa* only in deep water — 50-90 ft. (15-27 m) or more; both to great depths.
   Family: Umbonulidae, *Umbonula;* Cribrilinidae, *Cribrilina;* Escharellidae, *Escharella.*

SMITTINID CRUSTS *Smittina*   **Pl. 16**
and related genera
   Identification: Encrusting, white to yellowish, pink, or gray.

Opening round or oval with a tooth *inside* lower margin sometimes hidden by a beak or swelling.

A complex group with numerous shallow-water species in 4 genera; typical form of each genus shown on Plate 16. (1) *Rhamphostomella* species have an avicularium oriented *crosswise or diagonally,* and placed on a swelling below opening. (2) *Smittina* and (3) *Porella* species have an avicularium oriented *lengthwise* just below opening. (4) *Parasmittina* species have an avicularium placed to the *side* of the opening.

Similar species: Compare with beaked crusts (Plate 16).

Where found: All except *Parasmittina* species are Boreal or Arctic–Boreal; several occur subtidally at Cape Cod and range along shore northward. *Parasmittina* species cosmopolitan; along this coast common from Cape Cod south to Caribbean in lower intertidal zone and subtidally north to Arctic.

Family: Smittinidae.

Arrow Worms: Phylum Chaetognatha

Arrow worms are slender, torpedo-shaped, exclusively marine planktonic animals without special larval forms. They are predators on copepods, larval fish, and other zooplankters; sometimes abundant, but small and transparent. Their taxonomic relationship to other phyla is unclear.

ARROW WORMS *Sagitta* species **Pl. 33**

Identification: Members of this genus have *2 pairs* of lateral fins. Adults $\frac{3}{8}$–$\frac{3}{4}$ in. (9–19 mm). Several species fairly common inshore; microscopic study required to distinguish between them. *S. elegans* only shown.

Similar species: Other genera, all from deep water, have *1 pair* of lateral fins.

Where found: *S. elegans,* whole coast south at least to Chesapeake Bay; winter–spring at surface, in summer in deeper water north of Cape Cod; to minimum salinity of 11‰. *S. enflata,* chiefly south of Cape Cod; lower Chesapeake Bay in summer, winter–spring northward. *S. tenuis* and *S. hispida* are southern. *S. tenuis,* to Delaware Bay; summer–early fall; into mildly brackish water. *S. hispida,* to Long Island; summer–fall; sporadic. *S. tasmanica,* whole coast south to Va.; along shore.

Family: None designated.

Phoronid Worms: Phylum Phoronida

A small but distinctive phylum widely distributed in warm seas. Two traits ally these worms with bryozoans (p. 110) and brachiopods (below). The feeding apparatus in all 3 phyla is a *lophophore,* and the digestive tract recurves so that mouth and anus are close together.

PHORONIS *Phoronis architecta*   **Pl. 47**
   Identification: Wormlike with a horseshoe-shaped crown of tentacles (lophophore); see Fig. 43 opp. Plate 47. Translucent, pale peach color darkening in rear to yellowish red. Usually to 2 in. (50 mm) long, but very slender. Lophophore and lack of annulations distinguish Phoronis from other wormlike forms (see front left endpaper).
   Where found: N.Y. south at least to Beaufort, N.C. Chiefly subtidal in depths of 65 ft. (19.5 m) or more off ocean beaches northward, but in lower intertidal southward. In lower Chesapeake Bay in salinities as low as 18‰; not reported in Delaware Bay or brackish lagoons on N.J. coast.
   Remarks: This interesting worm makes vertical, chitinous burrows about twice its own length. It is rather sociable and may be found in densities of 90 per sq. yd. (0.9 m²). In mythology, Phoronis was the surname of the maiden Io, loved by Zeus and changed by Zeus's wife into a heifer; the logic of the present application of the name is unclear.
   Family: None designated.

Lamp Shells: Phylum Brachiopoda

Lamp shells had their heyday in Devonian time some 400 million years ago. More than 200 genera lived then; today there are just a few species on this coast, only one at all common in shallow water. Superficially they resemble bivalve mollusks (p. 142), but the shells are hinged dorsally and ventrally rather than laterally. Lower valve notched or pierced to make room for fleshy, stalklike *pedicel* that anchors animal to substratum. Internal anatomy includes a lophophore — a double-fringed structure with a conspicuous loop on each side; planktonic and detrital food particles trapped on lophophore filaments are moved by cilia along grooves to mouth. Sexes similar externally; hatchlings are trochophore-like (p. 61). Exclusively marine.

NORTHERN LAMP SHELL   **Fig. 39 opp. Pl. 24**
Terebratulina septentrionalis
   Identification: The larger, pear-shaped valve has a *notched beak;* shells thin with many fine radiating grooves. Pale yellowish to gray or brown. Stem (pedicel) *short,* attached to rocks, algae, or worm tubes. Usually ½ in. (12 mm), though reported to 1¼ in. (31 mm).

Where found: Locally common from Labrador south at least to Cape Cod. In lower intertidal zone northward but only subtidal in deep water at its southern limit. Sometimes overgrown by a brownish sponge, *Iophon nigricans*.
Family: Cancellothyrididae.

Mollusks: Phylum Mollusca

This phylum is 2nd in size only to Arthropoda with its horde of insect species. Two structures — the mantle and radula — are found in Mollusca and nowhere else in the animal kingdom. The *mantle* is a fold in the body wall that secretes the calcareous shell so typical of the phylum. The *radula* is a toothed, tongue- or ribbon-like organ variously modified for special feeding techniques. The *foot* is another distinctive molluscan feature. It is a solelike creeping structure in most snails, slugs, and chitons; somewhat hatchet-shaped in many bivalves. The various organ systems are contained in a *visceral mass. A head* region is usually clearly defined. Many mollusks lack one or another of these features; nevertheless, as a group they are easily recognizable, with only a few exceptions.

There are 6 classes. Two of these are not well represented in shallow water and merit only brief mention. Solenogasters (Class Aplacophora) are small, wormlike, somewhat questionably molluscan animals that burrow in soft bottoms in depths of 150 ft. (45 m) or more. Two species occur off this coast northward; both belong to the genus *Crystallophrisson.* Tusk shells (Class Scaphopoda) are more familiar mollusks, but in our latitude are confined to the outer part of the continental shelf and beyond. Several southern species are the most likely to occur inshore, but even these will only be found as occasional beach shells; live specimens are rare in less than 50 ft. (15 m). The genera *Dentalium* and *Cadulus* have been found. Tusk shells are well named; the shell resembles a miniature elephant's tusk usually less than 3 in. (75 mm) long.

The 4 main classes of Mollusca are Polyplacophora (below), Gastropoda (p. 124), Bivalvia (p. 142), and Cephalopoda (p. 161).

Chitons: Class Polyplacophora

Body oval with a fleshy marginal *girdle* (mantle); shell consists of 8 *valves* in a row. Chitons clamp themselves tightly to rocks, pilings, or other firm supports by a broad sole-shaped foot. The best way to dislodge them undamaged is to take them by surprise, quickly slipping a knife blade beneath the foot before they can contract. Dislodged chitons curl up like pill bugs. The end shells — *head* and *tail valves* — are semicircular in shape; the ones in between are rectangular or winged. Exposed parts of each valve have a median keel or triangular *jugum;* side sections are sometimes clearly divided into *central* and *lateral* areas. See Fig. 37 opp. Plate 19.

Sexes are usually separate but indistinguishable. Larvae are trochophores (p. 61). Adults have radular mouth parts and are sedentary browsers on algal films or other vegetation. Our species are small and inconspicuous. Marine only. **Note:** In some classifications Amphineura is used to include both chitons and solenogasters, in which case these groups are reduced to subclasses.

RED CHITON *Ischnochiton ruber*   **Pl. 19**

   Identification: Valves *reddish,* irregularly patterned with whitish and brown marks, *pink* inside; nearly smooth except for growth lines. Girdle light yellowish with red–brown bands, covered with *minute scales* (visible with 20X lens). Usually $\frac{5}{8}$ in. (16 mm), but up to 1 in. (25 mm).

   Similar species: (1) White Chiton, *I. albus* (Plate 19) is similar in form but valves are *whitish* or cream-colored, sometimes soiled with brown or black, *white* inside. Front slope of head valve is *straight* or slightly *concave* in profile (strongly *convex* in Red Chiton). To $\frac{1}{2}$ in. (12 mm). Massachusetts Bay to Arctic, but much less common intertidally in New England than Red Chiton. (2) Mottled Chiton, *Tonicella marmorea* (not shown) is superficially similar to Red Chiton but girdle is leathery, *without* scales or spines. Valves dull (microscopically granular), appear smooth except for growth lines. Central and lateral areas vaguely defined by a low, sometimes obscure ridge; head valve straight or only slightly convex. To $1\frac{1}{2}$ in. (38 mm). Massachusetts Bay to Arctic, chiefly subtidal. Family Lepidochitonidae.

   Where found: The most common intertidal chiton in New England. Arctic to Massachusetts Bay, locally and usually subtidally to e. L.I. Sound.

   Family: Ischnochitonidae.

BEE CHITON *Chaetopleura apiculata*   **Pl. 19**

   Identification: Valves whitish to cream-colored, soiled brown or gray. *Central and lateral areas well defined.* Rows of fine granules, running lengthwise, line the central areas; lateral portions with granules either scattered or in rows radiating outward, or worn smooth. Girdle banded, with minute scales and scattered *short hairs.* To $\frac{3}{4}$ in. (19 mm).

   Similar species: White Chiton (Plate 19) has nearly smooth valves without defined areas; girdle without hairs.

Where found: S. Maine to Fla.; chiefly subtidal in shallow water on stones and shells.
Family: Ischnochitonidae.

Gastropods: Class Gastropoda

The largest molluscan class includes a diversity of forms. Most have a single spiral shell, but many are shell-less, and a recently found Caribbean genus is actually bivalved.

The soft body has clearly defined regions: head, foot, mantle, and visceral mass (see general account of mollusks, p. 122). The head has a varying complement of sense organs —tentacles and eyes — and a mouth that is armed with a rasplike *radula* and (sometimes) jaws. The foot is a flat, creeping sole. The *mantle,* which is the shell-secreting structure, often includes a tubular respiratory *siphon*; in some snails the mantle is developed in lobes that can be extended to cover the shell. Deviations from all of these standard features occur, since gastropods have indulged in a certain amount of evolutionary experimentation.

Shelled Gastropods

Details of soft anatomy are important for the definition of subclasses and orders, but genera and species are mainly identified by differences in the form and color of the hard shell.

The typical gastropod (snail) shell is a spirally wound cone. Most snails are right-handed or *dextral*: with the spire uppermost and the opening facing the observer, the outer lip is on the right. *Sinistral* is the opposite (left-handed); a few species have such shells and occasional individuals of normally dextral species have sinistral shells. The separate turns of the shell are called *whorls.* The mantle of the living animal lines the *body whorl;* the remaining whorls form the *spire.* Grooves separating whorls are called *sutures.* Markings or modeled details are *spiral* when they follow the turns of the whorls and *axial* when they cross the whorls and are parallel to the main growth axis. This axis is defined by the central *columella* which coils around a hollow core called the *umbilicus.* The umbilicus has a surface opening in some snails (see Plate 22), not in others. The shell *aperture* often has a notch or scooplike channel below; this is the *anterior canal* and contains the siphon of the live snail. Many snails have a horny or calcareous *operculum* attached to the foot that serves as a trapdoor to seal the aperture when the animal retreats within.

The more primitive snails shed their eggs singly, but most deposit theirs in gelatinous masses or more elaborately formed capsules, some of which are commonly found cast ashore or attached to firm supports. Marine, freshwater, and terrestrial.

GASTROPOD STRUCTURES Fig. 27.

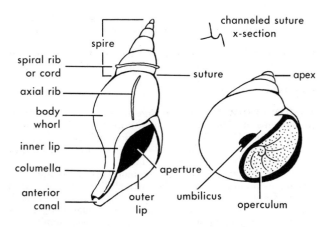

TORTOISESHELL LIMPET *Acmaea testudinalis* **Pl. 19**
 Identification: Our only common *intertidal* limpet. Shell a simple flattened cone, *inside* and out; round to oblong-oval. Variably marked with radiating lines or at least a checkered border. Usually 1 in. (25 mm), rarely to 2 in. (50 mm).
 Similar species: (1) Keyhole limpets (not shown) have a hole at apex. Little Keyhole Limpet, *Diodora cayenensis,* is southern, rarely north to Chesapeake Bay; has many fine, radial lines. To 1½ in. (38 mm); intertidal. Noah's Punctured Shell, *Puncturella noachina,* is *subtidal;* n. Mass. to Arctic. Plain white; ½ in. (12 mm). Family Fissurellidae. (2) Cup-and-Saucer Limpet and (3) slipper shells (all Plate 19) have twisted or strongly offset apex and either a platform or "tongue" *inside.*
 Where found: L.I. Sound to Arctic, intertidal to subtidal at shallow depths. Locally common on rocks, kelp stipes, or Eelgrass.
 Remarks: The limpet form — a more or less conical, tight-clinging shell — has been adopted by quite unrelated gastropods. Removal of firmly clamped limpet may injure the snail. Take them by surprise by quickly slipping a knife blade under shell.
 Family: Acmaeidae.

CHINK SHELL *Lacuna vincta* **Pl. 20**
 Identification: Periwinkle-like but shell *thin, translucent,* often delicately banded; the spire darker in life. Umbilicus a *narrow*

slit parallel to columella. To $\frac{1}{2}$ in. (12 mm), but smaller shells more common.

Similar species: 2 additional, Boreal species, *L. pallidula* and *L. parva* (neither shown), are recorded but rare; both have a low spire.

Where found: Staten Island, N.Y., to Arctic. Subtidal but commonly dredged on Eelgrass bottoms or hidden among algal holdfasts.

Family: Lacunidae.

COMMON PERIWINKLE *Littorina littorea*   **Pl. 20**

Identification: The most common northern rock and wharf-piling winkle. Has a *lower spire* than Gulf Periwinkle; *flatter whorls* and less deeply indented sutures than Rough Periwinkle. Columella pale. To $1\frac{1}{4}$ in. (31 mm).

Similar species: (1) Young of Common Periwinkles are not as smooth as adults and must be distinguished with care from Rough Periwinkle, *L. saxatilis* (Plate 20); both are variable in color and sculpturing, have similar ranges. Rough Periwinkle is smaller, usually less than $\frac{1}{2}$ in. (12 mm), or exceptionally — as at Montauk, Long Island — to $\frac{5}{8}$ in. (16 mm). Has taller spire, lives higher on shore than Common Periwinkle and is ovoviviparous — produces live young instead of aquatic eggs and larvae. (2) Ranges of *live* Common and Gulf Periwinkles (Plate 20) do not overlap; see next account.

Where found: Md. to Labrador; said to have been brought to Nova Scotia from w. Europe more than a century ago. Abundant intertidally, attached to any solid substratum.

Remarks: Periwinkles are vegetarians, browsing on algal films and the like. Withstand long periods without food or water. They are sold in Italian fish markets; edible after light boiling in sea water.

Family: Littorinidae.

GULF PERIWINKLE *Littorina irrorata*   **Pl. 20**

Identification: Abundant in southern marshes clinging to salt grasses and sedges, sometimes on rocks and jetties. Spire more pointed than Common Periwinkle and has spiral rows of dark flecks. Columella dark. To 1 in. (25 mm).

Similar species: See the preceding account.

Where found: Md. to n. Fla. and Gulf of Mexico. Formerly north to Mass., where *dead* shells are sometimes found.

Family: Littorinidae.

SMOOTH PERIWINKLE *Littorina obtusata*   **Pl. 20**

Identification: A small *round* periwinkle, common among rockweeds; somewhat like a small moon shell (Plate 22) but *without* umbilicus. Color variable — yellow, orange, brown,

even green or black; sometimes banded. Spire very low; whorls smooth. To ½ in. (12 mm).
Where found: W. Long Island to Arctic; reported south to Ocean City, N.J., but certainly not common on N.J. coast.
Family: Littorinidae.

COMMON WORM SHELL *Vermicularia spirata*   **Fig. 28**
Identification: Shell is mostly uncoiled — a twisted, wormlike tube with only the closed end tightly spiraled and auger-like. To 4 in. (100 mm), larger southward.
Similar species: (1) Beach specimens are frequently broken off at base of closed coil and may be mistaken for other auger-like species such as Common Auger (Plate 22) or the small shells shown on Plate 21. (2) See annelid tube worms (Plate 42).
Where found: A Caribbean species but known for more than a century from s. New England with old records from New Bedford and Buzzards Bay. It is said to be more common on Martha's Vineyard than elsewhere in Northeast. Sometimes considered a separate species, *V. radicula.*
Family: Turritellidae.

COMMON WORM SHELL

Fig. 28.

BITTIUMS *Bittium* species   **Pl. 21**
Identification: Gray to *blackish* or reddish brown spires have 6–8 whorls crosshatched with spiral lines and axial riblets. Small, to ¼ in. (6 mm).
   2 species. (1) Alternate Bittium, *B. alternatum,* is darker, more strongly sculptured, and lacks the rib (*varix*) usually present on body whorl of (2) Variable Bittium, *B. varium.*
Similar species: A host of small snails have spirelike shells. Common Auger (Plate 22) has a well-developed *anterior canal;* bittiums have a *slight* notchlike anterior canal; most others lack even this. See Additional Small Gastropods p. 135.
Where found: (1) Alternate Bittium, Va. north to Massachusetts Bay, also Gulf of St. Lawrence. (2) Variable Bittium, Md. to Texas. Extremely abundant on Eelgrass and quiet-water algae.
Family: Cerithiidae.

WENTLETRAPS *Epitonium* species   **Pl. 21**
Identification: Shell a tall spire with 8-20 vanelike riblets (called *costae*). White and polished; some species stained or banded brown. To $\frac{3}{4}$ in. (19 mm).

Several species in shallow water; 6 others deep, in 40 ft. (12 m) or more; only Lined Wentletrap shown. To distinguish species, count costae on body whorl. (1) Crowded Wentletrap, *E. multistriatum,* has more numerous costae than others, 16-19 (*40 or more near apex*). (2) Champion's Wentletrap, *E. championi,* and (3) New England Wentletrap, *E. novangliae,* have *spiral lines* as well as costae; other species do not (or not visible without magnification). New England Wentletrap usually has 12 costae (9-16) which are *angled* above; may be brown-banded. Champion's Wentletrap has 8-9 costae (not angled above), is narrower, and lacks bands. (4) Lined Wentletrap, *E. rupicola,* had 10-16 costae, is pinkish and often *brown-banded.* (5) Angled Wentletrap, *E. angulatum,* and (6) Humphrey's Wentletrap, *E. humphreysi,* are narrower, with 8-10 costae; those of Angled Wentletrap distinctly angled above. Sizes are: (1, 2, 3) to $\frac{1}{2}$ in. (12 mm); (4, 5, 6) to $\frac{3}{4}$ in. (19 mm).
Where found: Generally rather scarce and more often found ashore as dead shells. Lined Wentletrap is probably the commonest; local in shallow waters of bays and sounds. Greenland Wentletrap, *E. greenlandicum* (not discussed above) ranges from Arctic to Long Island and has been recorded on Cape Cod but is seldom found in less than 50 ft. (15 m). None of our shallow-water species ranges north of Cape Cod and New England Wentletrap's northern limit is Cape Henry despite its name.
Family: Epitoniidae.

VIOLET SNAIL *Janthina janthina*   **Fig. 38 opp. Pl. 22**
Identification: A beautiful little shell, translucent *violet,* paler above. Shell *wider* than long. Fragile. To $1\frac{1}{2}$ in. (38 mm).
Similar species: Globe Violet Snail, *J. globosa* (Fig. 38) is less common, more evenly colored and *longer* than wide. To $\frac{3}{4}$ in. (19 mm).
Where found: A visitor from far offshore — a Gulf Stream drifter supported at sea by a froth of bubbles. Washes ashore north to Cape Cod.
Family: Janthinidae.

COMMON SLIPPER SHELL *Crepidula fornicata*   **Pl. 19**
Identification: Shell has a *platform* extending about $\frac{1}{2}$ *way* across opening, edge sinuous. This is the "deck" from which these shells derive another common name, boat shells. Apex *turned* to one side. To $1\frac{1}{2}$ in. (38 mm).
Similar species: (1) Convex Slipper Shell, *C. convexa* (Plate 19) has *concave-edged* platform covering $\frac{1}{3}$ *of opening.* Apex

centered. A smaller—to ¹/₂ in. (12 mm)—strongly convex slip-per shell. (2) Flat Slipper Shell, *C. plana* (Plate 19) is pure white (others brownish or gray with darker marks); usually flattish, or curved to fit *inside* big moon shells, whelks, and such. To 1 in. (25 mm).

Where found: Gulf of Mexico north to Massachusetts Bay, locally to Gulf of St. Lawrence, in lower intertidal zone. Accidental in Europe.

Remarks: Found attached to almost any available hard object, often arranged in small to large stacks undergoing sex reversal: older, larger ones are female; younger, male; hermaphrodites in between. A nuisance when abundant on oyster beds. A common beach shell especially along protected bays and sounds.

Family: Calyptraeidae.

CUP-AND-SAUCER LIMPET   Pl. 19
Crucibulum striatum

Identification: Somewhat conical, with *twisted apex;* top deeply lined. Opening with an off-center tongue-like cup. To 1 in. (25 mm).

Where found: Nova Scotia to Fla. Reportedly common in lower intertidal zone northward, but subtidal and rare south of Cape Cod.

Family: Calyptraeidae.

LOBED MOON SHELL *Polinices duplicatus*   Pl. 22

Identification: This large moon shell, also called Sharkeye, has its umbilicus almost completely *covered* by a dark callus. Operculum *horny.* Color gray to tan. To 3 in. (75 mm).

Similar species: (1) Miniature Moon Shell, *Natica pusilla* (not shown) is a small — ¹/₄ in. (6 mm) — species with a completely callus-covered umbilicus and is the only shallow-water moon shell with a *limy* operculum. Cape Cod to West Indies; chiefly subtidal. (2) See Northern Moon Shell (Plate 22). (3) Smooth Periwinkle (Plate 20) is moon-shell-like but lacks an umbilicus; a very small snail.

Where found: Massachusetts Bay to Gulf of Mexico; most common large moon shell of southern beaches, replacing Northern Moon Shell from N.J. south, less common north to Bay of Fundy. Sandy beaches, intertidal zone to subtidal in shallow water.

Remarks: See the following account.

Family: Naticidae, including *Natica.*

NORTHERN MOON SHELL *Lunatia heros*   Pl. 22

Identification: Easily distinguished from the preceding species by its *open umbilicus.* Color gray to tan. To 4 in. (100 mm).

Similar species: The following species also have open umbilicus. (1) Spotted Moon Shell, *L. triseriata* (Plate 22) is smaller — ⅞ in. (22 mm) — and often handsomely ringed with bands of brown or purplish spots; Gulf of St. Lawrence to N.C.; common in shallow bays in Gulf of Maine, less common and in deeper water south of Cape Cod. Formerly regarded as juvenile Northern Moon Shell and unmarked individuals hard to distinguish from same. (2) Immaculate Moon Shell, *Polinices immaculatus* (not shown) resembles Northern Moon Shell but is smaller — ⅜ in. (9 mm) — and glossy white under a *greenish periostracum;* Gulf of St. Lawrence to N.C.; subtical at moderate depths but more likely to come ashore than the several other deeper-water moon shells.

Where found: Labrador to N.C. The most common large moon shell from Long Island north, a deep-water species southward, to more than 1200 ft. (360 m).

Remarks: Moon shells are common on beaches. "Sand collars" (see Fig. 3, p. 22) containing their eggs are also found ashore. (Note: Sand collars very fragile when dried.) Live shells are often seen plowing along, half-buried, on wet beach flats. They are predatory on other mollusks, which they drill neatly, making a beveled hole. The foot is enormous but can be completely retracted.

Family: Naticidae, including *Polinices.*

EAR SHELL *Sinum perspectivum*   **Pl. 22**
  Identification: This thin, *flat,* milky-white shell of southern beaches cannot be confused with any other species. Has a tan-colored *periostracum* and huge foot. To 1½ in. (38 mm).
  Where found: Va. to West Indies. Reported north to N.J. but not common north of Cape Henry. A subtidal sand burrower, and a common beach shell southward.
  Family: Naticidae.

SCOTCH BONNET *Phalium granulatum*   **Pl. 22**
  Identification: This southern species is a common beach shell on N.C. shores and is frequently inhabited by the Striped Hermit Crab (see p. 243). A handsome shell, spirally grooved with a distinct *columella shield;* shield development varies with age (shell shown is about half-grown). Color whitish with brown *squarish spots* in spiral series. To 4 in. (100 mm).
  Where found: N.C. to Brazil.
  Family: Cassididae.

OYSTER DRILL *Urosalpinx cinerea*   **Pl. 20**
  Identification: The common Oyster Drill has an *open, flaring* anterior canal. Adults usually 1 in. (25 mm) but twice that size in Chincoteague, Va., area.
  Similar species: Thick-lipped Oyster Drill, *Eupleura caudata* (Plate 20) has a thick, strongly toothed outer lip and a *long,*

tubular anterior canal; to ¾ in. (19 mm). Cape Cod to Fla.; usually less abundant than Oyster Drill.

Where found: Cape Cod to Fla.; locally north to Gulf of St. Lawrence. Accidentally introduced on Pacific Coast, Britain, and Europe. Intertidal to subtidal down to about 50 ft. (15 m); in brackish water to minimum salinity of 15‰.

Remarks: This major pest of oysters commonly destroys *60% or more* of the seed crop in parts of L.I. Sound and lower Chesapeake Bay. Reduced salinity protects seed grounds in fresher parts of tidewaters. The drill bores a neat hole in the oyster's shell and sucks out the soft parts of the oyster.

Family: Muricidae, including *Eupleura.*

DOGWINKLE *Thais lapillus*   **Pl. 20**
   Identification: Variable in shape, sculpturing, and color. Commonly dull white with rounded spiral ridges; aperture large with strong flaring lips (right shell, Plate 20). Variants are rougher or have scaly axial ridges; sometimes uniformly bright orange, yellow, dark brown, or banded with white (Plate 20, center and left). To 1½ in. (38 mm).

   Similar species: (1) Compare with young Waved Whelk (Plate 22); *soft parts* white with black flecks; shell with strong axial ribs and differently shaped aperture and anterior canal. (2) Florida Rock Shell, *T. haemastoma* (not shown) is a southern species reported from lower Chesapeake Bay but chiefly south of Cape Hatteras to Fla.; has a nearly straight columella and a row of low spiral bumps high on body whorl. To 2 in. (50 mm). (3) Northern Hairy-keeled Snail, *Trichotropis borealis* (Plate 21) has proportionately larger aperture, yellow-brown *periostracum,* hairy along spiral ridges. To ½ in. (12 mm). *Subtidal* at moderate depths; found in fish stomachs. Cape Cod north to Labrador. Family Trichotropidae.

   Where found: Eastern L.I. Sound to Arctic; also n. Europe. Chiefly intertidal.

   Remarks: This common drill (see preceding account) preys on other intertidal mollusks, especially Blue Mussels, and barnacles. Changes of diet are reflected in color changes: Dogwinkles that have fed on barnacles are whitish; mussel-eaters are brown or purplish. Dogwinkles secrete a purple dye, like Tyrian purple of the ancients and similarly used by American Indians. The straw-colored egg capsules are the size of rice grains; abundant in rock crevices and under seaweeds.

   Family: Thaididae.

MUD DOG WHELK *Nassarius obsoletus*   **Pl. 20**
   Identification: A dull, dark, weakly sculptured dog whelk, usually with eroded apex. Aperture brown-black with glazed inner lip; columella with a fold. To 1 in. (25 mm).

   Similar species: Other *Nassarius* species have body whorl separated from anterior canal by a groove. (1) Mottled Dog Whelk, *N. vibex* (Plate 20) has a strong inner lip and thick, toothed outer lip; sutures *not* channeled. Aperture and columella pale. To $\frac{1}{2}$ in. (12 mm). A southern species, local north of Cape Hatteras to Cape Cod (reported to s. Maine), on muddier bottoms than the next species. (2) New England Dog Whelk, *N. trivittatus* (Plate 20) has *channeled* sutures and finely *beaded whorls;* outer lip thin. To $\frac{3}{4}$ in. (19 mm). The most common New England species, Gulf of St. Lawrence south to Fla.; chiefly subtidal in quiet water on sand or grassy flats.

Where found: Cape Cod to Gulf of Mexico, locally north to Gulf of St. Lawrence. Intertidal to subtidal at shallow depths on muddy bottoms.

Remarks: Dog whelks are scavengers and may be attracted to a bait of dead fish.

Family: Nassariidae.

WAVED WHELK *Buccinum undatum*   **Pl. 22**

Identification: Shell with both *axial* ribs and *spiral* ridges (cords); aperture opening in a wide arc. Usually dull whitish to buff-toned but sometimes more colorful. Soft parts white with black flecks. Commonly to $2\frac{1}{2}$ in. (62 mm); exceptionally to 4 in. (100 mm).

Similar species: Compare young with Dogwinkle (Plate 20), which usually has a more constricted anterior canal.

Where found: Arctic south in w. Atlantic Ocean to N.J.; uncommon and only in deep water south of Cape Cod. Young are common in Maine tide pools and shallow water; adults chiefly subtidal to 600 ft. (180 m).

Remarks: Masses of egg capsules (called "sea wash balls") often found on beaches produce a soapy lather if scrubbed with water. This is the common edible whelk of Europe and Britain; a scavenger on dead fish, regarded as a bait stealer by lobstermen.

Family: Buccinidae.

COLUS WHELKS *Colus* species   **Pl. 22**

Identification: Spindle-shaped with extended spire and anterior canal equal to $\frac{1}{2}$ the length of the shell.

Several species, difficult to distinguish. Stimpson's Whelk, *C. stimpsoni,* is the most commonly reported species; handsome when fresh with a *dark* periostracum; to 5 in. (125 mm). Hairy Whelk, *C. pubescens* (not shown) is smaller — to $2\frac{1}{2}$ in. (62 mm) — with longer aperture; Pygmy Whelk, *C. pygmaea* (not shown) is smaller still — $\frac{3}{4}$ in. (19 mm) — and has a *paler* periostracum. Additional species are found offshore.

Where found: All are Boreal shells ranging from Labrador or Gulf of St. Lawrence southward, some species to the Carolinas in deep water. Found usually as much-worn beach shells north of Cape Cod and only from offshore dredgings or fish stomachs southward.

Family: Buccinidae.

TEN-RIDGED WHELK *Neptunea decemcostata*   **Pl. 22**
Identification: An elegant, spindle-shaped shell with 7–10 strong reddish brown spiral ridges (cords) on the body whorl. To 4 in. (100 mm).
Where found: Nova Scotia to Cape Cod. Subtidal in 8–200 ft. (2.4–60 m) or more. A beach shell after storms from Massachusetts Bay northward, rarely on Cape Cod; sometimes caught in lobster pots.
Family: Buccinidae.

CHANNELED WHELK *Busycon canaliculatum*   **Pl. 22**
Identification: A large whelk with *channeled* sutures; adults have square-shouldered whorls and yellowish aperture. To at least 7 in. (175 mm).

Whelks, even young ones, are not likely to be confused with any other sea snails; the short spire, large body whorl, and long anterior canal are distinctive.
Similar species: (1) Knobbed Whelk, *B. carica* (Plate 22) has more distinctly developed knobs on body whorl and spire; shoulders rounded and aperture orange; sutures *not* channeled; to at least 9 in. (225 mm); less common than Channeled Whelk. (2) Lightning Whelk, *B. contrarium* (not shown) is normally *sinistral,* which distinguishes it from the typically *dextral* Channeled Whelk. Lightning Whelk largely replaces Knobbed and Channeled Whelks south of Cape Hatteras; also reported in deep water as far north as N.J.
Where found: Reported north to Casco Bay, but chiefly Cape Cod to n. Fla. and Gulf of Mexico. Lower intertidal to subtidal down to 60 ft. (18 m); along bay and ocean beaches in salinities above 20‰.
Remarks: These are the largest sea snails on this coast, well known as beach shells and common in shallow water. The strings of egg capsules (Fig. 3, p. 22) are also familiar. Whelks are attracted to lobster bait but feed mainly on bivalves, which they attack by inserting the anterior canal between the prey's valves and using their shells as a hammer to chip away an opening. Whelks and conchs of various species (not necessarily related) are eaten in West Indies and Europe. The main culinary problem is overcoming the mollusk's rubbery consistency. Northern whelks are sold in Italian markets as the main ingredient of *scungili.*
Family: Melongenidae.

Fig. 29. LETTERED OLIVE

LETTERED OLIVE *Oliva sayana* **Fig. 29**
Identification: Our only large olive shell; strong, cylindrical, with darker scrawled markings. To 2½ in. (62 mm).
Similar species: *Olivella* species (not shown) have proportionately *longer* spires, shorter apertures, are somewhat more miter-shaped than cylindrical. To ½ in. (12 mm). Several tropical species, reported north to N.C. in shallow water.
Where found: N.C. to Fla.; fairly common in Cape Hatteras area as a beach shell.
Family: Olividae, including *Olivella*.

COMMON AUGER *Terebra dislocata* **Pl. 22**
Identification: A long, narrowly tapered shell with 20 or more axial ribs per whorl and a distinct anterior canal. Columella has 2 folds. To 1¾ in. (44 mm).
Similar species: No other small auger-shaped shell has so distinct an anterior canal (see Plate 21). See also Common Worm Shell account (p. 127).
Where found: Va. to Gulf of Mexico. Generally subtidal, but a common shell on ocean beaches southward.
Family: Terebridae.

SOLITARY GLASSY BUBBLE *Haminoea solitaria* **Pl. 20**
Identification: Shell extremely fragile with *fine spiral grooves* visible with hand lens. Spire *completely depressed* (not protruding above body whorl); outer lip elevated. Dull whitish to amber. Live bubbles are grayish and sluglike. When extended, soft parts nearly cover shell. To ½ in. (12 mm).
Similar species: Additional, very small — less than ¼ in. (6 mm) — shallow-water bubbles may be dredged on soft bottoms. One of the more common, Channeled Barrel Bubble, *Retusa canaliculata* (not shown) is cylindrical, with spire protruding above body whorl. Whole coast. Family Retusidae.
Where found: Mt. Desert I. to S.C.; intertidal pools to subtidal down to 30 ft. (9 m), in oozy mud.
Family: Atyidae.

SALT-MARSH SNAIL *Melampus bidentatus* **Pl. 20**
Identification: Shell *top-shaped,* rather fragile. Fresh shells richly colored, light brown with darker bands, fading after death. A common salt-marsh species among grasses and under debris. To ½ in. (12 mm).
Similar species: Oval Marsh Snail, *Ovatella myosotis* (Plate 20) is a small — ¼ in. (6 mm) — easily overlooked snail. Translucent, brownish, with more deeply indented sutures and toothed columella, the lower tooth somewhat cleft. In wood crevices in upper intertidal zone, Nova Scotia to West Indies.
Where found: Gulf of St. Lawrence to Gulf of Mexico. Intertidal.
Family: Ellobiidae, including *Ovatella.*

Fig. 30.

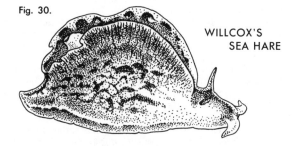

WILLCOX'S
SEA HARE

WILLCOX'S SEA HARE *Aplysia willcoxi* **Fig. 30**
Identification: *Internal shell* weakly calcified but can be *felt* as a nutlike firmness within fleshy body. Winglike folds extend along back on each side, join at rear. Emits a harmless purple dye when handled. Rich brownish with fine black reticulations (network of lines), lighter silvery blotches and specks. To 9 in. (225 mm).
Where found: Gulf of Mexico to Cape Cod but rare north of Carolinas. Shallow water.
Remarks: These spectacular mollusks can be found crawling among the seaweeds on which they browse, or swimming with languid beats of their soft wings.
Family: Aplysidae.

Additional Small Gastropods **Pl. 21**

There are hosts of tiny snails, mostly from deeper water. The following sampling of shells — usually less than ¼ in. (6 mm) — includes some of the commoner small species of various families. See Plate 21 for species shown.

Caecums, *Caecum* species, are tubular or slightly curved. *C. johnstoni,* nearly smooth; Beautiful Caecum, *C. pulchellum,* with raised rings; Cooper's Atlantic Caecum, *C. cooperi,* with lengthwise grooves. *C. johnstoni* and *pulchellum* to $\frac{1}{16}$ in. (1.6 mm); *cooperi* to $\frac{3}{16}$ in. (5 mm). Young have a coiled *nuclear whorl* at tip. Look for these shells in dead sponges or among sand grains. Cape Cod southward. Extralimital species sometimes accidentally imported in ballast sand. Family Caecidae.

Pearly Top Shells, *Margarites* species, somewhat resemble periwinkles (Plate 20) but have a distinct *open umbilicus;* differ from moon shells (Plate 22) in being *pearly iridescent* inside. Smooth Top Shell, *M. helicinus,* is *unridged,* yellowish brown. Ridged Top Shell, *M. cinereus,* white, tinted rose or green, and Greenland Top Shell, *M. groenlandicus,* reddish brown; both have *spiral ridges.* Smooth and Ridged Top Shells to $\frac{1}{2}$ in. (12 mm); Greenland Top Shell to $\frac{5}{16}$ in. (8 mm). All are Boreal, subtidal. Family Trochidae.

Swamp Hydrobia, *Hydrobia minuta,* has rather tall spire, with sutures deeply impressed. Nearly smooth; translucent yellowish brown. Common in salt-marsh pools. $\frac{1}{8}$ in. (3 mm). N.J. northward. Family Hydrobiidae.

Black Triphora, *Triphora nigrocincta,* is one of our few *sinistral* snails. Fairly tall spire with spiral rows of beads. To $\frac{1}{4}$ in. (6 mm). Shallow water, under stones and shells; often found with ceriths. Cape Cod to West Indies. Family Triphoridae.

Green's Cerith, *Cerithiopsis greeni,* is broader than preceding, *miter-shaped.* Resembles *Bittium* species (Plate 21), but compare shape of apertures. To $\frac{3}{16}$ in. (5 mm). Shallow water, sand and mud. Cape Cod to Fla. Family Cerithiidae.

Wood Screw Shell, *Seila adamsi,* does indeed resemble a wood screw; each of about 12 whorls has 3 or 4 spiral threads. Lacks axial ribs of Common Auger (Plate 22). To $\frac{1}{2}$ in. (12 mm). Cape Cod to West Indies. Family Cerithiidae.

Crescent Mitrella, *Mitrella lunata,* suggests Mud Dog Whelk (Plate 20) in shape, but is smooth, translucent, brightly marked when wet. Outer lip toothed inside but often eroded smooth. To $\frac{1}{4}$ in. (6 mm). Common on mud bottoms among seaweeds and Eelgrass in quiet water. Caribbean north at least to Casco Bay. An unspotted form, Banded Mitrella, *M. zonalis,* ranges from Maine to Conn. Family Columbellidae.

Dove shells, *Anachis* species, somewhat resemble preceding in shape but are more slender; have axial folds or ribs. 4 species, differing in shape and sculpture. $\frac{1}{4}$-$\frac{1}{2}$ in. (6-12 mm). Shallow water. Greedy Dove Shell, *A. avara,* N.J. to Fla.; Fat Dove Shell, *A. obesa,* Va. to West Indies; Haliaect's Dove Shell, *A. haliaecti,* Maine to N.C.; Well-ribbed Dove Shell, *A. translirata,* Cape Cod to Fla. Family Columbellidae.

Pyramid shells: Mostly parasitic on other invertebrates. They are numerous, hard to identify and classify. Odostomes,

Odostomia species: Moderately broad to narrow spires; usually with *1 fold* on columella; shells smooth to sculptured. Numerous species; most whitish and $\frac{1}{8}$ in. (3 mm) or less. Whole coast. Pyrams, *Pyramidella* species: Generally more slender and sharply tapered than preceding with *2–3 folds* on columella. Several species; most $\frac{1}{4}$ in. (6 mm) or less. Whole coast. Turbonilles, *Turbonilla* species: Resemble preceding in shape but most have *axial ribbing;* columella *without* folds; nuclear whorl (tip) has crosswise curl. About 20 species; most are $\frac{1}{4}$ in. (6 mm) or less. Whole coast. Family Pyramidellidae.

Sea Butterflies

The old ordinal name, Pteropoda, has been abandoned, and the shelled and shell-less sea butterflies are now thought to be related only in having similar planktonic habits. These unusual gastropods are more common offshore, where they sometimes gather in swarms sufficient to feed the large baleen whales. Parts of the ocean bottom, usually at depths of more than 6000 ft. (1800 m), are covered with an oozy layer of pteropod shells. The shells are very lightly calcified, and when fresh are transparent and colorless to yellowish brown, turning opaque and whitish in preservative. The pteropod foot has winglike flaps called *parapodia,* used for swimming. Both shelled and shell-less species have them.

SHELLED SEA BUTTERFLIES *Limacina*   Pl. 33
and related genera

   Identification: Shell thin, colorless to transparent yellowish brown; *sinistral.* Foot with parapodia. To $\frac{1}{4}$ in. (6 mm).
   Similar species: Numerous species of shelled sea butterflies have been recorded off this coast; they form a separate gastropod order, Thecosomata, and are classified in 4 families. While the shells of *Limacina* and *Peraclis* (not shown)are recognizably snail-like, those of other genera range from simple awl-shaped cones to more complex shapes (see *Field Guide to Shells of the Atlantic and Gulf Coasts*).
   Where found: Planktonic and chiefly oceanic, sporadically in shallow water. *L. retroversa,* one of the more frequently reported species, is common offshore, mostly at depths of 60 ft. (18 m) or more in Gulf of Maine; it surfaces at night and can be found inshore (particularly in fall) south of Cape Cod. May be abundant when present at all. Other shelled sea butterflies common in Gulf Stream.
   Family: Limacinidae.

NAKED SEA BUTTERFLY *Clione limacina*   Pl. 33
   Identification: Body sluglike, with pair of winglike parapodia at front end. Head with a pair of tentacles and *3 pairs of short*

cone-like projections. Pale grayish or salmon-colored. To 1 in. (25 mm).
Similar species: Additional shell-less species are found offshore.
Where found: Arctic south to Delaware Bay, occasionally to Va. Pelagic and chiefly offshore. May–July.
Family: Clionidae.

Shell-less Gastropods:
Nudibranchs and Sacoglossans

In several gastropod orders the evolutionary trend is toward a reduced shell. Bubbles (p. 134) and related forms generally have a weakly calcified shell; the mantle lobes may be extended upward to cover it, but the animal can still withdraw inside at will. In sea hares (p. 135) the shell no longer serves a protective function and is buried within the soft body. Many gastropods have no trace of a shell when adult though they do have one in their larval stage.

Most of these species are sluglike. Shell-less pteropods, however, are very peculiar indeed; they are planktonic and are discussed with shelled forms that have similar habits under the heading "Sea Butterflies" (p. 137).

Shell-less gastropods, also known as sea slugs, are considerably more varied than garden slugs. In particular the upper surface is commonly ornamented with tubercles, gills, or club-shaped respiratory structures called *cerata.* The head is well developed and usually has 2 pairs of tentacles differentiated as a frontal pair called *oral tentacles* and another, farther back, called *rhinophores.*

The 2 distinct orders of shell-less gastropods differ in feeding habits. Sacoglossans (Order Sacoglossa), comprising the families Stiligeridae (p. 142), Elysiidae (p. 139), and Limapontiidae (not represented here) are herbivorous. Nudibranchs (Order Nudibranchia) are carnivorous, and individual family groups tend to specialize in certain types of prey. Thus, doridaceans feed mainly on sponges, tunicates, or bryozoans, while dendronotaceans prefer hydroids or anemones. Some nudibranchs are able to ingest hydroids without causing their sting cells to discharge; these then find their way into the tips of the cerata and resume their protective function for the sea slug's benefit.

Species identification may be difficult. It is critical to study these creatures alive. The grace and beauty is lost in pickled specimens, and unless the living animals are carefully prepared with narcotization, they may be useless except for study of the radula and internal anatomy. Young and variant individuals frequently do not fit established descriptions, and much work remains to be done in clarifying species definitions.

SACOGLOSSAN SLUGS *Elysia* species   **Pl. 44**
Identification: Back has a pair of *lateral folds;* otherwise slug-like, without gill plumes or cerata; 1 pair of tentacles. Greenish.
2 species. (1) Eelgrass Slug, *E. catula,* is broadly rounded in front; has folds for $\frac{2}{3}$ body length — *not* reaching tail end or touching across back. To $\frac{3}{8}$ in. (9 mm). (2) *E. chlorotica* (not shown) has folds *reaching* tail end, *overlapping* across back. Front corners of foot extended, sharp-angled. To $1\frac{1}{8}$ in. (28 mm).
Similar species: *Alderia harvardiensis* (not shown) is also a sacoglossan, but not otherwise similar; see Additional Plumed Shell-less Gastropods, p. 142.
Where found: (1) *E. catula,* Massachusetts Bay south at least to Chesapeake Bay on Eelgrass. (2) *E. chlorotica,* Bay of Fundy south to Chesapeake Bay or beyond, in salt- and brackish-water marshes where it feeds on the algae *Vaucheria* (p. 49) and *Cladophora* (p. 51).
Family: Elysiidae.

LIMPET NUDIBRANCH *Doridella obscura*   **Not shown**
Identification: Mantle smooth, broadly oval, caplike, covering head and body. 2 short tentacles above. Gills *on underside* behind foot. To $\frac{5}{16}$ in. (8 mm).
Where found: Cape Cod to Gulf of Mexico. Very obscure, but often abundant on encrusting bryozoans in shallow water.
Family: Corambidae.

ROUGH-MANTLED NUDIBRANCHS *Onchidoris*   **Pl. 44**
and related genera
Identification: Mantle roughened with tubercles, broadly *oval,* covering head and body. A pair of rhinophores near head and a *gill ring at rear,* both retractile.
4 common intertidal species; others subtidal. (1) *Onchidoris bilamellata,* a tough-bodied species with *rounded* tubercles *varying* in size; strong color pattern with contrasting dark brown and whitish or cream-colored marks. To 1 in. (25 mm). (2) *Onchidoris muricata* is similar but softer-bodied and more uniformly colored, whitish to pale lemon-yellow or creamy; to $\frac{1}{2}$ in. (12 mm). (3) *Acanthodoris pilosa* has soft, *conical* tubercles nearly *equal* in size; gills fluffy, with *secondary branchlets* (preceding species have *simple* pinnate gills). Color varies, whitish to purple or brown. To $1\frac{1}{4}$ in. (31 mm). (4) *Doris verrucosa,* an exclusively southern species, has *rounded* tubercles *varying* in size. Dingy orange. To $1\frac{3}{4}$ in. (44 mm).
Similar species: Note Limpet Nudibranch (preceding account) with gills hidden *beneath* mantle.
Where found: (1) *O. bilamellata,* Bay of Fundy to R.I.; commonly exposed on intertidal rocks. (2) *O. muricata,* same range

but more secretive, hidden under rocks and in crevices, especially on encrusting bryozoans. (3) *A. pilosa,* Arctic south to L.I. Sound and locally to Chesapeake Bay; lower intertidal zone under stones and on seaweeds, among fouling organisms on jetties. (4) *D. verrucosa,* Brazil to Gulf of Mexico and locally north to Cape Cod; on pilings, lower intertidal zone to subtidal at shallow depths, especially on sponges.

Families: Onchidoridae, *Onchidoris* and *Acanthodoris;* Dorididae, *Doris.*

RIM-BACKED NUDIBRANCH *Polycera dubia*   **Pl. 44**
  Identification: Gills in a rosette on *middle of back;* a low *rim* or series of raised projections along each side. To $\frac{3}{4}$ in. (19 mm).
  Similar species: *Ancula* species (Plate 44) also have a gill ring near midbody with several ceratalike projections *on each side,* but lack lateral ridges. To $\frac{1}{2}$ in. (12 mm). Arctic to Cape Cod; from lower intertidal zone northward to subtidal at shallow depths. Family Anculidae.
  Where found: L.I. Sound north at least to Labrador; under stones from lower intertidal zone to subtidal at shallow depths; usually with bryozoans.
  Family: Polyceridae.

GULFWEED NUDIBRANCH *Scyllaea pelagica*   **Pl. 44**
  Identification: 2 pairs of narrow, straplike swimming fins on back identify this species. Color varies, matching Gulfweed. To $1\frac{3}{8}$ in. (34 mm).
  Similar species: *Fiona pinnata* (not shown) is also found on Gulfweed and other Gulf Stream flotsam but is not otherwise similar. It has numerous, close-crowded cerata, each with a wavy membrane along one edge. To 1 in. (25 mm). Family Fionidae.
  Where found: With drifting Gulfweed (p. 37).
  Family: Scyllaeidae.

BUSHY-BACKED NUDIBRANCH   **Pl. 45**
Dendronotus frondosus
  Identification: Easily identified by double row of *bushy cerata* along back. Body usually blotched with brown or rust but sometimes pure white. To 3 in. (75 mm).
  Where found: Arctic south to Cape Cod and (less commonly) at least as far as Barnegat Inlet, N.J.
  Remarks: This elegant species is one of the commonest New England nudibranchs; from lower intertidal zone to subtidal at shallow depths, in tide pools among fine seaweeds, and especially with hydroids.
  Family: Dendronotidae.

RED-GILLED NUDIBRANCHS *Coryphella* species   **Pl. 45**
Identification: To 100 cerata per side, each with a *red core* (shading to chocolate-brown in variants) and tipped with an opaque white ring or spot. Front edge of foot extended at sides, *sharp-angled* or *tentaclelike.* To $1^3/_{16}$ in. (30 mm). Several species listed from New England northward; typical form shown.
Similar species: Other species with *numerous fingerlike cerata* include: (1) *Catriona aurantia* (not shown), which is smaller — to $5/_8$ in. (16 mm) — and has a *rounded foot without projections;* cerata may be orange-tipped. Common in spring and summer with *Tubularia* species hydroids (p. 75); L.I. Sound north at least to N.H. Family Cuthonidae. *Cuthona concinna* (not shown), a British species reported from the same area, is similar in form and size but its foot is *blunt-angled* at the front. Family Cuthonidae. (2) *Facelina bostoniensis* (not shown) has a range similar to the preceding and is likewise reported on *Tubularia,* but is distinctive in having its rhinophores *roughened with raised rings.* To 1 in. (25 mm). Family Facelinidae. (3) See Striped Nudibranch (Plate 45 and next account).
Where found: South shore of Cape Cod north to Arctic. Very common among hydroids and seaweeds from the lower intertidal zone to subtidal into deep water.
Family: Coryphellidae.

STRIPED NUDIBRANCH *Cratena pilata*   **Pl. 45**
Identification: Cerata numerous but *less than* 100 per side. Color pattern distinctive: pale grayish or greenish-gray with white margins and a central *broken stripe* or series of elongate spots of rusty brown; cerata with dark, grayish, knotted core. To $1^3/_{16}$ in. (30 mm).
Similar species: See Maned and Red-Gilled Nudibranchs (both Plate 45) for comparisons with other plumed slugs.
Where found: Massachusetts Bay south at least to N.C. Chiefly estuarine among hydroids and other fouling organisms on pilings, buoys, and among red weeds in shallow water.
Family: Favorinidae.

CLUB-GILLED NUDIBRANCHS   **Pl. 45**
Eubranchus species
Identification: These pretty little nudibranchs have thickened, *club-shaped* cerata.
    2 species. (1) *E. exiguus* has 5–10 *banded* cerata per side. To $5/_{16}$ in. (8 mm). (2) *E. pallidus* has 30 or more cerata on each side; they are *blotched* with gold and red, as is the back. To $1/_2$ in. (12 mm).
Similar species: *Tergipes despectus* (Plate 45) has 5–8 cerata in a zigzag down the back; they are dark-cored with an orange

ring near the tip. To $\frac{5}{16}$ in. (8 mm). Arctic to south shore of Cape Cod. Family Cuthonidae.
Where found: Arctic south to R.I., usually with hydroids.
Family: Eubranchidae.

MANED NUDIBRANCH *Aeolidia papillosa* **Pl. 45**
Identification: Cerata *very numerous,* to 400 per side. When crawling, this elegant nudibranch has a well-combed look with cerata streaming back along sides; contracted (at rest) it suggests a sea anemone. Color varies, pinkish to smoky-gray or brown. To 4 in. (100 mm).
Where found: Bay of Fundy to Cape Cod and rarely south to Ocean City, Md., or beyond. Locally common in tide pools and shallow water, usually with sea anemones.
Family: Aeolidiidae.

Additional Plumed Shell-less Gastropods

None shown

Several small species can be found among hydroids and fine, bushy, red algae in lower intertidal zone and subtidally in shallow water. They have only a single pair of tentacles.

Idulia coronata has 5-9 club-shaped cerata in a single row on each side; each is ringed with 4-7 circlets of red-dotted tubercles. Tentacles emerge from trumpetlike sheaths. To $\frac{1}{2}$ in. (12 mm). Labrador south at least to N.J. Family Dotodae.

Tenellia fuscata has a broad shovel-like fin or velum in place of a first pair of tentacles. Its cerata are in 5-6 clumps along each side, with 2-3 cerata per clump. To $\frac{1}{4}$ in. (6 mm). S. Maine to Cape Cod. Family Cuthonidae.

Alderia harvardiensis (a sacoglossan) has paired cerata in 6-7 clusters on each side. To $\frac{1}{2}$ in. (12 mm). Reported from brackish water in muddy bays, Bay of Fundy to Massachusetts Bay. Family Stiligeridae.

Bivalves: Class Bivalvia

Bivalves are not likely to be confused with any other marine animals except brachiopods (p. 121).

The soft body consists of a *visceral mass,* a hatchet-shaped *foot* flanked by a pair of gills, and a mantle lobe next to each shell. The mantle lobes secrete the shell. Usually they are fused below to enclose a mantle cavity, leaving an opening for the foot. The foot is located toward the front of the body; this appendage is well developed in clams and other strong burrowers but is almost nonexistent in scallops and oysters. The rear part of the bivalve is defined by a pair of tubes or *siphons.* One of these siphons carries

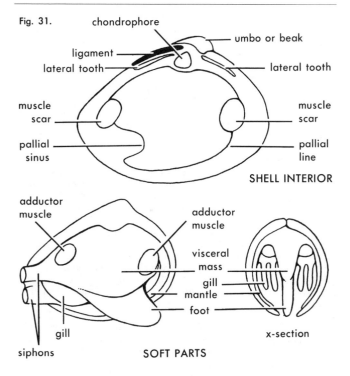

Fig. 31.

chondrophore

umbo or beak

ligament

lateral tooth

lateral tooth

muscle scar

muscle scar

pallial sinus

pallial line

SHELL INTERIOR

adductor muscle

adductor muscle

visceral mass

gill

mantle

foot

gill

siphons

SOFT PARTS

x-section

BIVALVE STRUCTURES

water in, while the other pumps water out; in the process the bivalve receives oxygen and food items and eliminates wastes. The siphons may be unequally developed; sometimes there is only one, or none at all. Other details of soft anatomy are used to define orders within the class, although malacologists differ in their views on these arrangements. Shell structure is the principal means of defining genera and species.

The shells or *valves* are joined by a hinge that is usually toothed and has a tough but elastic, dark brown *ligament* and 1 or 2 *adductor muscles*. In a cleaned shell the muscle scars are joined by a *pallial line* that often has a notch or *sinus*. The valves are usually asymmetrical, and right and left sides may be unequal in size or shape. With a few exceptions the beak or *umbo* points toward the front; the ligament is behind it, and the pallial sinus, whose development is related to that of the siphon musculature, is also at the rear. By keeping these points in mind it is usually possible to tell whether a shell in the hand is the left or right valve, a point of some importance for species identification. Differences in hinge teeth, including the presence or absence of *lateral teeth,* are also a very useful diagnostic feature. The ligament is sometimes divided into 2 distinct parts, with the inner part seated in a spoonlike *chondrophore.* In life the outside of the shell is covered by a filmy coating called the *periostracum;* this layer may be colored and conspicuous, or barely detectable. It flakes off with hard wear.

VEILED CLAM *Solemya velum* **Pl. 23**

   Identification: Shells oval-oblong with a shiny, dark olive to brown periostracum that *overhangs* shell (hence the alternate common name of Awning Clam) and is split and curled along edge. Weak ribs or lines radiate from low, off-center beaks. To 1½ in. (38 mm).

   Similar species: Northern Veiled Clam, *S. borealis* (not shown) is larger — to 3 in. (75 mm) — and has about 40 slender fingerlike projections around the siphonal opening (Veiled Clam has about 16). L.I. Sound to Nova Scotia. Subtidal.

   Where found: Nova Scotia to Fla.; on soft bottoms of coastal ponds and bays from lower intertidal zone to subtidal at shallow depths.

   Remarks: Veiled Clam is an active swimmer (along with razor clams and scallops), traveling in short, jet-propelled spurts. The weakly calcified shell is incredibly fragile and must have special care in collections; keep loosely bedded in soft cotton.

   Family: Solemyacidae.

NEAR NUT SHELL *Nucula proxima* **Pl. 23**

   Identification: A small, thick, triangular shell with a dull olive or yellow-gray periostracum. Hinge *strongly toothed,* inner margin *finely toothed.* To ⅜ in. (9 mm).

   Similar species: (1) Thin Nut Shell, *N. tenuis,* and (2) Delphinula Nut Shell, *N. delphinodonta* (neither shown) are *smooth-rimmed,* the 1st fragile and more oval, the 2nd similar to Near Nut Shell in shape. Both small — ¼ in. (6 mm) — and in somewhat deeper water than Near Nut Shell; Labrador south to Md. and N.J., respectively.

   Where found: Maine to Fla.; subtidal in 10 ft. (3 m) or more.

   Remarks: Nut shells are locally common on muddy bottoms of bays and sounds, where they are eaten by bottom-feeding fish and diving ducks. Also washed up on bay shores.

   Family: Nuculidae.

YOLDIAS *Yoldia* species **Pl. 23**

   Identification: Valves ax- or wedge-shaped or tapered behind.

Hinge with a more or less distinct *chondrophore* and filelike (taxodont) hinge teeth.

Numerous species, several in shallow water. (1) Ax Yoldia, *Y. thraciaeformis,* is stronger than following species, ax-shaped, with darker periostracum and distinct *diagonal fold.* 12–14 teeth on each side of chondrophore. To 2 in. (50 mm). (2) File Yoldia, *Y. limatula,* (3) Short Yoldia, *Y. sapotilla,* and (4) Oval Yoldia, *Y. myalis* (not shown) are rather thin, *tapered* or wedge-shaped, with pale greenish or olive periostracum. Species differ in number of teeth on each side of chondrophore: File Yoldia has about 20; Short Yoldia 50 or more, and Oval Yoldia 12–14. Sizes are 2½ in. (62 mm), 1 in. (25 mm), and 1 in. (25 mm), respectively.

Similar species: *Nuculana* species (not shown) also have taxodont hinge teeth but are distinctly *spouted* or *pointed* behind; see Gould's Pandora, p. 160.

Where found: (1) Ax Yoldia, Arctic south to N.C.; subtidal in 50 ft. (15 m) or more. (2) File Yoldia, the most frequently reported New England species, ranges from Gulf of St. Lawrence to L.I. Sound (or perhaps in deep water to N.C.); subtidal in 6 ft. (1.8 m) or more. (3) Short Yoldia, Labrador to Cape Cod and in deep water at least to e. L.I. Sound; found in somewhat deeper water than File Yoldia, as is the following cold-water species. (4) Oval Yoldia, Labrador to Cape Cod. All are mud burrowers.

Family: Nuculanidae, including *Nuculana.*

PONDEROUS ARK *Noetia ponderosa* **Pl. 26**
Identification: The broad, flat, radial ribs are *doubled* along margin. Shell thick and heavy, somewhat rectangular, with broad ligament. Shell white, periostracum velvety black. To 2½ in. (62 mm).

Similar species: Arks are generally distinguished from other radially ribbed clams by their *taxodont* (filelike) hinge teeth. (1) Transverse Ark, *Anadara transversa* (Plate 26) is similar but less massive with weaker beaks, ligament, and hinge. To 1½ in. (38 mm). Gulf of Mexico to Cape Cod (reported in s. Maine); subtidal from shallow water down to over 100 ft. (30 m) on various bottoms. (2) Blood Ark, *Anadara ovalis* (Plate 26) usually has a more rounded form, relatively weak beaks and ligament; hinge teeth only extend a little in front of beaks. To 2 in. (50 mm). Cape Cod (or rarely Massachusetts Bay) to Gulf of Mexico; subtidal from shallow water down to 150 ft. (45 m), chiefly on mud bottoms. (3) Several additional southern arks may be found in Cape Hatteras area, including Mossy Ark, *Arca imbricata* (not shown), an elongate rock-dwelling species. Another, the Incongruous Ark, *Anadara brasiliana* (not shown) resembles Ponderous Ark but has strongly *beaded* ribs and unequal valves.

Where found: A beach shell, Cape Cod to Gulf of Mexico;

shells found north of Va. are probably *fossils*.

Remarks: Some of the southern species attach themselves firmly to the underside of rocks by a strong byssal network, but our arks burrow in sand or sandy mud. The blood of some arks, including Blood Ark, contains hemoglobin — hence the name; most bivalve bloods have no specific oxygen-carrying compound and are colorless.

Family: Arcidae, including *Arca* and *Anadara*.

BLUE MUSSEL *Mytilus edulis*   **Pl. 24**

Identification: The common *smooth-shelled* mussel with pointed *terminal* beaks, edged inside with fine teeth. Outside usually glossy bluish or bluish black, sometimes paler brownish or rayed; inside violet. To 4 in. (100 mm).

Similar species: (1) Horse Mussel (Plate 24) has *subterminal* beaks. (2) Platform Mussel, *Congeria leucopheata* (Plate 24) is small — $\frac{3}{4}$ in. (19 mm) — and brownish; beaks terminal with *shelf* inside. Hudson R. (upper Manhattan north to fresh water) and in similar situations south to Texas. Not a true mussel but grows in the same manner; lower intertidal to subtidal at shallow depths. Family Dreissenidae.

Where found: Circumpolar, south in w. Atlantic Ocean to S.C. From slightly brackish estuaries to depths of several hundred feet offshore.

Remarks: Mussels moor themselves with tough threads, clinging tenaciously to any firm support available. Blue Mussels compete with barnacles and seaweeds to cover intertidal rocks and pilings. Given a foothold of scattered stones or shells, they form shoals, even on muddy tidal flats.

Though little used in America, Blue Mussels are deliciously edible. In prime habitats full growth comes in a year; elsewhere 2–5 years are needed.

Family: Mytilidae.

RIBBED MUSSEL *Modiolus demissus*   **Pl. 24**

Identification: A salt-marsh mussel with *subterminal* beaks and rough *radial ribs*. Periostracum greenish or yellowish brown. To 4 in. (100 mm).

Similar species: Bent Mussel, *Brachidontes recurvus* (Plate 24) is also radially ribbed, but has *terminal* beaks, is smaller — $1\frac{1}{2}$ in. (38 mm) — and *sharply* bent; in brackish water with oysters or on rocks and pilings; lower Chesapeake Bay to Gulf of Mexico, locally and probably accidentally (with oysters) to L.I. Sound or Mass.

Where found: Fla. to Cape Cod and locally to Gulf of St. Lawrence. Intertidally in brackish water.

Remarks: This mussel is abundant in tidal banks and flats,

where it lives half-buried in the peat or muck among the roots of marsh grasses. Inedible.
Family: Mytilidae, including *Brachidontes*.

HORSE MUSSEL *Modiolus modiolus*   **Pl. 24**
   Identification: This large Boreal mussel has *subterminal* beaks. Periostracum shaggy, flaky, brownish or bluish-black; shell whitish or tinged with mauve. To 6 in. (150 mm).
   Similar species: Blue Mussel (Plate 24) has terminal beaks.
   Where found: Circumpolar, south in w. Atlantic Ocean to Long Island or Staten Island, N.Y. Extends up into lower intertidal in e. Maine but chiefly subtidal in deeper water — to 240 ft. (72 m) — southward; scarce south of Cape Cod.
   Remarks: Seen mainly as a beach shell, often cast ashore in the grip of laminarian seaweed holdfasts. Considered inedible.
   Family: Mytilidae.

BAY SCALLOP *Aequipecten irradians*   **Pl. 26**
   Identification: This is the small *coarsely ribbed* scallop of weedy shallows; marginal wings nearly *equal* in size. Color extremely variable. To 3 in. (75 mm).
   Differences in shape and ribbing, as well as range, separate subspecies: (1) *A. i. concentricus* (N.J. to Ga.) is more inflated, has 19–21 *squarish* ribs; (2) *A. i. irradians* (N.Y. northward) is flatter, with 17–18 *rounded* ribs.
   Similar species: (1) Iceland Scallop, *Chlamys islandica* (not shown) has unequal wings and *50 or more* ribs. Variable in color. To 4 in. (100 mm). Arctic Ocean to Casco Bay and locally to Cape Cod. Reported in shallow water in Bay of Fundy but in 60 ft. (18 m) or more southward. (2) Calico Scallop, *A. gibbus* (not shown), a common beach shell *south of Cape Hatteras,* is more colorful than Bay Scallop; has about 20 *rounded* ribs. To 2 in. (50 mm).
   Where found: Gulf of Mexico to Cape Cod, locally to Massachusetts Bay (reported to Nova Scotia). From low tide line down to 50 ft. (15 m) on a variety of bottoms; often a beach shell.
   Remarks: The "blue-eyed scallop" of much-deserved gustatory fame. Young scallops are sedentary, attaching themselves by threads to Eelgrass or other supports to escape the stifling muck of bay bottoms. The Eelgrass blight (see p. 52) dealt near disaster to the Bay Scallop and in some areas neither grass nor scallop have fully recovered. Unlike other bivalves, scallops are highly motile; sharp contractions of the adductor muscle (the main edible feature; see p. 143) produce jetlike pulses of water from the mantle cavity and a rather erratic bouncing locomotion. Bay scallops grow quickly, breeding when a year old and rarely living even 2 years.

Family: Pectinidae, including *Chlamys*.

DEEP-SEA SCALLOP *Placopecten magellanicus*   **Pl. 26**
  Identification: A large scallop with flattish, *finely* ribbed valves. To 8 in. (200 mm).
  Where found: Labrador to Cape Cod, subtidal in 12 ft. (3.6 m) or more, and locally southward to N.C. in deeper water — to 600 ft. (180 m).
  Remarks: This common sea scallop is found in snorkeling depths in Maine, but is usually taken commercially from deeper water. Broken shells are found on ocean beaches after winter storms.
  Family: Pectinidae.

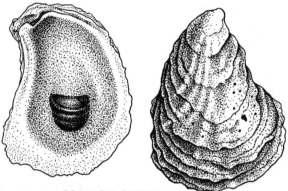

Fig. 32.   COMMON OYSTER

COMMON OYSTER *Crassostrea virginica*   **Fig. 32**
  Identification: Extremely variable in shape. Shells massive, rough, and unequal; lower valve cemented to any hard object available; upper valve smaller and flatter. A *single* violet muscle scar. To 10 in. (250 mm).
  Where found: Gulf of Mexico to Cape Cod, locally north to s. Maine; also in Gulf of St. Lawrence. In sounds and estuaries with salinity between 5 and 30‰. Intolerant of prolonged exposure to fresh water or marine salinities. Intertidal to subtidal at shallow depths.
  Remarks: The larvae go through trochophore and veliger stages (see p. 61) before the young oysters, called "spat," settle (or "set") into beds.
  So many enemies, diseases, and other calamities afflict this

most famous of bivalves that it is amazing the species survives. (Annual production of up to about 100 million eggs per female helps.) Sea stars, drills, crabs, flatworms (*Stylochus* species), fishes (such as drums and rays), Oyster-catchers, scoters and other sea ducks, as well as man, prey on oysters. Sponges (*Cliona* species), boring clams (*Diplothyra*), mud worms (*Polydora*), and crabs (*Pinnotheres*) are commensals that harm or interfere with normal life. Various protozoans and microbes cause disease, and a host of associates compete for space.

Oysters are harvested either with hand tongs or with mechanical tongs or dredges. In N.Y., N.J., and Conn. particularly, oysters are farmed on leased beds. In other states there are extensive public beds, and in Md. some of these are dredged by large sloops *under sail.* The Indians esteemed oysters and some middens attest to a wider prehistoric distribution northward. More recently such famous beds as those off Princess Bay, N.Y.; Jamaica Bay, Long Island; Quinnipiac R., Conn.; Barnegat and Great bays, N.J., have been destroyed or rendered unusable by pollution and mismanagement. Many others are threatened. **Family:** Ostreidae.

JINGLE SHELL *Anomia simplex*   Pl. 24
Identification: Valves dissimilar. Upper valve variably shaped and colored, often irregular, thin, translucent, glossy. Color whitish or silvery, yellow, orange, brownish, or stained black. Lower valve flat, fragile, with a large *hole.* To 3 in. (75 mm), though usually only $\frac{1}{2}$ that size.
Similar species: Prickly Jingle Shell, *A. aculeata* (not shown) is smaller — to $\frac{3}{4}$ in. (19 mm) — more fragile, with rows of fine, prickly scales. Labrador to Long Island, reported to N.C. but scarce south of Cape Cod; subtidal from shallow water down to 240 ft. (72 m) on rocks and seaweed holdfasts.
Where found: Caribbean to Cape Cod; generally replaced northward by Prickly Jingle Shell but reported locally to Nova Scotia. Subtidal from shallow water down to 60 ft. (18 m).
Remarks: Live jingles may be found attached to rocks or shells in the lower intertidal zone, but are probably more familiar as beach shells. A bundle of byssal threads passes through the lower valve to anchor the live animal.
Family: Anomiidae.

BLACK CLAM *Arctica islandica*   Pl. 28
Identification: Very similar to Quahog in shape and hinge but lacks a pallial sinus. Periostracum *black;* inside without purple coloring. To 4 in. (100 mm).
Similar species: Black clams without periostracum could easily be confused with Quahog (Plate 28) or related species.

Where found: Newfoundland to Cape Cod and in deep water to N.C. Subtidal to 500 ft. (150 m) but a common beach shell from Cape Cod north. Little-used commercially though it is edible. **Family:** Arcticidae.

CAROLINA MARSH CLAM Pl. 28
Polymesoda caroliniana
Identification: A broadly rounded, sturdy, fresh- to brackish-water clam with greenish to brownish, rather shaggy periostracum. Beaks frequently eroded. To $1\frac{1}{2}$ in. (38 mm).
Similar species: (1) Black Clam (Plate 28) has a dark periostracum but is otherwise quite different; also note distributions. (2) Compare with Wedge Rangia (Plate 28), another southern, brackish-water clam.
Where found: Va. to Texas, on marshy borders of coastal bays and rivers. Intertidal to subtidal in shallow water, to *maximum* salinity of 15‰. Look for these clams along the James R. off Colonial Parkway between Jamestown and Williamsburg, Va.
Family: Corbiculiidae.

CHESTNUT ASTARTE *Astarte castanea* Pl. 25
Identification: Commonest astarte in shallow water. Shell triangular, heavy and thick; hinge strong, pallial line *without* sinus. Inner margin *crenulated.* Outside *almost smooth* with a toughly adherent yellow-brown, chestnut, or blackish periostracum. Live clam has bright orange foot. To 1 in. (25 mm).
Similar species: (1) Waved Astarte, *A. undata* (not shown) is similar in size, shape, and range, though much less common; shell with 10–20 deeply incised concentric *ridges.* (2) Additional Boreal astartes found in deeper water; also fossil forms. The genus is distinctive; individual species are not. (3) Thickened Crassinella, *Crassinella mactracea* (not shown), a small — $\frac{1}{4}$ in. (6 mm) — weakly ribbed, astartelike relative, has a chalky, white or yellowish white exterior. Shells more sharply triangular. Massachusetts Bay to Fla.; subtidal from shallow water down to 150 ft. (45 m). Uncommon or easily overlooked. Family Crassatellidae.
Where found: Nova Scotia to Ocean City, N.J. Subtidal in 25 ft. (7.5 m) or more but commonly washed ashore on *ocean* beaches, particularly along the south shore of Martha's Vineyard, Nantucket, and outer Cape Cod. Look for them after winter storms.
Remarks: Astarte was the Phoenician goddess of love.
Family: Astartidae.

NORTHERN CARDITA *Cyclocardia borealis* Pl. 26
Identification: Shells heart-shaped, thick and strong with about 20 radial ribs. Outside dirty gray or whitish with dull

gray-brown or rusty periostracum. To $1\frac{1}{2}$ in. (38 mm).

Similar species: Northern Cardita is somewhat astartelike in form (Plate 25) but astartes are smooth or *concentrically* ribbed. The only other shallow-water Boreal bivalves with radial ribs are the *more weakly hinged* and *thin-shelled* cockles. (1) Little Cockle, *Cerastoderma pinnulatum* (Plate 26) is small — to $\frac{1}{2}$ in. (12 mm) — with 22–28 weak ribs that have *raised scales;* outside pale brownish cream-colored, inside even paler. Labrador to Cape Cod and less commonly to N.C., subtidal in 12–500 ft. (3.6–150 m) or more. (2) Iceland Cockle, *Clinocardium ciliatum* (Plate 26) is larger — to 2 in. (50 mm) — and has sharper, more numerous (32–38) ribs *without scales*. Banded inside and out with gray-brown, pale yellowish, and white; periostracum dirty-gray. Greenland to Mass., subtidal in 20 ft. (6 m) or more. Little Cockle and Iceland Cockle both Family Cardiidae. (3) Glandular Bean Mussel, *Crenella glandula* (Fig. 40 opp. Plate 26) is a tiny — $\frac{1}{2}$ in. (12 mm) — mussel with fine radial ribs; yellowish tan; *note hinge*. Labrador to N.C., sometimes in lower intertidal zone northward. Family Mytilidae.

Where found: Labrador to south shore of Cape Cod, and in deep water south to Sandy Hook (occasionally to S.C.); subtidal in 12–300 ft. (3.6–90 m) or more.

Remarks: Carditas and cockles are commonly found in the stomachs of fishes caught in northern waters.

Family: Carditidae.

CROSSHATCHED LUCINE   Pl. 25
Divaricella quadrisulcata

Identification: Shells round, quite strong, glossy white, with closely spaced *chevronlike* scratches crossing broad concentric growth ridges. To 1 in. (25 mm).

Similar species: See Disk Shell and White Semele (both Plate 25); have beaks turned *forward* and lack chevrons.

Where found: Cape Cod to Brazil. Subtidal in 6 ft. (1.8 m) or more. A beach shell; rare northward.

Family: Lucinidae.

GREAT HEART COCKLE *Dinocardium robustum*   Pl. 26

Identification: A large — to 5 in. (125 mm) — *southern* cockle with about 35 scaly radial ribs. Shell heart-shaped, swollen. Yellowish outside with rusty-brown marks; pinkish inside.

Similar species: (1) Most other radially ribbed cockles (Plate 26) are Boreal; see Northern Cardita, p. 150. (2) Three-toothed Cardita, *Venericardia tridentata* (Fig. 40 opp. Plate 26) is a small — $\frac{1}{4}$ in. (6 mm — shell with about 15 strongly beaded radial ribs. Delaware Bay to Fla., subtidal in 3–100 ft. (0.9–30 m). Family Carditidae.

Where found: Fla. and Gulf of Mexico north to N.C. or Cape Henry. Subtidal in 3–90 ft. (0.9–27 m) but a common beach shell southward.

Family: Cardiidae.

MORTON'S EGG COCKLE *Laevicardium mortoni*   **Pl. 25**
Identification: A small, light, *smooth-shelled* cockle. Inside of fresh shells bright *yellow* with a chestnut or purplish mark to one side; outside glossy whitish, soiled with gray or pale brown and often marked with *wavy brown bands*. Old shells are dull with faded colors but fresh ones are very pretty indeed. To almost 1 in. (25 mm).
Where found: Cape Cod to Gulf of Mexico, locally north to Nova Scotia. A bay clam in sand or sandy mud, lower intertidal zone to subtidal at shallow depths; often washed ashore.
Remarks: This little cockle is one of several "duck clams" sought by scaup and other diving ducks.
Family: Cardiidae.

GREENLAND COCKLE *Serripes groenlandicus*   **Pl. 28**
Identification: A cockle with *weak radial ribbing* at both ends; shell thin, slightly truncated at rear. Inside without pallial sinus; margin smooth. Has pale grayish or yellowish brown periostracum. To 4 in. (100 mm).
Where found: Greenland to Cape Cod, subtidal in 30 ft. (9 m) or more.
Family: Cardiidae.

QUAHOG or HARD-SHELLED CLAM   **Pl. 28**
Mercenaria mercenaria
Identification: Shells thick and strong, broadly oval, with beaks shifted *forward*. Inside white with *purple stain* at rear; outside dull whitish but often stained. External sculpturing changes with age; young have sharply-raised concentric ridges, older clams relatively smooth. Have a pallial *sinus* and *toothed* inner margin. Usually to 4 in. (100 mm), exceptionally to 6 in. (150 mm).
    M. m. notata, a named variant, lacks purple; has wavy, brownish markings. More common southward.
Similar species: (1) Southern Quahog, *M. campechiensis* (not shown), usually listed as a separate species, is larger, rarely purple-stained. *M. mercenaria* shells become smooth in central area as they age; *campechiensis* do not. Hybrids are common; variants difficult to distinguish. Chesapeake Bay to Texas. (2) Black Clam (Plate 28) *lacks* purple stain and pallial sinus, has blackish periostracum. (3) An easily overlooked beach shell, False Quahog, *Pitar morrhuana* (Plate 28) is like a small — to 2 in. (50 mm) — Quahog but weaker; lacks purple stain, and has

smooth inner margin. Outside often stained rusty or orange. Prince Edward I., Canada, to N.C.; sandy bottoms, subtidal in 20 ft. (6 m) or more. (4) Note Greenland Cockle (Plate 28) with weak *radial ribbing* at both ends. No pallial sinus.

Where found: Gulf of Mexico to Cape Cod, less commonly in Massachusetts Bay and locally in warm bays to Bar Harbor, Maine, reappearing in Gulf of St. Lawrence. Intertidal to subtidal down to about 60 ft. (18 m). Chiefly in salinities higher than 15‰. Habitat varies — sand or muddy sand in bays and along ocean beaches.

Remarks: New Englanders are as firm about calling this clam Quahog as they are about keeping tomatoes and other contaminants out of clam chowder. Southward it is called the Round or Hard-shelled Clam. Commercial names for this clam are based on size: Littleneck to about 1½ in. (38 mm), Cherrystone to 2 in. (50 mm), and Chowder to 3 in. (75 mm) or more. Clams grow quickly, but may live 20–25 years. *Mercenaria* comes from the shell's use in making Indian money or wampum.

Family: Veneridae, including *Pitar*.

GEM SHELL *Gemma gemma*   **Pl. 25**

Identification: A minute — usually less than ⅛ in. (3 mm) — *triangular* clam with nearly smooth, glossy valves; the inner margin *finely crenulated,* a trait easily seen with hand lens. Whitish or gray, often tinted with purple.

Similar species: See Chestnut Astarte (Plate 25) and Thickened Crassinella (p. 150, under Chestnut Astarte). These larger bivalves of similar shape have a pallial line *without* a sinus.

Where found: Nova Scotia to Texas. Tidal flats to subtidal at shallow depths in salinities as low as 5‰. A handsome and often common bay clam, easily overlooked because of its small size.

Family: Veneridae.

DISK SHELL *Dosinia discus*   **Pl. 25**

Identification: A neat, round, flat-valved clam with pointed beaks, hooked *forward.* Shell off-white, glossy, with fine, closely spaced, concentric ridges. To 3 in. (75 mm).

Similar species: (1) See Crosshatched Lucine (Plate 25). (2) White Semele, *Semele proficua* (Plate 25) has a *broad U-shaped* pallial sinus compared to wedge-shaped sinus of Disk Shell. Note differences in hinges. Inside often yellow or pale orange, speckled with reddish or purple (Disk Shell white). To 1½ in. (38 mm). Reported Va. to West Indies but accidental north of Cape Hatteras; subtidal. Family Semelidae. (3) Many-lined Lucine, *Lucina multilineata* (not shown) is very similar to White Semele in shape but only ¼–⅜ in. (6–9 mm). *Swollen* valves have many fine concentric lines and barely per-

ceptible radial lines outside, marginal teeth inside; pallial line *without* a sinus. Chesapeake Bay to Fla.; subtidal from shallow depths to 600 ft. (180 m). Family Lucinidae.
Where found: Va. to Gulf of Mexico. Subtidal in 6 ft. (1.8 m) or more but sometimes found in beach drift.
Family: Veneridae.

WEDGE RANGIA *Rangia cuneata* Pl. 28

Identification: A very strong, triangular, *brackish-water* clam; beaks very prominent; rear slope flattened. Periostracum silky, yellowish or brownish gray. To 2 in. (50 mm).
Similar species: Note Carolina Marsh Clam (Plate 28) with similar range.
Where found: N. Chesapeake Bay (Md.) to Texas. In tidal marshes.
Family: Mactridae.

SURF CLAM *Spisula solidissima* Pl. 28

Identification: Shells moderately strong, somewhat triangular. Hinge with distinct cuplike chondrophore and strong lateral teeth *crenulated on inner side,* visible with hand lens even in very small — $\frac{3}{8}$ in. (9 mm) — specimens. Outside nearly smooth; fresh shells have yellowish-olive periostracum. To 8 in. (200 mm).
Similar species: (1) Stimpson's Surf Clam, *S. polynyma* (not shown) is very similar but lateral teeth are shorter and *smooth.* To 4 in. (100 mm); R.I. to Arctic. (2) Little Surf Clam, *Mulinia lateralis* (Plate 25) is much smaller — to $\frac{3}{4}$ in. (19 mm) — closely similar, but shells more swollen and have *flattened backslope;* lateral hinge teeth *not* crenulated. E. Canada to West Indies; in shallow bays, mud bottoms, at salinities above 8‰. (3) Arctic Wedge Clam (Plate 28) has beaks strongly displaced from center to rear; lateral hinge teeth crenulated on *both* sides.
Where found: Nova Scotia or Labrador to S.C. Very low in the intertidal zone to subtidal down to 100 ft. (30 m).
Remarks: The most common clam shell on ocean beaches south of Cape Cod. A favorite of scavenging gulls, who drop them from on high until the shells break. Formerly little-valued commercially, surf clams recently accounted for 70% of the U.S. clam crop; usually taken by hydraulic dredge off N.J. and Md. shores. Most of the catch is canned.
Family: Mactridae, including *Mulinia.*

CHANNELED DUCK *Labiosa plicatella* Pl. 28

Identification: A beach shell, usually found in fragments. *Thin, fragile,* and purest white, with concentric ribs outside and

grooves within. Lopsided-triangular; beaks pointed and hinge with a chondrophore. To 3 in. (75 mm).
Where found: N.C. and southward on ocean beaches. In 6–40 ft. (1.8–12 m).
Family: Mactridae.

ARCTIC WEDGE CLAM *Mesodesma arctatum*   **Pl. 28**
Identification: Shells more or less oval but with prominent beaks well to rear. Hinge with deep chondrophore and *strong lateral teeth* crenulated on *both* sides (visible even in small and badly worn shells). Outside often roughened with growth ridges, chalky or with smooth yellowish periostracum. To $1\frac{1}{2}$ in. (38 mm).
Similar species: (1) See Surf Clam (Plate 28) and (2) Little Surf Clam (Plate 25). (3) Also suggests a dull, more robust Coquina (Plate 25) but latter lacks a chondrophore, and ranges overlap only slightly.
Where found: Gulf of St. Lawrence to e. Long Island (Patchogue and eastward) though reported to Va. Subtidal to 300 ft. (90 m), but sometimes common on ocean beaches, especially on outer Cape Cod.
Family: Mesodesmatidae.

TELLINS *Tellina* species   **Pl. 25**
Identification: Shells oval, compressed, and *thin*. Outside white or tinged with pink or yellow; shiny, sometimes slightly iridescent. Hinge weak, with lateral teeth at least in front. Northern species small — none exceeds $\frac{5}{8}$ in. (16 mm). Larger tellins, prized by collectors, occur south of Cape Hatteras. The posterior twist seen in larger tellins is barely evident in smaller northern ones.

In the absence of authoritatively identified shells for comparison, it is difficult to distinguish species positively. Typical form shown on Plate 25.
Similar species: (1) See Narrowed Macoma, next account. (2) Common Cumingia, *Cumingia tellinoides* (Plate 25) is dull and ridged outside, glossy within; hinge with a *spoonlike chondrophore*. To $\frac{3}{4}$ in. (19 mm). Nova Scotia to Fla., on shallow mud bottoms. Family Semelidae.
Where found: Dwarf Tellin, *T. agilis,* the common species in the North, Massachusetts Bay to Ga., and locally north to Gulf of St. Lawrence; DeKay's Dwarf Tellin, *T. versicolor,* from Cape Cod to West Indies. Additional small southern tellins range north to Cape Hatteras or just beyond; *T. mirabilis* and Iris Tellin, *T. iris,* are 2 species found in shallow water.
Remarks: Unlike most bivalves, which feed by filtration of planktonic particles, tellins are *deposit feeders* (see p. 62). The very long, inhalant siphon is snaked over the bottom to draw in

bits of organic debris. Look for dead shells in beach drift; live tellins dwell subtidally in shallow water, where they wander about as active burrowers.

Family: Tellinidae.

MACOMA CLAMS *Macoma* species   **Pl. 25**

Identification: Shells oval, broad or narrow; somewhat compressed and thin; often *asymmetrical,* with a posterior twist and unequal pallial sinuses. Outside chalky, with yellow-gray flaky periostracum. Hinges weak; lateral teeth *lacking* (in contrast to tellins, which have them).

3 species. (1) Baltic Macoma, *M. balthica,* and (2) Chalky Macoma, *M. calcarea,* are broadly oval, differing mainly in shape of pallial sinus. Baltic Macoma is smaller — to 1½ in. (38 mm) — less asymmetrical, and often tinged pinkish. Chalky Macoma to 2 in. (50 mm). See Fig. 33. (3) Narrowed Macoma, *M. tenta* (not shown) is small — ½ in. (12 mm) — narrow, and tellinlike, but lacks lateral teeth and is twisted.

Where found: (1) Baltic Macoma, Ga. to Arctic; in shallow water of quiet bays in salinities as low as 5‰; commonly washed ashore. (2) Chalky Macoma, from w. Long Island to Arctic; subtidal in 6 ft. (1.8 m) or more. (3) Narrowed Macoma, Cape Cod to West Indies, locally to Prince Edward I., Canada; subtidal. Macomas are mud dwellers and resemble tellins in habits (see preceding account).

Family: Tellinidae.

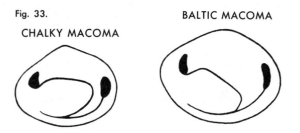

Fig. 33.

CHALKY MACOMA   BALTIC MACOMA

MUSCLE SCARS AND PALLIAL LINES

COQUINA *Donax variabilis*   **Pl. 25**

Identification: A burrower on wave-churned ocean beaches. Shells small, strong, with *beak offset* forward; inner margins *minutely toothed.* Color varies — yellow, orange, red, brown, purple, often rayed or banded; sometimes all white. To ¾ in. (19 mm).

Plates

THE SPECIES shown on the following 64 plates are grouped according to visual similarities. The scale varies; many are reduced, others enlarged, and some are about life size. Actual dimensions are given in each of the species accounts. Note, however, that these are the *maximum* recorded sizes; specimens found are likely to be smaller.

When several species that are very difficult to distinguish are presented together as a group and none in particular is identified as "shown" on the plate, then a *typical form* has been illustrated.

Keep in mind that the descriptions given on the legend pages provide only general information. See the text for thorough accounts with details necessary for making a positive species identification.

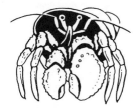

Plate 1

GREEN SEAWEEDS

Scale varies. Measurements are maximum recorded length of whole plants. Fragments or whole plants shown as indicated.

SEA LETTUCE   *Ulva lactuca*   p. 28
Ruffled or lobed sheets, usually unattached. To 3 ft. (900 mm). See text for similar species. Whole plant.

HOLLOW GREEN WEEDS   *Enteromorpha* species   p. 27
Tubular, at least in part; often containing air bubbles. *E. intestinalis* shown; to 1 ft. (300 mm). See text for other species. Whole plants.

CHAETOMORPHA MELAGONIUM
Coarsely filamentous with cells visible to naked eye, unbranched. Stiff, wiry, blue-green. To 1 ft. (300 mm). See under Filamentous Seaweeds, p. 50. Fragments.

GREEN SEA FERN   *Bryopsis plumosa*   p. 29
Delicately bushy; fernlike with regular branching. To 4 in. (100 mm). See text for similar species. Fragment.

SPONGOMORPHA species
Filamentous in ropy tangles. To 6 in. (150 mm). See under Filamentous Seaweeds, p. 51. Whole plant.

GREEN FLEECE   *Codium fragile*   p. 28
Coarsely bushy with thick spongy branches. To 3 ft. (900 mm). Fragment.

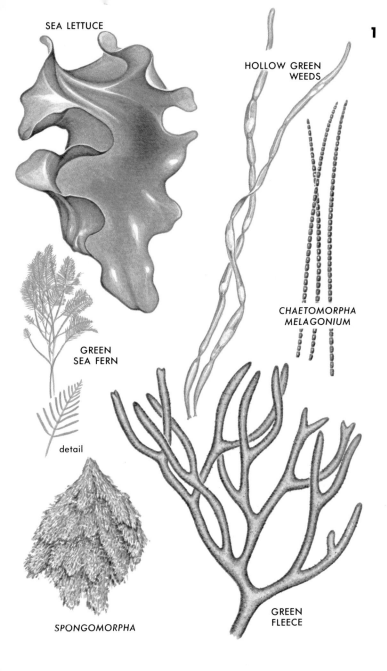

SEA LETTUCE

HOLLOW GREEN WEEDS

CHAETOMORPHA MELAGONIUM

GREEN SEA FERN

detail

SPONGOMORPHA

GREEN FLEECE

1

Plate 2
ROCKWEEDS AND RELATED BROWN SEAWEEDS

Scale varies. Measurements are maximum recorded length of whole plants. Only fragments are shown. Yellowish- or golden-brown to deep olive.

ROCKWEEDS   *Fucus* species   p. 36
Blades have a distinct midrib. To 3 ft. (900 mm).

F. vesiculosus. The only species with air bladders, usually in pairs within blade. Blades may be spiraled or bladders scarce to absent in some variants found in quiet water or in places exposed to heavy surf. Receptacles swollen, berry-shaped.

The following species may resemble variant *F. vesiculosus;* best identified by receptacles, though even these vary.

F. spiralis. Blades usually twisted in spiral form; receptacles ridged. On upper mid-littoral rocks.

F. evanescens. Receptacles short, flattened. In quiet places, subtidal in shallow water.

F. edentatus. Receptacles long, flattened. On mid- to lower-littoral rocks exposed to surf.

F. filiformis. Receptacles long, swollen; blades slender. In tide pools in upper intertidal zone.

KNOTTED WRACK   *Ascophyllum nodosum*   p. 35
Blades narrow, compressed, with single air bladders and short branchlets. Receptacles short, berrylike. Commonly to 2 ft. (600 mm), sometimes much longer. A runty quiet-water variant called **scorpioides** is also shown.

ASCOPHYLLUM MACKAII
A dwarfed form, distinguished by long receptacles. To 8 in. (200 mm). See under Knotted Wrack, p. 35. Receptacle only shown.

GULFWEED   *Sargassum* species   p. 37
Blades narrow, round, with air bladders on stalks, and with midrib. To 2 ft. (600 mm) or more.

S. filipendula. Blades have small, scattered, dark spots. An attached form, growing in lower intertidal zone or below.

S. natans. Leaves have few or no spots. Berries have a spike. Only found floating free. See text for *S. fluitans,* the other common pelagic species of Gulfweed.

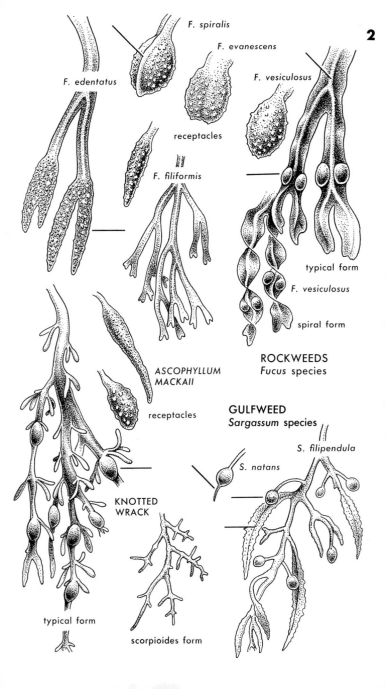

2

F. spiralis

F. evanescens

F. edentatus

F. vesiculosus

receptacles

F. filiformis

typical form

F. vesiculosus

spiral form

ROCKWEEDS
Fucus species

ASCOPHYLLUM MACKAII

receptacles

GULFWEED
Sargassum species

S. natans

S. filipendula

KNOTTED WRACK

typical form

scorpioides form

Plate 3

KELP

Greatly reduced. Measurements are maximum recorded length of whole plants. Dark brown. Attachment is a branched holdfast.

SEA COLANDER *Agarum cribrosum* p. 34
Blade ribbed, riddled with holes. To 6 ft. (1.8 m).

HORSETAIL KELP *Laminaria digitata* p. 34
Blade ribless, divided in straplike fingers. To 3½ ft. (1.1 m). See text for ecological variants.

EDIBLE KELP *Alaria* species p. 33
Blade ribbed, with bladelets basally. To 10 ft. (3 m). *A. esculenta,* the common species in our area, shown; see text for others.

HOLLOW-STEMMED KELP *Laminaria longicruris*
Blade ribless, stem hollow and swollen above. To 15 ft. (4.5 m) or more. See under Common Southern Kelp, p. 34.

COMMON SOUTHERN KELP *Laminaria agardhii* p. 34
Blade ribless, stem solid. Blade has ruffled edge in spring–summer; is oarlike, unruffled, in winter. To 10 ft. (3 m). See text for similar species.

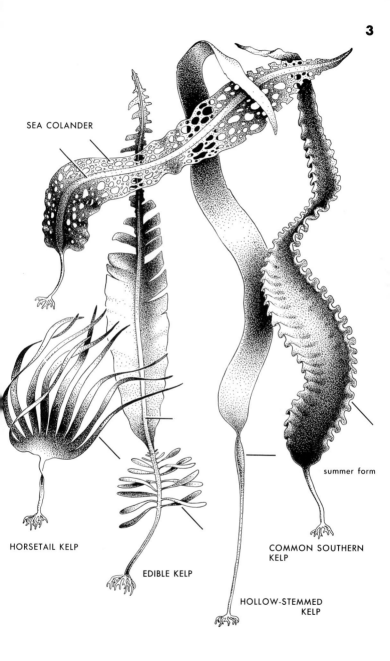

SEA COLANDER

HORSETAIL KELP

EDIBLE KELP

summer form

COMMON SOUTHERN
KELP

HOLLOW-STEMMED
KELP

Plate 4

CONFUSING BROWN SEAWEEDS

Reduced; scale varies. Measurements are maximum recorded length of whole plants; often much smaller. Whole plants or fragments shown as indicated.

SMOOTH CORD WEED *Chorda filum* p. 33
 Whiplike, without branches; with furlike colorless hairs in spring, bare in summer. To 15 ft. (4.5 m). (Smaller *C. tomentosa* has dark fur all year; see text.) Whole plant.

BOTTLEBRUSH *Cladostephus verticillatus* p. 29
 Bushy, with whorls of tiny, curving branchlets. To 10 in. (250 mm). Fragment.

Largest branches *longer* than main axis.

BLACK WHIP WEED *Chordaria flagelliformis* p. 29
 Dark. Main branches with few or no secondary branches. To 2 ft. (600 mm). See text for similar species. Whole plant.

ACROTHRIX NOVAE-ANGLIAE
 Pale. Main branches with many secondary branches. To 1½ ft. (450 mm). See under Black Whip Weed, p. 29. Whole plant.

Largest branches *shorter* than main axis.

SPINY SOUR WEED *Desmarestia aculeata* p. 31
 Main branches stiff, alternating on main axis; has tufts of fine filaments in spring, short spiny branchlets in summer. To 18 in. (450 mm). Whole plant.

SOFT SOUR WEED *Desmarestia viridis* p. 31
 Main branches soft, opposite each other on main axis at regular intervals and cylindrical throughout. Sour smelling. To 2 ft. (600 mm). Whole plant.

FALSE SOUR WEED *Dictyosiphon foeniculaceus*
 Main branches stiffer but finer than preceding; placed at random on main axis. Chiefly epiphytic on other seaweeds. To 2 ft. (600 mm). See under Soft Sour Weed, p. 31. Whole plant.

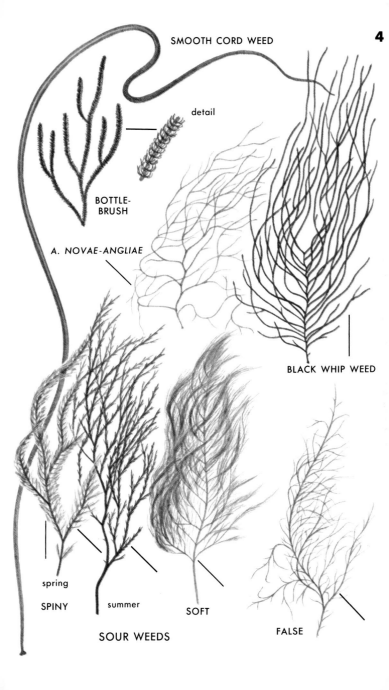

4

SMOOTH CORD WEED

detail

BOTTLE-BRUSH

A. NOVAE-ANGLIAE

BLACK WHIP WEED

spring

SPINY

summer

SOFT

FALSE

SOUR WEEDS

Plate 5
SEVERAL BROWN AND SOME RED SEAWEEDS

Reduced; scale varies. Measurements are maximum recorded length of whole plants; often much smaller. Whole plants or fragments shown as indicated.

SEA POTATO   *Leathesia difformis*   p. 30
  Lumpy, hollow; texture rubbery. To 4 in. (100 mm). Whole plant.

ROUGH TANGLE WEED   *Stilophora rhizodes*
  Branches roughened with fine bumps; pale brown. To 1 ft. (300 mm). See under Slippery Tangle Weed, p. 31. Fragment.

SLIPPERY TANGLE WEED   p. 31
Sphaerotrichia divaricata
  Branches smooth, slimy; end branchlets wide-angled. To 20 in. (500 mm). See text for similar species. Fragment.

BROWN SLIME WEEDS   *Eudesme* species   p. 30
  Soft, gelatinous; light brown to greenish. *E. virescens* shown; to 14 in. (350 mm) with branches ³⁄₈ in. (9 mm) thick. See text for individual species. Fragment.

RED SLIME WEED   *Nemalion multifidum*
  Soft, gelatinous; red to reddish brown. To about 10 in. (250 mm). See under Brown Slime Weeds, p. 30. Fragment.

SAUSAGE WEED   *Scytosiphon lomentaria*   p. 33
  Hollow, unbranched, and constricted at intervals. To 2 ft. (600 mm). Whole plant.

ROUGH HOLLOW WEED   *Asperococcus echinatus*
  Blades hollow, unbranched, varying in width; with gritty surface. To 20 in. (500 mm). See under Sausage Weed, p. 33. Whole plant.

HALOSACCION RAMENTACEUM
  Blades hollow, with short branchlets. An extremely variable species, other variants resemble Dumont's Red Weed (Plate 6). To 1 ft. (300 mm). See under Sausage Weed, p. 33, and Dumont's Red Weed, p. 38. Whole blades.

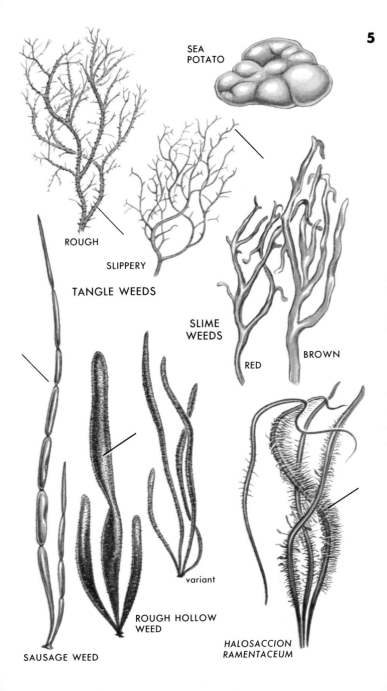

5

SEA POTATO

ROUGH

SLIPPERY

TANGLE WEEDS

SLIME WEEDS

RED BROWN

variant

ROUGH HOLLOW WEED

SAUSAGE WEED

HALOSACCION RAMENTACEUM

Plate 6
LEAFY RED AND BROWN SEAWEEDS

Scale varies. Measurements are maximum recorded length of whole plants; often much smaller. Whole plants or fragments shown as indicated.

FRAYED WEED   *Rhodophyllis dichotoma*
Blade ribless, forking above; margin lined with short bladelets. To 3 in. (75 mm). See under Dulse, p. 44. Whole plant.

DUMONT'S RED WEED   *Dumontia incrassata*   p. 38
Coarsely branching; axis and branches hollow and twisted at ends. To 1 ft. (300 mm). See text for similar species. Whole plant.

SEA OAK   *Phycodrys rubens*   p. 46
Leaflike, deeply lobed, with midrib, lateral ribs, and riblets. To 6 in. (150 mm). See text for similar species. Fragment.

RIBBED LACE WEEDS   *Membranoptera* species
Narrow-lobed with midrib dividing into main lobes but without smaller riblets. To 8 in. (200 mm). See under Sea Oak, p. 46. Fragment.

GRINNELL'S PINK LEAF   *Grinnellia americana*   p. 46
Filmy, elongate blade with fine midrib, no lobes. To 2 ft. (600 mm). Whole frond.

RIBBON WEEDS   *Punctaria* species   p. 32
Blade straplike, ribless, with padlike holdfast. See text for similar species.

Delicate Ribbon Weed, *P. latifolia.* Filmy; base of blade tapers abruptly. To 1 ft. (300 mm). Base of blade.

Coarse Ribbon Weed, *P. plantaginea.* Base of blade tapers gradually. To 1 ft. (300 mm). Whole blade.

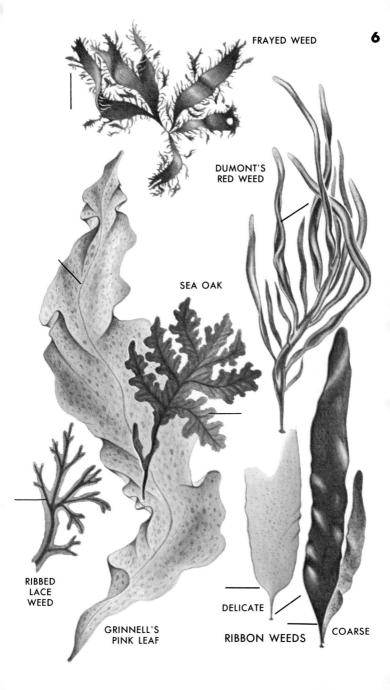

FRAYED WEED

6

DUMONT'S
RED WEED

SEA OAK

RIBBED
LACE
WEED

GRINNELL'S
PINK LEAF

DELICATE

RIBBON WEEDS

COARSE

Plate 7

COMMON RED SEAWEEDS, MOSTLY NORTHERN

Scale varies. Measurements are maximum recorded length of whole plants; often much smaller. Whole plants or fragments shown as indicated.

LACY RED WEED   *Euthora cristata*   p. 39
Blade delicately lacy, without midrib. To 2 in. (50 mm). See text for similar species. Fragment.

WIRE WEED   *Ahnfeltia plicata*   p. 42
In tangles like steel wool, wiry and stiff, with random branching. To 8 in. (200 mm), branches less than $\frac{1}{16}$ in. (1.6 mm) thick. See text for similar species. Fragment.

TWIG WEED   *Polyides caprinus*
More flexible and robust than the preceding, with regular, Y-shaped branches. To 8 in. (200 mm), branches $\frac{1}{16}$ in. (1.6 mm) thick. See under Wire Weed, p. 42. Fragment.

LEAF WEEDS   *Phyllophora* species   p. 42
Thalli 2-parted, consisting of a stalk and ribless, wedge-shaped or forked blades. To 6 in. (150 mm). See text for individual species. Fragments.

LAVER   *Porphyra* species   p. 38
Blade ribless, filmy and nearly transparent, undivided. To 1 ft. (300 mm). See text for individual species. Whole plant.

DULSE   *Rhodymenia palmata*   p. 44
Blade flat and ribless, rubbery, nearly opaque in life; often forking and with marginal bladelets. To 1 ft. (300 mm). See text for similar species. Fragment.

IRISH MOSS   *Chondrus crispus*   p. 43
Blades flat and ribless, profusely forking. Variable in form and color, often showing bluish iridescence underwater. To 7 in. (175 mm). Whole blades and fragments.

TUFTED RED WEED   *Gigartina stellata*   p. 43
Blades flat or partly curled, ribless and covered with short tufts. To 3 in. (75 mm). Whole blade.

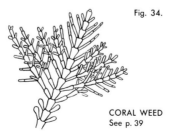

Fig. 34.

CORAL WEED
See p. 39

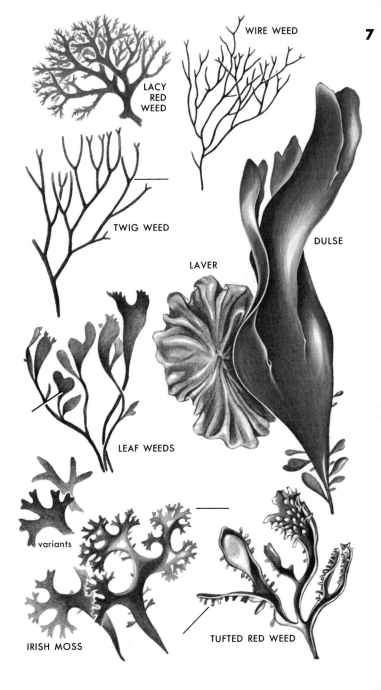

WIRE WEED

LACY RED WEED

TWIG WEED

DULSE

LAVER

LEAF WEEDS

variants

IRISH MOSS

TUFTED RED WEED

Plate 8
COARSELY BUSHY RED SEAWEEDS

Fragments shown. Measurements are maximum recorded length of whole plants; often much smaller. Largest branches of mature plants usually more than $\frac{1}{16}$ in. (1.6 mm) thick; see Plate 9 for more delicate forms. All are quite variable and should be identified in close consultation with the main text accounts.

BRUSHY RED WEED *Cystoclonium purpureum* p. 41
With many fine branchlets on outer parts. Shown also are a pigtail variant with finely coiled outer branchlets, and a faded individual with fruiting bodies (reddish bumps). To 2 ft. (600 mm). See text for similar species.

HOOKED WEED *Hypnea musciformis* p. 41
Sparsely bushy with spiky branchlets; some branches ending in strong hooks. To 1½ ft. (450 mm). See text for similar species.

CHENILLE WEED *Dasya pedicellata* p. 47
Few to many slender branches with a furry coating of fine, short branchlets. To 2 ft. (600 mm) or more.

GRACEFUL RED WEED *Gracilaria foliifera* p. 40
Coarsely bushy with at least parts of some branches flattened. To 1 ft. (300 mm).

AGARDH'S RED WEED *Agardhiella tenera* p. 40
Coarsely bushy with rounded branches tapering at base; fruiting bodies only slightly protuberant (see Fig. 35, below). To 1 ft. (300 mm). See text for similar species.

FALSE AGARDHIELLA *Gracilaria verrucosa*
Similar to the preceding but branches not tapered basally; fruiting bodies more protuberant. To 1 ft. (300 mm). See under Agardh's Red Weed and Graceful Red Weed, both p. 40.

Fig. 35.

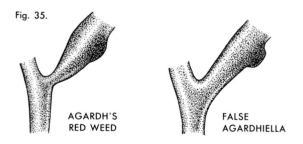

AGARDH'S
RED WEED

FALSE
AGARDHIELLA

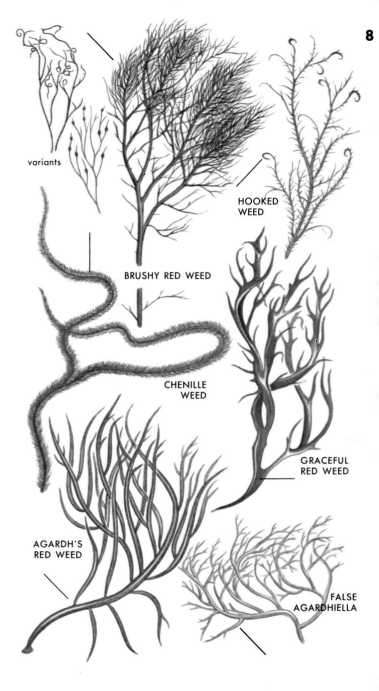

variants

HOOKED WEED

BRUSHY RED WEED

CHENILLE WEED

GRACEFUL RED WEED

AGARDH'S RED WEED

FALSE AGARDHIELLA

Plate 9

FINELY BUSHY RED SEAWEEDS

Fragments shown about life size, details enlarged. Measurements are maximum recorded length of whole plants; often much smaller. Largest branches of mature plants usually less than $\frac{1}{16}$ in. (1.6 mm) thick; see Plate 8 for coarser forms.

PINK BEAD *Griffithsia globulifera* p. 45
Segmented, with segments varying in shape in different parts of plant. Commonly to $2\frac{1}{2}$ in. (62 mm). See text for similar species.

BARREL WEED *Champia parvula* p. 44
Segmented, with segments all about as broad or broader than long, diminishing toward ends; branching less regular than in preceding species. To 3 in. (75 mm).

POD WEEDS *Chondria* species p. 47
Smaller branches short, club- to spindle-shaped. 4–10 in. (100–250 mm). See text for individual species.

BANDED WEEDS *Ceramium* species p. 44
Species vary in form but are clearly banded at least in youngest branches; end branchlets usually form pincers. *C. rubrum* shown; 4–16 in. (100–400 mm).

RED FERN *Ptilota serrata* p. 45
Branches flattened, fernlike, with alternate short and long branchlets. To 6 in. (150 mm). See text for similar species.

TUBED WEEDS *Polysiphonia* species p. 47
Species vary in form but have fine cross and lengthwise partitions usually visible with a hand lens on some part of plant. Commonly to 16 in. (400 mm) tall. *P. harveyi* and *P. denudata* shown. See text for other species and related genera.

SPYRIDIA FILAMENTOSA
Coarser than most tubed weeds (preceding). Distinctive cellular structure is visible with a good hand lens. Smallest branches appear banded but lack pincer arrangement. To 1 ft. (300 mm). See under Tubed Weeds, p. 47.

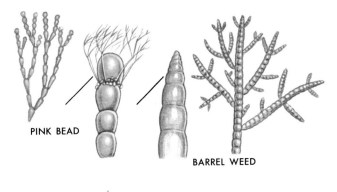

9

PINK BEAD

BARREL WEED

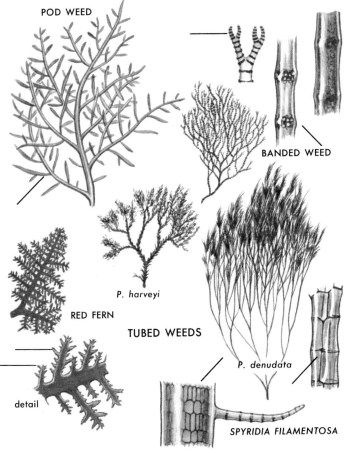

POD WEED

BANDED WEED

RED FERN

P. harveyi

TUBED WEEDS

detail

P. denudata

SPYRIDIA FILAMENTOSA

Plate 10
SPONGES AND OTHER SESSILE ANIMALS

Scale varies. Measurements are maximum recorded height or width, whichever is greater. Note, however, that adjoining sponge colonies may be hard to recognize as separate masses. Positive identification of some animals requires study of microscopic spicules; see p. 64.

ORGAN-PIPE SPONGES   *Leucosolenia* species   p. 65
   Tubular or vaselike, usually branching. To $\frac{3}{8}$ in. (9 mm) tall.
VASE SPONGES   *Scypha* species
   Unbranched; opening surrounded by a fringe of spicules. To $\frac{1}{8}$ in. (3 mm) tall. See under Organ-pipe Sponges, p. 65.
EGG SPONGE   *Mycalecarmia ovulum*   p. 66
   Forms an egg-shaped "knot" on seaweed, bryozoan, or hydroid stems. To $\frac{5}{8}$ in. (16 mm) long.
BORING SPONGES   *Cliona* species   p. 69
   Bores holes in mollusk shells, sometimes overgrowing host completely. *C. celata* shown; largest pores $\frac{3}{16}$ in. (5 mm). See text for other species.
LOOSANOFF'S HALICLONA   *Haliclona loosanoffi*   p. 66
   Yellow to gold or pinkish. Oscula on raised chimneys. Mainly south of Cape Cod. To 3 in. (75 mm) wide. See text for other species.
BOWERBANK'S HALICHONDRIA   p. 67
Halichondria bowerbanki
   Usually yellow to gold but varies to brown, cinnamon, or olive. Crusts raised in irregular masses. To 3 in. (75 mm) tall. See text for similar species.
CRUMB OF BREAD SPONGE   p. 67
Halichondria panicea
   Color varies. Resembles Loosanoff's Haliclona (above) but has larger spicules. Mainly north of Cape Cod. Colonies can extend over several feet. See text for similar species.
RUBBERY BRYOZOANS   *Alcyonidium* species   p. 111
   Fleshy irregular lobes with zooids; surface finely puckered. No spicules. To 1 ft. (300 mm) or more. *A. verrilli* shown; see text for other species.
DEAD MAN'S FINGERS   *Alcyonium digitatum*   p. 92
   Fleshy fingerlike lobes embedded with tiny whitish zooids. Has distinct internal spicules (see text). To 8 in. (200 mm).
SANDY-LOBED AMAROUCIUM   p. 268
Amaroucium pellucidum
   Colonies in cauliflowerlike, sand-coated lobes. To 8 in. (200 mm). See text for similar species.
SEA PORK   *Amaroucium stellatum*   p. 268
   Colonies are hard rubbery lumps with zooids in circular systems. See text for similar species. To 1 ft. (300 mm).
WHITE CRUSTS   *Didemnum* species   p. 267
   Colonies are tough whitish crusts with internal spicules. To 4 in. (100 mm).
GOLDEN STAR TUNICATE   *Botryllus schlosseri*   p. 267
   Colonies are soft, flat patches or lobes. Color varies. No spicules. To 4 in. (100 mm).

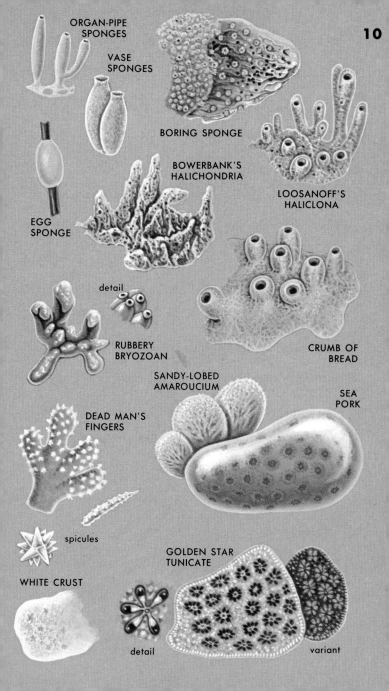

10

ORGAN-PIPE SPONGES

VASE SPONGES

BORING SPONGE

EGG SPONGE

BOWERBANK'S HALICHONDRIA

LOOSANOFF'S HALICLONA

detail

RUBBERY BRYOZOAN

CRUMB OF BREAD

DEAD MAN'S FINGERS

SANDY-LOBED AMAROUCIUM

SEA PORK

spicules

WHITE CRUST

GOLDEN STAR TUNICATE

detail

variant

Plate 11
LARGER SPONGES, OCTOCORALS

Scale varies. Measurements are maximum recorded height or width, whichever is greater. Larger pores are called *oscula*. Positive identification of some sponges requires study of microscopic spicules (see p. 64).

FIG SPONGE   *Suberites ficus*   p. 68
Surface smooth, shiny, liverlike. Oscula inconspicuous. To 14 in. (350 mm) tall.

FINGER SPONGE   *Haliclona oculata*   p. 65
Oscula conspicuous. Branches usually rounded, fingerlike. Yellowish to gray-brown. To 18 in. (450 mm) tall. See text for similar species.

PURPLE SPONGE   *Haliclona permollis*   p. 66
Purple, with raised oscula. To 4 in. (100 mm) or more wide.

SEA WHIP   *Leptogorgia virgulata*   p. 93
A slender whiplike octocoral. Color varies, purple to orange-yellow, tan, or red. To 3 ft. (900 mm) tall. See text for similar species.

PALMATE SPONGES   *Isodictya* species
Base and branches usually broad and thick. Yellowish to dark reddish. To 18 in. (450 mm) tall. See under Red Beard Sponge, p. 68.

RED BEARD SPONGE   *Microciona prolifera*   p. 68
Red to orange. Colony encrusting when young, raised in irregular lobes when mature. To 8 in. (200 mm) tall.

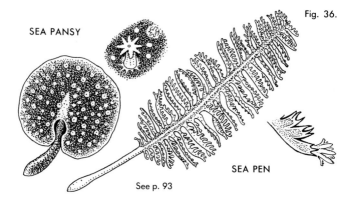

Fig. 36.

SEA PANSY

SEA PEN

See p. 93

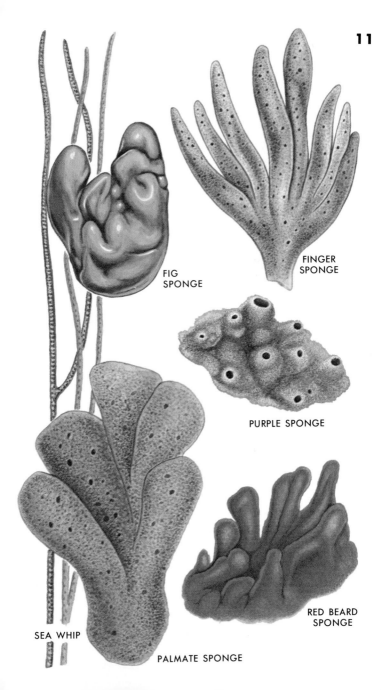

11

FIG SPONGE

FINGER SPONGE

PURPLE SPONGE

RED BEARD SPONGE

SEA WHIP

PALMATE SPONGE

Plate 12

SEA ANEMONES

Scale varies. Measurements are maximum recorded height or width of column, whichever is greater. Make identifications in close consultation with text.

FRILLED ANEMONE *Metridium senile* p. 97
Tentacles fine, numerous; disk lobed. To 4 in. (100 mm) tall.

GHOST ANEMONE *Diadumene leucolena* p. 98
Pale, translucent. To 1½ in. (38 mm) tall.

STRIPED ANEMONE *Haliplanella luciae* p. 97
Column dark green with cream-colored to red stripes. To ¾ in. (19 mm) tall.

SILVER-SPOTTED ANEMONE *Bunodactis stella* p. 97
Color varies; an opaque silver-white spot at base of most tentacles. Column has sticky bumps. Often found buried up to disk in crevices or sandy pools. To 2 in. (50 mm) wide.

NORTHERN RED ANEMONE *Tealia felina* p. 96
Color varies; tentacles usually banded. Column smooth, completely contractile. To 3 in. (75 mm) wide, larger in deep water.

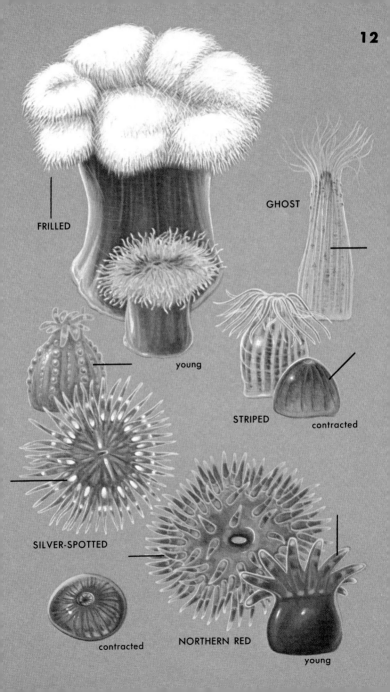

12

FRILLED

GHOST

young

STRIPED

contracted

SILVER-SPOTTED

contracted

NORTHERN RED

young

Plate 13

HYDROIDS AND ENTOPROCTS

Colony form shown in silhouette; details of individual zooids enlarged. Measurements are maximum recorded height of whole colony or zooid as indicated. *Gonophores* are marked "g." *Hydranth* not protected by a *hydrotheca,* but see bougainvillia hydroids (below). For species with a hydrotheca see Plate 14.

TUBULARIAN HYDROIDS   p. 75
Tubularia and related genera
  Tentacles in separate groups; 1 whorl of long ones below; 1 or more whorls of short ones above. Zooids long-stemmed; to 6 in. (150 mm). **T. crocea** shown. See text for other tubularian hydroids and related species.

CLUB HYDROID   *Clava leptostyla*   p. 76
  Tentacles 20–30; filiform and scattered on the hydranth. Zooids on unbranched stems; to $\frac{3}{8}$ in. (9 mm). See text for similar species.

CLAPPER HYDROID   *Sarsia tubulosa*   p. 76
  Tentacles 10–20; capitate (knobbed) and scattered on the hydranth. Zooids to $\frac{3}{4}$ in. (19 mm). See text for similar species.

FRESHWATER HYDROID
Cordylophora caspia
  Hydranth similar to Club Hydroid (above), but stem annulated (ringed) and branched. Colony to $2\frac{3}{8}$ in. (59 mm). See under Club Hydroid, p. 76.

BOUGAINVILLIA HYDROIDS   p. 78
Bougainvillia and related genera
  Periderm (stem wall) forms a cuplike *pseudohydrotheca* at base of hydranth. Tentacles filiform.
  B. carolinensis. Often has stems bound together in bundles (fascicled). Colony to 1 ft. (300 mm).
  Garveia species. Stems *not* fascicled. To 3 in. (75 mm). See text for other differences and related species.

FEATHER HYDROID   *Pennaria tiarella*   p. 76
  1 whorl of filiform tentacles below, 4–5 whorls of capitate (knobbed) ones on the hydranth. Colony to 6 in. (150 mm).

ENTOPROCTS   *Barentsia and Pedicellina* species   p. 110
  Zooids tiny, to $\frac{3}{8}$ in. (9 mm); stems unbranched.

STICK HYDROIDS   *Eudendrium* species   p. 79
  Similar to bougainvillia hydroids (above), but periderm doesn't form a cup. Colony to 6 in. (150 mm). **E. carneum** and **E. ramosum** shown. See text for similar species.

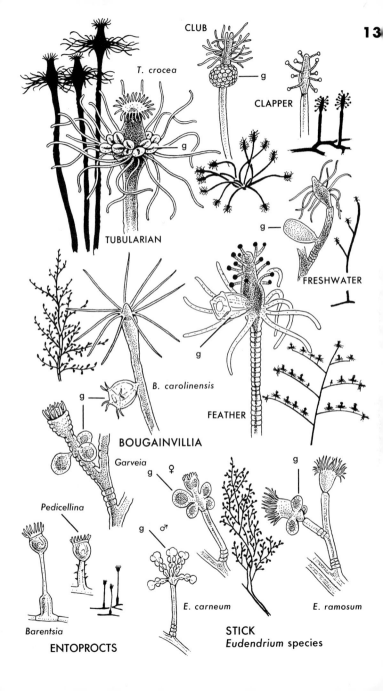

13

CLUB

T. crocea

g

CLAPPER

g

TUBULARIAN

FRESHWATER

g

B. carolinensis

g

FEATHER

BOUGAINVILLIA

g — *Garveia*

g ♀

g ♂

Pedicellina

Barentsia

ENTOPROCTS

E. carneum

g

E. ramosum

STICK
Eudendrium species

Plate 14

HYDROIDS

Colony form shown in silhouette; details of individual zooids enlarged. Measurements are maximum recorded height of whole colony or zooid as indicated. *Gonophores* (encapsuled in rigid *gonothecae*) are marked "g." *Hydranth* retracts into a *hydrotheca;* for hydroids without hydrothecae or gonothecae see Plate 13.

CAMPANULARIAN HYDROIDS p. 80
Campanularia and related genera
  Hydrothecae cuplike, with rim smooth or toothed. Colony to 1 ft. (300 mm). See text for genera and species.

LOVENELLID HYDROIDS p. 81
Lovenella and related genera
  Hydrothecae have a cone- or wedge-shaped lid or operculum. ***Lovenella*** and ***Opercularella*** shown. Colony to 2 in. (50 mm). See text for other genera.

HALECIUM HYDROIDS *Halecium* species p. 84
  Hydrothecae short, with flared or trumpetlike opening. Stems and branches divided by nodes but usually not annulated (ringed). 3 species shown: ***H. gracile, H. tenellum,*** and ***H. beani.*** Colony to 3 in. (75 mm).

PLUMED HYDROID *Schizotricha tenella* p. 85
  Hydrothecae are short stemless cups set above one edge of stem or branch. Nematophores present. Colony to 4 in. (100 mm). See text for similar species.

AGLAOPHENIA species
  Similar to preceding, but hydrothecae rims are toothed. Found on Gulfweed. Colony to ½ in. (12 mm). See under Plumed Hydroid, p. 85.

GARLAND HYDROIDS p. 84
Sertularia and related genera
  Hydrothecae are short bent tubes on opposite sides of branches or stems.
  Abietinaria species. Hydrothecae bottle-shaped in alternate to nearly opposite pairs. Colony to 1 ft. (300 mm).
  Sertularia argentea. Hydrothecae alternate. Colony to 1 ft. (300 mm).
  Sertularia cornicina. Hydrothecae in opposite pairs. Colony to ½ in. (12 mm), rarely to 2 in. (50 mm).
  Sertularia pumila and ***Diphasia*** species. Similar to preceding, but note differences in gonothecae. *S. pumila* colony to 2 in. (50 mm); *Diphasia* species to 4 in. (100 mm).

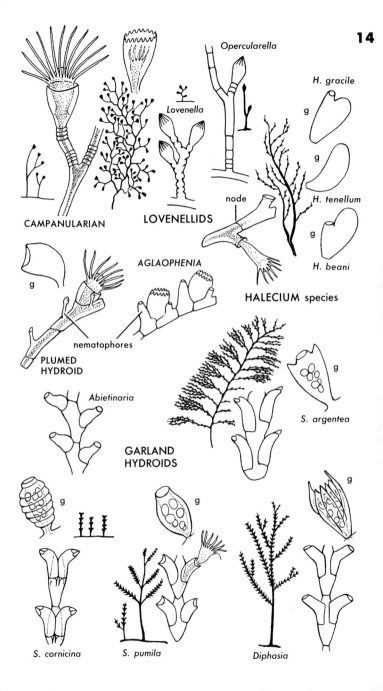

14

CAMPANULARIAN

Opercularella

Lovenella

LOVENELLIDS

node

H. gracile

g

g

H. tenellum

g

H. beani

HALECIUM species

g

PLUMED HYDROID

nematophores

AGLAOPHENIA

Abietinaria

GARLAND HYDROIDS

g

S. argentea

g

g

g

S. cornicina

S. pumila

Diphasia

Plate 15

BUSHY BRYOZOANS

Colony form shown in outline; details of individual zooecia enlarged. Measurements are maximum recorded height of whole colony; although individual zooecia are usually less than $\frac{1}{50}$ in. (0.5 mm) long, they can easily be seen with a hand lens. Nodes indicated by "n."

1. **SHELLED BRYOZOAN**   *Eucratea loricata*   p. 115
    Zooecia paired, back to back. Colony to 10 in. (250 mm).
2. *BICELLARIELLA CILIATA*
    Zooecia side by side, spiny. Colony whitish, feathery; to 1 in. (25 mm). See under Bushy Bugula, p. 116.
3. **BUSHY BUGULA**   *Bugula turrita*   p. 116
    Colony bushy, yellowish to yellow-orange; to 1 ft. (300 mm). See text for similar species.
4. *DENDROBEANIA MURRAYANA*
    Individual zooecia similar to preceding, but opening spiny. Colony leafy; to $1\frac{1}{2}$ in. (38 mm). See under Fan Bugula, p. 117.
5. **LEAFY BRYOZOAN**   *Flustra foliacea*   p. 112
    Colony a flat leafy frond; creamy to pale brown. To 4 in. (100 mm) or more.
6. **BRISTLY BRYOZOAN**   *Flustrellidra hispida*   p. 112
    Colony a whiskery brownish swelling on seaweed stems. $\frac{4}{5}$–2 in. (20–50 mm).
7. **SHIELDED BRYOZOAN**   *Scrupocellaria scabra*   p. 117
    Each zooecium opening protected by a flat shield. Colony twiggy; to $\frac{5}{8}$ in. (16 mm). See text for similar species.
8. *TRICELLARIA TERNATA*
    Zooecia similar to preceding but shields smaller. See under Shielded Bryozoan, p. 117.
    SPIRAL BRYOZOANS   *Amathia* species   p. 113
    Zooecia in double file, wound around stems and branches.
9. *A. convoluta* has zooecia extending almost entire distance between nodes. Colony to 6 in. (150 mm).
10. *A. vidovici* has zooecia extending less than $\frac{1}{2}$ the distance between nodes. Colony to 2 in. (50 mm).
11. **JOINTED-TUBE BRYOZOANS**   *Crisia* species   p. 115
    Zooecia tubular, with 1 or more pairs between nodes. Colony to $\frac{3}{4}$ in. (19 mm). *C. eburnea* shown. See text for other species.
12. *CABEREA ELLISII*
    Zooecia in 2–4 rows, some with whiplike *vibraculae*. See under Bushy Bugula, p. 116.
    PINNATE BRYOZOANS   *Aeverrillia* species   p. 114
    Zooecia paired, on opposite sides of slender branches. Colony 2–$2\frac{4}{5}$ in. (50–70 mm).
13. *A. setigera* has tiny hook at base of each zooecium.
14. *A. armata* does not.
15. **PANPIPE BRYOZOANS**   p. 114
    Tubulipora and related genera
    Zooecia tubular, in crusts or erect antlerlike colonies; to 1 in. (25 mm) or more. *Idmonea atlantica* shown. See text for other species.

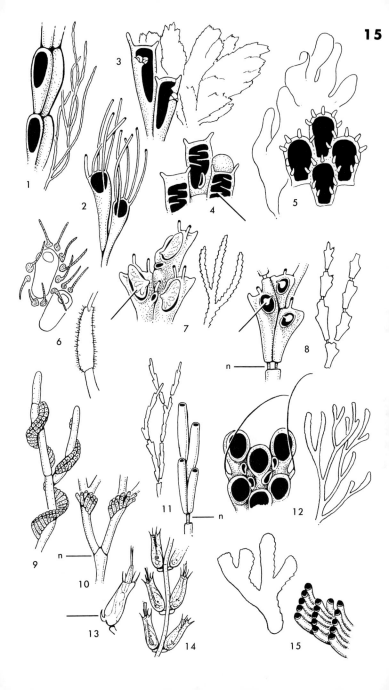

Plate 16

ENCRUSTING BRYOZOANS

Colonies form flat to raised, nodular crusts. Individual zooecia (shown on plate) are visible with a hand lens but are usually less than $\frac{1}{50}$ in. (0.5 mm) long. Avicularia marked "a"; ooecia, "o"; see p. 111.

1-5. **RED CRUSTS** p. 118
    Cryptosula and related genera
        Colonies usually orange to red, brown, or purple. (1) ***Cryptosula pallasiana*** has broad-based zooecia openings, with a tooth on each side near base. (2) ***Schizoporella unicornis,*** (3) ***Stephanosella*** species, (4) ***Stomachetosella sinuosa,*** and (5) ***Schizomavella auriculata*** have openings round or broadly oval with a central notch at bottom. See text.

  6. **MICROPORE CRUST**   *Microporella ciliata*   p. 119
        Opening archlike, with a raised pore below it. Usually silvery white.

  7. **GLASSY HIPPOTHOA**   *Hippothoa hyalina*   p. 118
        Zooecia glassy, without pores. Opening round, with a notch at bottom. See text for similar species.

8-10. **BEAKED CRUSTS** p. 119
    Umbonula and other genera
        Opening has a beak or tooth over lower margin. Colonies usually whitish to gray. A difficult and variable group: (8) ***Cribrilina punctata*** (2 variants shown), (9) ***Umbonula arctica,*** (10) ***Escharella immersa.*** See text.

11-14. **SMITTINID CRUSTS** p. 119
    Smittina and related genera
        Zooecia opening has a tooth inside lower margin, sometimes hidden by a beak or swelling. Colonies usually whitish to yellowish, pink, or gray. (1) ***Rhamphostomelia*** species, (12) ***Smittina*** species, (13) ***Parasmittina*** species, and (14) ***Porella*** species. See text.

15-21. **LACY CRUSTS** p. 115
    Membranipora and related genera
        Colonies form lacy crusts. Zooecia box- or coffin-like, with or without spines; frontal wall wholly or partly membranous. A variable and difficult group: (15) ***Membranipora tenuis,*** (16) ***Membranipora tuberculata,*** (17) ***Conopeum truitti,*** (18) ***Electra pilosa,*** (19) ***Electra crustulenta,*** (20) ***Tegella unicornis,*** and (21) ***Callopora craticula.*** See text.

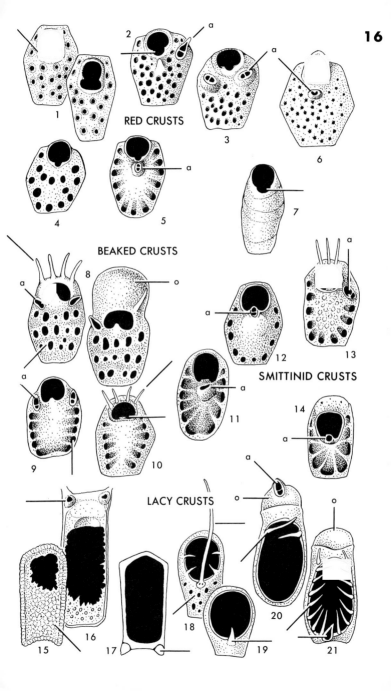

16

RED CRUSTS

BEAKED CRUSTS

SMITTINID CRUSTS

LACY CRUSTS

Plate 17
SEA SQUIRTS, GOOSE BARNACLES, AND SESSILE JELLYFISH

Scale varies. Measurements are maximum recorded size.

SEA VASE   *Ciona intestinalis*   p. 270
  5–7 muscle bands visible on each side. To 2½ in. (62 mm).

SEA PEACH   *Halocynthia pyriformis*   p. 271
  Surface clean, yellowish-white to orange-red. Siphons 4-lobed.
  To 2½ in. (62 mm).

SEA GRAPES   *Molgula* species   p. 272
  1 siphon 4-lobed, other 6-lobed. Often encrusted with debris.
  Shown are ***M. citrina,*** to ⁵⁄₁₆ in. (8 mm), and ***M. manhattensis,***
  to 1⅜ in. (34 mm). See text for other species.

ROUGH SEA SQUIRT   *Styela partita*   p. 271
  Rough-skinned and gristly; siphons 4-lobed, sometimes striped.
  See text for a related southern species. To 1⅛ in. (28 mm).

BLOOD DROP SEA SQUIRT   *Dendrodoa carnea*   p. 270
  Resembles a drop of blood; siphons low, 4-lobed. To ⅜ in.
  (9 mm). See text for a related northern species.

CACTUS SEA SQUIRT   *Boltenia echinata*   p. 271
  Spiny. To ½ in. (12 mm).

STALKED SEA SQUIRT   *Boltenia ovifera*   p. 271
  Stalk is 2–4 times longer than body. To 3 in. (75 mm).

STALKED JELLYFISH   *Haliclystus auricula*   p. 91
  Top divided into 8 lobes with clusters of tentacles at tip of each
  lobe; base a narrow stalk. To 1¼ in. (31 mm) tall. See text for
  similar species.

STRIPED GOOSE BARNACLE   p. 217
Conchoderma virgatum
  Shells vestigial; body striped. To 3 in. (75 mm).

EARED GOOSE BARNACLE   *Conchoderma auritum*
  Shells vestigial; body dark colored. Top with earlike lobes. To
  6 in. (150 mm). See under Striped Goose Barnacle, p. 217.

PELAGIC GOOSE BARNACLES   *Lepas* species   p. 217
  Shells well-developed. *L. anatifera* shown; to 1¾ in. (44 mm).
  See text for similar species.

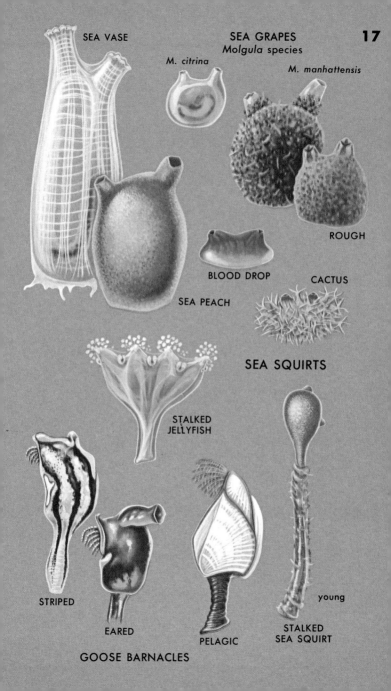

SEA VASE

SEA GRAPES
Molgula species

M. citrina

M. manhattensis

ROUGH

BLOOD DROP

CACTUS

SEA PEACH

SEA SQUIRTS

STALKED
JELLYFISH

STRIPED

EARED

PELAGIC

young

STALKED
SEA SQUIRT

GOOSE BARNACLES

17

Plate 18

ACORN BARNACLES

Scale varies. Measurements are maximum recorded height or base width, whichever is greater. Make identifications in close consultation with text. See p. 214 for definition of terms.

LITTLE GRAY BARNACLE *Chthamalus fragilis* p. 215
Dingy gray, fragile. Basis (base) membranous; side plates overlap both end plates. Mainly a southern species, found in upper intertidal zone. To ⅜ in. (9 mm).

NORTHERN ROCK BARNACLE p. 215
Balanus balanoides
Common intertidal barnacle north of Cape May in nearly undiluted seawater. Basis (base) membranous; one end plate overlaps side plates. To 1 in. (25 mm).

CRENATE BARNACLE *Balanus crenatus* p. 216
Radii narrow. Plate walls have 1 groove opposite each tube. A northern, mainly subtidal species. To 1 in. (25 mm).

ROUGH BARNACLE *Balanus balanus*
Radii wide. Plate walls have multiple grooves (compare with preceding species). Tough and craggy; adheres very strongly to substratum. Northern, mainly subtidal. To 2 in. (50 mm). See under Crenate Barnacle, p. 216.

STRIPED BARNACLE *Balanus amphitrite*
Usually striped gray and white in North, purple and white south of Cape Hatteras; radii wide. To ⅜ in. (9 mm). See under Ivory Barnacle, p. 215.

BAY BARNACLE *Balanus improvisus*
Radii narrow. Brackish to almost fresh water. To ½ in. (12 mm). See under Ivory Barnacle, p. 215.

IVORY BARNACLE *Balanus eburneus* p. 215
Smooth and ivory white; scuta grooved lengthwise, radii fairly wide. Tergum deeply notched. Estuarine. To 1 in. (25 mm).

TURTLE BARNACLE *Chelonibia testudinaria*
Radii distinct, notched or grooved. Found on sea turtles. To 2 in. (50 mm). See under Crab Barnacle, p. 216, for similar species.

CRAB BARNACLE *Chelonibia patula* p. 216
Found on crabs southward. Terga and scuta smaller than opening. To ¾ in. (19 mm).

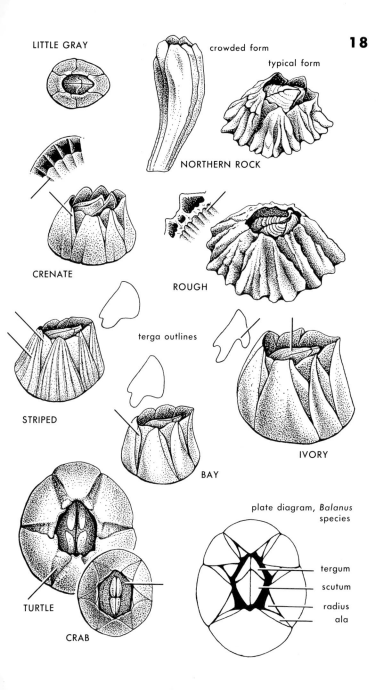

18

LITTLE GRAY

crowded form

typical form

NORTHERN ROCK

CRENATE

ROUGH

STRIPED

terga outlines

IVORY

BAY

TURTLE

CRAB

plate diagram, *Balanus* species

tergum

scutum

radius

ala

Plate 19

SLIPPER SHELLS, LIMPETS, AND CHITONS

Measurements are maximum recorded length.

COMMON SLIPPER SHELL   *Crepidula fornicata*   p. 128
Platform covers about ½ of aperture, edge sinuous. Often found in stacks. To 1½ in. (38 mm).

CONVEX SLIPPER SHELL   *Crepidula convexa*
Platform covers about ⅓ of aperture, edge concave. To ½ in. (12 mm). See under Common Slipper Shell, p. 128.

FLAT SLIPPER SHELL   *Crepidula plana*
Pure white; usually flat, or curved to fit inside larger snail shells. To 1 in. (25 mm). See under Common Slipper Shell, p. 128.

TORTOISESHELL LIMPET   *Acmaea testudinalis*   p. 125
A simple flattened cone, inside and out; markings and shape vary. Commonly to 1 in. (25 mm). See text for similar species.

CUP-AND-SAUCER LIMPET   p. 129
Crucibulum striatum
A flattened cone with apex twisted to one side and a tongue-like cup inside. To 1 in. (25 mm).

RED CHITON   *Ischnochiton ruber*   p. 123
Valves reddish, smooth; girdle minutely scaly. Front slope of head valve curved. To 1 in. (25 mm). See text for similar species.

WHITE CHITON   *Ischnochiton albus*
Valves whitish; girdle minutely scaly. Front slope of head valve nearly straight. To ½ in. (12 mm). See under Red Chiton, p. 123.

BEE CHITON   *Chaetopleura apiculata*   p. 123
Valves whitish, with clearly defined central and lateral areas; girdle has minute scales and short hairs. To ¾ in. (19 mm).

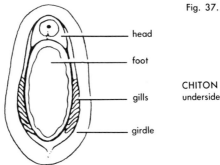

Fig. 37.

head

foot

gills

girdle

CHITON
underside

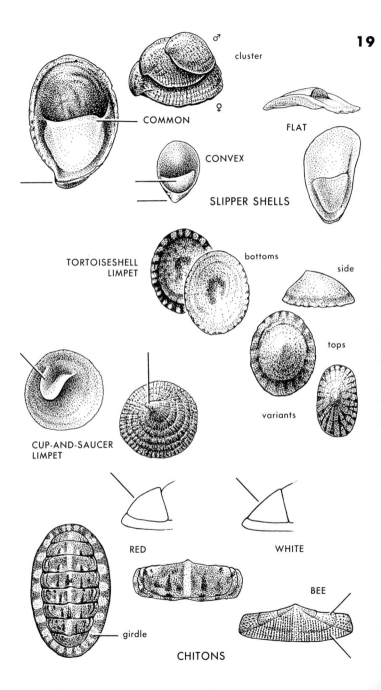

19

cluster

♂

♀

COMMON

CONVEX

FLAT

SLIPPER SHELLS

TORTOISESHELL LIMPET

bottoms

side

tops

variants

CUP-AND-SAUCER LIMPET

RED

WHITE

BEE

girdle

CHITONS

Plate 20
INTERTIDAL AND SHALLOW-WATER SNAILS

Scale varies. Measurements are maximum recorded length.

COMMON PERIWINKLE   *Littorina littorea*   p. 126
Spire blunt, columella pale. To $1\frac{1}{4}$ in. (31 mm).

GULF PERIWINKLE   *Littorina irrorata*   p. 126
Spire pointed, columella dark; has spiral rows of dark flecks. To 1 in. (25 mm).

ROUGH PERIWINKLE   *Littorina saxatilis*
Sutures deeply cut, whorls grooved. To $\frac{5}{8}$ in. (16 mm). See under Common Periwinkle, p. 126.

SMOOTH PERIWINKLE   *Littorina obtusata*   p. 126
Spire very low, whorls smooth. Color variable. To $\frac{1}{2}$ in. (12 mm).

CHINK SHELL   *Lacuna vincta*   p. 125
Thin, translucent; slitlike groove on columella. To $\frac{1}{2}$ in. (12 mm).

DOGWINKLE   *Thais lapillus*   p. 131
Variable color and form. To $1\frac{1}{2}$ in. (38 mm). See text for similar species.

MUD DOG WHELK   *Nassarius obsoletus*   p. 131
Aperture and columella dark; apex eroded. To 1 in. (25 mm).

MOTTLED DOG WHELK   *Nassarius vibex*
Aperture and columella pale; body whorl and anterior canal separated by sharp groove. To $\frac{1}{2}$ in. (12 mm). See under Mud Dog Whelk, p. 131.

NEW ENGLAND DOG WHELK   *Nassarius trivittatus*
Whorls beaded, sutures channeled. Sharp groove as in Mottled Dog Whelk. To $\frac{3}{4}$ in. (19 mm). See under Mud Dog Whelk, p. 131.

OYSTER DRILL   *Urosalpinx cinerea*   p. 130
Anterior canal open, flaring. Commonly to 1 in. (25 mm).

THICK-LIPPED OYSTER DRILL   *Eupleura caudata*
Anterior canal tubular. To $\frac{3}{4}$ in. (19 mm). See under Oyster Drill, p. 130.

SALT-MARSH SNAIL   *Melampus bidentatus*   p. 135
Top-shaped, fragile. To $\frac{1}{2}$ in. (12 mm).

OVAL MARSH SNAIL   *Ovatella myosotis*
Columella distinctly toothed. To $\frac{1}{4}$ in. (6 mm). See under Salt-marsh Snail, p. 135.

SOLITARY GLASSY BUBBLE   p. 134
Haminoea solitaria
No protruding spire. To $\frac{1}{2}$ in. (12 mm). See text for similar species.

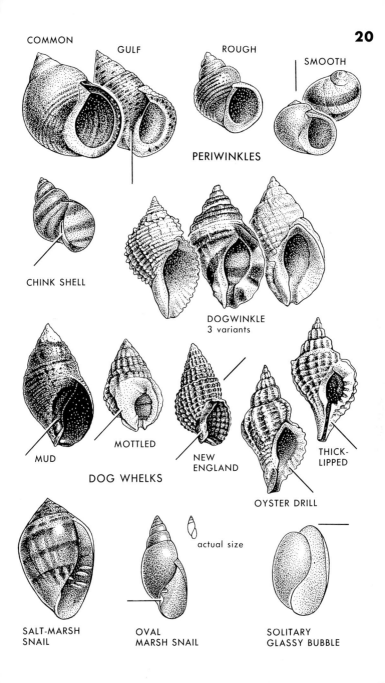

20

COMMON

GULF

ROUGH

SMOOTH

PERIWINKLES

CHINK SHELL

DOGWINKLE
3 variants

MUD

MOTTLED

NEW
ENGLAND

THICK-
LIPPED

DOG WHELKS

OYSTER DRILL

SALT-MARSH
SNAIL

OVAL
MARSH SNAIL

actual size

SOLITARY
GLASSY BUBBLE

Plate 21

VERY SMALL SNAILS

Measurements are maximum recorded length or height, whichever is greater. Unless otherwise indicated, see Additional Small Gastropods, p. 135, for text accounts.

WOOD SCREW SHELL   *Seila adamsi*
Like a fine wood screw, with 30 or more spiral threads. To $\frac{1}{2}$ in. (12 mm).

CAECUMS   *Caecum* species
Tubular or slightly curved. **Beautiful Caecum,** *C. pulchellum,* shown; to $\frac{1}{16}$ in. (1.6 mm). See text for other species.

PEARLY TOP SHELLS   *Margarites* species
Like small periwinkles or moon shells but have a pearly iridescence inside; umbilicus open. **Greenland Top Shell,** *M. groenlandicus,* shown; to $\frac{5}{16}$ in. (8 mm). See text for other species.

PYRAMID SHELLS

  Turbonilles, *Turbonilla* species. A slender cone, usually with axial ribbing. Undamaged tip has a crosswise nuclear whorl; columella without folds. Usually $\frac{1}{4}$ in. (6 mm). 20 known species.
  Odostomes, *Odostomia* species. Cone variable, narrow to broad; columella has 1 fold. Usually $\frac{1}{8}$ in. (3 mm). Numerous species.

NORTHERN HAIRY-KEELED SNAIL   *Trichotropis borealis*
Aperture broad, open. Fresh shell has hairy periostracum. To $\frac{1}{2}$ in. (12 mm). See under Dogwinkle, p. 131.

DOVE SHELLS   *Anachis* species
Moderately broad cone with axial folds or ribs. To $\frac{1}{2}$ in. (12 mm). **Greedy Dove Shell,** *A. avara,* shown; see text for other species.

CRESCENT MITRELLA   *Mitrella lunata*
Smooth, miter-shaped. Translucent; markings most visible in fresh, wet shells. To $\frac{1}{4}$ in. (6 mm).

SWAMP HYDROBIA   *Hydrobia minuta*
Smooth, translucent, yellowish brown. Sutures deeply impressed. To $\frac{1}{8}$ in. (3 mm).

WENTLETRAPS   *Epitonium* species   p. 128
Spire tall, with 8–20 vanelike riblets. To $\frac{3}{4}$ in. (19 mm). **Lined Wentletrap,** *E. rupicola,* shown. Numerous species; see text.

BLACK TRIPHORA   *Triphora nigrocincta*
Sinistral. Whorls beaded. To $\frac{1}{4}$ in. (6 mm).

BITTIUMS   *Bittium* species   p. 127
Gray to blackish, crosshatched with spiral lines and axial riblets. To $\frac{1}{4}$ in. (6 mm). Shown are **Variable Bittium,** *B. varium,* which usually has a rib (*varix*) on back of body whorl, and **Alternate Bittium,** *B. alternatum,* which does not.

GREEN'S CERITH   *Cerithiopsis greeni*
Miter-shaped with strongly beaded whorls. Compare aperture with those of preceding 2 species. To $\frac{3}{16}$ in. (5 mm).

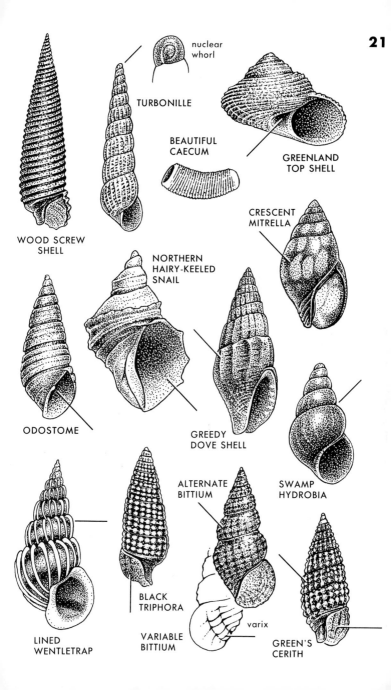

21

WOOD SCREW SHELL

TURBONILLE

nuclear whorl

BEAUTIFUL CAECUM

GREENLAND TOP SHELL

CRESCENT MITRELLA

NORTHERN HAIRY-KEELED SNAIL

ODOSTOME

GREEDY DOVE SHELL

SWAMP HYDROBIA

LINED WENTLETRAP

BLACK TRIPHORA

ALTERNATE BITTIUM

VARIABLE BITTIUM

varix

GREEN'S CERITH

Plate 22

LARGER BEACH SNAILS

Reduced; scale varies. Measurements are maximum recorded length or height, whichever is greater.

CHANNELED WHELK   *Busycon canaliculatum*   p. 133
Sutures deeply channeled. To 7 in. (175 mm). See text for similar species.

KNOBBED WHELK   *Busycon carica*
Sutures not channeled; body whorl and spire with knobs. To 9 in. (225 mm). See under Channeled Whelk, p. 133.

TEN-RIDGED WHELK   *Neptunea decemcostata*   p. 133
Whitish, with strong reddish-brown spiral cords. To 4 in. (100 mm).

STIMPSON'S WHELK   *Colus stimpsoni*
Spindle-shaped; anterior canal equals $\frac{1}{2}$ shell length. To 5 in. (125 mm). See Colus Whelks, p. 132.

EAR SHELL   *Sinum perspectivum*   p. 130
Thin, flat, milky white. To $1\frac{1}{2}$ in. (38 mm).

COMMON AUGER   *Terebra dislocata*   p. 134
Screw-shaped with distinct anterior canal. To $1\frac{3}{4}$ in. (44 mm). See text for similar species.

WAVED WHELK   *Buccinum undatum*   p. 132
Has both axial ribs and spiral chords; aperture wide, flaring. To 4 in. (100 mm), but usually smaller.

LOBED MOON SHELL   *Polinices duplicatus*   p. 129
Umbilicus almost completely closed by callus. To 3 in. (75 mm). See text for similar species.

NORTHERN MOON SHELL   *Lunatia heros*   p. 129
Umbilicus open; shell grayish, not conspicuously marked. To 4 in. (100 mm). See text for similar species.

SPOTTED MOON SHELL   *Lunatia triseriata*
Usually banded with dark spots. To $\frac{7}{8}$ in. (22 mm). See under Northern Moon Shell, p. 129.

SCOTCH BONNET   *Phalium granulatum*   p. 130
Fine spiral and axial grooves form checkerboard or beaded pattern; columella (inner lip) has distinct shield. To 4 in. (100 mm).

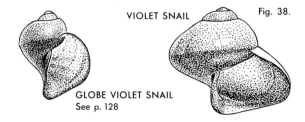

VIOLET SNAIL   Fig. 38.

GLOBE VIOLET SNAIL
See p. 128

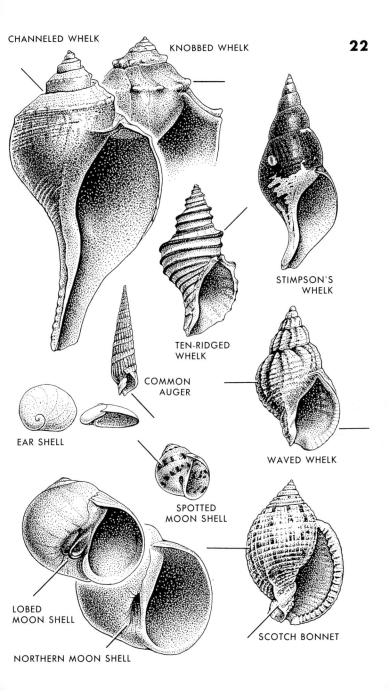

22

CHANNELED WHELK

KNOBBED WHELK

STIMPSON'S WHELK

TEN-RIDGED WHELK

COMMON AUGER

EAR SHELL

WAVED WHELK

SPOTTED MOON SHELL

LOBED MOON SHELL

NORTHERN MOON SHELL

SCOTCH BONNET

Plate 23

YOLDIAS, SPOON SHELLS, AND RELATED BIVALVES

Scale varies. Measurements are maximum recorded length.

YOLDIAS   *Yoldia* species   p. 144
    Ax- or wedge-shaped; hinge has filelike (taxodont) teeth.
    Ax Yoldia, *Y. thraciaeformis.* 12–14 teeth per side; shell has a diagonal fold, *dark* periostracum. To 2 in. (50 mm).
    File Yoldia, *Y. limatula.* Teeth coarse, about 20 per side. To $2\frac{1}{2}$ in. (62 mm).
    Short Yoldia, *Y. sapotilla.* Teeth fine, about 50 per side. To 1 in. (25 mm).
    See text for similar species.

NEAR NUT SHELL   *Nucula proxima*   p. 144
    Hinge strongly toothed, inner margin fine-toothed. To $\frac{3}{8}$ in. (9 mm). See text for similar species.

GLASSY LYONSIA   *Lyonsia hyalina*   p. 159
    Shell thin, glassy; marginally coated with sand grains. Note simple hinge without filelike teeth. To $\frac{3}{4}$ in. (19 mm).

GOULD'S PANDORA   *Pandora gouldiana*   p. 160
    Shells flat, with spoutlike rear. To 1 in. (25 mm). See text for similar species.

SPOON SHELLS   *Periploma* species   p. 161
    Shells thin, unequal; hinge has distinct chondrophore.
    Paper Spoon Shell, *P. papyratium.* Shells almost equally bowed, chondrophore points down. To 1 in. (25 mm).
    Lea's Spoon Shell, *P. leanum.* 1 shell nearly flat, other bowed; chondrophore almost horizontal. To $1\frac{1}{2}$ in. (38 mm).

CONRAD'S THRACIA   *Thracia conradi*   p. 161
    Beak of right valve notched to receive beak of left. To 4 in. (100 mm).

VEILED CLAM   *Solemya velum*   p. 144
    Shiny periostracum overhangs extremely fragile shell. To $1\frac{1}{2}$ in. (38 mm).

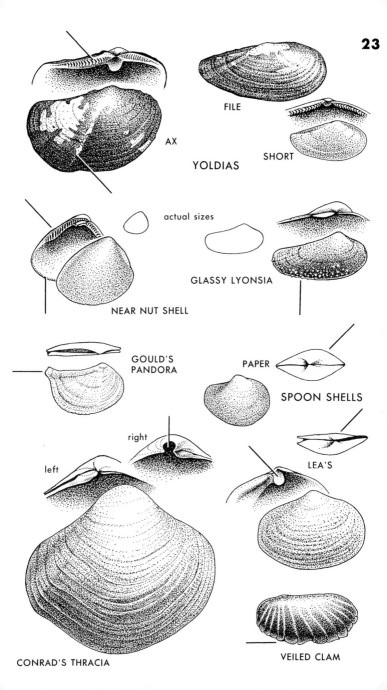

23

AX

FILE

SHORT

YOLDIAS

actual sizes

GLASSY LYONSIA

NEAR NUT SHELL

GOULD'S PANDORA

PAPER

SPOON SHELLS

left   right

LEA'S

CONRAD'S THRACIA

VEILED CLAM

Plate 24

MUSSELS, RAZOR CLAMS, AND
OTHER BIVALVES

Measurements are maximum recorded length.

HORSE MUSSEL *Modiolus modiolus* p. 147
  Beaks subterminal. To 6 in. (150 mm).

BLUE MUSSEL *Mytilus edulis* p. 146
  Beaks terminal, edged inside with fine teeth. To 4 in. (100 mm).

PLATFORM MUSSEL *Congeria leucopheata*
  Beaks terminal, with a shelf inside. To $\frac{3}{4}$ in. (19 mm). A brackish-water species. See under Blue Mussel, p. 146.

RIBBED MUSSEL *Modiolus demissus* p. 146
  Beaks subterminal; shell radially ribbed. To 4 in. (100 mm).

BENT MUSSEL *Brachidontes recurvus*
  Beaks terminal; shell strongly curved, radially ribbed. To $1\frac{1}{2}$ in. (38 mm). See under Ribbed Mussel, p. 146.

RIBBED POD *Siliqua costata*
  Hinge off-center forward, with a strong rib inside. To 2 in. (50 mm). See under Stout Tagelus, p. 157.

PURPLISH TAGELUS *Tagelus divisus*
  Fragile. Hinge near middle, with a weak rib inside. To $1\frac{1}{2}$ in. (38 mm). See under Stout Tagelus, p. 157.

STOUT TAGELUS *Tagelus plebeius* p. 157
  Hinge near middle, with 2 small teeth inside. To 4 in. (100 mm).

JINGLE SHELL *Anomia simplex* p. 149
  Valves dissimilar, thin, translucent, glossy. To 3 in. (75 mm). See text for similar species.

COMMON RAZOR CLAM *Ensis directus* p. 157
  About 6 times longer than wide; hinge line slightly bowed. Left hinge has 2 teeth. To 10 in. (250 mm).

LITTLE GREEN RAZOR CLAM *Solen viridis*
  About 4 times longer than wide, hinge line straight. Both hinges have 1 tooth. To 2 in. (50 mm). See under Common Razor Clam, p. 157.

Fig. 39.

lophophore

pedicel

NORTHERN LAMP SHELL
See p. 121

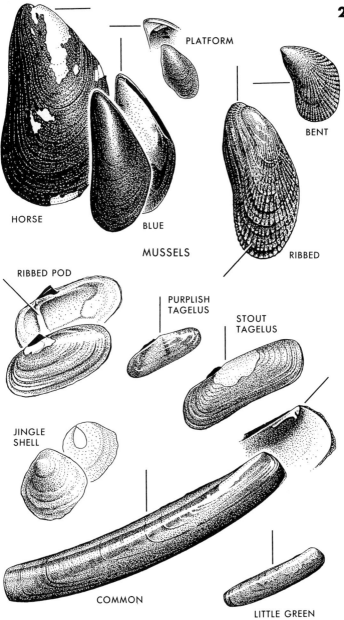

24

PLATFORM

BENT

HORSE

BLUE

RIBBED

MUSSELS

RIBBED POD

PURPLISH TAGELUS

STOUT TAGELUS

JINGLE SHELL

COMMON

LITTLE GREEN

RAZOR CLAMS

Plate 25

SMALLER CLAMS

Measurements are maximum recorded length or height, whichever is greater.

1, 2. **MACOMA CLAMS** *Macoma* species p. 156
    Shells thin, dull, twisted; hinge without lateral teeth. (1) **Baltic Macoma,** *M. balthica,* and (2) **Chalky Macoma,** *M. calcarea,* shown. To 1½ in. (38 mm) and 2 in. (50 mm), respectively. See text to differentiate between these and other, similar species.

3. **TELLINS** *Tellina* species p. 155
    Shells thin, shiny, white to yellowish or pink, with lateral teeth (at least in front). To ⅝ in. (16 mm).

4. **MORTON'S EGG COCKLE** p. 152
    Laevicardium mortoni
    Inside yellow with dark mark to one side. To almost 1 in. (25 mm).

5. **COMMON CUMINGIA** *Cumingia tellinoides*
    Somewhat tellin-like but shell is deeper and has a spoon-like chondrophore. To ¾ in. (19 mm). See under Tellins, p. 155.

6. **LITTLE SURF CLAM** *Mulinia lateralis*
    Backslope flattened, lateral teeth not crenulated. Hinge has cuplike chondrophore. To ¾ in. (19 mm). See under Surf Clam, p. 158.

7. **GEM SHELL** *Gemma gemma* p. 153
    Shell triangular, glossy, often tinted purple; inner margin finely crenulated. To ⅛ in. (3 mm).

8. **COMMON BASKET CLAM** *Corbula contracta* p. 158
    Shells unequal; right hinge has a hook inside. To ½ in. (12 mm).

9. **COQUINA** *Donax variabilis* p. 156
    Inner margin finely toothed; color highly variable. On ocean beaches. To ¾ in. (19 mm). See text for similar species.

10. **CHESTNUT ASTARTE** *Astarte castanea* p. 150
    Shell triangular, thick, and strong; inner margin crenulated. Dark periostracum. To 1 in. (25 mm). See text for similar species.

11. **CROSSHATCHED LUCINE** p. 151
    Divaricella quadrisulcata
    Shell round, white, strong, marked with chevronlike scratches. To 1 in. (25 mm).

12. **WHITE SEMELE** *Semele proficua*
    Beak less hooked than in next species; compare hinges. To 1½ in. (38 mm). See under Disk Shell, p. 153.

13. **DISK SHELL** *Dosinia discus* p. 153
    Beak hooked forward; compare hinges with preceding species. To 3 in. (75 mm). See text for similar species.

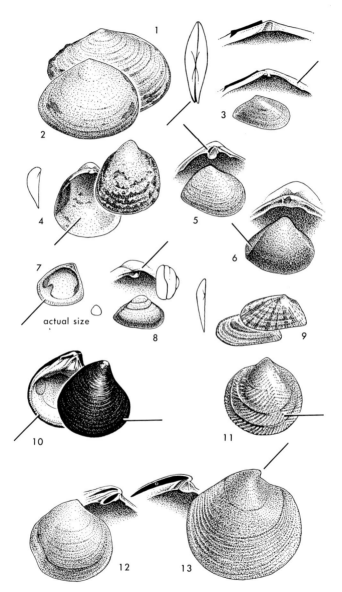

actual size

Plate 26
ARKS, COCKLES, AND SCALLOPS

Measurements are maximum recorded height or length, whichever is greater. All shells are radially ribbed. Arks have filelike (taxodont) teeth.

TRANSVERSE ARK   *Anadara transversa*
Beaks, ligament, and hinge weaker than in Ponderous Ark. To 1½ in. (38 mm). See under Ponderous Ark, p. 145.

BLOOD ARK   *Anadara ovalis*
Shell rounded, teeth only extend a little in front of beak; ligament narrow. To 2 in. (50 mm). See under Ponderous Ark, p. 145.

PONDEROUS ARK   *Noetia ponderosa*   p. 145
Teeth extend well beyond beak on both sides; ligament broad. Ribs doubled along margin. To 2½ in. (62 mm). See text for similar species.

NORTHERN CARDITA   *Cyclocardia borealis*   p. 150
Shell thick, about 20 ribs. Compare hinge with those of other species on this plate. To 1½ in. (38 mm).

GREAT HEART COCKLE   *Dinocardium robustum*   p. 151
Shell thick; about 35 scaly ribs. To 5 in. (125 mm). A southern beach shell.

LITTLE COCKLE   *Cerastoderma pinnulatum*
Shell thin, with about 22–28 scaly ribs. To ½ in. (12 mm). See under Northern Cardita, p. 150.

ICELAND COCKLE   *Clinocardium ciliatum*
Shell thin; about 35 ribs. To 2 in. (50 mm). See under Northern Cardita, p. 150.

BAY SCALLOP   *Aequipecten irradians*   p. 147
Coarsely ribbed with equal marginal wings. To 3 in. (75 mm). See text for similar species.

DEEP-SEA SCALLOP   *Placopecten magellanicus*   p. 147
Shell flattish, finely ribbed. To 8 in. (200 mm).

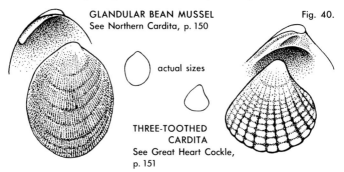

GLANDULAR BEAN MUSSEL
See Northern Cardita, p. 150

Fig. 40.

actual sizes

THREE-TOOTHED
CARDITA
See Great Heart Cockle,
p. 151

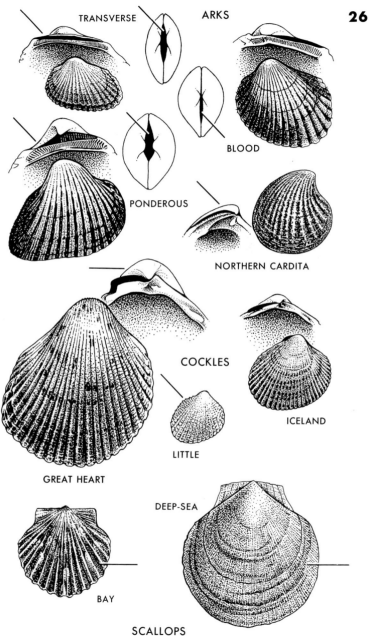

26

ARKS

TRANSVERSE

BLOOD

PONDEROUS

NORTHERN CARDITA

COCKLES

GREAT HEART

LITTLE

ICELAND

DEEP-SEA

BAY

SCALLOPS

Plate 27

BORING CLAMS

Scale varies. Measurements are maximum recorded length.

SHIPWORMS   *Teredo* and related genera   p. 159
Wormlike wood borers with T-shaped shells at front end, a pair
of pallets at rear. **Common Shipworm,** *T. navalis,* and pallet
of **Gould's Shipworm,** *B. gouldia,* shown. Shell and pallets to
about $\frac{1}{4}$ in. (6 mm); whole worm several inches long.

ARCTIC ROCK BORER   *Hiatella arctica*   p. 158
Shell thick, dirty white; siphons bright red. To $1\frac{1}{2}$ in. (38 mm).

WOOD PIDDOCKS   *Martesia* species   p. 160
Peg-shaped, with a diagonal groove near front end. **Striate
Wood Piddock,** *M. striata,* shown; to 2 in. (50 mm).

GREAT PIDDOCK   *Zirfaea crispata*   p. 160
Shell divided by diagonal groove. To 3 in. (75 mm).

TRUNCATE BORER   *Barnea truncata*
Resembles Angel Wing (below) but shell wedge-shaped forward,
and note hinge. To 2 in. (50 mm). See under Great Piddock,
p. 160.

FALSE ANGEL WING   *Petricola pholadiformis*
Resembles next species, but note hinge. To 2 in. (50 mm). See
under Angel Wing, p. 159.

ANGEL WING   *Cyrtopleura costata*   p. 159
Hinge most distinctive. Usually found as a broken beach shell.
To 7 in. (175 mm).

WING SHELL   *Pholas campechiensis*
Compare hinge with those of preceding 2 species. To 4 in.
(100 mm). See under Angel Wing, p. 159.

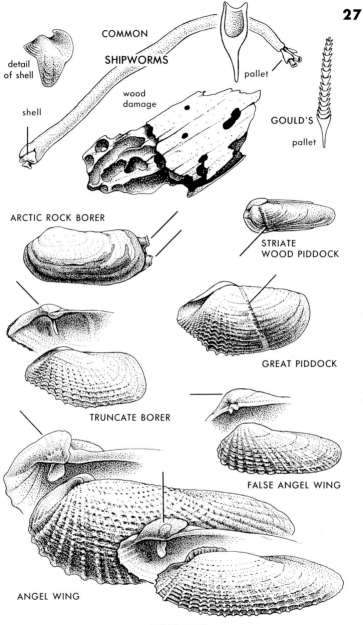

COMMON

SHIPWORMS

detail
of shell

shell

wood
damage

pallet

GOULD'S

pallet

ARCTIC ROCK BORER

STRIATE
WOOD PIDDOCK

GREAT PIDDOCK

TRUNCATE BORER

FALSE ANGEL WING

ANGEL WING

WING SHELL

Plate 28

LARGER CLAMS

Reduced. Measurements are maximum recorded length.

ARCTIC WEDGE CLAM   *Mesodesma arctatum*   p. 155
  Hinge has deep chondrophore and strong lateral teeth. To
  $1\frac{1}{2}$ in. (38 mm).

CAROLINA MARSH CLAM   p. 150
Polymesoda caroliniana
  Shell broadly rounded, with shaggy periostracum. A fresh- to
  brackish-water clam. To $1\frac{1}{2}$ in. (38 mm).

WEDGE RANGIA   *Rangia cuneata*   p. 154
  Beaks thick, swollen; shell very strong, with silky periostracum.
  Brackish water. To 2 in. (50 mm).

SOFT-SHELLED CLAM   *Mya arenaria*   p. 158
  Shells thin, gaping. Left side of hinge has tongue-like chondrophore, right has heart-shaped pit. To 4 in. (100 mm), occasionally larger. See text for similar species.

CHANNELED DUCK   *Labiosa plicatella*   p. 154
  Fragile, white; with concentric ribs and grooves. Usually found
  as a broken beach shell. To 3 in. (75 mm).

QUAHOG or HARD-SHELLED CLAM   p. 152
Mercenaria mercenaria
  Inside white with a purple stain, margin toothed. To 4 in.
  (100 mm), sometimes larger. See text for similar species.

BLACK CLAM   *Arctica islandica*   p. 149
  Resembles Quahog (preceding) but lacks pallial sinus and purple
  stain. Periostracum black. To 4 in. (100 mm).

FALSE QUAHOG   *Pitar morrhuana*
  Similar to Quahog (above) but shell more delicate, lacks purple
  stain and marginal teeth. To 2 in. (50 mm). See under Quahog,
  p. 152.

SURF CLAM   *Spisula solidissima*   p. 154
  A large clam often washed ashore on ocean beaches; shell has
  strong chondrophore. To 8 in. (200 mm). See text for similar
  species.

GREENLAND COCKLE   *Serripes groenlandicus*   p. 152
  Shell has weak radial ribbing at both ends; inside without pallial
  sinus. Note hinge. To 4 in. (100 mm).

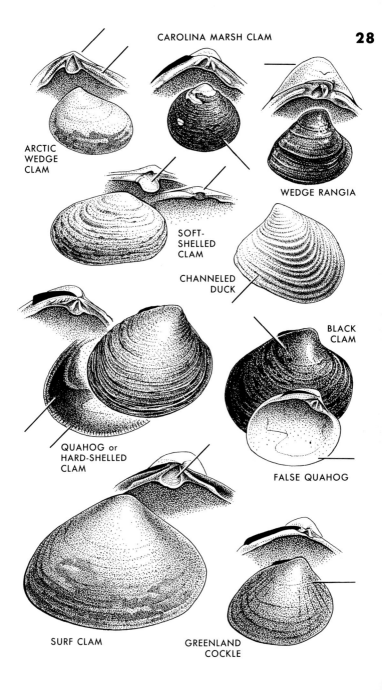

ARCTIC
WEDGE
CLAM

WEDGE RANGIA

SOFT-
SHELLED
CLAM

CHANNELED
DUCK

BLACK
CLAM

QUAHOG or
HARD-SHELLED
CLAM

FALSE QUAHOG

SURF CLAM

GREENLAND
COCKLE

Plate 29
SMALLER HYDROMEDUSAE AND
A JELLYFISH

Scale varies. Measurements are maximum recorded height or width of bell, whichever is greater. In many species of hydromedusae the free-swimming *medusoid* stage alternates with a fixed, nonswimming *hydroid* stage; see p. 71 for details.

TOWER HYDROMEDUSA *Turritopsis nutricola* p. 77
Tentacles numerous, up to 85 on a ⅛ in. (3 mm) bell. Mouth 4-lipped. To ³⁄₁₆ in. (5 mm). See text for similar species.

BOUGAINVILLIA HYDROMEDUSAE p. 78
Bougainvillia and related genera
Tentacles in 4 clusters. Mouth has branching tentacles. *B. carolinensis* shown; to ³⁄₁₆ in. (5 mm). See text for similar species.

RATHKEA OCTOPUNCTATA
Tentacles in 8 clusters of 3–5 each. To ³⁄₁₆ in. (5 mm). See under Bougainvillia Hydroids, p. 78.

PROBOSCIDACTYLA ORNATA
Radial canals branch toward margin. To ³⁄₁₆ in. (5 mm). See under Additional Hydromedusae, p. 85, for this and similar species.

CLAPPER HYDROMEDUSA *Sarsia tubulosa* p. 76
Manubrium long, pendulous. Tentacles roughened, warty. To ¼ in. (6 mm). See text for similar species.

ONE-ARMED HYDROMEDUSAE p. 75
Hybocodon species
Has only 1 tentacle (don't confuse with damaged medusae of other species). Bell has 5 radial rows of nematocysts. To ¼ in. (6 mm). *H. pendula* shown; see text for similar species.

OBELIA **species**
Bell nearly flat, with numerous short tentacles; no visible velum. To ¼ in. (6 mm). Top view shown. See under Campanularian Hydroids and Hydromedusae, p. 80.

BRANCHLET HYDROMEDUSA p. 82
Eucheilota ventricularis
Each tentacle has 1–3 short cirri emerging from base; 8–12 marginal vesicles between tentacles. To ½ in. (12 mm).

CRADLE HYDROMEDUSA *Cunina octonaria* p. 74
Tentacles stiff, emerging halfway up side of bell. To ¼ in. (6 mm).

CROWN JELLY *Nausithoe punctata* p. 89
Umbrella divided by a horizontal groove; top is caplike. Margin has 16 deeply scalloped lappets; 8 tentacles. To ⅝ in. (16 mm).

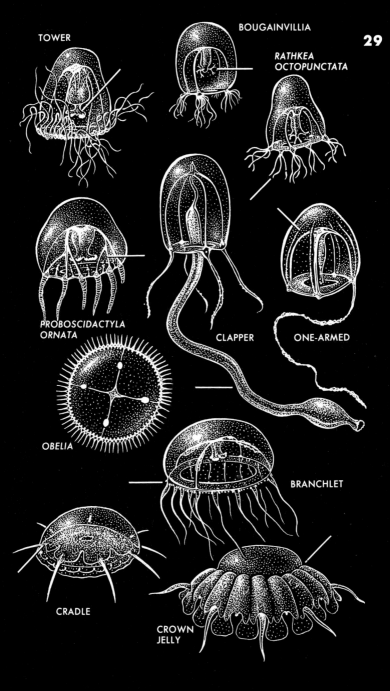

TOWER

BOUGAINVILLIA

29

RATHKEA OCTOPUNCTATA

PROBOSCIDACTYLA ORNATA

CLAPPER

ONE-ARMED

OBELIA

BRANCHLET

CRADLE

CROWN JELLY

Plate 30
LARGER HYDROMEDUSAE, SEA WASP

Scale varies. Measurements are maximum recorded height or width of bell, whichever is greater. In many species of hydromedusae the free-swimming *medusoid* stage alternates with a fixed, nonswimming *hydroid* stage; see p. 71 for details.

ELEGANT HYDROMEDUSA   *Tima formosa*   p. 84
Manubrium long, clapperlike; mouth has 4 frilly lips. 32 tentacles, varying in size. To 4 in. (100 mm) wide. See text for similar species.

SPLENDID HYDROMEDUSA   *Aglantha digitale*   p. 74
About $1\frac{1}{2}$ times taller than wide. 8 radial canals and up to 100 tentacles. To $1\frac{1}{8}$ in. (28 mm).

ANGLED HYDROMEDUSA   *Gonionemus vertens*   p. 74
Tentacles sharply bent near outer end. To $1\frac{3}{4}$ in. (44 mm). Top view shown.

PHIALIDIUM species
Tentacles (up to 32) alternate with small bulbs or vesicles along margin. Mouth 4-lipped. Most species $\frac{1}{4}$ in. (6 mm) or less. See under Campanularian Hydroids and Hydromedusae, p. 80.

CATABLEMA VESICARIUM
Bell has a large apical process. To 1 in. (25 mm). See under Additional Hydromedusae, p. 86, for this and similar species.

EIGHT-RIBBED HYDROMEDUSA   p. 83
Melicertum octocostatum
Has 8 radial canals, 64–72 tentacles when mature. To $\frac{1}{2}$ in. (12 mm).

SEA WASP   *Tamoya haplonema*   p. 89
Has four 2-part tentacles, each with paddlelike base and strong filament. Bell rigid. A strong stinger. To $3\frac{1}{2}$ in. (88 mm).

BLACK-EYED HYDROMEDUSA   p. 82
Tiaropsis multicirrata
Tentacles numerous, 24 on $\frac{1}{16}$-in. (1.6 mm) bell, and up to 200 on mature, $1\frac{1}{8}$-in. (28 mm) medusa. Tiny black dots alternate with tentacles along margin. See text for similar species.

MANY-RIBBED HYDROMEDUSAE   p. 83
Aequorea species
Radial canals numerous, (about 24–100 when mature), with $1\frac{1}{2}$–3 times as many tentacles and even more numerous marginal vesicles. To 7 in. (175 mm). See text for similar species.

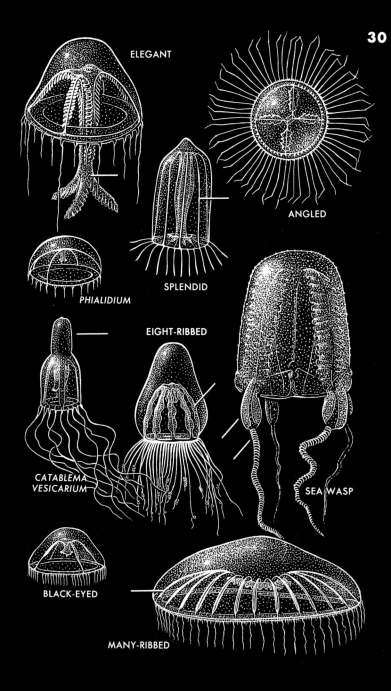

30

ELEGANT

ANGLED

SPLENDID

PHIALIDIUM

EIGHT-RIBBED

CATABLEMA
VESICARIUM

SEA WASP

BLACK-EYED

MANY-RIBBED

Plate 31

JELLYFISH

Reduced; scale varies. Measurements are maximum recorded umbrella diameters.

PORTUGUESE MAN-OF-WAR *Physalia physalia* p. 87
Balloonlike float with feeding, defensive, and other specialized structures suspended below. Float to more than 1 ft. (300 mm), fully extended tentacles to 50 ft. (15 m).

BY THE WIND SAILOR *Velella velella* p. 87
Colony an oval raft with triangular sail. To 4 in. (100 mm). See text for similar species.

SEA NETTLE *Chrysaora quinquecirrha* p. 90
Usually with more than 8 tentacles, emerging from marginal clefts. Ocean and bay forms differ; see text. To 7½ in. (188 mm).

PURPLE JELLYFISH *Pelagia noctiluca*
No more than 8 tentacles, emerging from marginal clefts; bell warty above. A stray from deep water. To 2 in. (50 mm). See under Sea Nettle, p. 90.

MOON JELLY *Aurelia aurita* p. 90
Numerous short tentacles form a marginal fringe; 4 horseshoe-shaped gonads. To 10 in. (250 mm). Top view shown.

LION'S MANE *Cyanea capillata* p. 89
Tentacles in 8 clusters on underside, well in from margin of umbrella. Size and color vary geographically; see text.

MUSHROOM CAP *Rhopilema verrilli* p. 89
Without tentacles. To more than 1 ft. (300 mm).

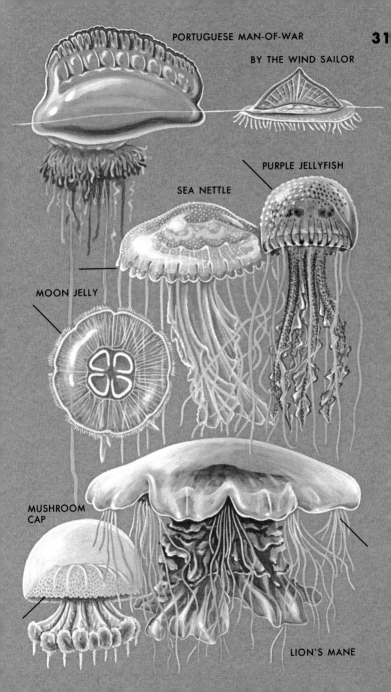

PORTUGUESE MAN-OF-WAR

31

BY THE WIND SAILOR

PURPLE JELLYFISH

SEA NETTLE

MOON JELLY

MUSHROOM
CAP

LION'S MANE

Plate 32

COMB JELLIES

Scale varies. Measurements are maximum recorded length with comb jellies extended. Differ from jellyfish in having 8 rows of comblike ciliary plates and biradial symmetry. They do not sting.

LEIDY'S COMB JELLY   *Mnemiopsis leidyi*   p. 100
  Lobes longer than body. Southern. To 4 in. (100 mm).

COMMON NORTHERN COMB JELLY   p. 100
Bolinopsis infundibulum
  Lobes shorter than body. Northern. To 6 in. (150 mm).

BEROE'S COMB JELLIES   *Beroe* species   p. 100
  Body flattened, saclike, without lobes or tentacles. To $4\frac{1}{2}$ in. (112 mm). See text for individual species.

SEA GOOSEBERRY   *Pleurobrachia pileus*   p. 99
  Spherical, firm-bodied; has 2 long retractile tentacles. To $1\frac{1}{8}$ in. (28 mm). See text for similar species.

VENUS GIRDLE   *Cestum veneris*   p. 101
  Ribbonlike. Tropical and oceanic. To 5 ft. (1.5 m).

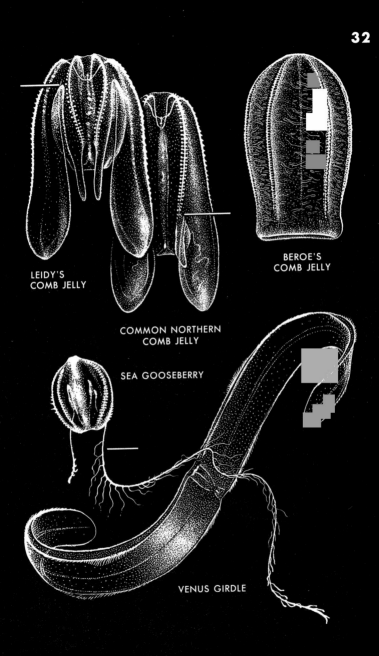

32

LEIDY'S
COMB JELLY

BEROE'S
COMB JELLY

COMMON NORTHERN
COMB JELLY

SEA GOOSEBERRY

VENUS GIRDLE

Plate 33

MISCELLANEOUS PLANKTERS

Scale varies. Measurements are maximum recorded.

SIPHONOPHORES

Colonial hydrozoans with 1 or more pneumatic bells and a chain of specialized structures; see p. 86. Shown are representatives of 2 principal suborders.

Stephanomia cara. Has 1 terminal float preceded by 4 pairs of swimming bells. Float to $\frac{1}{16}$ in. (1.6 mm) long; colony to 3 in. (75 mm) or more. See p. 87.

Diphyes dispar. Has 2 swimming bells, larger one to $\frac{3}{4}$ in. (19 mm). See p. 86.

SHELLED SEA BUTTERFLIES   p. 137
Limacina and related genera

Foot with winglike flaps (parapodia). Shell thin; transparent, colorless to yellow-brown; sinistral. *L. retroversa* shown; shell to $\frac{1}{4}$ in. (6 mm) long.

NAKED SEA BUTTERFLY   *Clione limacina*   p. 137
Shell-less, sluglike. To 1 in. (25 mm).

ARROW WORMS   *Sagitta* species   p. 120
Transparent, torpedo-shaped, with 2 pairs of side fins. *S. elegans* shown; to $\frac{3}{4}$ in. (19 mm). See text for other genera and species.

PLANKTON WORM   *Tomopteris helgolandica*   p. 168
Transparent, with bilobed parapodia (lateral feet) and 2 long tentacular cirri. To $3\frac{1}{2}$ in. (88 mm).

OIKOPLEURA   *Oikopleura* species   p. 274
Animal somewhat tadpole-like, resides in a complex "house" of its own construction. Body to $\frac{3}{8}$ in. (9 mm); tail $3\frac{1}{2}$–4 times longer; house is cherry-sized or larger. See text for individual species and similar forms.

SALPS   *Thalia* and *Salpa* species   p. 273
Transparent, barrel-shaped, with hooplike muscular bands. *T. democratica* shown; to 1 in. (25 mm). See text for other species.

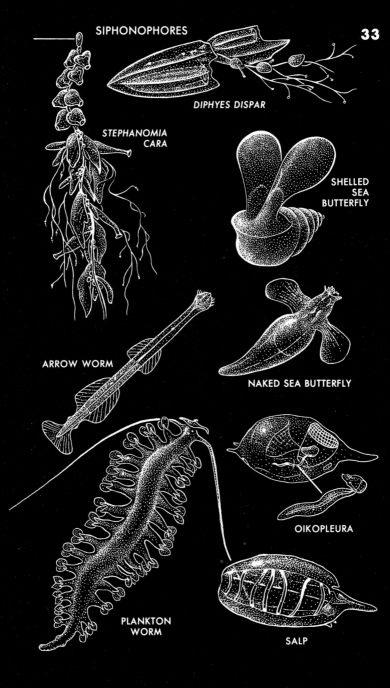

SIPHONOPHORES

33

DIPHYES DISPAR

STEPHANOMIA
CARA

SHELLED
SEA
BUTTERFLY

ARROW WORM

NAKED SEA BUTTERFLY

OIKOPLEURA

PLANKTON
WORM

SALP

Plate 34

MICROPLANKTERS

Scale varies. Measurements are maximum recorded length.

WATER FLEAS p. 211

Podon species. Carapace short, rounded. To less than $\frac{1}{16}$ in. (1.6 mm).

Evadne species. Carapace more elongated, pointed. To less than $\frac{1}{16}$ in. (1.6 mm).

Leptodora kindti. (See bottom of plate). Elongated, without a carapace. To $\frac{3}{4}$ in. (19 mm).

CRUSTACEAN LARVAE p. 210

Mantis Shrimp larva. Second thoracic appendages are predatory claws. To $\frac{1}{4}$ in. (6 mm).

Anomuran Crab zoea. Most species lack a dorsal spine; usually less than $\frac{3}{16}$ in. (5 mm). Mole Crab zoea shown. See p. 243.

Crab zoea. Most species have a dorsal spine; $\frac{1}{8}$ in. (3 mm) long.

Crab megalopa. Crablike form apparent but abdomen extended rather than carried tightly pressed against underside. To $\frac{3}{8}$ in. (9 mm).

Nauplius. Teardrop-shaped with 3 pairs of appendages; less than $\frac{1}{50}$ in. (0.5 mm) long.

COPEPODS p. 211

A typical calanoid copepod shown. $\frac{1}{16}$–$\frac{1}{2}$ in. (1.6–12 mm).

JELLYFISH EPHYRAE

Wheel-like animals with 8 radiating arms. Larvae of scyphozoan jellyfish. To $\frac{3}{16}$ in. (5 mm) diameter. See under Jellyfish, p. 87.

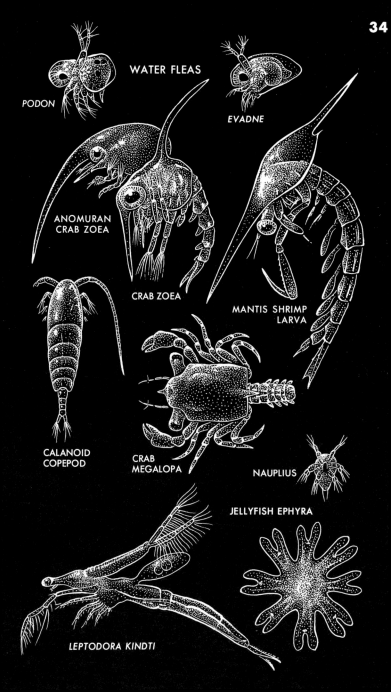

34

PODON

WATER FLEAS

EVADNE

ANOMURAN
CRAB ZOEA

CRAB ZOEA

MANTIS SHRIMP
LARVA

CALANOID
COPEPOD

CRAB
MEGALOPA

NAUPLIUS

JELLYFISH EPHYRA

LEPTODORA KINDTI

Plate 35

SQUIDS, NAUTILUS

Scale varies. Measurements are maximum recorded length.

BOREAL SQUID   *Illex illecebrosus*   p. 162
  Fins short, only ⅓ or more of mantle length. Skin over eyes
  pierced by a hole with a notch in front. Mantle to 9 in.
  (225 mm). Whole squid and mantle outline shown.

LONG-FINNED SQUID   *Loligo pealei*   p. 162
  Fins extend ½ or more of mantle length. Skin over eyes transparent with a small (sometimes obscure) hole in front. Mantle
  to 17 in. (425 mm). Mantle outline only shown.

BRIEF SQUID   *Lolliguncula brevis*
  Similar to preceding but fins shorter, less than ½ of mantle
  length, and more rounded. Mantle to 5 in. (125 mm). Mantle
  outline only shown. (Notched tail is not a significant identification trait.) See under Long-finned Squid, p. 162.

SPIRULA   *Spirula spirula*
  Flat-coiled, chambered shells common on southern beaches. To
  1 in. (25 mm) in diameter. Live animal lives at great depths
  offshore. See Additional Cephalopod Species, p. 163.

PAPER NAUTILUS   *Argonauta argo*
  Shells paper-thin; to 1 ft. (300 mm) across. See Additional
  Cephalopod Species, p. 163.

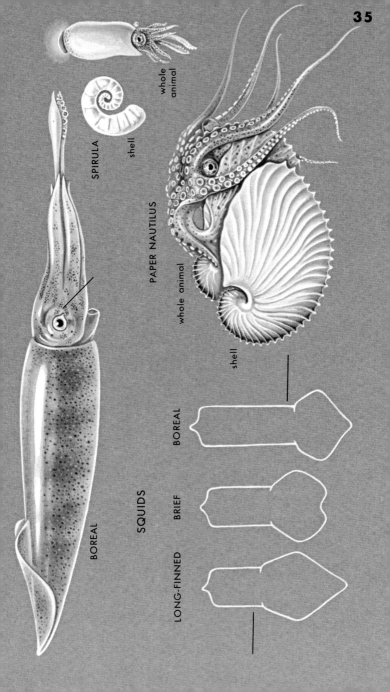

SPIRULA

whole animal

shell

PAPER NAUTILUS

whole animal

shell

BOREAL

SQUIDS

BOREAL

BRIEF

LONG-FINNED

Plate 36

FLATWORMS

Scale varies. Measurements are maximum recorded lengths with worms extended. Most of these worms are highly contractile.

HORNED FLATWORM   *Prosthecereaus maculosus*   p. 103
Has a pair of tentacles on front margin. To ½ in. (12 mm).

GULFWEED FLATWORM   *Gnesioceros sargassicola*   p. 103
2 small tentacles well within margin; eyespots on tentacles and in 2 groups on head in front of tentacles. To ⅜ in. (9 mm). See text for similar species.

SLENDER FLATWORM   *Euplana gracilis*   p. 102
Has 2 rows of 4–5 eyespots, plus a pair of spots behind each row. To ⅜ in. (9 mm).

OYSTER FLATWORM   *Stylochus ellipticus*   p. 102
Eyespots in a band along ⅓ or more of front margin. A pair of tiny tentacles well within margin. To 1 in. (25 mm). See text for similar species.

ZEBRA STYLOCHUS   *Stylochus zebra*
Dark and light crossbands. To 1½ in. (38 mm). See under Oyster Flatworm, p. 102.

CORONADENA MUTABILIS
Similar to Oyster Flatworm (above) but has marginal eyespots along front half and in 4 distinct clusters on head. To ¾ in. (19 mm). Head only shown. See under Oyster Flatworm, p. 102.

LIMULUS LEECH   *Bdelloura candida*   p. 102
Sucker at rear end, 2 eyespots at front. On book gills of horseshoe crabs. To ⅝ in. (16 mm). See text for similar species.

SPECKLED FLATWORM   *Notoplana atomata*   p. 102
Eyespots in 4 clusters, none along margin. To 1 in. (25 mm). See text for similar species.

SMALLER NEMERTEANS

LEECH NEMERTEAN   *Malacobdella grossa*
Has a sucker at rear; front margin notched. To 1⁹⁄₁₆ in. (39 mm). See under Additional Nemertean Species, p. 107.

FOUR-EYED NEMERTEANS   *Tetrastemma* species p. 106
Have 4 distinct eyespots. Color and pattern vary in different species. To 1³⁄₁₆ in. (30 mm), most smaller. **T. candidum** and **T. elegans** shown; see text for other species.

MANY-EYED NEMERTEANS   p. 106
Amphiporus and *Zygonemertes* species
Have numerous eyespots in rows or scattered on head. Head grooves transverse or obliquely angled, but often hard to detect. Color and pattern vary with species. To 6 in. (150 mm) but most are smaller. **A. ocraceus** (head only) and **A. angulatus** shown; see text for other species.

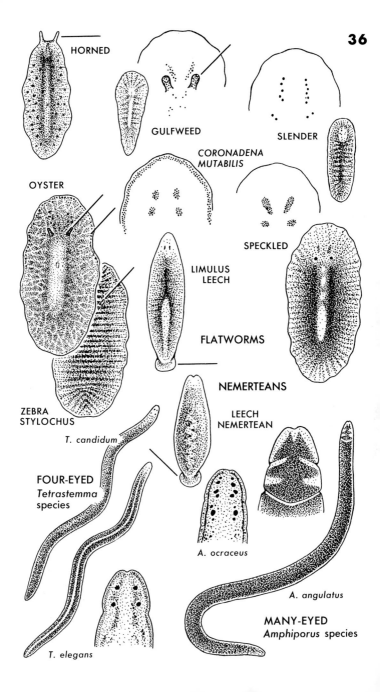

36

HORNED

GULFWEED

SLENDER

CORONADENA MUTABILIS

OYSTER

SPECKLED

LIMULUS LEECH

FLATWORMS

NEMERTEANS

ZEBRA STYLOCHUS

LEECH NEMERTEAN

T. candidum

FOUR-EYED
Tetrastemma species

A. ocraceus

A. angulatus

MANY-EYED
Amphiporus species

T. elegans

Plate 37
LARGER NEMERTEANS AND ACORN WORM

Scale varies. Measurements are maximum recorded length with worms extended.

MILKY RIBBON WORM *Cerebratulus lacteus* p. 105
  Head grooved lengthwise; mouth (on underside) a small slot; cirrus may be present. No eyespots. To 4 ft. (1.2 m), occasionally much larger. See text for similar species.

LINED NEMERTEANS *Lineus* species p. 104
  Head grooved lengthwise; eyespots present. No cirrus. Head end only shown. See text for similar species.
  1. **Striped Lineus,** *L. bicolor.* Green with pale median stripe. To 2 in. (50 mm).
  2. **Sandy Lineus,** *L. arenicola.* Rosy, sand-colored. To 4 in. (100 mm).
  3. **Social Lineus,** *L. socialis.* Color varies; similar to next species but contracts in coils. To 6 in. (150 mm).
  4. **Red Lineus,** *L. ruber.* Color varies; contracts by shortening and thickening. To 6 in. (150 mm).

MICRURAN NEMERTEANS *Micrura* species p. 105
  Head grooved lengthwise; mouth (on underside) round. No eyespots; cirrus may be present. **Leidy's Micruran,** *M. leidyi,* shown; to 1 ft. (300 mm). See text for other species.

SHARP-HEADED NEMERTEAN p. 105
Zygeupolia rubens
  Head long, pointed; no eyespots or head grooves. To 3 in. (75 mm). Head outline only shown.

KOWALEWSKY'S ACORN WORM p. 265
Saccoglossus kowalewskii
  Body (easily fragmented) has 3 distinct regions. Unsegmented and without appendages. To 6 in. (150 mm).

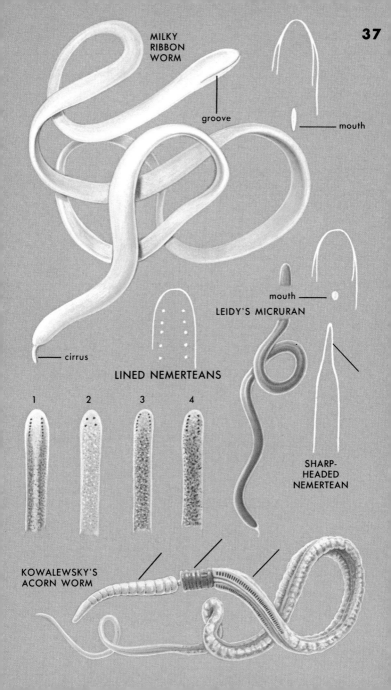

MILKY RIBBON WORM

groove

mouth

cirrus

LEIDY'S MICRURAN

mouth

LINED NEMERTEANS

1 2 3 4

SHARP-HEADED NEMERTEAN

KOWALEWSKY'S ACORN WORM

Plate 38
ERRANT POLYCHAETES (1)

Scale varies. Measurements are maximum recorded length with body extended. Most have well-developed head appendages. *Palps* are marked "p"; *tentacular cirri,* "tc"; *dorsal cirri,* "dc," and *ventral cirri,* "vc."

CLAM WORMS   *Nereis* species   p. 176
Head has 1 pair of short, thick palps, 4–5 pairs of tentacular cirri, an eversible proboscis with sicklelike jaws. See text for individual species; *N. virens* shown. To 8 in. (200 mm) or more. **Note:** Some species have a highly modified breeding stage called a *heteronereis* (head only shown). Palps visible from above.

DUMERIL'S CLAM WORM   p. 178
Platynereis dumerilii
Similar to preceding, but tentacular cirri longer. To 3 in. (75 mm). Heteronereis (breeding) stage has palps on underside of head (not visible from above). Head only shown.

SPRING WORM   *Lycastopsis pontica*   p. 179
Similar to clam worms (above), but tentacular cirri shorter. High intertidal. To 2¼ in. (56 mm).

SWIFT-FOOTED WORM   *Podarke obscura*   p. 175
Head has 3 antennae, 1 pair of slender, jointed palps, 6 pairs of long tentacular cirri, and even longer cirri on parapodia. To 1½ in. (38 mm). See text for similar species.

SIGAMBRA   *Sigambra* species   p. 175
Head has 1 pair of short, thick palps, 3 antennae, 2 pairs of tentacular cirri. To 1½ in. (38 mm). See text for individual species.

CABIRA INCERTA
Related to preceding, but maggotlike with poorly developed appendages. To ¾ in. (19 mm). See under Sigambra, p. 175 .

SYLLID WORMS   *Syllis* and related genera   p. 174
Head has 1 pair of palps, 3 antennae, 2 pairs of tentacular cirri; parapodia uniramous. Breeding stage (*epitokes*) often highly modified. See text for other syllids.

  Amblyosyllis finmarchica. Short-bodied with very long cirri. To ⅜ in. (9 mm). This and *Exogone* species (below) represent extreme variations in syllid body types.

  Autolytus species. Parapodia with dorsal cirri, no ventral cirri; antennae and tentacular cirri sometimes coiled. To 1 in. (25 mm). Head only shown.

  Exogone species. Threadlike with rudimentary cirri. To ⅜ in. (9 mm). Front end shown.

  Syllis species. Parapodia with long dorsal cirri, short ventral cirri. To 2 in. (50 mm).

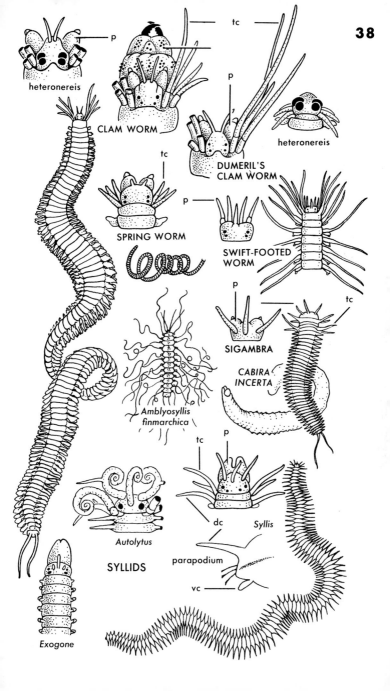

38

heteronereis

CLAM WORM

p

tc

heteronereis

DUMERIL'S CLAM WORM

tc

SPRING WORM

p

SWIFT-FOOTED WORM

p

SIGAMBRA

tc

CABIRA INCERTA

Amblyosyllis finmarchica

p

tc

Syllis

dc

parapodium

vc

Autolytus

SYLLIDS

Exogone

Plate 39

ERRANT POLYCHAETES (2)

Scale varies. Measurements are maximum recorded length with worms extended. All species shown have well-developed head appendages. *Tentacular cirri* are marked "tc"; *median antenna,* "ma."

PLUMED WORM   *Diopatra cuprea*   p. 179
  Head has 7 antennae (frontal pair short). A ruff of plumelike gills along each side toward head. Debris-encrusted tube projects aboveground. To 1 ft. (300 mm). See text for similar species.

RED-GILLED MARPHYSA   *Marphysa sanguinea*   p. 180
  Head cleft in front, with 5 short antennae. Gills have 2–8 filaments. To 2 ft. (600 mm). See text for similar species.

FOUR-EYED DORVILLEA   p. 182
Schistomeringos rudolphi
  Head has a pair of segmented antennae and a thicker pair of curving palps below. To 2 in. (50 mm) or more. Front end only shown. See text for similar species.

PADDLE WORMS   *Phyllodoce* and related genera   p. 166
  Head has at least 4 antennae at front; parapodia have paddle-shaped cirri. Front end only shown, except for *Phyllodoce arenae.* See also Fig. 49, p. 167.

  Eteone species. Only 2 pairs of tentacular cirri; other genera have 4 pairs. *E. trilineata* shown; to ³⁄₈ in. (9 mm). See text for other species.

  Eulalia sanguinea. Has a median antenna; 2 segments with tentacular cirri visible from above. To 2³⁄₈ in. (59 mm).

  Eulalia viridis. Has a median antennae as in preceding species, but 3 segments with tentacular cirri visible from above. To 6 in. (150 mm). See text for other species.

  Nereiphylla fragilis. Prostomium squarish. To 3¹⁄₈ in. (78 mm).

  Paranaitis speciosa. Has backward projection on prostomium. To ⁵⁄₈ in. (16 mm).

  Phyllodoce arenae. Prostomium notched behind. To 4 in. (100 mm). See text for other species.

Fig. 41.

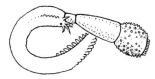

PADDLE WORM
showing proportions
of everted proboscis

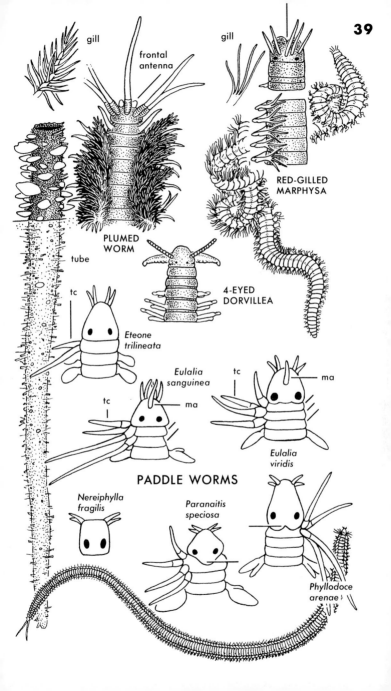

39

gill

frontal antenna

gill

RED-GILLED MARPHYSA

tube

PLUMED WORM

4-EYED DORVILLEA

tc

Eteone trilineata

Eulalia sanguinea

tc

ma

tc

ma

Eulalia viridis

PADDLE WORMS

Nereiphylla fragilis

Paranaitis speciosa

Phyllodoce arenae

Plate 40
ERRANT POLYCHAETES (3)

Scale varies. Measurements are maximum recorded length with worms extended. Head with small or no appendages.

BLOOD WORMS   *Glycera* species   p. 171
Head tapered, with 4 tiny antennae. Proboscis bulbous, with 4 black fangs. *G. dibranchiata* shown, whole worm and details; to 15 in. (375 mm). See text for other species.

OPAL WORM   *Arabella iricolor*   p. 180
Head conical, without appendages. Parapodia similar throughout. To 2 ft. (600 mm). Whole worm and details shown.

NOTOCIRRUS SPINIFERUS
Similar to preceding, but parapodia have barely visible golden aciculae. To 4⅜ in. (109 mm). Parapodium only shown. See under Opal Worm, p. 180.

LUMBRINERID THREAD WORMS   p. 181
Lumbrineris and *Ninoe* species
Similar to preceding but some setae are hooks. Body thickness varies in different species. Parapodium of *L. fragilis* shown — note black, imbedded acicula; to 15 in. (375 mm). See text for other species.

CHEVRON WORMS   *Goniada* and related genera   p. 172
Similar to blood worms (above) but parapodia stronger. Proboscis only shown for both of the following; see text for other species.
Goniada maculata. Proboscis has papilla ring, circlets of small teeth at end; a row of 9 V's on each side near base. To 4 in. (100 mm).
Glycinde solitaria. Proboscis has bushy patch along edge. To 1⅜ in. (34 mm).

RED-LINED WORMS   *Nephtys* species   p. 173
Head (left) has flattened, shovel-like prostomium with 2 short antennae at front (2nd pair close-by or hidden underneath). Proboscis (right) with soft papillae at front, wartlike papillae on sides. Whole worm and details shown. To 1 ft. (300 mm). Species identification difficult; see text.

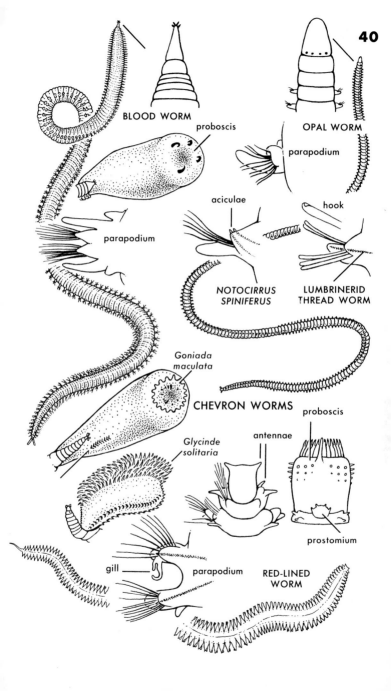

40

BLOOD WORM

OPAL WORM

proboscis

parapodium

aciculae

hook

*NOTOCIRRUS
SPINIFERUS*

LUMBRINERID
THREAD WORM

parapodium

*Goniada
maculata*

CHEVRON WORMS

proboscis

*Glycinde
solitaria*

antennae

prostomium

gill

parapodium

RED-LINED
WORM

Plate 41

SEDENTARY POLYCHAETES (1)

Scale varies. Measurements are maximum recorded length with worms extended. Head with small or no appendages.

BAMBOO WORMS   *Clymenella* and related genera   p. 186
Head blunt-ended or hoodlike. Body cylindrical, segments usually longer than wide. See text for other species.

  Clymenella torquata. Crownlike pygidium (tail). 4th segment with collar. To 6 in. (150 mm) or more.

  Asychis elongata. Scoop-shaped pygidium (tail). To 1 ft. (300 mm). Pygidium only shown.

OWENIA FUSIFORMIS
Head has frilly membrane; pygidium (tail) rounded. To 4 in. (100 mm). See under Bamboo Worms, p. 186, for this and related species.

ORBINIID WORMS   *Orbinia* and related genera   p. 183
Head rounded or conical, without appendages. 2 body regions: flattened thorax, with ridges of setae at sides; cylindrical abdomen, with tapered cirri on upperside.

  Haploscoloplos robustus. Head conical. To 14¾ in. (369 mm). Whole worm and head shown. See text for other species.

  Naineris quadricuspida. Head rounded. To 3⅛ in. (78 mm). Head only shown.

  Orbinia ornata. Has fringe of papillae behind ridges of setae. To 10 in. (250 mm). Side view of thoracic segments shown.

OPHELIID WORMS   *Ophelia* and related genera   p. 187
Spindle-shaped. To 3 in. (75 mm).

  Travisia carnea. Short and stout. Lacks body grooves.

  Ophelia denticulata. Sides deeply grooved from segments 10–12 to tail; 18 pairs of gills. See text for 2nd species.

  Ophelina acuminata. Side grooves extend whole length.

CAPITELLID THREAD WORMS   p. 184
Capitella and related genera
Earthwormlike; tiny parapodia; weakly defined body regions.

  Notomastus latericeus. Setae-bearing ridges almost touch at midline. To 1 ft. (300 mm). Cross section shown. See text for other species.

  Capitella capitata. 5–7 segments have capillary setae (see top right of plate). To 4 in. (100 mm).

LUGWORMS   *Arenicola* species   p. 184
Gill tufts along sides. *A. cristata* shown; to 1 ft. (300 mm). See text for other species.

PARAONID WORMS   *Aricidea* and *Paraonis* species
Head conical. Body regions weakly defined; 7–30 pairs of slender gills on upperside toward head. To 1 in. (25 mm). See under Orbiniid Worms, p. 183.

  Aricidea species. Have a median antenna. Head only shown.

  Paraonis species. Lack median antenna. Whole worm shown.

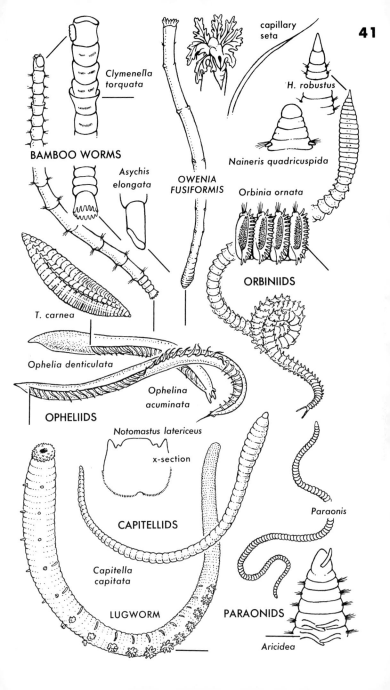

41

capillary seta

H. robustus

Clymenella torquata

BAMBOO WORMS

Naineris quadricuspida

Asychis elongata

OWENIA FUSIFORMIS

Orbinia ornata

ORBINIIDS

T. carnea

Ophelia denticulata

Ophelina acuminata

OPHELIIDS

Notomastus latericeus

x-section

CAPITELLIDS

Paraonis

Capitella capitata

LUGWORM

PARAONIDS

Aricidea

Plate 42
SEDENTARY POLYCHAETES (2)

Scale varies. Measurements are maximum recorded length with worms extended. Head with well-developed appendages.

HARD TUBE WORMS p. 195
Spirorbis and related genera
    Tube limy, hard. One tentacle of head forms a plug or operculum. Tubes and typical head shown.
    Spirorbis species. Tube forms flattened coils, $\frac{1}{8}$ in. (3 mm) in diameter.
      S. spirillum tube coils right-handed; **S. borealis** left-handed. See text for other species.
    Hydroides dianthus. Tube straggles over surface, not regularly coiled. To 3 in. (75 mm) long.
    Filograna implexa. Tubes joined in bundles. To several inches long, but less than $\frac{1}{16}$ in. (1.6 mm) in diameter.

SAND BUILDER WORM   *Sabellaria vulgaris* p. 189
Tubes made of cemented sand grains; form thick mats or colonies. To 1 in. (25 mm). Tubes, whole worm, and head shown.

GLASSY TUBE WORM   *Spiochaetopterus costarum*
Tube is transparent, ringed. Worm has 3-part body, middle longest; head with 2 long palps. To $2\frac{3}{8}$ in. (59 mm). Tube and head shown. See under Parchment Worm, p. 188.

PARCHMENT WORM   *Chaetopterus variopedatus* p. 188
Body complexly divided into regions, with 3 paddles on upperside near middle. To 10 in. (250 mm).

TRUMPET WORM   *Pectinaria gouldii* p. 191
Tube slender, conical. Head has a fan of golden setae. To 2 in. (50 mm). Tube, whole worm, and head shown.

ROSY MAGELONAS   *Magelona* species p. 190
Head spadelike, with 2 long tentacles at back. To 2 in. (50 mm). *M. rosea* shown; see text for other species.

MUD WORMS   *Polydora* and related genera p. 187
Head has a pair of long palps, often coiled. At least 10 genera, 24 species; see text.
    Polydora ligni. 5th setiger distinctly modified. To 1 in. (25 mm). See text for other species.
    Spiophanes bombyx. T-shaped head. To $2\frac{3}{8}$ in. (59 mm). Head only shown.

FAN WORMS   *Sabella* and related genera p. 194
Head has feathery tentacles (radioles) in 2 lobes. 6 genera, at least 8 species; see text.
    1. ***Sabella microphthalma.*** Numerous eyespots in 2 irregular rows along each radiole. To $1\frac{3}{16}$ in. (30 mm). Whole worm shown.
    2. ***Euchone elegans.*** Collar at base of branchial crown. To 1 in. (25 mm). Collar detail shown.
    3. ***Potamilla reniformis.*** Row of 1–8 eyespots on each radiole. To 4 in. (100 mm). Detail of radiole shown.
    4. ***Myxicola infundibulum.*** Radioles joined by a membrane almost to their tips. To 8 in. (200 mm). Detail of radiole shown.

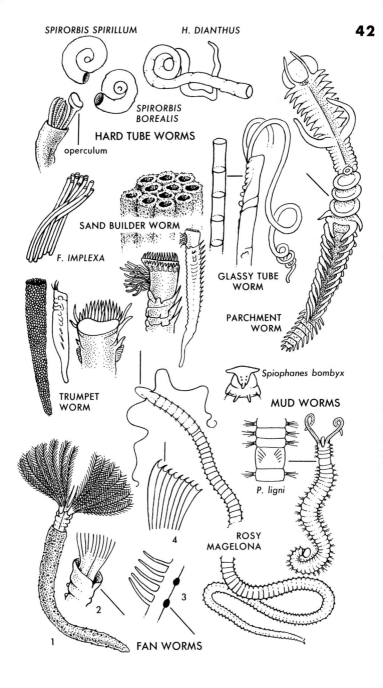

42

SPIRORBIS SPIRILLUM

H. DIANTHUS

SPIRORBIS BOREALIS

HARD TUBE WORMS

operculum

SAND BUILDER WORM

F. IMPLEXA

GLASSY TUBE WORM

PARCHMENT WORM

TRUMPET WORM

Spiophanes bombyx

MUD WORMS

P. ligni

4

3

2

1

FAN WORMS

ROSY MAGELONA

Plate 43
SEA MOUSE, SCALE WORMS AND OTHER POLYCHAETES

Scale varies. Measurements are maximum recorded length.

SEA MOUSE *Aphrodita hastata* p. 169
  Furry coat conceals scales. To 6 in. (150 mm), rarely to 9 in.
  (225 mm).

FIFTEEN-SCALED WORMS *Harmothoe* species p. 170
  Scales in 15 pairs. *H. imbricata* shown; color and pattern vary;
  to 2½ in. (62 mm). See text for other species.

TWELVE-SCALED WORMS *Lepidonotus* species p. 169
  Scales in 12–13 pairs. *L. squamatus* shown; to 2 in. (50 mm).
  See text for other species.

BURROWING SCALE WORMS p. 171
Sthenelais and related genera
  Long and slender with 20 pairs of scales or more. Without cirri,
  which are present in preceding 2 groups. Scales only shown. See
  text for other species.
  1. *Sthenelais boa.* Outer scale margin with simple papillae. To
     8 in. (200 mm).
  2. *Sthenelais limicola.* Outer scale margin (head end) with
     irregular papillae; rear scales notched. To 4 in. (100 mm).
  3. *Sigalion arenicola.* Outer scale margin with "feathered"
     papillae. To 1 ft. (300 mm).

FRINGED WORMS *Cirratulus* and related genera p. 190
  Head conical, with appendages at rear. See text for other species.

  Cirratulus cirratus. Head appendages similar; no thickened
    palps. To 4¾ in. (119 mm).
  Dodecaceria corallii. 2 types of head appendages including a
    pair of thickened palps. To ½ in. (12 mm).

AMPHARETID WORMS p. 191
Ampharete and related genera
  See text for comparison with next group. Head of an *Ampharete*
  species is shown. To 1 in. (25 mm). See text for other genera and
  species.

TEREBELLID WORMS p. 192
Amphitrite and related genera
  Head has numerous soft, contractile tentacles, and red gills.
  A. johnstoni shown; to 10 in. (250 mm). See text for other gen-
  era and species.

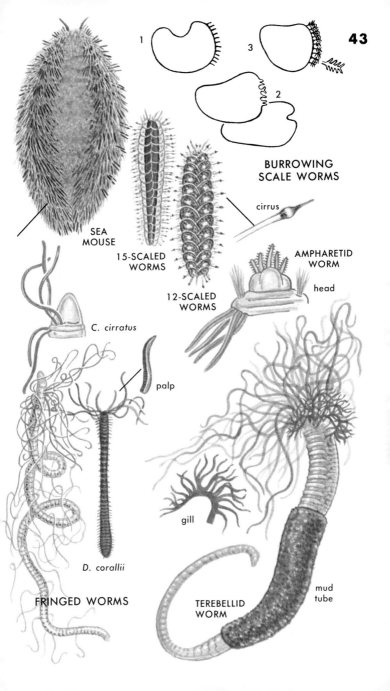

43

1

3

2

BURROWING
SCALE WORMS

SEA
MOUSE

15-SCALED
WORMS

12-SCALED
WORMS

cirrus

AMPHARETID
WORM

head

C. cirratus

palp

D. corallii

FRINGED WORMS

gill

TEREBELLID
WORM

mud
tube

Plate 44
SHELL-LESS GASTROPODS

Enlarged; scale varies. Measurements are maximum recorded length with body extended.

ROUGH-MANTLED NUDIBRANCHS   p. 139
Onchidoris and related genera
Top roughened with tubercles, a pair of tentacles at the front and a gill ring at the rear, both retractile.
  Onchidoris bilamellata. Tubercles rounded, varying in size; strongly patterned, firm-bodied. To 1 in. (25 mm).
  Onchidoris muricata. Similar to preceding but softer bodied and more uniformly pale-colored. To $\frac{1}{2}$ in. (12 mm).
  Acanthodoris pilosa. Tubercles conical, about equal in size; gills fluffy, with secondary branchlets (rather than simply pinnate as in the preceding 2 species). Color highly variable. To $1\frac{1}{4}$ in. (31 mm).
  Doris verrucosa. Tubercles rounded, varying in size. A southern species. To $1\frac{3}{4}$ in. (44 mm).

GULFWEED NUDIBRANCH   *Scyllaea pelagica*   p. 140
2 pairs of straplike fins, tentacles similar. On Gulfweed. To $1\frac{3}{8}$ in. (34 mm). See text for other Gulfweed species.

EELGRASS SLUG   *Elysia catula*
Greenish with a pair of lateral folds along $\frac{2}{3}$ body length. To $\frac{3}{8}$ in. (9 mm). See Sacoglossan Slugs, p. 139.

RIM-BACKED NUDIBRANCH   *Polycera dubia*   p. 140
Back has a rim of tubercles on each side; gill ring near midbody. To $\frac{3}{4}$ in. (19 mm).

***ANCULA* species**
Gill ring near midbody with ceratalike projections on each side. To $\frac{1}{2}$ in. (12 mm). See under Rim-backed Nudibranch, p. 140.

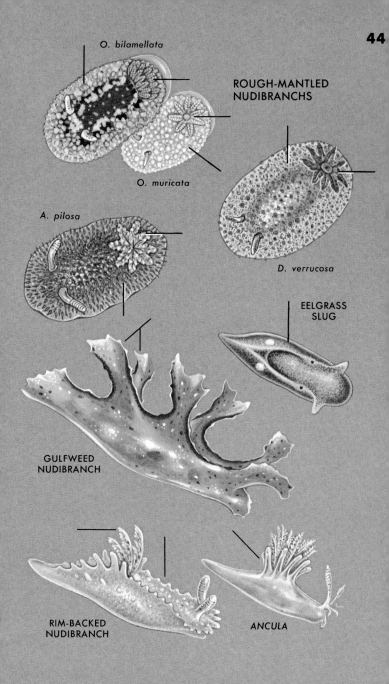

44

O. bilamellata

ROUGH-MANTLED
NUDIBRANCHS

O. muricata

A. pilosa

D. verrucosa

EELGRASS
SLUG

GULFWEED
NUDIBRANCH

RIM-BACKED
NUDIBRANCH

ANCULA

Plate 45
SHELL-LESS GASTROPODS: NUDIBRANCHS

Most species shown enlarged; scale varies. Measurements are maximum recorded length with body extended. Cerata are club- or finger-like gills.

RED-GILLED NUDIBRANCHS   *Coryphella* species   p. 141
    To 100 cerata per side, each with a red to chocolate-brown core and an opaque white ring or spot near tip. To $1\frac{3}{16}$ in. (30 mm). See text for similar species.

MANED NUDIBRANCH   *Aeolidia papillosa*   p. 142
    To 400 cerata per side; color variable. To 4 in. (100 mm).

STRIPED NUDIBRANCH   *Cratena pilata*   p. 141
    Cerata numerous but less than 100 per side, each with a dark core; broken stripe or row of reddish-brown spots down mid-back. To $1\frac{3}{16}$ in. (30 mm).

TERGIPES DESPECTUS
    5–8 cerata in a zigzag down the back. To $\frac{5}{16}$ in. (7 mm). See under Club-gilled Nudibranchs, p. 141.

CLUB-GILLED NUDIBRANCHS   p. 141
Eubranchus species
    Cerata club-shaped.
    E. exiguus. 5–10 banded cerata per side. To $\frac{5}{16}$ in. (8 mm).
    E. pallidus. 30 blotched cerata per side. To $\frac{1}{2}$ in. (12 mm).

BUSHY-BACKED NUDIBRANCH   p. 140
Dendronotus frondosus
    Cerata bushy, in a double row. To 3 in. (75 mm).

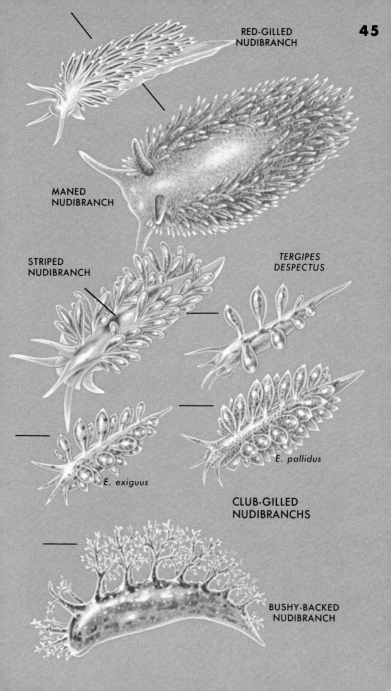

45

RED-GILLED
NUDIBRANCH

MANED
NUDIBRANCH

STRIPED
NUDIBRANCH

*TERGIPES
DESPECTUS*

E. exiguus

E. pallidus

CLUB-GILLED
NUDIBRANCHS

BUSHY-BACKED
NUDIBRANCH

Plate 46

SEA CUCUMBERS

Measurements are maximum recorded length. Body shape very changeable; tentacles and tube feet variably contractile. Microscopic deposits are shown on Fig. 42, below.

SYNAPTAS *Leptosynapta* species p. 255
Wormlike, transparent, with 12 pinnate tentacles; no tube feet. Color varies; deposits include anchors. **Pink Synapta,** *L. roseola,* shown; to 4 in. (100 mm). See text for other species.

SILKY CUCUMBER *Chiridota laevis* p. 256
Wormlike, translucent; with 12 peltate tentacles; no tube feet. Deposits (in raised papillae) are wheels. To 6 in. (150 mm).

RAT-TAILED CUCUMBER *Caudina arenata* p. 256
Pale, pink to purplish; with 15 tentacles, each with 4 short digits; no tube feet. To 7 in. (175 mm). Detail of tentacle also shown. See text for similar, blackish species.

SCARLET PSOLUS *Psolus fabricii* p. 254
Red, scaly; anus ringed by 5–6 large granular scales. To 8 in. (200 mm). Sole also shown. See text for similar, deep-water species.

HAIRY CUCUMBER *Sclerodactyla briareus* p. 254
Dark; body nearly covered with slender tube feet. Deposits scarce, mostly tables. To 6 in. (150 mm) or more. See text for paler, more distinctly tailed species.

ORANGE-FOOTED CUCUMBER p. 254
Cucumaria frondosa
Tube feet in 5 bands; with 10 bushy tentacles. Deposits scarce, mostly plates. To 10 in. (250 mm), much larger offshore. See text for similar species with tube feet in bands.

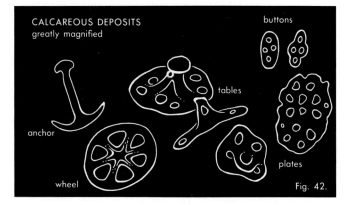

CALCAREOUS DEPOSITS
greatly magnified

buttons

tables

anchor

wheel

plates

Fig. 42.

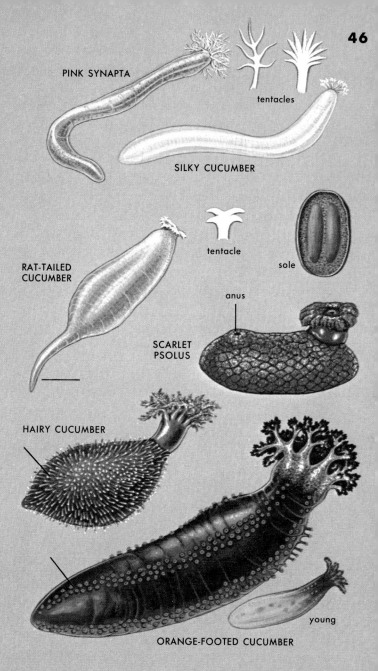

46

PINK SYNAPTA

tentacles

SILKY CUCUMBER

RAT-TAILED
CUCUMBER

tentacle

sole

anus

SCARLET
PSOLUS

HAIRY CUCUMBER

young

ORANGE-FOOTED CUCUMBER

Plate 47
BURROWING ANEMONES AND
MISCELLANEOUS WORMS

Scale varies. Measurements are maximum recorded length. Body (column) and tentacles highly contractile.

ATHENARIAN BURROWING ANEMONES   p. 95
Edwardsia and related genera
> Bottom end rounded or formed into a digging physa. Oral disk has 1 whorl of up to 20 tentacles.
> **Nematostella vectensis.** Smooth, without physa or collar. To ³⁄₄ in. (19 mm).
> **Edwardsia elegans.** 3-part column (collar, middle section, physa); about 16 tentacles. To 1³⁄₈ in. (34 mm).
> **Haloclava producta.** About 20 rows of coarse warts, 20 knobbed tentacles. To 6 in. (150 mm).

THENARIAN BURROWING ANEMONES   p. 96
Actinothoe species
> Bottom end has adhesive pedal disk. Oral disk with numerous (48–64) tentacles in several cycles. **A. modesta** shown; to 2¹⁄₂ in. (62 mm). See text for other species.

CERIANTHARIAN ANEMONES   p. 98
Cerianthus and *Ceriantheopsis* species
> Tentacles very numerous in 2 distinct whorls. **Ceriantheopsis americanus** shown; to 8 in. (200 mm). See text for other species.

GOULD'S SIPUNCULID   *Phascolopsis gouldii*   p. 198
> Skin silky, wrinkled but not segmented; head has fingerlike tentacles; see Fig. 43, below. To 1 ft. (300 mm).

PHORONIS   *Phoronis architecta*   p. 121
> Translucent, unsegmented. Has horseshoe-shaped crown of tentacles (lophophore); see Fig. 43, below. To 2 in. (50 mm).

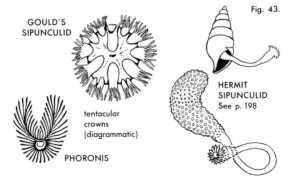

Fig. 43.

GOULD'S SIPUNCULID

tentacular crowns (diagrammatic)

PHORONIS

HERMIT SIPUNCULID
See p. 198

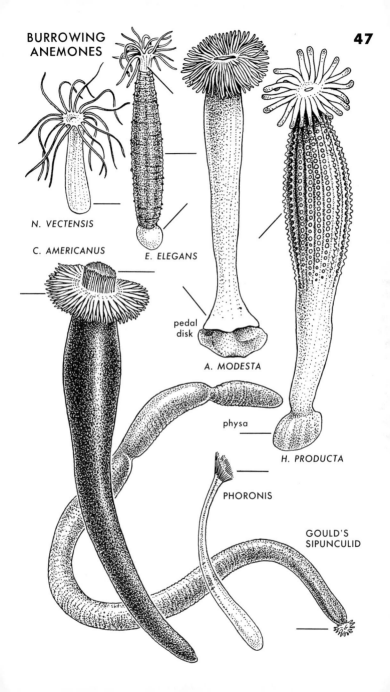

47

BURROWING ANEMONES

N. VECTENSIS

C. AMERICANUS

E. ELEGANS

A. MODESTA

pedal disk

H. PRODUCTA

physa

PHORONIS

GOULD'S SIPUNCULID

Plate 48

SEA SPIDERS

Scale varies. Measurements are maximum recorded body length.

ANEMONE SEA SPIDER   *Pycnogonum littorale*   p. 202
  Proboscis conical, without appendages. To $\frac{3}{16}$ in. (5 mm).

SARGASSUM SEA SPIDER   *Endeis spinosa*
  More slender than preceding; with longer proboscis, also without
  appendages. To $\frac{1}{4}$ in. (6 mm). Found on Gulfweed. See under
  Anemone Sea Spider, p. 202.

LONG-NECKED SEA SPIDER   p. 201
Callipallene brevirostris
  Proboscis has slender neck and short, thick chelifores. To $\frac{1}{16}$ in.
  (1.6 mm). Proboscis only shown.

RINGED SEA SPIDER   *Tanystylum orbiculare*   p. 201
  Proboscis has palpi and stubby chelifores. Leg span to $\frac{1}{4}$ in.
  (6 mm).

LENTIL SEA SPIDER   p. 201
Anoplodactylus lentus
  Proboscis thick at base, with slender chelifores. To $\frac{1}{4}$ in. (6 mm).

CLAWED SEA SPIDER   *Phoxichilidium femoratum*
  Similar to preceding, though less slender. Terminal claws on legs
  have distinct auxiliary claw. To $\frac{1}{8}$ in. (3 mm). Claw only
  shown. See under Lentil Sea Spider, p. 201.

INSECTS

See under Arachnids and Insects, pp. 203–205.

ANURIDA MARITIMA
  Wingless, blue-gray; often in rafts of many individuals on surface of tide pools. To $\frac{1}{8}$ in. (3 mm) long.

BITING FLIES
  Sand Flies, *Culicoides* species. Minute; generally less than $\frac{1}{8}$ in.
  (3 mm) long. Cause persistent, very itchy bites in susceptible
  individuals, who may not be aware of being bitten.
  Horse and Deer Flies, *Tabanus* and *Chrysops* species. The
  large-headed, hard-biting flies of dunes and marshes. Day
  fliers. To 1 in. (25 mm). **Salt-marsh Greenhead Fly,**
  T. nigrovittatus, shown.
  Stable Fly, *Stomoxys calcitrans.* Looks like a House Fly but
  bites. Commonly found near windrows of dead Eelgrass or
  other drifting weeds. To $\frac{1}{4}$ in. (6 mm).

SALTWATER MOSQUITOES
  Culex and *Aedes* species rest with body parallel to surface.
  Biting beak flanked by short palpi and feathery antennae.
  Aedes species have banded legs; *Culex* species do not.
  Anopheles species rest with body angled to surface. Usually
  have dark-spotted wings; palpi are about as long as beak. See
  Fig. 10, p. 61, for larval insects.

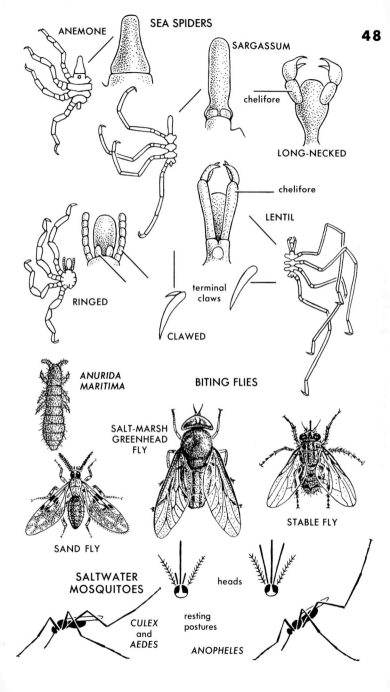

SEA SPIDERS

ANEMONE

SARGASSUM

chelifore

LONG-NECKED

chelifore

LENTIL

RINGED

terminal claws

CLAWED

48

ANURIDA MARITIMA

BITING FLIES

SALT-MARSH GREENHEAD FLY

STABLE FLY

SAND FLY

SALTWATER MOSQUITOES

heads

CULEX and *AEDES*

resting postures

ANOPHELES

Plate 49
PARASITIC AND OTHER ISOPODS

Scale varies. Measurements are maximum recorded length. Tail fan-shaped except in bopyrids.

AEGA PSORA
Eyes large; first 3 pairs of legs hooklike. Found on fishes. To 2 in. (50 mm). See under Parasitic Isopods, p. 224.

CYMOTHOIDS *Cymothoa* and related genera
Eyes small in adults; all 7 pairs of walking legs hooklike. Larvae differ from adults and are not easily identifiable to species; note large eyes. Distinguish the following by differences in body form: (1) **Olencira praegustator,** to $\frac{3}{8}$ in. (9 mm); (2) **Cymothoa excisa,** to 1 in. (25 mm); (3) **Lironeca ovalis,** to $\frac{7}{8}$ in. (22 mm); (4) **Nerocila acuminata,** to $\frac{7}{8}$ in. (22 mm). See under Parasitic Isopods, p. 224.

GREEDY ISOPODS *Cirolana* species   p. 221
First 3 pairs of legs hooklike. Scavengers on dead animals.
C. borealis. Inner blade of uropod and telson rounded. To $\frac{1}{2}$ in. (12 mm). Detail of telson and left uropod only shown.
C. concharum. Inner blade of uropod and telson notched. To 1 in. (25 mm). Detail of telson and left uropod only shown.
C. polita. Inner blade of uropod notched, telson rounded. To $\frac{5}{8}$ in. (16 mm). Whole animal and detail shown.

BOPYRID ISOPODS *Probopyrus* and related genera
Adult females degenerate, permanently attached to crabs or shrimps; males minute, found with females. *P. pandalicola* shown; forms a bump under host shrimp's carapace. To $\frac{3}{8}$ in. (9 mm). See under Parasitic Isopods, p. 224.

PARASITIC COPEPODS, FISH LICE

All are found on fishes.

RIBBON LICE *Lernaeenicus* species   p. 212
Head imbedded in fish's flesh; slender body trails free. To 2 in. (50 mm). See text for similar species.

LAZY FISH LICE *Argulus* species   p. 213
Body flattened, with a pair of suckers on underside. Sometimes free-swimming. To $\frac{1}{2}$ in. (12 mm).

BOOTED FISH LICE *Caligus* and related genera   p. 212
Eyes small, immobile; tail has a pair of caudal rami. Sometimes free-swimming. To 2 in. (50 mm). Whole female and tail of male shown.

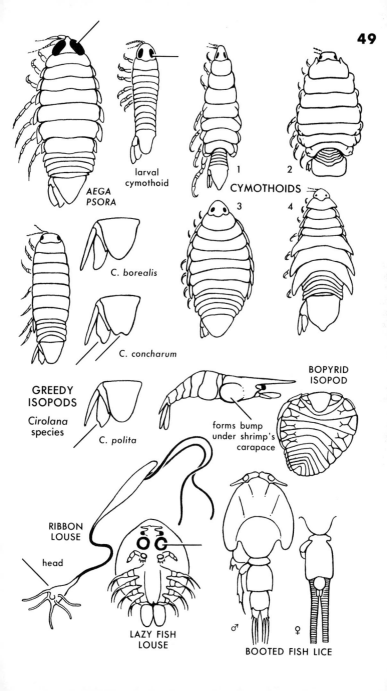

AEGA PSORA

larval cymothoid

CYMOTHOIDS

1

2

3

4

C. borealis

C. concharum

GREEDY ISOPODS

Cirolana species

C. polita

BOPYRID ISOPOD

forms bump under shrimp's carapace

RIBBON LOUSE

head

LAZY FISH LOUSE

♂ ♀

BOOTED FISH LICE

Plate 50

TANAIDS AND ISOPODS

Scale varies. Measurements are maximum recorded length.

TANAIS CAVOLINII   p. 220
Cylindrical; abdomen has bundles of dense bristles; uropods spiky, no telson. To $\frac{3}{16}$ in. (5 mm). See text for similar species.

SLENDER ISOPOD   *Cyathura polita*   p. 221
Cylindrical; telson and uropods fanlike. To 1 in. (25 mm). See text for similar species.

In the following species the uropods fold neatly against the underside of the telson.

***ERICHSONELLA* species**
Body slender; antennae long, large-jointed to tips. ***E. attenuata*** has more slender body than ***E. filiformis***. To $\frac{1}{2}$ in. (12 mm). See under *Idotea* species, p. 222.

***CHIRIDOTEA* species**
Abdominal segments separate (not fused); body broadly oval; eyes on top of head. To $\frac{3}{8}$ in. (9 mm). See under *Idotea* species, p. 222.

***EDOTEA* species**
Abdominal segments fused; antennae large-jointed to tips. To $\frac{1}{4}$ in. (6 mm). ***E. triloba*** shown. See under *Idotea* species, p. 222.

***IDOTEA* species**   p. 222.
Abdominal segments separate (not fused); body slender; eyes at side of head. To 1 in. (25 mm). 3 species, easily distinguished by differences in shape of telson: ***I. phosphorea, I. metallica,*** (telson of these 2 species only shown) and ***I. baltica.*** Color and pattern of *I. baltica* extremely variable; see Fig. 63, p. 223.

SEA PILL BUG   *Sphaeroma quadridentatum*   p. 222
Body mottled with white. Rolls in a ball when disturbed. To $\frac{3}{8}$ in. (9 mm). See text for similar species.

LITTLE SHORE ISOPOD   *Jaera marina*   p. 224
Uropods very short, set in a notch in telson. To $\frac{1}{8}$ in. (3 mm).

SEA ROACH   *Ligia exotica*   p. 224
Uropods long, terminal (set at back of telson). An active, conspicuous species on pilings and rocks southward. To $1\frac{1}{4}$ in. (31 mm). See text for similar species.

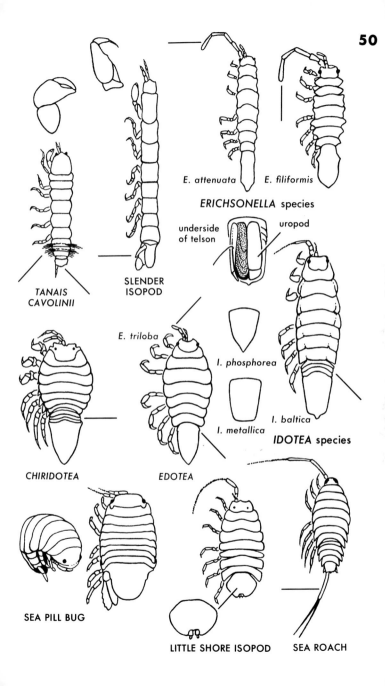

50

E. attenuata   *E. filiformis*

ERICHSONELLA species

underside of telson   uropod

TANAIS CAVOLINII

SLENDER ISOPOD

E. triloba

I. phosphorea

I. metallica   *I. baltica*

IDOTEA species

CHIRIDOTEA   **EDOTEA**

SEA PILL BUG

LITTLE SHORE ISOPOD   **SEA ROACH**

Plate 51
AMPHIPODS AND A CUMACEAN

Scale varies. Measurements are maximum recorded length.

BIG-EYED AMPHIPODS *Hyperia* species   p. 226
  Eyes large, bulging. Planktonic. To ¾ in. (19 mm). *H. galba*
  shown; see text for other species.

DIGGER AMPHIPODS   p. 228
Haustorius and related genera
  Legs modified for digging. To ¾ in. (19 mm). *H. canadensis*
  shown; see text for other species.

PLANKTONIC AMPHIPOD   p. 226
Calliopius laeviusculus
  Antennae brushlike; telson not notched. Planktonic. To ½ in.
  (12 mm). Whole animal and details shown.

PONTOGENEIA INERMIS
  Gnathopods differ in shape from preceding species; base of antennae brushlike in males; telson notched. Planktonic. To ½ in.
  (12 mm). Tail and gnathopod only shown. See under Planktonic Amphipod, p. 226.

SCUDS *Gammarus* and related genera   p. 227
  Telson usually longer than wide, deeply split. Antennae about
  equal length, or 1st pair longer. To 1¼ in. (31 mm).
  G. mucronatus. Spiny back; lives in brackish water. Abdomen
  only shown.
  G. oceanicus. A large tide-pool species common on the New
  England shore.

BEACH FLEAS *Talorchestia* and *Orchestia* species   p. 226
  Pale, sand-colored; high jumpers found near high tide line on
  beaches. Telson slightly notched; 3rd uropods unbranched. To
  1³⁄₁₆ in. (30 mm). **T. longicornis** has longer 2nd antennae and
  smaller eyes than **T. megalophthalma** (head only shown). See
  text for related brownish amphipods found under wave-tossed
  debris.

SHARP-TAILED CUMACEAN *Oxyurostylis smithi* p. 219
  Carapace short, leaving 4–5 leg-bearing (thoracic) segments
  exposed. Telson abruptly tapered, ending in a sharp point. To
  ⁵⁄₁₆ in. (8 mm). See text for similar species.

Fig. 44.

CHELURA TEREBRANS
a wood-boring amphipod
See Gribbles, p. 221

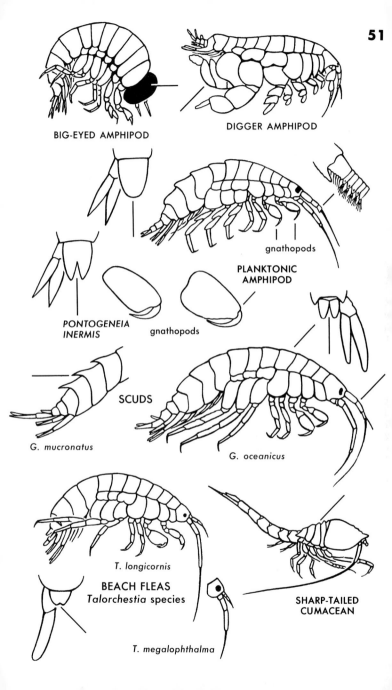

51

BIG-EYED AMPHIPOD

DIGGER AMPHIPOD

PLANKTONIC AMPHIPOD

gnathopods

PONTOGENEIA INERMIS

gnathopods

SCUDS

G. mucronatus

G. oceanicus

T. longicornis

BEACH FLEAS
Talorchestia species

T. megalophthalma

SHARP-TAILED CUMACEAN

Plate 52

TUBICOLOUS AMPHIPODS

Enlarged; scale varies. Measurements are maximum recorded length. Males and females differ in limb development, but individuals are gregarious and females may be identified by associated males. Telson marked "t"; 3rd uropods "u." See p. 228 for the species below.

SLENDER TUBE MAKERS   *Corophium* and other genera
Coxal plates small, body depressed (top to bottom). Second gnathopods usually stronger than 1st except in *M. gryllotalpa*.
> ***Corophium*** species. 2nd antennae powerfully developed; 3rd uropods and telson minute. To $\frac{3}{16}$ in. (5 mm).
> ***Erichthonius*** species. 1st and 2nd antennae about equal. Uropods, telson larger than in preceding species. To $\frac{1}{2}$ in. (12 mm). Details only shown.
> ***Microdeutopus gryllotalpa.*** 1st antennae larger than 2nd; 3rd uropods branched. To $\frac{5}{16}$ in. (8 mm). Details only shown.

MOTTLED TUBE MAKER   *Jassa falcata*
Males have very powerfully developed 2nd gnathopods. To $\frac{3}{8}$ in. (9 mm).

OTHER TUBE MAKERS   *Ampithoe* and other genera
Coxal plates well developed, body less depressed than in slender tube makers (above).
> ***Leptocheirus pinguis.*** 3rd uropods with slender branches. To $\frac{1}{2}$ in. (12 mm).
> ***Ampithoe*** species. 3rd uropods with short branches, hooklike spines (microscopic) at top of outer ones. To $\frac{3}{4}$ in. (19 mm). See text for related species.

OTHER AMPHIPODS

FOUR-EYED AMPHIPODS   p. 227
Ampelisca and *Byblis* species
> Have 4 beadlike eyes. To $\frac{5}{8}$ in. (16 mm). Head end of typical *Ampelisca* shown.

SEED AMPHIPODS   *Stenothoe* and related genera   p. 227
1–3 coxal plates exceptionally large. *Parametopella cypris* shown; to $\frac{1}{16}$ in. (1.6 mm). See text for other species.

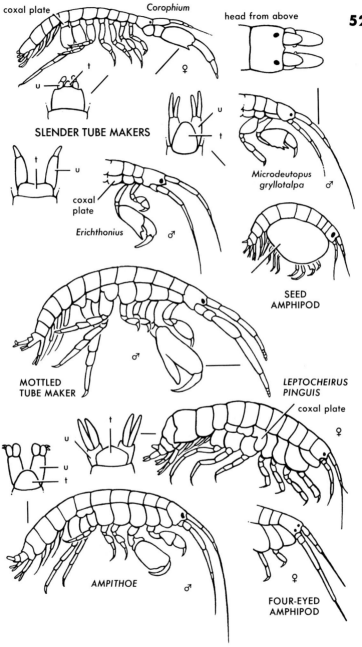

52

coxal plate

Corophium

head from above

t

u

♀

SLENDER TUBE MAKERS

u

t

t

u

Microdeutopus gryllotalpa ♂

coxal plate

Erichthonius ♂

SEED AMPHIPOD

MOTTLED TUBE MAKER ♂

LEPTOCHEIRUS PINGUIS

coxal plate ♀

t

u

u

t

AMPITHOE ♂

♀

FOUR-EYED AMPHIPOD

Plate 53

MISCELLANEOUS SHRIMPS

Enlarged; scale varies. Measurements are maximum recorded length, front of carapace to end of abdomen.

HORNED KRILL SHRIMP   p. 231
Meganyctiphanes norvegica
     Antennal peduncle has an upright leaf; 7 pairs of walking legs biramous. To 1½ in. (38 mm). A euphausiid shrimp; see text for other species.

BENT MYSID SHRIMP   *Praunus flexuosus*   p. 230
     Inner uropod has statocyst. To 1 in. (25 mm). A mysid shrimp; see text for similar species.

NEBALIA SHRIMP   *Nebalia bipes*   p. 217
     Carapace bivalve-like; abdomen ends in caudal rami. To ½ in. (12 mm). A phyllocarid shrimp.

LONG-EYED SHRIMP   *Ogyrides alphaerostris*   p. 236
     Eyestalks long and slender. To 1 in. (25 mm). A caridean shrimp; see text for similar species.

ACETES AMERICANUS
     Similar to the next species, but carapace shorter. To 1 in. (25 mm); front end only shown. A penaeid shrimp; see under Lucifer Shrimp, p. 234.

LUCIFER SHRIMP   *Lucifer faxoni*   p. 234
     Carapace long, necklike. To ½ in. (12 mm). A penaeid shrimp.

SKELETON SHRIMPS   p. 229
Caprella and related genera
     Shrimplike amphipods. Commonly to ¾ in. (19 mm); largest to 2 in. (50 mm) or more.

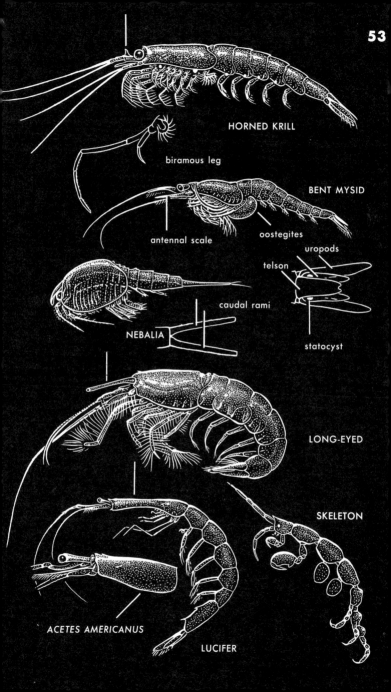

53

HORNED KRILL

biramous leg

BENT MYSID

antennal scale

oostegites

uropods

telson

caudal rami

NEBALIA

statocyst

LONG-EYED

SKELETON

ACETES AMERICANUS

LUCIFER

Plate 54

NORTHERN CARIDEAN SHRIMPS

Scale varies. Measurements are maximum recorded length, front of carapace (tip of rostrum) to end of abdomen. See Fig. 58, p. 206, for structural diagram of shrimp.

For further details of first 3 generic groups see Additional Caridean Species, p. 238. In all 3 genera, carpus of 2nd pair of walking legs has 7 segments. To identify species note differences in rostrum.

EUALUS species
No supraorbital spines. Sizes are: **E. gaimardii,** $3\frac{3}{8}$ in. (84 mm); **E. pusiolus,** 1 in. (25 mm); **E. fabricii,** 2 in. (50 mm). Details only shown for *gaimardii* and *fabricii.*

LEBBEUS species
1 supraorbital spine. Sizes are: **L. groenlandicus,** $3\frac{3}{8}$ in. (84 mm); **L. polaris,** $2\frac{1}{4}$ in. (56 mm); **L. zebra,** 2 in. (50 mm). Note differences in relative lengths of antennal peduncle and rostrum in *polaris* and *zebra;* details only shown.

SPIRONTOCARIS species
2 supraorbital spines. Sizes are: **S. spinus,** $2\frac{5}{6}$ in. (70 mm); **S. phippsii,** $1\frac{1}{2}$ in. (38 mm). Details only shown.

RED SAND SHRIMP   *Sclerocrangon boreas*
Similar to Sand Shrimp (below), but carapace rougher; 3–4 teeth on midline of carapace. To 5 in. (125 mm). See under Sand Shrimp, p. 236.

BOREAL RED SHRIMPS   *Pandalus* species   p. 237
Rostrum at least $1\frac{1}{4}$ times longer than carapace. To 5 in. (125 mm). Detail of *P. borealis* shown. See text for other species; see also Plate 56.

SAND SHRIMP   *Crangon septemspinosa*   p. 236
Rostrum short; claws of 1st pair of walking legs subchelate. 1 tooth on midline of carapace. To $2\frac{3}{4}$ in. (69 mm).

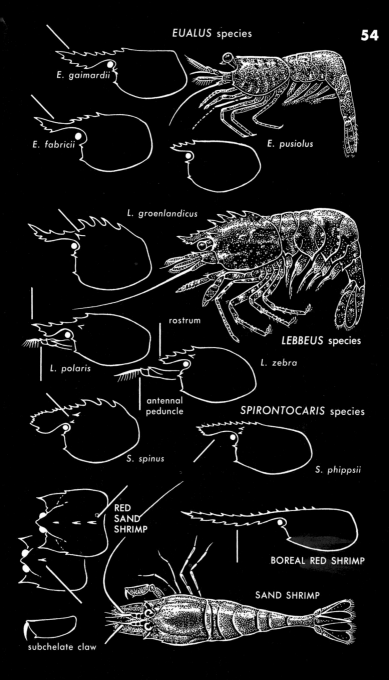

EUALUS species **54**

E. gaimardii

E. fabricii

E. pusiolus

L. groenlandicus

rostrum

L. polaris

L. zebra

antennal
peduncle

LEBBEUS species

SPIRONTOCARIS species

S. spinus

S. phippsii

RED
SAND
SHRIMP

BOREAL RED SHRIMP

SAND SHRIMP

subchelate claw

Plate 55
MOLE CRAB AND SOUTHERN SHRIMPS

Enlarged; scale varies. Measurements are maximum recorded length, front of carapace (tip of rostrum) to end of abdomen. See Fig. 58, p. 206, for structural diagram of shrimp.

MOLE CRAB *Emerita talpoida* p. 244
  Egg-shaped. On ocean beaches. To 1 in. (25 mm).

SOUTHERN COMMERCIAL SHRIMPS p. 233
Penaeus species
  3 pairs of legs with weak claws. To 8 in. (200 mm). Head end only shown. See text for individual species; see also Pink Shrimp, Plate 56.

SOUTHERN CARIDEAN SHRIMPS

SHORE SHRIMPS *Palaemonetes* species p. 234
  Claws on 1st and 2nd legs, 2nd pair strongest and longest. To 2 in. (50 mm). **Common Shore Shrimp,** *P. vulgaris,* shown. See text for other species and similar forms.

VEINED SHRIMP *Hippolysmata wurdemanni*
  Claws on 1st and 2nd pair of legs; 2nd pair longer but weaker. Carpus has about 30 segments. To $2\frac{1}{8}$ in. (53 mm). Head end only shown. See under Shore Shrimps, p. 234.

GULFWEED SHRIMP *Latreutes fucorum* p. 238
  Rostrum bladelike, toothless except at tip. To $\frac{3}{4}$ in. (19 mm). See text for other species found on Gulfweed.

GRASS SHRIMPS *Hippolyte* species p. 238
  Claws on 1st and 2nd pair of legs; 2nd pair longer but weaker. Carpus has 3 segments. Color varies as shown. To $\frac{3}{4}$ in. (19 mm). See text for individual species.

ARROW SHRIMP *Tozeuma carolinense* p. 237
  Rostrum long, spiky, toothless on upperside. Color varies. To 2 in. (50 mm).

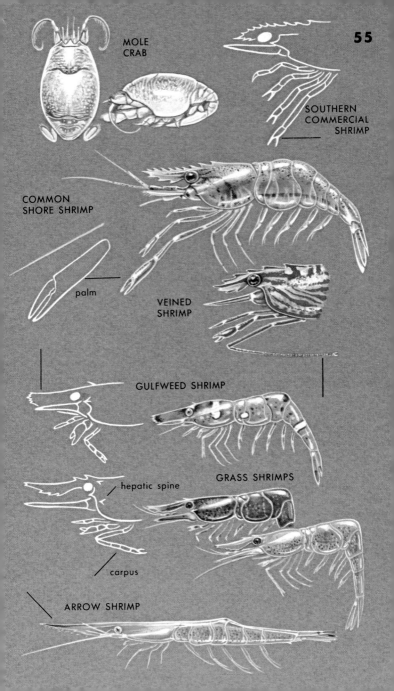

MOLE CRAB

55

SOUTHERN COMMERCIAL SHRIMP

COMMON SHORE SHRIMP

palm

VEINED SHRIMP

GULFWEED SHRIMP

GRASS SHRIMPS

hepatic spine

carpus

ARROW SHRIMP

Plate 56
MISCELLANEOUS LARGER ARTHROPODS

Reduced; scale varies. Measurements are maximum recorded length, front of carapace or tip of rostrum to end of abdomen or tail.

BOREAL RED SHRIMPS   *Pandalus* species   p. 237
 No claws (or only microscopic ones) on 1st legs; 2nd legs unequal, with small claws; none on 3rd legs. *P. borealis* shown; to 5 in. (125 mm). See text for other species; see also Plate 54.

PINK SHRIMP   *Penaeus duorarum*
 1st 3 pairs of walking legs have small claws. To 8 in. (200 mm). See Southern Commercial Shrimps, p. 233.

MANTIS SHRIMP   *Squilla empusa*   p. 218
 Short carapace, mantislike claws, 3 pairs of weak walking legs. To 10 in. (250 mm).

ATLANTIC HORSESHOE CRAB   p. 202
Limulus polyphemus
 Horseshoe-shaped front end, spiny midbody, spike-like tail. To 2 ft. (600 mm) including tail.

NORTHERN LOBSTER   *Homarus americanus*   p. 239
 3 pairs of limbs have claws, with huge pincers on 1st pair. To 3 ft. (900 mm).

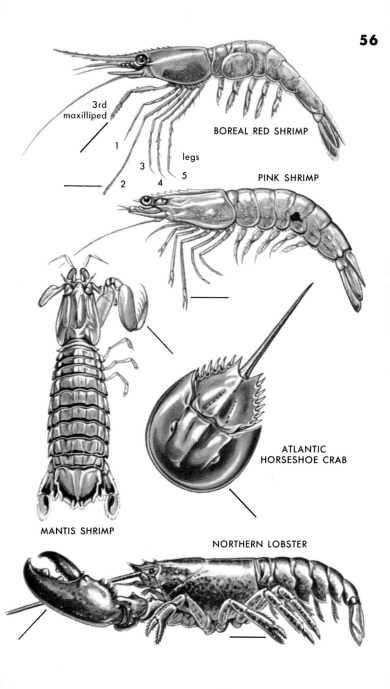

3rd
maxilliped

1

2

3

4

5

legs

BOREAL RED SHRIMP

PINK SHRIMP

MANTIS SHRIMP

ATLANTIC
HORSESHOE CRAB

NORTHERN LOBSTER

Plate 57

HERMIT CRABS AND MUD SHRIMPS

Scale varies. Measurements for hermit crabs are maximum recorded carapace length (see Fig. 68, p. 241), and for mud shrimps, maximum length from front of carapace to end of abdomen.

ACADIAN HERMIT CRAB   *Pagurus acadianus*   p. 242
  Major claw moderately wide (width more than half the length); orange-striped. To $1\frac{1}{4}$ in. (31 mm).

HAIRY HERMIT CRAB   *Pagurus arcuatus*   p. 242
  Major claw wide, ridged, hairy. To $1\frac{1}{4}$ in. (31 mm). See text for similar species.

LONG-CLAWED HERMIT CRAB   p. 241
Pagurus longicarpus
  Major claw narrower than Acadian Hermit Crab (above), nearly hairless; brown- or gray-striped. To $\frac{3}{8}$ in. (9 mm). See text for similar species.

FLAT-CLAWED HERMIT CRAB   p. 242
Pagurus pollicaris
  Major claw broad and flat. To $1\frac{1}{4}$ in. (31 mm).

STRIPED HERMIT CRAB   *Clibanarius vittatus*   p. 243
  Claws nearly equal; walking legs boldly striped. To $1\frac{1}{4}$ in. (31 mm).

NAUSHON MUD SHRIMP   *Naushonia crangonoides*
  1st legs with subchelate claws; none on 2nd. To $1\frac{3}{8}$ in. (34 mm). Head end only shown. See under Short-browed Mud Shrimp, p. 240.

FLAT-BROWED MUD SHRIMP   *Upogebia affinus* p. 240
  Front of carapace flat-topped. To 4 in. (100 mm).

SHORT-BROWED MUD SHRIMP   p. 240
Callianassa atlantica
  1st and 2nd legs have claws. To $2\frac{1}{2}$ in. (62 mm). Head end only shown.

BIG-CLAWED SNAPPING SHRIMP   p. 236
Alpheus heterochelis
  1st and 2nd legs have claws, 2nd pair weak and slender. To 2 in. (50 mm). Head end only shown. See text for similar species.

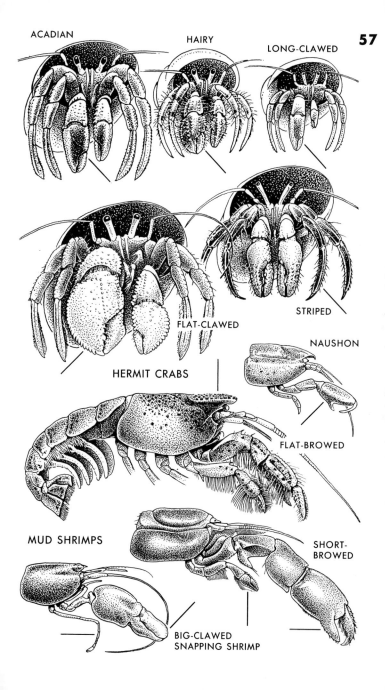

ACADIAN

HAIRY

LONG-CLAWED

FLAT-CLAWED

STRIPED

HERMIT CRABS

NAUSHON

FLAT-BROWED

MUD SHRIMPS

SHORT-BROWED

BIG-CLAWED
SNAPPING SHRIMP

Plate 58
GHOST, MARSH, AND FIDDLER CRABS

Scale varies. Measurements are maximum recorded carapace width. Shell squarish or tapered somewhat behind, with a single marginal tooth or none. Mostly intertidal or semiterrestrial crabs.

GHOST CRAB   *Ocypode quadrata*   p. 251
Pale, sand-colored; burrows on sandy beaches. Space between eyes narrow. To 2 in. (50 mm).

GULFWEED CRAB   *Planes minutus*   p. 251
Yellow-olive to reddish-brown with white spots and darker flecks. On Gulfweed or oceanic flotsam. To $\frac{3}{4}$ in. (19 mm).

WHARF CRAB   *Sesarma cinereum*
Paler than next species and lacking marginal notch. To 1 in. (25 mm). Partial outline of shell shown. See under Marsh Crab, p. 251.

MARSH CRAB   *Sesarma reticulatum*   p. 251
Purplish to black; with marginal notch. Space between eyes broad. To $1\frac{1}{8}$ in. (28 mm).

FIDDLER CRABS   *Uca* species   p. 252
Males have 1 claw enormously enlarged; space between eyes much shorter than eyestalks.
Sand Fiddler, *U. pugilator.* Palm of large claw smooth. To 1 in. (25 mm). Claw only shown.
Mud Fiddler, *U. pugnax.* Palm of large claw has an oblique row of tubercles. To $\frac{7}{8}$ in. (22 mm).
Brackish-water Fiddler, *U. minax.* Palm of large claw has an oblique ridge of tubercles; joints red. Shell with a distinct groove behind each eye. To $1\frac{1}{2}$ in. (38 mm).

Fig. 45.

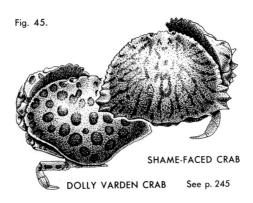

SHAME-FACED CRAB

DOLLY VARDEN CRAB   See p. 245

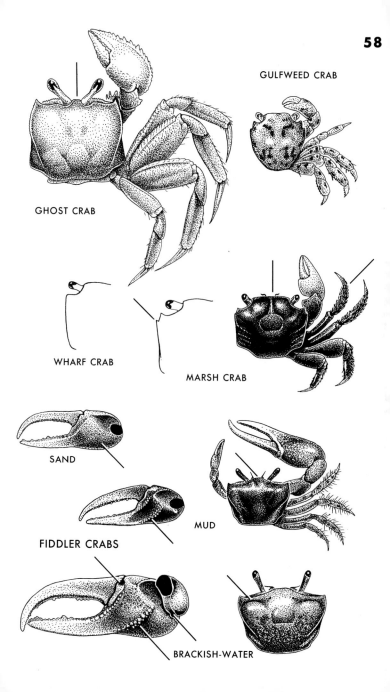

GULFWEED CRAB

GHOST CRAB

WHARF CRAB

MARSH CRAB

SAND

MUD

FIDDLER CRABS

BRACKISH-WATER

Plate 59

MUD CRABS

Scale varies. Measurements are maximum recorded carapace width. Mud crabs have 5 marginal teeth, the first 2 partially fused; frontal margin notched.

WHITE-FINGERED MUD CRAB   p. 250
Rhithropanopeus harrisii
  Fingers lighter than palm. Found in fresh to brackish water. To $3/4$ in. (19 mm). Partial outline of shell and claw shown.

BLACK-FINGERED MUD CRABS   p. 249
Panopeus and related genera
  Fingers black.

  Panopeus herbstii. Movable finger of major claw toothed but wrist ungrooved. Inner surface of 3rd maxilliped has a red mark in males, sometimes in females (1). To $1\frac{1}{2}$ in. (38 mm). Claw and maxilliped shown.

  Hexapanopeus angustifrons. Movable finger of major claw with a strong tooth; wrist grooved. Inner surface of 3rd maxilliped unmarked. To $1\frac{1}{8}$ in. (28 mm). Claw only shown.

  Neopanopeus sayi. Dark color of fixed finger extends broadly on palm. Inner surface of 3rd maxilliped sometimes has a red dot (2). Fingers of minor claws edged like cutting pliers. To $7/8$ in. (22 mm). Claw and maxilliped shown.

  Eurypanopeus depressus. Black markings similar to preceding. Inner surface of 3rd maxilliped has a large red spot (3). Fingers of minor claw spooned. To $3/4$ in. (19 mm). Claw and maxilliped shown.

COMMENSAL CRABS

Very small crabs—to $3/4$ in. (19 mm). Shell round or oval, without marginal teeth. Live as commensals or parasites in bivalves and other invertebrates. See p. 250 for species below.

OYSTER CRAB   *Pinnotheres ostreum*
  Shell round to oval or longer than wide. Tips of walking legs pointed. To $5/8$ in. (16 mm).

PINNIXA **species**
  Shell about twice as wide as long. *P. chaetopterana* and *P. retinens* have *propodus* (second joint from end) of 3rd walking legs slightly longer than wide (4); *P. cylindrica,* propodus length and width about equal (5); *P. sayana,* propodus slender (6). *P. chaetopterana* has fingers bent down (7); *P. retinens* has them straight (8). To $3/4$ in. (19 mm).

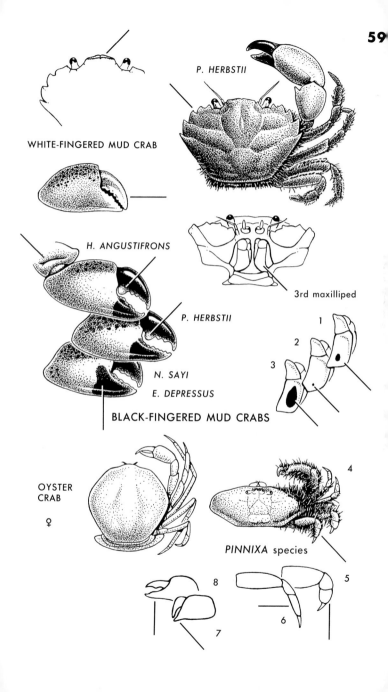

59

WHITE-FINGERED MUD CRAB

P. HERBSTII

H. ANGUSTIFRONS

P. HERBSTII

N. SAYI

E. DEPRESSUS

3rd maxilliped

1
2
3

BLACK-FINGERED MUD CRABS

OYSTER
CRAB
♀

PINNIXA species

4
5
6
7
8

Plate 60

SPIDER CRABS AND OTHERS

Scale varies. Measurements are maximum recorded length of carapace. Shell triangular or globular with front usually developed as a projecting rostrum.

LIBINIA DUBIA
About 6 spines on center line; rostrum longer than in next species. To 4 in. (100 mm). See under Common Spider Crab, p. 246.

COMMON SPIDER CRAB *Libinia emarginata* p. 246
About 9 spines along center of back. To 4 in. (100 mm).

PURSE CRAB *Persephona punctata* p. 245
Shell globular, with 3 spines behind. To 2 in. (50 mm).

RED-SPOTTED SPIDER CRAB *Pelia mutica* p. 245
Shell without spines or tubercles, often covered with sponge; rostrum deeply forked. To $\frac{1}{2}$ in. (12 mm).

TOAD CRAB *Hyas araneus* p. 245
Shell with row of tubercles at sides and scattered on top; orbits with projecting wings behind. To $3\frac{3}{4}$ in. (95 mm).

HYAS COARCTATUS
Compare orbital wings with preceding species. To $1\frac{1}{4}$ in. (31 mm). Detail only shown. See under Toad Crab, p. 245.

CHIP CRAB *Heterocrypta granulata* p. 246
Shell broadly triangular, without marginal teeth, strongly ridged above. To $\frac{3}{4}$ in. (19 mm).

ANOMURAN CRABS

4th walking legs vestigial, concealed beneath abdomen or tightly folded against shell.

LITHODES MAIA p. 243
Shell is strongly spined; abdomen asymmetrical. To 4 in. (100 mm).

PARCHMENT WORM POLYONYX p. 243
Polyonyx gibbesi
Shell broadly oval; gray, unpatterned. To $\frac{5}{8}$ in. (16 mm).

SPOTTED PORCELAIN CRAB *Porcellana sayana*
Shell narrowly oval, longer than wide; reddish brown with pale spots. To $\frac{1}{2}$ in. (12 mm). See under Parchment Worm Polyonyx, p. 243.

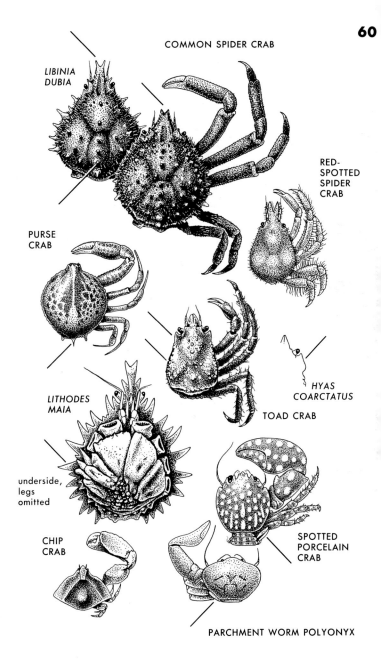

60

COMMON SPIDER CRAB

LIBINIA DUBIA

RED-SPOTTED SPIDER CRAB

PURSE CRAB

HYAS COARCTATUS

TOAD CRAB

LITHODES MAIA

underside, legs omitted

CHIP CRAB

SPOTTED PORCELAIN CRAB

PARCHMENT WORM POLYONYX

Plate 61

SWIMMING AND ROCK CRABS

Reduced. Measurements are maximum recorded width of carapace.

ROCK CRAB *Cancer irroratus* p. 246
9 marginal teeth, smooth to finely granulate-edged. To 5¼ in. (131 mm).

JONAH CRAB *Cancer borealis*
Similar to preceding but marginal teeth rough-edged. To 6¼ in. (156 mm). Teeth only shown. See under Rock Crab, p. 246.

GREEN CRAB *Carcinus maenas* p. 247
5 marginal teeth; last walking legs flattened but not paddle-shaped. Males and young crabs yellow to greenish underneath, females red-orange. To 3 in. (75 mm).

LADY CRAB *Ovalipes ocellatus* p. 248
Carapace only slightly broader than long; last legs paddle-shaped. Marked with clusters of speckles. To 3 in. (75 mm). See text for similar species.

BLUE CRAB *Callinectes sapidus* p. 247
Claws and legs bright blue, young paler. To 9 in. (225 mm). See text and Fig. 46 (below) for similar species.

SPECKLED CRAB *Arenaeus cribrarius*
Brown with whitish spots. To 4½ in. (112 mm). See under Blue Crab, p. 247.

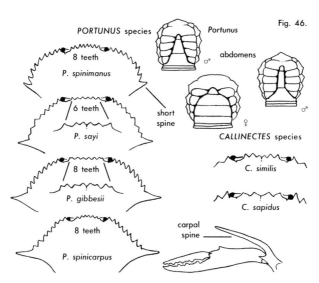

PORTUNUS species
P. spinimanus — 8 teeth
P. sayi — 6 teeth
P. gibbesii — 8 teeth
P. spinicarpus — 8 teeth
short spine
carpal spine

Portunus abdomens
♂ ♀ ♂

CALLINECTES species
C. similis
C. sapidus

Fig. 46.

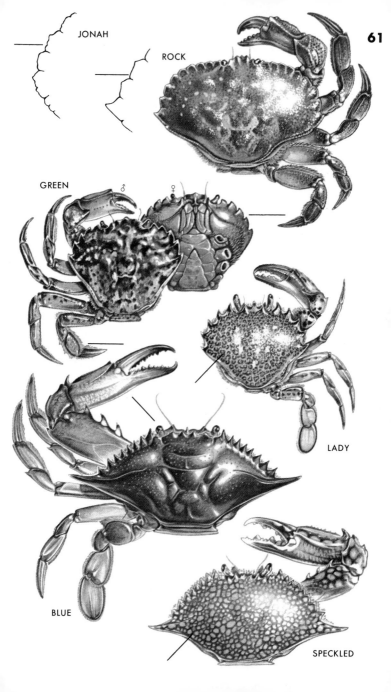

JONAH

ROCK

61

GREEN

♂ ♀

LADY

BLUE

SPECKLED

Plate 62
SEA URCHINS AND SAND DOLLARS

Reduced. Measurements are maximum recorded length or width of test, whichever is greater.

GREEN SEA URCHIN p. 257
Strongylocentrotus droebachiensis
    Spines no longer than ⅓ test width; periproct has many small plates (see Fig. 47, below). To 3 in. (75 mm).

PURPLE SEA URCHIN   *Arbacia punctulata*   p. 257
    Spine length equals about ½ test width; periproct has 3–5 plates (see Fig. 47, below). To 2 in. (50 mm).

HEART URCHIN   *Moira atropos*   p. 258
    Egg- or heart-shaped with 5 deep grooves. To 2 in. (50 mm).

SAND DOLLAR   *Echinarachnius parma*   p. 258
    Flat with 5-petaled pattern; color variable. To 3 in. (75 mm).

KEYHOLE URCHIN   *Mellita quinquiesperforata*
    Flat with 5 slitlike holes. To 3 in. (75 mm) or more. See under Sand Dollar, p. 258.

Fig. 47.

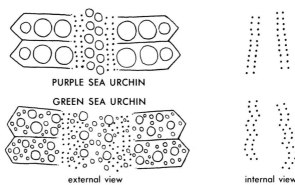

PURPLE SEA URCHIN

GREEN SEA URCHIN

external view   internal view

test details showing tubercles (circles) for
attachment of spines, and pores (dots) for tube feet

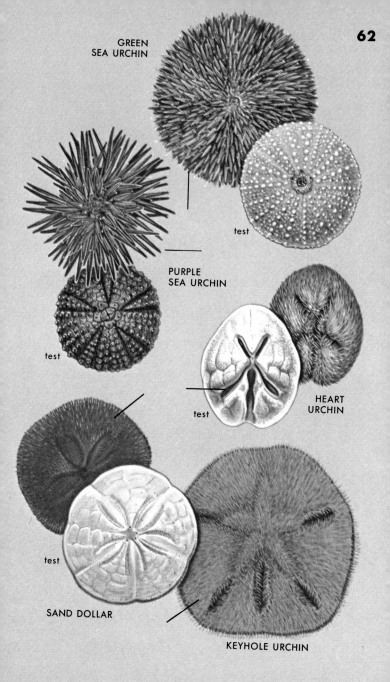

62

GREEN
SEA URCHIN

test

PURPLE
SEA URCHIN

test

HEART
URCHIN

test

test

SAND DOLLAR

KEYHOLE URCHIN

Plate 63

SEA STARS

Reduced. Measurements are *radius* measured from center of disk to tip of arm.

ASTERIID SEA STARS   p. 261
Asterias and *Leptasterias* species
  Tube feet in 4 rows. Skin with tiny pincerlike pedicellariae (see Fig. 70, p. 259).
  Forbes' Asterias, *A. forbesii.* Madreporite usually orange; note broadly rounded pedicellariae. To 5 in. (125 mm).
  Boreal Asterias, *A. vulgaris.* Madreporite usually yellow; note elongated pedicellariae. To 8 in. (200 mm).
  Polar Sea Star, *L. polaris.* Usually 6-armed. To 5 in. (125 mm).

MUD STAR   *Ctenodiscus crispatus*   p. 260
  Pentagonal; arms have distinct marginal plates, each with a flat spine. To 2 in. (50 mm). See text for similar species.

BLOOD STARS   *Henricia* species   p. 261
  Covered above with granular spines; color varies. To 2 in. (50 mm).

MARGINED SEA STARS   *Astropecten* species   p. 260
  With marginal plates, the lower ones fringed with slender spines. *A. articulatus* shown; to 5 in. (125 mm). See text for other species.

SLENDER SEA STAR   *Luidia clathrata*   p. 259
  Covered with blocklike paxillae (see Fig. 70, p. 259). To 4 in. (100 mm).

SUNSTARS   *Solaster* and *Crossaster* species   p. 260
  Surface covered with bristles or prickles called pseudopaxillae (see Fig. 70, p. 259).
  Spiny Sunstar, *C. papposus.* Usually 10–12 arms; with coarsely bristly pseudopaxillae. To 7 in. (175 mm).
  Purple Sunstar, *S. endeca.* Usually 9–10 arms; with short, prickly pseudopaxillae. To 8 in. (200 mm).

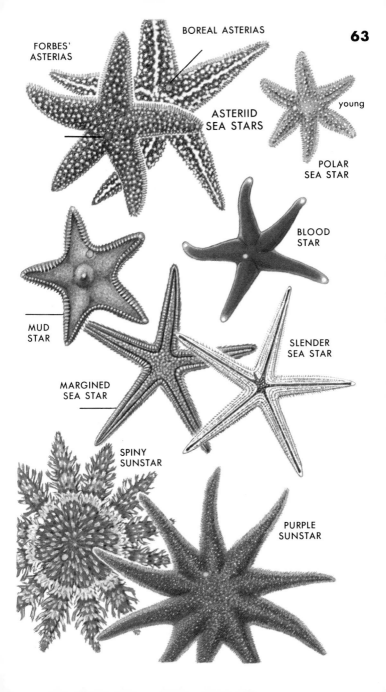

63

FORBES' ASTERIAS

BOREAL ASTERIAS

ASTERIID SEA STARS

young

POLAR SEA STAR

BLOOD STAR

MUD STAR

SLENDER SEA STAR

MARGINED SEA STAR

SPINY SUNSTAR

PURPLE SUNSTAR

Plate 64

BRITTLE STARS

Whole animals reduced; details enlarged. Measurements are maximum recorded dimensions.

DWARF BRITTLE STAR   *Axiognathus squamata*   p. 264
Disk scaly, to $\frac{3}{16}$ in. (5 mm), arms about 5 times longer. See text for other species with scaly disk.

BURROWING BRITTLE STAR   *Amphioplus abditus*
Similar to preceding but larger, arms longer. Disk to $\frac{1}{2}$ in. (12 mm), arms 12–16 times longer. See under Dwarf Brittle Star, p. 264.

DAISY BRITTLE STAR   *Ophiopholis aculeata*   p. 263
Arm plates ringed by small scales. Disk covered with fine, blunt spines and large plates. Disk to $\frac{3}{4}$ in. (19 mm), arms about $4\frac{1}{2}$ times longer. Color extremely variable.

SHORT-SPINED BRITTLE STAR   p. 263
Ophioderma brevispina
Arm spines short, held close to sides. Disk covered with fine granules. Disk to 5/8 in. (16 mm), arms about 4 times longer.

BASKET STAR   *Gorgonocephalus arcticus*   p. 263
Arms branch profusely. Disk to $1\frac{1}{2}$ in. (38 mm).

SPINY BRITTLE STAR   *Ophiothrix angulata*   p. 263
Arms and disk have long glassy spines edged with fine teeth. Disk to $\frac{1}{2}$ in. (12 mm), arms about 5 times longer.

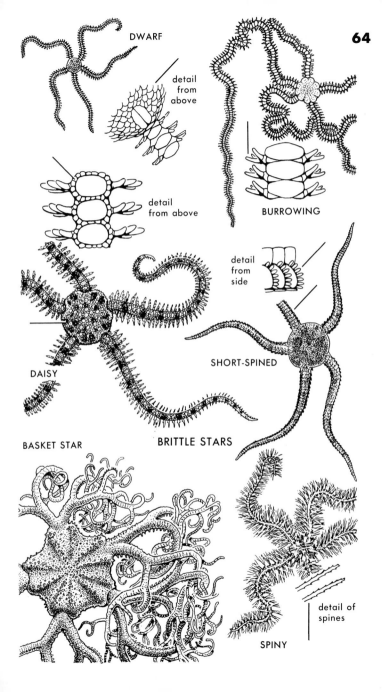

DWARF

detail from above

detail from above

BURROWING

detail from side

DAISY

SHORT-SPINED

BRITTLE STARS

BASKET STAR

SPINY

detail of spines

Similar species: (1) Fossor Coquina, *D. fossor* (not shown and *doubtfully distinct*) is smaller — ½ in. (12 mm) — smooth rather than finely striated, and less variable in color, tending to yellowish or purple. Occurs sporadically, Long Island to Cape Hatteras. (2) Compare with tellins (Plate 25), which are smaller, more fragile, and have inner shell margin *smooth*. (3) See also Arctic Wedge Clam. (Plate 28).

Where found: Del. to Gulf of Mexico, irregular north of Cape Hatteras. Intertidal on ocean beaches.

Remarks: One of the few inhabitants of the surf zone on sandy beaches. Coquinas burrow when waves recede, emerging with the next surge. In summer on southern beaches, irregular northward but usually abundant when present — sometimes in hundreds or thousands per sq. yd. They make a delicate chowder.

Family: Donacidae.

STOUT TAGELUS *Tagelus plebeius*   Pl. 24

Identification: Shells oblong (length about 3 times greater than width), gaping; hinge near *middle* with 2 small teeth. Outside chalky with thin yellowish brown periostracum. To 4 in. (100 mm).

Similar species: (1) Purplish Tagelus, *T. divisus* (Plate 24) is smaller — to 1½ in. (38 mm) — fragile, with a *weak* radial rib inside. Periostracum yellowish, glossy, usually with purple rays. Gulf of Mexico to Cape Cod but scarce and local on our coast. Burrows in sand; intertidal to subtidal at shallow depths. (2) Ribbed Pod, *Siliqua costata* (Plate 24) is elongate, oval; hinge off-center forward with a *strong* rib inside; periostracum glossy to iridescent, purplish-tinged. To 2 in. (50 mm). Cape Hatteras to Casco Bay, rarely or locally to Gulf of St. Lawrence; subtidal on sandy bottoms. Family Solenidae.

Where found: Cape Cod to Gulf of Mexico. Burrows in sandy mud to a depth of 18 in. (450 mm) on bay beaches.

Family: Sanguinolariidae.

COMMON RAZOR CLAM *Ensis directus*   Pl. 24

Identification: The large jackknife or (straight) razor clam is about *6 times* longer than wide; hinge line *bowed*. Beaks at front end, left hinge with 2 teeth. To 10 in. (250 mm).

Similar species: Little Green Razor Clam, *Solen viridis* (Plate 24) is smaller and only about *4 times* longer than wide, with straighter hinge line; both hinges have 1 tooth. To 2 in. (50 mm). Fla. to Cape Cod, but uncommon north of N.J.

Where found: Labrador to Ga. Lower intertidal to subtidal down to 120 ft. (36 m); sandy mud, often in colonies.

Remarks: In *Stalking the Blue-Eyed Scallop,* Euell Gibbons gives several ingenious methods for catching these elusive clams

and recipes for cooking them afterwards. They burrow deeply and hold on tenaciously; the fully extended foot is nearly as long as the shell and can be used to swim as well as burrow.
Family: Solenidae, including *Solen.*

ARCTIC ROCK BORER *Hiatella arctica*   **Pl. 27**
Identification: Shell elongate, thick, dirty white; roughened with growth ridges. Siphons *bright red.* To 1½ in. (38 mm).
Where found: Arctic south to West Indies. Young are common in lower intertidal zone northward; scarce and subtidal south of Cape Cod.
Remarks: Colorful siphons are conspicuous, but are promptly withdrawn if disturbed. The clams wedge themselves or bore into crevices, among seaweed holdfasts and such.
Family: Hiatellidae.

SOFT-SHELLED CLAM *Mya arenaria*   **Pl. 28**
Identification: Shells elongate, thin, gaping. Hinge asymmetrical, left side with a *tongue-like chondrophore,* right with a heart-shaped pit. Chalky white with dull brownish or yellowish periostracum. To 3–4 in. (75–100 mm), exceptionally to 6 in. (150 mm).
Similar species: Truncate Soft-shelled Clam, *M. truncata* (not shown) has a broad U-shaped pallial sinus compared to the tongue-shaped one of Soft-shelled Clam. Shells *truncated* behind, but variant Soft-shelled Clam is similar. To 3 in. (75 mm). Arctic to Cape Cod; lower intertidal in Bay of Fundy, southward subtidal to 100 ft. (30 m).
Where found: Subarctic to Cape Hatteras, less commonly to S.C.; introduced on Pacific Coast. In bays and sounds, intertidal to subtidal to about 30 ft. (9 m), in minimum salinity of 5‰. Usually on muddier bottoms than Quahog (p. 152).
Remarks: Called simply "the clam" in New England, where it is usually fried. This species is known as the Steamer, Long Clam, Gaper, or Nannynose south of Cape Cod. It is the clam that squirts at you on tideflats, providing another, less delicate name. Diving ducks, whistling swans (which can extract them from deep burrows), raccoons, and cownose rays, as well as man, are fond of soft clams. In Chesapeake Bay, where the clams are harvested by hydraulic dredge, the annual catch is about twice as large as in New England.
Family: Myacidae.

COMMON BASKET CLAM *Corbula contracta*   **Pl. 25**
Identification: A small, thick, *asymmetrical* clam, with lower edge of right valve curling over left at the posterior end. Right hinge has a *strong hook* inside. To ½ in. (12 mm).
Where found: Cape Cod to West Indies. A bay and sound

species, subtidal in 3-100 ft. (0.9-30 m) or more. Not rare, but easily overlooked.
Family: Corbulidae.

ANGEL WING *Cyrtopleura costata* **Pl. 27**
Identification: Usually found as a broken beach shell; thin, brittle, and pure white. Scaly ribs at rear as well as forward. To 7 in. (175 mm). Compare *beaks* and *hinges* with the similar species listed below.
Similar species: (1) Wing Shell, *Pholas campechiensis* (Plate 27) is smaller — to 4 in. (100 mm) — with weaker sculpture, especially at rear. N.C. to Brazil, uncommon north of Cape Hatteras. Subtidal. (2) False Angel Wing, *Petricola pholadiformis* (Plate 27) smaller still — to 2 in. (50 mm) — with weaker ribbing. *More common* in our range than either Angel Wing or Wing Shell. Bores in stiff mud or peaty clay. Gulf of Mexico to Massachusetts Bay, locally to Gulf of St. Lawrence. *Intertidal.* Family Petricolidae. Note also (3) Truncate Borer and (4) Great Piddock (both Plate 27).
Where found: Cape Cod to Brazil; subtidal in mud and clay.
Family: Pholadidae, including *Pholas.*

SHIPWORMS *Teredo* and related genera **Pl. 27**
Identification: *Wormlike* wood-boring bivalves with small, somewhat T-shaped shells at front end, and a pair of calcareous projections called *pallets* at rear. Shell and pallets to $\frac{1}{4}$ in. (6 mm); whole worm several inches.
Teredo, Psiloteredo, and *Teredora* species have *paddle-shaped* pallets $\frac{3}{16}$-$\frac{3}{8}$ in. (5-9 mm) long; those of Gould's Shipworm, *Bankia gouldi,* are slender and *segmented.*
Where found: Common Shipworm, *Teredo navalis,* whole coast but chiefly south of Massachusetts Bay, in pilings and other immersed timbers. Other species are carried north in driftwood. Into moderately brackish water.
Remarks: Filelike edges of valves are used in boring; pallets seal the open end of burrow. Shipworms are one of the few animals that exist mainly on digested cellulose. They are a menace to untreated pilings and wooden boats, particularly in warm water. On his 4th voyage Columbus was marooned for a year in Jamaica when 2 of his ships succumbed to teredos.
Family: Teredinidae.

GLASSY LYONSIA *Lyonsia hyalina* **Pl. 23**
Identification: A thin glassy shell with swollen beaks, usually *coated marginally with sand grains.* Gray-yellow periostracum. To $\frac{3}{4}$ in. (19 mm).
Similar species: Species of *Yoldia* (Plate 23) and *Nuculana* (not shown) are also slender and thin but have filelike (taxo-

dont) hinges. For *Nuculana* species see Gould's Pandora (next account).

Where found: Nova Scotia to S.C. in soft shallows of bays and coastal ponds. Often with Morton's Egg Cockle (p. 152) on Eelgrass bottoms.

Family: Lyonsiidae.

GOULD'S PANDORA *Pandora gouldiana*   **Pl. 23**
Identification: A small, *very flat* bivalve with spoutlike rear. Shells unequal: right flat; left slightly swollen, with diagonal line. White, or pearly when eroded. Hinge with 3 strong teeth. To 1 in. (25 mm).

Similar species: Additional species (none shown) with valves narrowed or spoutlike behind include: (1) Several southern species of *Pandora* that are rare. (2) Dipper Shells, *Cuspidaria* species, subtidal in 100 ft. (30 m) or more. Family Cuspidariidae. (3) Nut Shells, *Nuculana* species, most of which live in deep water; all have *filelike* (taxodont) hinge teeth. 2 shallow-water *Nuculana* species are Pointed Nut Shell, *N. acuta,* and Sulcate Nut Shell, *N. tenuisulcata.* Both are slim, comma-shaped, to $\frac{1}{2}$ in. (12 mm). Pointed Nut Shell has sharp spout; Sulcate Nut Shell has a blunt one. Pointed Nut Shell, Massachusetts Bay to West Indies; Sulcate Nut Shell, R.I. to Gulf of St. Lawrence. See Near Nut Shell, p. 144. Family Nuculanidae.
Where found: Whole coast. Subtidal in shallow water off ocean beaches and in bays; generally uncommon.
Family: Pandoridae.

WOOD PIDDOCKS *Martesia* species   **Pl. 27**
Identification: Wedge- or peg-shaped with front swollen, broadly rounded; outside with diagonal groove *near front end* and fine, filelike concentric ridges.

2 species. (1) Wood Piddock, *M. cuneiformis* (not shown) is short, stubby; to $\frac{3}{4}$ in. (19 mm). (2) Striate Wood Piddock, *M. striata,* is longer — to 2 in. (50 mm).
Where found: Cape Hatteras to Brazil, but both are wood borers and may be carried north in driftwood.
Family: Pholadidae.

GREAT PIDDOCK *Zirfaea crispata*   **Pl. 27**
Identification: *Diagonal groove* divides shell; forward part with scaly ribs; rear with concentric ridges only. To 3 in. (75 mm).
Similar species: (1) Truncate Borer, *Barnea truncata* (Plate 27) lacks groove, has progressively weaker ribs to rear. To 2 in. (50 mm). A more fragile shell, it resembles Angel Wing and similar species on Plate 27, but differs in shape and hinge; also called Fallen Angel Wing. Cape Cod to Fla.; intertidal to sub-

tidal at shallow depths. (2) See wood piddocks (Plate 27 and preceding account), with diagonal groove nearer front end.
Where found: Long Island, or rarely N.J., north to Labrador. Intertidal to subtidal at shallow depths, in wood as well as clay, peat, or soft rocks.
Family: Pholadidae, including *Barnea.*

CONRAD'S THRACIA *Thracia conradi* Pl. 23
Identification: This large, strongly bowed clam has a distinctive hinge: beak of right valve has a deep notch and is pierced by beak of left valve. Hinges toothless. To 4 in. (100 mm).
Where found: L.I. Sound to Gulf of St. Lawrence. A deep burrower in sand or mud, subtidal in 15–90 ft. (4.5–27 m).
Family: Thraciidae.

SPOON SHELLS *Periploma* species Pl. 23
Identification: Shells somewhat unequal, *thin,* white, rounded at front, squared behind. Hinge has a distinct chondrophore.
2 species in shallow water, others deeper. (1) Paper Spoon Shell, *P. papyratium,* has almost equally bowed valves; chondrophore points down. To 1 in. (25 mm). (2) Lea's Spoon Shell, *P. leanum,* has distinctly unequal valves — left nearly flat, right bowed. Chondrophore projects almost horizontally. To 1½ in. (38 mm).
Similar species: See Soft-shelled Clam (Plate 28), also with chondrophore.
Where found: (1) Paper Spoon Shell, Labrador to R.I.; subtidal in 20 ft. (6 m) or more. (2) Lea's Spoon Shell, Gulf of St. Lawrence to N.C.; commonly found washed ashore but lives subtidally in 15 ft. (4.5 m) or more.
Family: Periplomatidae.

Squids and Octopuses:
Class Cephalopoda

These are among the most highly evolved invertebrates. Eye development, for example, rivals that of bony animals in complexity and efficiency. Cephalopods are active, fast-moving, and seemingly intelligent.

Prehistoric cephalopods called ammonoids, which were most prevalent in the Age of Dinosaurs, and other, even more ancient forms, were heavily shelled. The modern Chambered Nautilus of the South Pacific also has a strong shell. Most cephalopods living today, however, do not. Squids found on this coast have a flexible, plasticlike "pen" — an internal shell-like structure — buried deep in the body. (See accounts of Spirula and Paper Nautilus, p. 163.)

The head and body (*mantle*) are clearly differentiated in squids, less so in octopuses. The mouth is armed with a pair of strong parrotlike beaks; presumably even our small species can bite if carelessly handled, but this does not appear to be a common occurrence. Squids are predatory on fishes, crustaceans, and other squids. The mouth is surrounded by 8 arms (octopuses) or 8 arms and 2 tentacles (squids), all with suckers. One of the arms in males is modified to transfer elaborately formed spermatophores to the female when mating.

The body has a mantle cavity into which water can be drawn and then expelled forcefully through a tubular siphon, simulating jet propulsion. When the animal is threatened, an ink sac ejects its contents through the siphon, providing a smoke screen for escape. Cephalopods have a phenomenal ability to change color, and do so according to mood and the need for camouflage. Out of water, squids are soft and flaccid, a sorry transformation from their grace and alertness in life.

BOREAL SQUID *Illex illecebrosus*   **Pl. 35**
Identification: Fins short (only $\frac{1}{3}$ *or more* of mantle length), triangular; skin covering eyes pierced by a hole with notch in front. Mantle to 9 in. (225 mm).
Similar species: See Long-finned Squid (Plate 35).
Where found: Arctic Ocean south to Cape Cod and in very deep water to Gulf of Mexico.
Remarks: This species replaces Long-finned Squid north of Cape Ann. It is common inshore in summer, feeding especially on herring, mackerel, and krill shrimps. Squids are traditionally the preferred bait of the North Atlantic cod fisheries.
Family: Ommastrephidae.

LONG-FINNED SQUID *Loligo pealei*   **Pl. 35**
Identification: Fins elongate (to $\frac{1}{2}$ *or more* of mantle length), triangular; eyes covered by transparent skin with a small pore in front that is not always easy to find. Mantle to 17 in. (425 mm).
Similar species: (1) Brief Squid, *Lolliguncula brevis* (Plate 35) is short-bodied and has *rounded* fins that are *less than* $\frac{1}{2}$ mantle length. Mantle to 5 in. (125 mm). Delaware Bay to Brazil. (2) Boreal Squid (Plate 35) has skin over eye with an opening, *notched* in front.
Where found: The most common squid between Cape Hatteras and Cape Cod, but ranging south to Caribbean and north to Cape Ann; less frequently to Penobscot Bay, Maine, or even Bay of Fundy.
Remarks: An abundant shallow-water species during warmer months (April–Nov. in s. New England). Heavily preyed on by bluefish, sea bass, mackerel, and other fishes, and taken commercially for bait and for sale in Italian fish markets. Communal egg clusters contain hundreds of 2-in. (50 mm), banana-

shaped, gelatinous capsules with up to 200 eggs in each; attached to seaweeds and bottom debris; commonly trawled in summer.

Family: Loliginidae, including *Lolliguncula.*

Additional Cephalopod Species   Pl. 35

More than 36 species of cephalopods have been recorded off this coast. Some of these live on or near the bottom, far out on the continental shelf or beyond; others swim suspended in the darkness above the abyss of the deep sea. The following are among the few that *might* be found along our beaches.

Spirula, *Spirula spirula.* The flat-coiled *chambered* shells, up to 1 in. (25 mm) in diameter, are common on ocean beaches from N.C. southward and exceptionally north to Nantucket. In life the gas-filled internal shell buoys a squidlike body; at its tail end Spirula has a luminous disk to light its sunless habitat 600–3000 ft. (180–900 m) down. Family Spirulidae.

Common Atlantic Shore Octopus, *Octopus vulgaris* (not shown). Has an average arm span of 2–3 ft. (600–900 mm), but 10-ft. (3 m) giants live in deep water down to $\frac{1}{4}$ mile (400 m). Common from s. Fla. throughout the Caribbean, where small individuals can be found in crevices and under rocks intertidally. Two Long Island records (1945), presumably accidental. Family Octopodidae.

Offshore Octopus, *Bathypolypus arcticus* (not shown). A rough and warty species with a horn (*cirrus*) over each eye. 3rd right arm of males is spooned at end. Body to 2 ft. (600 mm). Whole coast in deep water but at trawling depth north of Cape Cod. Family Octopodidae.

Paper Nautilus, *Argonauta argo.* A deep-sea drifter, best known by the elegant paper-thin shells that wash ashore, chiefly on warm Atlantic beaches and sometimes as far north as Cape Cod. The shell — up to 1 ft. (300 mm) or more across — is secreted by 2 modified arms of the female as a brood chamber; males are only $\frac{1}{2}$ in. (12 mm) long and shell-less. Family Argonautidae.

Giant Squids, *Architeuthis* species (not shown). Normally live in the deep sea beyond the continental shelf, but have occasionally washed ashore, or been encountered at the surface *all around* the North Atlantic from Fla. north to Davis Strait, w. Europe, and Madeira. Adults probably reach a length of 60 ft. (18 m) or more with tentacles extended (head and mantle only $\frac{1}{4}$ of total length). This is one of the largest invertebrates, and reported encounters with live individuals almost rival the lurid tales of the Norse *Kraken* and other squidlike monsters. See Frank W. Lane's *Kingdom of the Octopus,* Jarrolds, London, 1960. Family Ommastrephidae.

Segmented Worms:
Phylum Annelida

Most annelids are wormlike, externally segmented, and have bristles or *setae*. However, no such simple definition describes all members of the phylum.

There are 4 annelid classes. Members of the class Myzostomaria are parasitic on or commensal with echinoderms, particularly crinoids or sea lilies which only live in deep water off this coast. *Protomyzostomus* is a genus found on the Basket Star (p. 263). Myzostomids are somewhat disklike and less than $3/8$ in. (9 mm) long. They have few setae and only internal signs of segmentation, but like other annelids they do have a trochophore larval stage.

Leeches make up another annelid class, Hirudinea. They are easily recognized as leeches (see left front endpaper) by a sucker at each end (some free-living flatworms, p. 102, have 1 sucker at the rear). They are atypical annelids in lacking setae and in being obscurely segmented externally. Marine leeches belong to a single family, Piscicolidae. Although not rare, they have been studied very little on this coast. Numerous genera are known; most parasitize or prey on fishes, but a few have been found on shrimps, crabs, sea turtles, and even sea spiders. Although popularly despised as parasites, leeches do not usually remain permanently attached to their prey. Size range is $3/8$–8 in. (9–200 mm). They will not be dealt with further in this guide.

The remaining annelid classes are Oligochaeta, aquatic earthworms (p. 196), and Polychaeta, bristle worms (below), which are the most numerous marine forms.

Bristle Worms:
Class Polychaeta

Polychaetes vary widely in body shape, but almost all are clearly segmented externally and have bristles or *setae*. These are usually grouped in bundles with a heavier supporting bristle called an *aciculum*. Setal bundles develop as part of the structure of the polychaete foot or *parapodium;* parapodia vary in appearance from inconspicuous pimplelike bumps to elaborately lobed appendages with *gills* (*branchiae*) or fingerlike *cirri*. Variations in detail are endless, but parapodia are best developed in swimming polychaetes and least so in burrowing forms. Often a parapodium has 2 main branches or lobes and is said to be *biramous;* the upper branch is called a *notopodium,* the lower a *neuropodium,* and their associated setae are *notosetae* and *neurosetae*. Not all segments

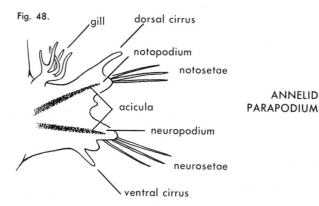

Fig. 48.

gill

dorsal cirrus

notopodium

notosetae

acicula

ANNELID
PARAPODIUM

neuropodium

neurosetae

ventral cirrus

have setae; those that do are called *setigers*. Setae vary greatly in form and detail, and serious taxonomic work relies heavily on their differences. Where necessary, setae will be described and illustrated, but their study usually requires a microscope.

The polychaete head poses problems in nomenclature; it too varies in form and function. Specialized feeding mechanisms have been developed by different species: some polychaetes are strong-jawed predators; others have structures for filtering and licking or for piercing and sucking; still others indiscriminately ingest mud or sand, leaving the sorting of digestible from indigestible items to their internal anatomy. The head reflects these varied talents. At the very front is a *prostomium* (not technically a segment) followed by a *buccal* segment (containing the mouth) and 1 or more succeeding trunk segments associated with head functions, the whole forming a *peristomium*. These structures often bear appendages that are variously termed antennae, tentacles, palpi (or palps), and cirri; gills may also be present. Also, there is often an *eversible proboscis* that is actually part of the foregut; it can be thrust out of the body or completely withdrawn.

Many polychaetes are conventionally "wormlike," with dozens or even hundreds of segments following one another with little variation from head to tail. In other species distinct body regions have evolved. The sexes are usually separate, but are not externally distinguishable in most families. A process called *epitoky* involves the metamorphosis of sexually inactive, benthic worms into sexually active, pelagic ones that are often quite different in appearance. The famed Palolo Worm of the Pacific exhibits epitokous swarming, and similar swarms occur on our coast, notably among syllids (p. 174) and clam worms (p. 176).

Sperm and ova are usually shed into the water, and offspring pass through a metamorphosis from swimming trochophore (see p. 61) to segmented larval stages, and finally to the mature worm. A few species brood their young. Many polychaetes have considerable ability to regenerate lost or damaged parts and break apart with distressing ease when handled. Some reproduce asexually. The bizarre chains of budding individuals of some kinds of syllids are examples (p. 174).

Classification of polychaetes is still in a state of flux. The arrangement and composition of families and orders varies with different authorities, and species and genera are continually being redefined. The segregation of polychaetes into Errantia and Sedentaria divisions is a classical one which is still in use and handy as a practical device, but condemned by many specialists as unnatural and obsolete; it is used here for convenience, but recognized as an artificial system. Polychaeta is one of the largest classes of marine invertebrates with well over 300 species in our area. They are treated in this section mainly by family groups, with the more common species given as examples.

Errant Polychaetes

The dictionary defines *errant* as "roving, especially in search of adventure." Errant polychaetes, therefore, are ones that get out and move about as opposed to the stay-at-home sedentary polychaetes (p. 182). The distinction is somewhat tenuous in the case of several borderline families. Typically the body of errant polychaetes is relatively long, slender, and wormlike; it is *not* divided into distinctly different regions. While the head varies in structure, it often has a muscular *eversible proboscis* with jaws. The setae are usually bristly and arranged in tufts along the side. Many errant polychaetes live in tubes, but usually they can leave them to move about. Most are carnivores.

PADDLE WORMS *Phyllodoce* and related genera   **Pl. 39**
  Identification: Leaf- or paddle-shaped *parapodial cirri* readily identify members of this family. The large eversible proboscis has papillae but no jaws. All genera have 4 frontal antennae. Body proportions vary; length about 15–70 times greater than width.

    5 genera (all Plate 39); 14 species discussed here. (1) *Eteone* (5 species) have *2 pairs of tentacular cirri;* other genera have 4 pairs. Species differ in proportions of tentacular cirri and shape of anal cirri and parapodia; color varies but is usually whitish to pale yellow. *E. lactea* has lower pair of tentacular cirri 2–3 times longer than upper pair; *E. trilineata* has upper pair twice as long. (Tentacular cirri about *equal* length in the other species.) *E. trilineata* to $\frac{3}{8}$ x $\frac{1}{16}$ in. (9 x 1.6 mm); *E. lactea* to 9 x $\frac{1}{8}$ in. (225 x 3 mm). *E. heteropoda* has *tapered* anal cirri; to

Fig. 49. **PADDLE WORMS**
PARAPODIA (setae omitted)

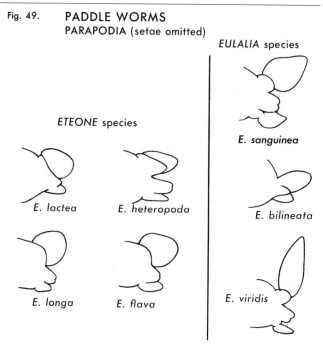

EULALIA species

ETEONE species

E. sanguinea

E. lactea   E. heteropoda

E. bilineata

E. longa   E. flava

E. viridis

Redrawn from Marian H. Pettibone's Marine Polychaetes of the New England Region

$3\frac{3}{4}$ x $\frac{1}{8}$ in. (94 x 3 mm). *E. flava* and *E. longa* have *short, blunt* anal cirri; *longa* is a more slender species. To 6 x $\frac{3}{16}$ in. (150 x 5 mm).

(2) *Eulalia* (3 species) have a *median antenna* (other genera do not); note differences in parapodia. *E. viridis* and *E. bilineata* have 3 segments with tentacular cirri visible from above, *E. sanguinea* only 2. *E. viridis* is greenish, sometimes spotted with brown; to 6 x $\frac{1}{8}$ in. (150 x 3 mm). *E. bilineata,* also greenish, has 2 dark lengthwise stripes; to 4 x $\frac{1}{16}$ in. (100 x 1.6 mm) — proportionately more slender than *E. viridis*. *E. sanguinea* varies in color through tones of brown, spotted or crossbanded with darker brown or green; to $2\frac{3}{8}$ x $\frac{3}{8}$ in. (59 x 9 mm).

(3) *Paranaitis,* (4) *Nereiphylla,* and (5) *Phyllodoce* have 4 pairs of tentacular cirri, lack median antenna, differ in shape of prostomium as shown. First 2 genera have only 1 species each in shallow water. *Paranaitis speciosa* is greenish, variably spotted or crossbanded with red; to $\frac{5}{8}$ x $\frac{1}{8}$ in. (16 x 3 mm). *Nereiphylla*

fragilis is greenish yellow; to 3 x $\frac{1}{8}$ in. (75 x 3 mm). Some authorities do not recognize *Nereiphylla* as a separate genus, placing *N. fragilis* in *Phyllodoce*. Species of *Phyllodoce* differ in shape of ventral cirri, color, and markings. *P. groenlandica* is greenish blue, irregularly marked with brown; to 18 x $\frac{3}{8}$ in. (450 x 9 mm). *P. maculata* is yellowish or green with brown spots on the midline above, and a somewhat diffuse lengthwise stripe on each side; to 4 x $\frac{1}{16}$ in. (100 x 1.6 mm). *P. mucosa* is white with 1–3 brown lengthwise stripes above; to 6 x $\frac{1}{8}$ in. (150 x 3 mm). *P. arenae* is white to green with a spindle-shaped crossband on each segment; to 4 x $\frac{1}{8}$ in. (100 x 3 mm).

Similar species: Do not confuse with clam worms (Plate 38), which also have paddlelike parapodia.

Where found: (1) *Eteone* species are all Boreal or Boreal–Arctic with southward limits as follows: *E. lactea,* Fla.; *E. heteropoda,* Gulf of Mexico; *E. longa,* Va.; *E. flava,* N.J.; *E. trilineata,* Cape Cod. *E. lactea* and *E. heteropoda* occur in estuarine waters in lower Chesapeake Bay. (2) *Eulalia* species, Arctic south to L.I. Sound and locally to N.C. *E. sanguinea* enters estuarine waters in lower Chesapeake Bay. (3) *Paranaitis speciosa,* Penobscot Bay, Maine, to N.C.; intertidal to subtidal in deep water and also in estuaries, particularly on mud bottoms. (4) *Nereiphylla fragilis,* lower Chesapeake Bay to S.C.; estuarine and subtidal to shallow depths. (5) *Phyllodoce* species are also Boreal–Arctic with southern limits as follows: *P. arenae,* N.C.; *P. mucosa,* Gulf of Mexico; *P. maculata,* N.J.; *P. groenlandica,* N.C. First 2 species estuarine in lower Chesapeake Bay. All species occur intertidally, at least northward, and many range to great depths.

Remarks: Species of *Eteone* and other paddle worms are commonly found creeping about in bottom debris, among sponges, barnacles, and other sessile animals and plants. They are active, carnivorous worms.

Family: Phyllodocidae.

PLANKTON WORM *Tomopteris helgolandica*   **Pl. 33**

Identification: Transparent, with little sign of segmentation. Parapodia long, paddlelike, bilobed, with a pair of long tentacle-like tentacular cirri. To $3\frac{1}{2}$ in. (88 mm).

Similar species: Other transparent planktonic polychaetes (none shown) seldom found inshore include: (1) *T. septentrionalis,* a smaller — to 1 in. (25 mm) — relative; lacks *T. helgolandica's* well-developed cylindrical *tail.* Mainly Arctic–Boreal but south to S.C. (2) *Vanadis longissima* is long, cylindrical, with a pair of *bulging red eyes,* small parapodia. To 8 in. (200 mm). Worldwide. Family Alciopidae. (3) *Travisiopsis* species lack parapodia but have body margined with broad *leafy* cirri. To $1\frac{3}{16}$ in. (30 mm). Nearly cosmopolitan. Family Typhloscolecidae.

Where found: Throughout Atlantic Ocean; also reported from Indian Ocean, Mediterranean Sea. Mainly offshore, occasionally in coastal plankton.

Remarks: Alister Hardy described this worm as a very active swimmer, saying it "appears to run through the water as a centipede runs along the ground." It rolls into a ball and sinks when disturbed. Migrates vertically to surface at night.

Family: Tomopteridae.

SEA MOUSE *Aphrodita hastata*   Pl. 43

Identification: A *short, stout* worm with a furry coat. Fur thickest along sides; consists of several types of setae: some very fine and downy; others stronger, hairlike, with a highly iridescent, silky sheen of gold, bronze, or greenish; still others thicker, dark, and bristly. 15 pairs of scales hidden beneath fur. To 6 x 3 in. (150 x 75 mm) including fur; exceptionally to 9 in. (225 mm).

Where found: Gulf of St. Lawrence south to N.J. or rarely to mouth of Chesapeake Bay. *Subtidal* from 6 ft. (1.8 m) to great depths, on mud.

Remarks: Well known because of its distinctive form but not very often seen; only found by dredging, or when it is washed ashore after storms.

Family: Aphroditidae.

MANY-SCALED WORM   Not shown
Lepidametria commensalis

Identification: A slender worm with 30–50 pairs of scales. Dark colored. To 4 x ⅜ in. (100 x 9 mm).

Similar species: Burrowing scale worms (Plate 43) are also slender with numerous scales. They lack *filiform dorsal cirri* which are characteristic of Many-scaled Worm and other polynoids.

Where found: Cape Ann south to Gulf of Mexico. Intertidal to subtidal at shallow depths; chiefly commensal with larger tube worms.

Family: Polynoidae.

TWELVE-SCALED WORMS *Lepidonotus* species   Pl. 43

Identification: These worms have only *12–13* pairs of scales; other scale worms have more, at least when adult.

(1) *L. squamatus* has scales roughened with *tubercles of different sizes.* Colored with various shades of brown, often mottled or spotted with yellow, red, or green. To 2 x ⅝ in. (50 x 16 mm). (2) *L. sublevis* (not shown) has scales roughened with *fine tubercles of about equal size,* more scattered than those of *L. squamatus,* or scales may appear nearly smooth. To 1⅜ x ⅜ in. (34 x 9 mm). (3) *L. variabilis* (not shown) appears to have *smooth scales* — tubercles microscopic. Distinguish from

L. *sublevis* by *row of fine papillae* along edge of each scale opposite fringe of fine hairs; papillae lacking in *sublevis*. To 1$\frac{3}{8}$ x $\frac{3}{8}$ in. (34 x 9 mm).

Where found: (1) *L. squamatus,* Gulf of St. Lawrence south at least to Chesapeake Bay; lower intertidal to subtidal in deep water, and in estuaries to 20‰ salinity. (2) *L. sublevis,* Cape Cod to Gulf of Mexico; commensal in shells of Flat-clawed Hermit Crab (Plate 57) and also found among oyster shells and bottom debris. Lower intertidal to subtidal in deep water and to 15‰ salinity. (3) *L. variabilis,* Delaware Bay to West Indies, to 16.5‰ salinity.

Remarks: *L. squamatus,* the most frequently encountered species, is common on all sorts of bottoms (except mud), in crevices, and among other fouling and sedentary animals and seaweeds. It loses scales less easily than most scale worms; rolls up like a pill bug when disturbed.

Family: Polynoidae.

FIFTEEN-SCALED WORMS *Harmothoe* species   **Pl. 43**
Identification: Readily distinguished from species in preceding account by *15 pairs* of scales.

Several species, 2 common in shallow water. (1) *H. imbricata* has 4 eyes *on underside* not visible from above except through head. To 2$\frac{1}{2}$ x $\frac{3}{4}$ in. (62 x 19 mm). (2) *H. extenuata* (not shown) has 4 eyes on *top* of head. To 3 x $\frac{3}{4}$ in. (75 x 19 mm). Both species have *nearly smooth,* thin scales; brown or black to greenish, mottled or speckled, or sometimes distinctly banded lengthwise. (3) *H. dearborni* (not shown) is a $\frac{1}{2}$-in. (12 mm) species found on Gulfweed. Additional species rare, local, or subtidal at considerable depths; found mainly by dredging.

Similar species: (1) *Gattyana cirrosa* (not shown) has 15 pairs of scales covered with fine tubercles that tend to collect a camouflage of fine debris; larger tubercles (under strong magnification) are *4-pronged.* To 1$\frac{7}{8}$ x $\frac{1}{2}$ in. (47 x 12 mm). Lives in bottom debris or commensal with various tube worms. Arctic to S.C.; habitat quite variable. Lower intertidal to subtidal at great depths. A 2nd species, *Gattyana amondseni* (not shown) is somewhat smaller, has *2-pronged* tubercles. Arctic to R.I.; mostly subtidal in our range. (2) Additional scale worms with 15 pairs of scales are found subtidally; most are less than 1 in. (25 mm) long. Mainly Boreal.

Where found: (1) *H. imbricata,* Labrador to New York Bight. (2) *H. extenuata,* Arctic to Chesapeake Bay. Both range from intertidal zone to subtidal down to more than a mile deep; also estuarine in salinities at least as low as 18‰. (3) *H. dearborni,* on drifting Gulfweed, mainly Cape Cod south.

Remarks: *H. imbricata* and *H. extenuata* occur together, often also with twelve-scaled worms. All are found in a wide range of habitats and associations, including commensally with tube worms and hermit crabs. *H. imbricata* is even found semi-pelagically as a competent swimmer. Female *imbricata* carry their eggs *under* their scales; female *extenuata* carry theirs between parapodia or under their body.

Family: Polynoidae, including *Gattyana.*

BURROWING SCALE WORMS *Sthenelais*   Pl. 43
and related genera

Identification: Long and slender with 20 pairs of scales or more when mature. Lack cirri. All except the last species are burrowers.

3 genera, 4 species. (1) *Sthenelais boa* has up to 100 pairs or more when adult; each scale has a row of *papillae along outer margin.* Color varies; scales opaque, often with a stripe down the back. To 8 x $\frac{3}{16}$ in. (200 x 5 mm). (2) *Sthenelais limicola* has scales near head with irregular papillae on part of outer margin; scales farther back on body lack papillae but have a *notch.* Scales translucent. A smaller, more delicate species than *S. boa;* to 4 x $\frac{3}{16}$ in. (100 x 5 mm). (3) *Sigalion arenicola* is pinkish, translucent; scales have 8–13 papillae on outer margin, each fringed to resemble the *feathered end of an arrow.* To 12 x $\frac{5}{16}$ in. (300 x 8 mm). (4) *Pholoe minuta* (not shown) is small — to 1 x $\frac{3}{16}$ in. (25 x 5 mm) — *very fragile,* and translucent. Has 12–60 pairs of scales, each margined with short papillae.

Similar species: Note Many-scaled Worm (p. 169).

Where found: (1) *Sthenelais boa,* Cape Cod to Brazil; from lower intertidal zone to subtidal at great depths, and into brackish water, sometimes among Eelgrass roots. (2) *Sthenelais limicola,* Cape Cod to Fla.; shallow water in sand or mud. (3) *Sigalion arenicola,* Cape Cod to Ga.; shallow water; rare. (4) *Pholoe minuta,* Arctic to S.C.; *not a burrower* but found under stones, on algal holdfasts, and among debris and sedentary animals in tide pools; also subtidally to great depths.

Family: Sigalionidae.

BLOOD WORMS *Glycera* species   Pl. 40

Identification: In life the pale translucent skin allows the red body fluid to show through, pulsing and flowing from one part of worm to another; hence the vernacular name. Head tapered, with 4 tiny antennae. Large bulbous proboscis, armed at end with *4 small black fangs,* can be completely withdrawn and as quickly extended, providing an alternate name, Beak Thrower.

4 species — first 2 common, last 2 much rarer. (1) *G. dibranchiata* has a *pair* of blunt fingerlike gills, one above and one below the bristly lobe of each parapodium. To 15 in. long by

$\frac{3}{8}$ in. thick (375 x 9 mm). (2) *G. americana* (not shown) has a *retractile, branching* gill at back of parapodium; size same as preceding. (3) *G. robusta* (not shown), a deep burrower in mud, has tiny, clear, *blisterlike* gills on top and back of parapodia. To 2 ft. (600 mm). (4) *G. capitata* (not shown) an Arctic species found mainly in deep water on our coast; lacks gills. To 6 in. (150 mm).

Similar species: See next account.

Where found: (1) *G. dibranchiata,* Gulf of St. Lawrence to Gulf of Mexico. (2) *G. americana,* Cape Cod to Argentina. (3) *G. robusta,* Gulf of St. Lawrence to Gulf of Mexico. All 3 species range from intertidal zone to subtidal down to more than 1000 ft. (300 m). (4) *G. capitata,* Arctic to New York Bight; subtidal in our area, in deep water.

Remarks: Blood worms (chiefly *G. dibranchiata*) are commonly sold for bait. They may be found in abundance on tidal flats, especially where there is some mud and organic debris mixed with sand. Fast burrowers, they literally screw themselves into the ground with the aid of their toothed proboscis. They can nip, and in severe cases their bite is as painful as a bee sting. Blood worms are poor swimmers. Lack a distinct epitokous form, but sexual swarmers may be found at water surface at night in summer. Tolerate low-oxygen conditions and minimum salinity of 5‰ or less (*G. dibranchiata*).

Family: Glyceridae.

CHEVRON WORMS *Goniada* and related genera   **Pl. 40**
Identification: Traits shared with blood worms (preceding account) include: slender form; conical head tipped with *4 minute antennae;* contractile, *balloonlike proboscis.* Differ in having somewhat stronger parapodia. Proboscis has rows of *tiny black V's* near base, circlets of *minute* teeth at outer end, or brushy rows of small *hooklets.* Body *divided into 2–3 regions* by differences in complexity of parapodia.

4 genera and species. (1) *Goniada maculata* is a *bicolored* worm — pale green at front end, yellow to orange at rear end. Proboscis has *row of 9 V's* on each side near base. To 4 in. (100 mm). (2) *Goniadella gracilis* (not shown) is pinkish to pale yellow, iridescent. Proboscis has *row of 26 V's.* This and preceding species also have 2 series of tiny teeth in short arcs near outer end of proboscis. To 2 in. (50 mm), but less than $\frac{1}{16}$ in. (1.6 mm) wide. (3) *Glycinde solitaria* is pale yellow to gray with greenish cast. Proboscis has brushy patch along one edge, 3 rows of knobs or hooklets along other. To $1\frac{3}{8}$ in. (34 mm). (4) *Ophioglycera gigantea* (not shown) is pinkish. Proboscis covered with tiny papillae, also with a pair of multi-toothed fangs and circlet of tiny teeth. To 30 in. long by $\frac{1}{2}$ in. (750 x 12 mm).

Where found: (1) *Goniada maculata,* Gulf of St. Lawrence to

R.I.; chiefly subtidal in 30 ft. (9 m) or more, on bottoms of mixed sediments. (2) *Goniadella gracilis,* Cape Cod to New York Bight, in sand or mixed bottoms; subtidal from shallow water down to 280 ft. (84 m) or more. (3) *Glycinde solitaria,* N.J. to West Indies, in sand or mud; lower intertidal to subtidal at shallow depths and into brackish water to 15‰ salinity. (4) *Ophioglycera gigantea,* Nova Scotia to New York Bight; rare. Reported at low tide line in Bay of Fundy; also swimming at surface.

Family: Goniadidae.

RED-LINED WORMS *Nephtys* species   **Pl. 40**

Identification: Body somewhat similar to clam worms (Plate 38) but head is quite different with the following diagnostic features: a small, *shovel-like* prostomium (squarish and flattened); *2 short antennae at front,* and another, nearly equal-sized pair below, either close-by or farther back, and not always visible from above; 2 dotlike eyes, or none; a cylindrical or barrel-shaped eversible proboscis, with a cluster of slender papillae at the front end and rows of tiny wartlike papillae along the sides. Parapodia well developed, distinctly bilobed. To 8–12 in. (200–300 mm).

At least 6 species in lower intertidal, others subtidal or rare; typical form shown. Identification may be difficult, requiring close examination of head and parapodia — preferably with positively identified specimens for comparison. Differences are subtle and easily misinterpreted; also, eversion of the proboscis tends to distort the proportions of the head and its setae-bearing lobes. Color is usually slate to pearly gray with a distinct red line (blood vessel) down the back and another on the belly. *N. picta* often has somewhat crescent-shaped, brownish crossbands near the head, and these may be joined by front and back markings to form a lengthwise band. Another common species, *N. bucera,* may also be banded but markings (absent in preserved specimens) are usually V-shaped.

Where found: Whole coast, from intertidal zone to subtidal at great depths; marine and estuarine. (1) *N. picta,* S.C. north to Cape Cod. (2) *N. incisa,* Chesapeake Bay north to Arctic; chiefly *subtidal,* often in very smelly mud; also estuarine. (3) *N. bucera,* Gulf of Mexico north to Isles of Shoals and locally to Gulf of St. Lawrence; also estuarine (in Chesapeake Bay to Cove Point, Md.). The preceding are the only common species found south of N.Y. *N. incisa* is also the most common New England species, inhabiting muddy bays and sounds. The remaining species range from the Arctic southward to the limits indicated: (4) *N. ciliata,* to south shore of Cape Cod. (5) *N. caeca,* to L.I. Sound. (6) *N. discors,* to e. Maine.

Remarks: These are common intertidal worms, active predators on other invertebrates, and burrowers in sand or mud. They may emerge to swim in sexual swarms (sometimes called shimmy worms) but do not have distinctive epitokous forms. **Family:** Nephtyidae.

SYLLID WORMS *Syllis* and *Autolytus* species   **Pl. 38**
Identification: NONBREEDING STAGE: Slender worms about 25–50 times longer than thick. Parapodia uniramous, with long, slender, dorsal cirri. Head has a pair of palps that are either thick and separate (*Syllis*) or fused and downturned to form a rim (*Autolytus*). Both genera have 3 antennae and 2 pairs of tentacular cirri; cirri and antennae often curled in *Autolytus*. Proboscis cylindrical with 1 or more teeth. *Syllis* species reach 2 in. (50 mm); *Autolytus* species $\frac{3}{4}$–1 in. (19–25 mm).

Several species plus *A. emertoni,* which is only known from breeding forms (*epitokes*); typical forms shown. Species identification may require microscopic study of setae, parapodia, and other small features but live or fresh material can often be identified by pattern details. Note pattern in following 4 species (bands run crosswise; stripes lengthwise):

> *S. gracilis* — banded with dots
> *A. prismaticus* — 3 long stripes
> *A. prolifer* — 2 narrow bands per segment
> *A. verrilli* — unmarked or 2 bands per segment

BREEDING STAGE (*epitokes*): A distinct, planktonic, epitokous stage occurs in many syllid genera; details vary. In some *Syllis* species, a series of setigers at the rear end form a *stolon*. These modified setigers are full of sperm or ova. The parapodia become better fitted for swimming, and a new head forms at the beginning of the stolon, which then breaks loose as a free-swimming worm. In *Autolytus prolifer* similar sexual budding produces chains of up to 8 worms. Male and female stolons of *Syllis* are externally similar, but in *Autolytus* they are different. Stolons are found mainly during summer months, but some species breed from early spring to fall. Species identification of epitokes will not be discussed, as it is a very difficult process. **Similar species:** Most other syllids, 10 genera and 20 or more species, are small — $\frac{1}{4}$–$\frac{5}{16}$ in. (6–8 mm) — and require microscopic study. The very slender *Exogone* species (typical form shown on Plate 38) are distinctive in having very short appendages; they are burrowers. To $\frac{3}{8}$ in. (9 mm); whole coast. *Amblyosyllis finmarchica* (Plate 38) is a very short worm with long appendages. To $\frac{3}{8}$ in. (9 mm); Maine northward. Several syllids are notably luminescent (bright green), including *Eusyllis blomstrandi* and *Odontosyllis fulgurans* (neither shown).
Where found: *S. gracilis,* cosmopolitan in warm seas; locally

Fig. 50.

SYLLID EPITOKE

north of Cape Cod to cen. Maine coast. *Autolytus* species are cool-water worms, although *A. verrilli* ranges south to N.C. and *A. prolifer* to Ga.; *A. prolifer* is an estuarine form.

Remarks: Syllids are common creeping annelids found among bottom debris, seaweeds, and benthic animals from lower intertidal to subtidal at great depths. Their mode of feeding is uncertain, since solid food has not been found in them. They are presumed to be predators that use a piercing-sucking technique (see p. 62).

Family: Syllidae, including *Exogone, Amblyosyllis, Eusyllis,* and *Odontosyllis.*

SWIFT-FOOTED WORM *Podarke obscura* **Pl. 38**

Identification: A moderately thickish worm (about 13 times longer than wide) with well-developed parapodia and head appendages. Parapodia biramous, with *long slender cirri* above. Head has 5 short appendages on prostomium (2 jointed palps and 3 antennae), and 6 pairs of long tentacular cirri behind. Color brown to blackish with lighter, narrow crossbands — usually 3 per segment; breeding males cream-colored. To 1½ in. (38 mm).

Similar species: *Nereimyra punctata* (not shown) is shorter and thicker, to 1 x ⅛ in. (25 x 3 mm). Has a similar appendage pattern but *no median antenna;* dorsal cirri even longer, and jointed. Whole coast, from lower intertidal zone to subtidal, creeping among debris. Other species in this small family are less than ⁵⁄₁₆ in. (8 mm).

Where found: Cape Cod to Caribbean. From lower intertidal zone to subtidal at great depths, creeping under and among a wide variety of bottom debris; also in Eelgrass beds and the like. Swarms on summer evenings.

Family: Hesionidae, including *Nereimyra.*

SIGAMBRA *Sigambra* species **Pl. 38**

Identification: Thickish worms (about 7–20 times longer than wide) with well-developed parapodia and head appendages. Parapodia are biramous, with moderately long, tapered dorsal cirri. Head has a pair of *peglike palps* set in swollen bases hardly distinguishable from the prostomium, then 3 antennae, followed by 2 pairs of long tentacular cirri. Proboscis cylindrical, ringed with papillae.

3 species, differing in how far back on the body *hooked notosetae* first appear. *S. tentaculata* has them starting on 4th setiger; *S. bassi* on setigers 11–15, *S. wassi* on setigers 23–30. Last 2 species to 1½ in. (38 mm); *S. tentaculata* to ⅝ in. (16 mm). Typical form shown on Plate 38.

Similar species: Other members of the family Pilargidae are subtidal and not superficially similar. *Cabira incerta* (Plate 38) does not look like an annelid worm, even under a hand lens; it is a *lumpish* cylindrical worm with *poorly developed* parapodia and head appendages. To ¾ x 1/16 in. (19 x 1.6 mm). Lower Chesapeake Bay to L.I. Sound.

Where found: *S. tentaculata,* L.I. Sound to Texas. *S. bassi,* N.C. southward. *S. wassi,* Chesapeake Bay. Burrowers in sand or mud from intertidal zone to subtidal at great depths.

Family: Pilargidae, including *Cabira.*

CLAM WORMS *Nereis* species   Pl. 38

Identification: Moderately elongate but robust worms with well-developed parapodia and head appendages. Head has 4–5 pairs of tentacular cirri, 1 pair of *short blunt palps,* usually 4 eyes, and an eversible 2-ringed proboscis with a pair of *large sicklelike jaws.*

7 species; *note differences in parapodia* (Fig. 51). (1) *N. virens,* the only species shown, is the principal New England form; standard bait-sized clam worms are 8 in. (200 mm) or more, but *virens* reportedly reaches 36 x 1⅝ in. (900 x 43 mm). (2) *N. succinea,* the common southern species, is seldom more than 5–6 in. (125–150 mm); distinguished from *N. virens* by parapodia, which are *smallish* toward head, longer and *straplike* at rear; *N. virens* has uniform parapodia, head to tail. Jaws pale amber in *succinea,* blackish in *virens.*

Less common species (none shown): (3) *N. diversicolor,* often with *2 darker lengthwise stripes* (may persist in preservative); to 8 in. (200 mm). (4) *N. acuminata,* small — 2¾ in. (69 mm) — transparent or *whitish.* (5) *N. pelagica,* variably colored but coloring not like that of the species above. Common on algae and especially *among fouling organisms* on pilings, buoys, and such; to 6 in. (150 mm). (6) *N. grayi,* small — 2⅜ in. (59 mm) — often found in association with bamboo worms. (7) *N. zonata,* an Arctic form found in deep water.

A highly modified breeding stage called *heteronereis* occurs in *N. succinea, N. pelagica,* and *N. zonata;* see next species account and Plate 38.

Similar species: Compare with Dumeril's Clam Worm (Plate 38).

Where found: (1) *N. virens,* Gulf of St. Lawrence south at least to Delaware Bay (reportedly to Va. but not listed for Chesapeake Bay); from upper intertidal to subtidal down to 500 ft. (150 m) deep or more. (2) *N. succinea,* tropics north to Cape Cod and locally to Gulf of St. Lawrence; chiefly an estuarine species, to salinity of 9‰ or less; upper intertidal to subtidal at shallow depths. (3) *N. diversicolor,* Gulf of St. Lawrence to Cape Ann; upper intertidal to subtidal at shallow depths, also in brackish water with salinity less than 1‰ to 25‰ or more; (4) *N. acuminata,* Fla. to Cape Cod; lower intertidal to subtidal down to 330 ft. (99 m) or more. (5) *N. pelagica,* Arctic south at least to New York Bight; lower intertidal to subtidal at great depths. Reported from many parts of the world by accidental transport. (6) *N. grayi,* Cape Cod south at least to Chesapeake Bay; lower intertidal to subtidal at shallow depths. (7) *N. zonata,* Arctic south to New York Bight; subtidal on this coast.

Remarks: These are perhaps our most familiar polychaetes. Large specimens, particularly of *N. virens,* are spectacularly elegant (for worms), with richly opalescent green and coppery-brown or red coloring. *N. diversicolor* and *N. acuminata* mate in their burrows, but others are strong swimmers and

Fig. 51.

NEREIS species
PARAPODIA
(examples from
midbody or tail)

spiniger (s)

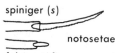

notosetae

falciger (f)

1–4 have s only
5,6 have s and f

1. *N. virens*

3. *N. diversicolor*

5. *N. pelagica*

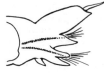

2. *N. succinea*

4. *N. acuminata*

6. *N. grayi*

emerge in breeding swarms during the dark of the moon, mainly June–September (*N. succinea*), or late March–June (*N. virens*), or erratically throughout the year (*N. pelagica*).

Clam worms are strong predators on many kinds of invertebrates, including other clam worms; they also feed on algae (*N. acuminata* especially) and are scavengers. They are, in turn, eaten by bottom-feeding fishes, skates, and crabs. These are active worms, found burrowing in a wide variety of bottoms; they form sandy tubes glued together with mucus. They are also tolerant of salinity changes and, as indicated above, are common estuarine animals.

Family: Nereidae.

DUMERIL'S CLAM WORM   Pl. 38
Platynereis dumerilii

Identification: NONBREEDING STAGE: Similar to clam worms (preceding account) but tentacular cirri *long*. Eye-bearing part of head narrow-oval rather than broad-rectangular or pear-shaped. Color varies but often spotted, blotched, or banded. Examined closely under magnification, 2nd ring of proboscis (behind jaws) has 2 tiny patches of comblike teeth on upperside. Clam worms (*Nereis* species) have stronger cone-shaped teeth in 3 patches on 2nd ring and in 5 patches on top and sides of 3rd ring. To 3 in. (75 mm).

BREEDING STAGE (*heteronereis*): Smaller; males to 1 in. (25 mm), females to almost twice that — $1\frac{7}{8}$ in. (47 mm). Head has *eyes greatly enlarged* and palps on *underside*. Body has 2 distinct regions with parapodia of rear section highly modified for swimming. Males greenish toward head, pink to red behind; females pale yellowish to white or pale green.

Similar species: Clam worms (Plate 38). *Nereis succinea, N. pelagica,* and *N. zonata* also have distinct *heteronereis* stages that are proportionately smaller than nonbreeding stages. Body has 2–3 regions with middle or rear modified for swimming (in 3-region forms the rear section often breaks off). Eyes enlarged but head less radically reorganized and palps still visible from above. (See preceding account for nonbreeding stage and swarming seasons.)

Where found: Whole coast; cosmopolitan. From lower intertidal zone to subtidal to 400 ft. (120 m); minimum salinity to 15‰.

Remarks: Look for this interesting worm on rockweeds and other seaweeds in the lower intertidal zone, on Eelgrass, or in drifting clumps of Gulfweed. It also lives among fouling organisms on pilings and mixed-bottom debris. Forms a transparent but tough, parchmentlike tube.

Reproductive swarms of this and several *Nereis* species are reminiscent of (unrelated) Palolo Worms of tropical waters.

Swarming takes place at night and often involves hordes of worms. *Nereis* species have external fertilization — eggs and sperm are shed and combine in sea water. Dumeril's Clam Worm has unique internal fertilization. Swarming males and females intertwine. Female seizes male's tail end in jaws, ingests sperm through her mouth; internal organs of *heteronereis* have been so thinned and weakened that sperm pass through walls of digestive tract to reach eggs in body cavity. Within seconds the now fertilized eggs escape through deteriorating body wall of female into the sea. Presumably both males and females die after mating. Swarming occurs in July–Aug. on south shore of Cape Cod, June–July southward, always during the dark of the moon. Swarmers are attracted to lights.
Family: Nereidae.

SPRING WORM *Lycastopsis pontica*   **Pl. 38**
Identification: A small — 2¼ in. (56 mm) — worm from the *high intertidal* zone, where it lives with such terrestrial invertebrates as sand fleas, pseudoscorpions, and marine earthworms (oligochaetes) under dead seaweed and other beach debris. Coils tightly, springlike. Head resembles clam worms (Plate 38) but has *short* appendages. Color whitish, tinted green or yellow; prominent red blood vessels, dark jaws.
Where found: Cape Cod to Brazil; estuarine.
Family: Nereidae.

PLUMED WORM *Diopatra cuprea*   **Pl. 39**
Identification: Distinctive *projecting tubes encrusted with bits of shell or other debris* draw attention to this worm. Tube is soft but tough, skinlike; opening ½–⅗ in. (12–15 mm) wide above, gradually tapering below; projects several inches aboveground, extending underground to 3 ft. (900 mm).

Head has 7 antennae, the 1st (frontal) pair short, others longer, with ringed bases; tentacular cirri in adults, not in young. Segments vary somewhat from head to tail, with 30–40 pairs of *red plumelike gills* starting behind head, and number gradually diminishing in segments farther back. Highly iridescent. To 12 x ⅜ in. (300 x 9 mm).
Similar species: Related *Nothria* species (none shown) are mostly subtidal, found by dredging on mud bottoms. All make skinlike tubes encrusted with debris, including large shell fragments. *N. conchylega* has a portable tube that it drags about, caddis-fly fashion; others bury their tubes like the Plumed Worm does. Pattern of head appendages resembles Plumed Worm, but gills are *simple filaments,* not bushy spirals. To 6 x ⅛ in. (150 x 3 mm). Whole coast but mainly subtidal in 30 ft. (9 m) or more.

Where found: Cape Cod Bay to Brazil; intertidal to subtidal down to 270 ft. (81 m).

Remarks: Poking up from tidal flats and rich clam beds, Plumed Worm chimneys are well camouflaged, resembling stumps of plants. When undisturbed, the worms protrude from their tubes to snag prey. To catch the worm, aim a shovel at a point a foot or so straight down from tube opening, plunge in, turn shovelful onto surface. Front and rear parts regenerate easily, so specimens may be found damaged. Live worms are truly elegant; can be kept in aquarium.

Family: Onuphidae, including *Nothria*.

RED-GILLED MARPHYSA *Marphysa sanguinea*　　　**Pl. 39**

Identification: Head bluntly rounded in front with a *central cleft* (actually formed by 2 cushion-shaped palps fused to the head); 5 short antennae. The segments of this worm are similar except for changes in gill structure. Iridescent. To 24 x $\frac{9}{16}$ in. (600 x 9 mm). Live worms break up into fragments when handled.

Similar species: (1) *M. belli* (not shown) has head rounded in front *without* cleft, gills comblike. To 8 in. (200 mm). (2) *Eunice* species (not shown) have a very similar head but segment behind it has a pair of short *tentacular cirri* on top. To 8 in. (200 mm). Several species; chiefly subtidal on mixed bottoms, often with corals. *E. pennata,* whole coast, subtidal at depths of 12 ft. (3.6 m) or more.

Where found: Cosmopolitan in warm seas; in w. Atlantic from West Indies north to Cape Cod and locally to Casco Bay. From lower intertidal zone to subtidal at shallow depths on a wide variety of bottoms, including Eelgrass and oyster beds. Form mucus-lined tunnels but no permanent tubes.

Family: Eunicidae, including *Eunice*.

OPAL WORM *Arabella iricolor*　　　**Pl. 40**

Identification: A *wiry* cylindrical worm with segments *similar throughout* except for minor changes in shape of the small parapodia. Head conical, without appendages. *Brilliantly iridescent* in life. To 24 x $\frac{3}{16}$ in. (600 x 5 mm).

Similar species: (1) *Notocirrus spiniferus* (Plate 40) is *very* similar in form and is best distinguished by microscopic study of parapodia, which have 1–3 *slightly* protruding, golden aciculae lacking in Opal Worm. Both species may have 4 eyes at base of prostomium, sometimes hidden when prostomium is contracted, and sometimes missing or reduced to 2 in *Notocirrus*. To $4\frac{3}{8}$ x $\frac{1}{8}$ in. (109 x 3 mm). Young are parasitic in body cavity of Plumed Worm (Plate 39). Cape Cod to N.C., from lower intertidal zone to subtidal at shallow depths, estuarine and marine. (2) See arabellid and lumbrinerid thread worms, below. (3) See

Plate 41 for cone-headed species with body more or less *divided into regions.*

Where found: Cosmopolitan in warm waters; in w. Atlantic common north to Cape Cod and (locally at least) to Bay of Fundy. From lower intertidal zone to subtidal at moderate depths in a wide variety of habitats, including estuarine Eelgrass and oyster bottoms.

Remarks: Adult Opal Worms are burrowing carnivores, but the young of some species are parasitic, usually in other worms.

Family: Arabellidae, including *Notocirrus.*

ARABELLID THREAD WORMS   Not shown
Drilonereis species

Identification: Several kinds of long, red, threadlike worms are found in fine sand or sandy mud. Their burrows intermingle in seemingly endless tangles, and it is almost impossible to get their elastic but easily fragmented bodies out in 1 piece.

   3 species. (1) *D. longa* grows to 2 ft. (600 mm) but is less than $\frac{1}{16}$ in. (1.6 mm) thick. *Head spatulate, without appendages.* Parapodia at head end reduced to slight pimples, gradually becoming larger farther back. Red, iridescent. (2) *D. filum,* a southern species common intertidally at least as far north as Va., can only be distinguished positively from *D. longa* by differences in jaw structure. (3) *D. magna* is less common, more robust, and has prominent parapodia. Distinguishable from Opal Worm (Plate 40) by flattened prostomium and presence of aciculae in parapodia.

Similar species: See next account, and also capitellid thread worms, p. 184.

Where found: (1) *D. longa,* West Indies north to Cape Cod and locally to Penobscot Bay; from intertidal zone to subtidal to great depths. (2) *D. filum,* Panama north to Va.; intertidal zone to subtidal at shallow depths. (3) *D. magna,* whole coast but mainly subtidal to great depths.

Family: Arabellidae.

LUMBRINERID THREAD WORMS   Pl. 40
Lumbrineris and *Ninoe* species

Identification: Resemble Opal Worm (Plate 40) in form, including conical to round prostomium, small parapodia. Also easy to confuse with arabellid thread worms (preceding account) except that latter have a flattened (*spatulate*) prostomium. Key difference — lumbrinerids have setae that are *hooks* (see Plate 40); arabellids do not. Body thickness varies in lumbrinerids from threadlike to stouter earthwormlike proportions. Color also varies, usually from shades of red or pink to tan or yellowish; sometimes patterned with whitish crossbands, and usually iridescent.

1 *Ninoe* species, 2 *Lumbrineris;* others in deep water. (1)
N. nigripes (not shown) is readily identified by *branching fingerlike gills* on parapodia toward the head (absent in *Lumbrineris*). To 4 x $\frac{3}{16}$ in. (100 x 5 mm). (2) *L. fragilis* resembles
the preceding in having setae dark at base, paler toward end, and
black aciculae imbedded in the translucent parapodia (visible
with hand lens). To 15 x $\frac{1}{2}$ in. (375 x 12 mm). (3) *L. tenuis* (not
shown) is smaller — to 6 x $\frac{1}{8}$ in. (150 x 3 mm) — with *yellow
aciculae and setae.*
Where found: (1) *N. nigripes,* Gulf of St. Lawrence to Gulf of
Mexico; chiefly subtidal, in mud. (2) *L. fragilis,* Arctic to Cape
Cod and subtidally south at least to N.C. (3) *L. tenuis,* Bay of
Fundy to Fla. Both *Lumbrineris* species from lower intertidal to
subtidal into deep water, burrowing in mud or mixed-bottom
debris.
Family: Lumbrineridae.

FOUR-EYED DORVILLEA *Schistomeringos rudolphi* **Pl. 39**
Identification: Head has a pair of thick, curving, ventral palps,
a pair of segmented antennae, 4 dotlike reddish eyes, and a
necklike structure consisting of 2 segments without parapodia or
setae. Segments otherwise similar. Males pinkish, females
gray-violet. Reach 2 x $\frac{1}{8}$ in. (50 x 3 mm) or more in life, but
shrink to half that when pickled.
Similar species: *Schistomeringos caecus* (not shown) is eye-
less, only to $\frac{5}{16}$ in. (8 mm) long. Gulf of St. Lawrence to N.C.
Chiefly subtidal, but in lower intertidal zone northward, in mud
or fine sand.
Where found: West Indies north to Cape Cod and (locally at
least) to Boothbay Harbor. Lower intertidal to subtidal in bays
and sounds, ranging into brackish water.
Remarks: Dorvilleids are carnivorous. They burrow in soft
bottoms, making temporary tubes under stones and such. May
be found swimming.
Family: Dorvilleidae.

Sedentary Polychaetes

Most sedentary polychaetes live in tubes. This confined existence
requires considerable specialization in structures for feeding, respi-
ration, and other basic activities. The body may be long and
typically wormlike, but often it is not. Characteristically it is
divided into regions; the front is called the *thorax* (its parts are
thoracic) and the rear, the *abdomen.* The distinction may only be
marked by changes in the parapodia and setae, but in more highly
modified worms there are proportional differences in body form
and segmentation as well. The head usually does not have an

eversible proboscis but is variously equipped with grooved, con-
veyor-belt-like palps or tentacles, tentaclelike gills, or other food-
gathering and respiratory devices. The setae, too, are often greatly
modified and varied. Most of these worms are *microphagous,*
feeding on plankton, detrital fragments, and other small particles.
Details are given in the accounts that follow.

ORBINIID WORMS *Orbinia* and related genera   **Pl. 41**
 Identification: Head has a conical or rounded prostomium
without appendages. Body fairly long and typically wormlike,
divided into 2 regions, though not very conspicuously so in some
species. Front (thoracic) region is thicker, somewhat flattened;
has *neuropodia forming vertical ridges,* armed with rows of
setae. Abdominal region longer, cylindrical; parapodia of upperside become more prominent, with *tapered fingerlike lobes*
and *cirri.*

4 genera, several species inshore, others deeper. (1) *Naineris
quadricuspida* has a *bluntly rounded* head (conical in other
genera). To $3\frac{1}{8}$ x $\frac{1}{8}$ in. (78 x 3 mm). (2) *Orbinia ornata* has
thoracic neuropodia with peglike setae forming short *filelike
ridges* on each side; behind them is a *fringe of soft papillae*
(lacking in the remaining genera). Deep red in life. To
10 x $\frac{1}{4}$ in. (250 x 6 mm). (3) *Haploscoloplos* and (4) *Scoloplos*
are similar genera and at times have been united; identification
requires careful examination of abdominal parapodia (at about
the 7th segment after the body changes form). *Haploscoloplos*
species have a small lobe — *interramal cirrus*—between the
neuropodium and adjoining lobe of notopodium. *Scoloplos
acutus* (not shown), the common representative of the genus,
lacks an interramal cirrus. A slender worm — $1\frac{1}{2}$ x $\frac{1}{16}$ in.
(38 x 1.6 mm); chiefly subtidal. *H. robustus* and *H. fragilis* (not
shown) are the 2 most frequently encountered *Haploscoloplos*
species. Both vary in color from flesh tones to yellow-brown,
ocher, or light red. *H. robustus* usually has a double row of
brown spots down back; *fragilis* doesn't. Positive identification
requires microscopic examination of differences in parapodia. As
names imply, *robustus* reaches a larger size, to $14\frac{3}{4}$ x $\frac{3}{8}$ in.
(369 x 9 mm); *fragilis* smaller, to 6 x $\frac{1}{8}$ in. (150 x 3 mm).
 Similar species: Paraonid worms, *Paraonis* and *Aricidea* species (typical forms shown on Plate 41) are similar in having a
conical head, weakly developed parapodia, and 7–30 pairs of
slender or leaflike gills on upperside toward the head. All are
small and threadlike — to 1 in. (25 mm) long — requiring microscopic study. Most are subtidal. *Paraonis* species (which lack a
median antenna) are found on sandy beaches and subtidally
from Maine to N.C., though evidently local south of Cape Cod.
Several species of *Aricidea* (with a slender median antenna)

occur subtidally from the Arctic southward along our whole coast. All are burrowers in mud or sand. Family Paraonidae.
Where found: (1) *Naineris quadricuspida,* Arctic to Cape Cod. (2) *Orbinia ornata,* s. Maine to Gulf of Mexico. (3) *Haploscoloplos robustus* and *H. fragilis,* both Gulf of St. Lawrence to Gulf of Mexico. (4) *Scoloplos acutus,* Arctic to Va. All except the first species enter brackish water; all except the last extend up into the intertidal zone.
Remarks: Orbiniids burrow in mud or sand and are deposit feeders, consuming much indigestible soil material along with organic debris. They spring into spiral coils when dug up and are very easily broken.
Family: Orbiniidae.

CAPITELLID THREAD WORMS *Capitella*   Pl. 41
and related genera
Identification: Somewhat earthwormlike, with vestigial parapodia. Body *weakly divided* into a swollen thorax and a longer, slimmer abdomen; regions otherwise distinguished by changes in parapodia and setae. Color often changes from dark red or purplish at head end to paler or yellowish at tail end.
3 genera, 4 species. (1) *Notomastus* species are more robust than other capitellids. Positive identification of species may require microscopic study of thoracic setae; all 11 thoracic setigers have capillary notosetae. *N. latericeus* has setae-bearing ridges on abdomen that *almost touch* at midline below, and triangular *flaplike gills* above; to 12 x $\frac{3}{16}$ in. (300 x 5 mm). *N. luridus* (not shown) has neither and is about half as large. (2) *Capitella capitata* has *setae on peristomium* and *9 thoracic setigers* (5–7 segments with fine-tipped capillary setae). To 4 x $\frac{1}{16}$ in. (100 x 1.6 mm). (3) *Heteromastus filiformis* (not shown) is as long as the preceding species but only half as thick; has 11 *thoracic setigers* (5 with capillary setae) and *no* setae on peristomium.
Where found: (1) *Notomastus latericeus,* whole coast; *N. luridus,* s. Maine south at least to L.I. Sound. (2) *Capitella capitata,* Arctic south to N.C. (3) *Heteromastus filiformis,* Arctic to Gulf of Mexico. All range into estuaries; also found from intertidal zone to subtidal at shallow depths and *N. latericeus* to abyssal depths.
Remarks: Capitellids feed in the same way earthworms do, literally eating their way through the substratum. They are tolerant of poor conditions on bay mud flats and harbor bottoms; *Capitella* and *Heteromastus* in particular seem to thrive in polluted situations.
Family: Capitellidae.

LUGWORMS *Arenicola* species   Pl. 41
Identification: Robust worms, thickest in the front half, taper-

ing toward the head and more gradually to the rear; an 8-in. worm is about $\frac{3}{8}$ in. thick (200 x 9 mm). 3 body regions. *Trunk* has weak parapodia bearing bundles of setae, and (starting roughly $\frac{1}{3}$ of the way back) a tuft of gills on each side. *Tail* region lacks setae and parapodia. *Head* small and contractile, lacks appendages but has an eversible proboscis armed with papillae.

3 species. (1) *A. marina* (not shown), the common species north of Cape Cod, has 12–13 pairs of gills; to 8 in. (200 mm). (2) *A. cristata,* the common species south of Cape Cod, has 11 pairs of gills; to 1 ft. (300 mm). (3) *A. brasiliensis* (not shown), also with 11 pairs of gills, is soft- rather than firm-bodied, and pale pinkish tan rather than dark greenish black; a frailer form generally than either of the preceding species. To 6 in. (150 mm). **Where found:** (1) *A. marina,* Arctic to Cape Cod (subtidal on south shore). (2) *A. cristata,* Cape Cod to Caribbean including brackish water (in Chesapeake Bay to mouth of Severn R.). (3) *A. brasiliensis,* only known on this coast along south shore of Cape Cod, but its range includes Brazil and parts of the Pacific Ocean.

Remarks: Lugworms make U-shaped burrows with openings at both ends. Front opening is usually a funnel-shaped depression; rear opening varies. *A. marina* and *A. brasiliensis* extrude earthwormlike coiled castings, but *A. cristata* produces a formless film or heap.

Although lugworms have been familiar biology course subjects for many years, *A. cristata* and *A. brasiliensis* were only recently separated taxonomically. They also differ in egg mass — a gelatinous streamer for *cristata,* firm and egg-shaped for *brasiliensis. A. cristata* also lives in quieter, muddier places. Lugworms feed on fine particles carried on currents pumped through their burrows.

Family: Arenicolidae.

T-HEADED WORM *Scalibregma inflatum* **Fig. 52**
Identification: Head small but distinctive in having a *pair of hornlike projections.* Body *divided* into regions: front half somewhat swollen, with vestigial parapodia and 4–5 pairs of

Fig. 52.

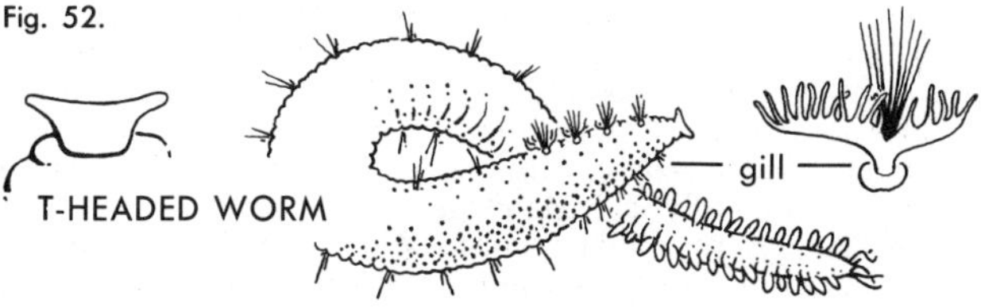

T-HEADED WORM

gill

branching gills; rear narrower, with double row of conical or fingerlike *cirri* along each side. Brick red. To 3 in. (75 mm). **Similar species:** *Polyphysia crassa* (not shown), a related little-known species, is short, maggotlike, with blunter horns; body *not* divided into regions. To 1³⁄₁₆ in. (30 mm). Arctic south at least to south shore of Cape Cod; subtidal.
Where found: Cosmopolitan. Arctic south at least to N.C., intertidal and subtidal in shallow water; deeper southward. In muddy sand. (Not known in Chesapeake Bay.)
Family: Scalibregmidae, including *Polyphysia.*

BAMBOO WORMS *Clymenella* and related genera   **Pl. 41**
 Identification: Aptly named! Body cylindrical; segments few and usually much longer than wide. Parapodia almost nonexistent. Head blunt-ended or hoodlike, without appendages. Most species subtidal in 30 ft. (9 m) or more.
 3 genera and species reach intertidal zone and are easily identified by differences in aciculae and in the head or tail ends (although it may not be immediately obvious which end is which). (1) *Asychis elongata* has tail end (*pygidium*) *scoopshaped* in profile, margin sharply angled; head end heavily speckled with black. To 12 x ⅛ in. (300 x 3 mm). (2) *Clymenella torquata* and (3) *Clymenella zonalis* (not shown) have a *crownlike* tail end (pygidium). *C. torquata* has a collar on 4th segment (indistinct in small specimens) and 6–8 acicular setae on 1st segment. The aciculae appear as black dots. *C. zonalis* lacks the collar and has 1–3 aciculae on 1st segment; also has dark *red bands* near head. *C. torquata* has 2 color forms, pale cream with red joints, and green. *C. zonalis* small, to ¾ in. (19 mm); *C. torquata* to more than 6 in. (150 mm).
Similar species: Oweniids have a similar body form but pygidium is rounded. (1) *Owenia fusiformis* (Plate 41) has a frilly membrane around mouth, lacking in (2) *Myriochele heeri* (not shown). *O. fusiformis* to 4 x ⅛ in. (100 x 3 mm), and *M. heeri* to 1³⁄₁₆ x ¹⁄₁₆ in. (30 x 1.6 mm). Both species are cosmopolitan in cool-temperate seas; on this coast *O. fusiformis* ranges south at least to N.C. and *M. heeri* to N.Y. or N.J. Both mainly subtidal in 30 ft. (9 m) or more, but *O. fusiformis* enters lower Chesapeake Bay. Family Oweniidae.
Where found: (1) *Asychis elongata,* Bar Harbor, Maine, south at least to Va.; in sandy mud in lower intertidal zone at least from L.I. Sound northward, and in estuaries in salinities as low as 15‰. A related species occurs south of Cape Hatteras. (2) *Clymenella torquata,* Bay of Fundy to N.C., mainly subtidal but extending into lower intertidal northward. (3) *Clymenella zonalis,* whole coast; also chiefly subtidal although reported intertidally in N.C.; estuarine and marine.
Remarks: Both bamboo worms and oweniids make sand- or mud-encrusted tubes and are "mud eaters" (deposit feeders),

although *O. fusiformis* also uses its frilly membrane to entrap suspended particles.
Family: Maldanidae.

OPHELIID WORMS *Ophelia* and related genera **Pl. 41**
Identification: Short, distinctive, *spindle-shaped* worms, usually tapered abruptly at both ends; most species *deeply grooved* along sides or bottom. Parapodia almost nonexistent, but *tapered gills* may be conspicuous along side grooves. Head conical, without appendages. Most are peach-colored to shades of red, often with an iridescent sheen. To 2–3 in. (50–75 mm).

3 genera, several species, 4 into shallow water. (1) *Travisia carnea* is short, stout, and grublike; lacks body grooves. (2) In *Ophelia* species, gills and grooves *begin* on segments 10–12; body is thus conspicuously *divided into 2 regions*. *O. denticulata* has 18 pairs of gills; *O. bicornis* (not shown) 11–15 pairs. (3) *Ophelina acuminata* has *full-length groove* on midbelly and 1 on each side; gills begin on 2nd setiger and are well developed.
Where found: (1) *Travisia carnea,* Cape Cod south at least to Va. (a similar species occurs south of Cape Hatteras); on sand flats, in estuarine waters and subtidal on soft bottoms. (2) *Ophelia* species: *O. denticulata,* Maine to N.C.; intertidal to subtidal at shallow depths; *O. bicornis,* a Boreal form, but south at least locally to Chesapeake Bay. (3) *Ophelina acuminata,* Arctic south at least to N.J.; mainly subtidal.
Remarks: Opheliids burrow headfirst into fairly clean sand, their belly and side grooves forming a channel for respiratory currents. Some are active swimmers when disinterred. Plump and grooveless *Travisia* species, on the other hand, are sluggish worms that burrow in muck.
Family: Opheliidae.

MUD WORMS *Polydora* and related genera **Pl. 42**
Identification: Tubes soft, mud- or sand-covered. Intact worms are readily distinguished by a *pair of long palps* that are often *coiled;* unfortunately these are easily broken off by rough handling. No other head appendages. Body typically wormlike, without distinct regions.

A formidable assemblage of *at least* 10 genera, 24 species. Following are some of the more common ones. (1) *Polydora* (10 species, others at both ends of our range and offshore), easily recognized by *modified 5th setiger; to* 1 in. (25 mm). *P. commensalis* (not shown), orange-red, found with hermit crabs; *P. websteri* (not shown), a pest in live oysters (see **Remarks,** below); *P. ligni,* one of the most frequently reported free-living (noncommensal) species. (2) *Spiophanes bombyx* has *T-shaped prostomium,* no gills; to $2\frac{3}{8}$ x $\frac{1}{16}$ in. (59 x 1.6 mm). (3) *Streblospio benedicti* (not shown), a very small species with 1 pair of *banded* gills; to $\frac{1}{4}$ in. (6 mm). (4) *Prionospio* (at least 5 species, none shown) has *4–5 pairs of gills* (following genera have 7 or more pairs); 1–3 in. (25–75 mm). *P. heterobranchia,* with 5 pairs, is a common estuarine species. *P. steenstrupi,* with 4 pairs, is common intertidally but also ranges subtidally to great depths. (5) *Scolecolepides viridis* (not shown) has gills beginning on 1st setiger, *absent* on rear $\frac{1}{3}$–$\frac{1}{2}$ of body. To 4 x $\frac{1}{8}$ in. (100 x 3 mm). (6) *Spio* species (none shown) have gills beginning on 1st setiger, *continuing* to rear end; 4 eyes, visible from above, form a square. *S. setosa* may attract attention by its fine sand chimneys on protected beaches and sand banks. To 3 x $\frac{1}{8}$ in. (75 x 3 mm). A 2nd *Spio* species, *S. filicornis,* is smaller and has fewer hooded hooks in its neuropodia — 6 as opposed to 16 in *S. setosa.* However, the number varies with age and on different segments of the same individual.

Where found: (1) *Polydora* species, whole coast. (2) *Spiophanes bombyx,* Fla. to Cape Cod and locally north to Boothbay Harbor. (3) *Streblospio benedicti,* Maine to Fla. (4) *Prionospio steenstrupi,* whole coast; *P. heterobranchia,* Cape Cod south to tropics. (5) *Scolecolepides viridis,* Newfoundland to S.C. (6) *Spio* species, whole coast.

Remarks: These worms build mud-covered tubes intertidally and subtidally at shallow depths. Some live in debris- or sediment-coated places on rocky shores, buoys, and pilings, among the benthic inhabitants of such places, but many are burrowers on soft grounds. Common preferences include: *Spio setosa,* sand; *Streblospio benedicti,* sandy mud; *Scolecolepides viridis,* mud; and *Polydora ligni,* mud-clay. Mud worms use their palps to sweep the bottom or the water itself for suspended food particles. In the process they collect bits of mud and debris, and may considerably alter their own environment. Oyster beds have been completely buried under several inches of mud accumulated by enormous numbers of *Polydora ligni* — about 430 per sq. in. (6.5 cm^2). *Polydora websteri* feeds in the same way other mud worms do and is not a parasite, but it does take up residence inside live oyster shells. The oyster in turn attempts to encapsule its visitor by forming a blister of shell material around it. These worms are not directly harmful, but in sufficient numbers they can smother the oysters.

Mud worms are common in estuaries, and all of the species discussed above range into brackish water — *Scolecolepides viridis* farther than the others, but *Polydora ligni* and *Prionospio heterobranchia* may be found in salinities lower than 5‰; *Spiophanes bombyx* and *Spio setosa* only to minimum salinity of 15‰.

Family: Spionidae.

PARCHMENT WORM *Chaetopterus variopedatus* **Pl. 42**
Identification: A flabby worm, very distinctive. Divided into 3 regions, most notably a middle region with *3 paddles* on upper-

side formed by fused notopodia. (Latin name refers to varied structure of parapodia in different parts of body.) Whole worm highly luminescent.

Tube, buried in mud, is U-shaped, parchmentlike, with chimneys at each end projecting aboveground. Worm to 10 x 1 in. (250 x 25 mm), occupies bottom of U.

Similar species: Glassy Tube Worm, *Spiochaetopterus costarum* (Plate 42) makes a *transparent tube, ringed like bamboo* and planted upright in mud bottoms. Worm is small — to $2\frac{3}{8}$ in. (59 mm) — and slender; a 1-in. (25 mm) tube is barely $\frac{1}{25}$ in. (1 mm) in diameter. Worm also 3-parted; middle region makes up most of body length, has long segments with small, inconspicuous parapodia — no paddles. Tail short; head has a pair of thick palps. 5th segment often brownish purple. Cape Cod to Gulf of Mexico on mud flats and protected banks; intertidal to subtidal at shallow depths and in estuaries to less than 5‰ salinity.

Where found: Cosmopolitan in warm seas although rare in West Indies. On this coast from N.C. to Cape Cod, and rarely to Knox region in Maine. Chiefly subtidal on mud bottoms and Eelgrass beds; to 15‰ salinity.

Remarks: Paddles keep water currents moving through the tube, aiding in highly specialized feeding technique. Enlarged notopodia at the front of the middle region produce a mucous bag that is really an ultrafine net sack for filtering plankton brought into the tube by a front-to-back current. Periodically pumping is briefly halted, the bag is detached, bundled up by a cuplike organ located just in front of the paddles, and sent back to the mouth in a ciliated groove along the back. With this ingenious arrangement the smallest planktonic particles can be harvested for food. Parchment Worm tubes frequently shelter commensal crabs, either Parchment Worm Polyonyx (Plate 60) or *Pinnixa chaetopterana* (Plate 59).

Family: Chaetopteridae, including *Spiochaetopterus*.

SAND-BUILDER WORM *Sabellaria vulgaris*   **Pl. 42**

Identification: Colonial worms whose well-cemented sand tubes form reeflike aggregations up to 1 ft. (300 mm) or more across, usually on a hard substratum; smaller patches coat oyster shells and pebbles. The worm is conical in shape, has a flattened head with *2 semicircular pads* of iridescent golden setae. To 1 x $\frac{1}{8}$ in. (25 x 3 mm).

Where found: Cape Cod to Ga. From lower intertidal to subtidal at shallow depths, including estuaries in salinities to 15‰. (Related species are responsible for "worm rocks" on the Fla. coast; *Phragmatopoma lapidosa* occurs between Cape Kennedy and Miami, *Sabellaria floridensis* along the Gulf north of Naples, Fla.)

Family: Sabellariidae.

ROSY MAGELONAS *Magelona* species   **Pl. 42**
   Identification: Long slender worms; head spadelike, has a pair
of tentacles *fringed with papillae on 1 side.* Body 2-parted;
short thorax of 8 setigers separated from tapered abdomen by a
slightly modified segment. Front part of body and tentacles
pink, otherwise pale.
    2 species. *M. papillicornis* (not shown) has 9th setiger modi-
fied with more pronounced lobes and specialized setae, absent in
M. rosea. To 2 x $\frac{1}{16}$ in. (50 x 1.6 mm); *papillicornis* larger in
Europe.
   Where found: Both species are found in w. Atlantic south of
Cape Cod, *M. papillicornis* to Brazil and *M. rosea* at least to
N.C. Muddy sand, subtidal in shallow water.
   Family: Magelonidae.

FRINGED WORMS *Cirratulus* and related genera   **Pl. 43**
   Identification: Body cylindrical, fairly elongate (20–40 times
longer than thick); *not* divided into regions. Head *conical;* some
species with 1 or more pairs of *tentacles or palps* plus 1 or more
pairs of threadlike *filamentous gills.* Handle gently; tentacles
and gills are delicate, easily broken off. Small damaged specimens will require microscopic study. Some genera have pelagic
epitokes.
    4 genera, 7 species; others in deep water. (1) *Dodecaceria
corallii* and (2) *Tharyx* species (none shown) have 1 pair of *thick,
grooved palps. D. corallii* is a small dark-colored worm that
burrows in dead shells and corals (including Star Coral, p. 93);
has 14–16 gills at head end. Its aciculae have spoon-shaped
tips. To $\frac{1}{2}$ in. (12 mm). *Tharyx* species are pale, have *more
numerous* gills than *D. corallii,* extending from just behind the
head to midbody or beyond. To $\frac{5}{8}$ in. (16 mm). Mostly in deep
water but *T. setigera, T. acutus,* and *T. annulosus* occur in
shallow water southward. (3) *Cirratulus cirratus* does *not* have
thick palps. Head with 2–9 pairs of black eyes sometimes joined
in 2 arcs. To $4\frac{3}{4}$ in. (119 mm). (4) *Cirriformia* species (none
shown), also *without* thick palps, are blind: *C. filigera* has tentacles on the 4th and 5th or 5th and 6th setigers; *C. grandis* on 1st
and 2nd. *C. filigera* to 10 in. (250 mm); *C. grandis* to 6 in.
(150 mm).
   Similar species: Damaged specimens (lacking appendages)
might be confused with other cone-headed worms; see Plates 40
and 41.
   Where found: (1) *Dodecaceria corallii,* Cape Cod to Gulf of
Mexico; in Star Coral and thus mainly subtidal; also in dead
shells. (2) *Tharyx* species, whole coast but mainly subtidal at
depths of 35 ft. (11 m) or more. *T. setigera,* intertidally or subtidally in shallow water from lower Chesapeake Bay southward.
T. acutus, Maine to New York Bight, abundant throughout L.I.

Sound. *T. annulosus,* N.C. north to New England and especially common from e. L.I. Sound to abyssal depths offshore. (3) *Cirratulus cirratus,* Cape Cod (subtidally on south shore) north at least to cen. Maine coast from lower intertidal to subtidal, under rocks. (4) *Cirriformia filigera,* a warm-water form reported north to Cape Hatteras and locally to N.Y., from lower intertidal zone to subtidal. *C. grandis,* N.C. to Cape Cod and locally to Penobscot Bay; intertidal mud flats to subtidal at moderate depths.

Remarks: Most fringed worms live buried in mud or in mud tubes attached to the underside of rocks. Like terebellid worms (p. 192) they use their tentacles to sweep the substratum for food. The gills are also thrust up through the mud and lie on the surface. *Tharyx acutus* and *annulosus* thrive in polluted areas and are among the most common polychaetes found in offshore dumping grounds.

Family: Cirratulidae.

TRUMPET WORM *Pectinaria gouldii*   Pl. 42

Identification: Head flattened in front with a *fan* of iridescent golden setae. Tube a long, slender, *slightly curved cone* neatly made of sand grains well cemented together; to 2 in. (50 mm) long; worm about $\frac{2}{3}$ as long.

Where found: Whole coast, at least as far north as Bay of Fundy; intertidal to subtidal at shallow depths and in estuaries to 15‰ salinity. (2 additional species found in deeper water north of Cape Cod.)

Remarks: In life this pretty little worm lies mostly buried, with only the small end of its cone exposed as a breathing tube. The golden bristles are used for digging and gathering food particles from the sand.

Family: Pectinariidae.

AMPHARETID WORMS *Ampharete*   Pl. 43
and related genera

Identification: Generally similar in form to terebellids (see next account) but tentacles can be *completely withdrawn* into mouth; also, gills (3–4 pairs) are *simply tapered* or *pinnate* rather than branching as in most shallow-water terebellids.

4 genera, several species. (1) *Ampharete* species (typical form shown) and (2) *Asabellides oculata* (not shown) have *pinnate* tentacles. *Ampharete* species have a conspicuous bundle of long golden setae (called *paleae*) just in front of gills; *Asabellides oculata* does not. *Ampharete* species to 1 in. (25 mm); *Asabellides oculata* to $\frac{3}{8}$ in. (9 mm). (Identity and distribution of 2 species of *Ampharete* have been confused. *A. arctica* is apparently the common species on this coast and *A. acutifrons* much rarer. *A. arctica* has 2 anal cirri, *acutifrons* has 10.)

(3) *Melinna cristata* and (4) *Hypaniola grayi* (neither shown) have *simple* tentacles, few paleae or none. *M. cristata* has a *long slender abdomen* of about 50 segments; to 2 in. (50 mm). *H. grayi* has a shorter abdomen with only half as many segments; to ⅝ in. (16 mm).

Where found: (1) *Ampharete* species, Arctic to tropics, but Maine records are only north to Penobscot Bay. (2) *Asabellides oculata,* Casco Bay south at least to Chesapeake Bay where it is reportedly abundant subtidally in sandy silt; in brackish water to 5‰ or less. (3) *Melinna cristata,* also in estuarine waters on Eelgrass beds and the like from Arctic to N.C., but the only Maine records are from Penobscot Bay area. (A 2nd species, *M. elisabethae,* reported in Boothbay Harbor, and a 3rd, *M. maculata,* from Va. to Gulf of Mexico.)   (4) *Hypaniola grayi,* cen. Maine coast south at least to N.J. in salt ponds and other brackish waters. All of the above species occur from lower intertidal zone to subtidal; others in deeper water.

Remarks: Like the terebellids, these worms gather food with sticky, grooved tentacles. Their tubes are made of mud or other debris, and are often attached to sponges, mollusk shells, or colonial tunicates.

Family: Ampharetidae.

TEREBELLID WORMS *Amphitrite* and related genera **Pl. 43**
Identification: Body *tapered,* divided (inconspicuously) into 2 regions; abdomen and thorax are differentiated by changes in setae, form of parapodia, and so forth. Head has *numerous soft, extensile tentacles* concentrated at the front and usually 1–3 pairs of gills behind them (on setigers 2–4). Form soft, sand- or mud-encrusted tubes. Largest species reach 18 in. (450 mm).

12 genera, at least 20 species, all with the general body form of *Amphitrite johnstoni* (only species shown on Plate 43) but differing in gill structure and in kinds and location of setae. The most frequently encountered genera are: (1) *Polycirrus,* 3 species, entirely without gills. To 2¾ in. (69 mm). (2) *Enoplobranchus sanguineus,* the only generic representative, has *no gills on head* but does have *branching gill-like parapodia* starting at about the 9th setiger and extending through midbody. Species name comes from characteristic blood-red color. A slender worm, about 50 times longer than thick (most other terebellids are 8–20 times longer than thick). To 13¾ in. (344 mm).

Remaining shallow-water genera have *gills on head*; usually 1–3 pairs are branching and *treelike.* Genera are distinguished initially by the number of setigers: *Pista, Nicolea,* and *Loimia* have 15–17; others usually 20 or more. (3) *Pista* species have 1–2 pairs of gills, and setigers toward the head have *lobes.* The most common species, *P. cristata,* has distinctive *pompomlike* gills; its rough tubes are encrusted with pebbles. To 3½ in.

(88 mm). (4) *Nicolea venustula,* the only common species of the genus, has 2 pairs of gills but *no* lobed setigers; to $2\frac{3}{8}$ in. (59 mm). (5) *Loimia* species have lobed setigers but *3 pairs* of gills (compared to 2 in *Pista*). *L. medusa* is the most commonly reported species; to $1\frac{1}{4}$ in. (31 mm). (6) *Amphitrite* species have setae on 20 or more segments — *A. johnstoni* has setae on 24–25 segments, *A. ornata* on 40–50. Both are large worms, *johnstoni* reaching 10 in. (250 mm), *ornata* 15 in. (375 mm). (7) *Terebella lapidaria* has setae extending to its tail end; to 2 in. (50 mm). **Similar species:** Compare with ampharetid worms, preceding account and Plate 43.

Where found: (1) *Polycirrus* species, whole coast. (2) *Enoplobranchus sanguineus,* N.C. to Cape Cod and locally to Gulf of St. Lawrence. *Pista* species, practically cosmopolitan but neither *P. cristata* nor *P. maculata* (another wide-ranging species) has been reported north of Casco Bay on this coast. *P. cristata* tolerates salinities as low as 18‰, and another species, *P. eximius,* is reported in even more brackish water on Eelgrass beds. (4) *Nicolea venustula,* Arctic south at least to N.J. (5) *Loimia* species, Cape Cod to tropics; *L. medusa* in salinities as low as 10‰ but chiefly subtidal. (6) *Amphitrite* species, whole coast. *A. ornata* is the common southern species, found intertidally on mud flats and in Eelgrass beds to 15‰ salinity; reported north to Bay of Fundy. *A. johnstoni* is the more common Boreal species but ranges south at least to N.J. Other species are subtidal. (7) *Terebella lapidaria,* Cape Cod to N.C. All of these species are shallow-water forms, extending from lower intertidal to subtidal.

Remarks: The larger species of *Amphitrite* are spectacular worms with crowns of yellowish-orange tentacles and blood-red fluffy gills. On soft grounds they lie buried in the substratum with only their heads exposed. Elsewhere their mud- or particle-encrusted tubes may be found attached to the underside of rocks. *Polycirrus* species are more commonly found under debris, in dead snail shells, and among algal holdfasts on soft mud bottoms. Terebellids typify the deposit feeding method used by polychaetes. The tentacles are grooved and coated with mucus; their cilia make a conveyor belt to carry food particles to the mouth. In some species these extraordinary tentacles can be extended many times the length of the worm's body and snaked over the substratum in all directions from the opening of the burrow.

Family: Terebellidae.

FLABELLIGERID WORMS *Flabelligera* Fig. 53
and related genera

Identification: Body relatively short, about 8–12 times longer than thick; club-shaped or maggotlike; usually *well-covered*

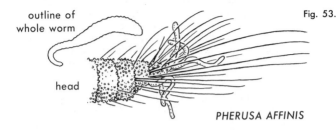

outline of whole worm

head

Fig. 53.

PHERUSA AFFINIS

with fine sticky papillae to which mud and other debris adhere. Body narrows behind to form a tail-like appendage but is not otherwise divided into regions. Head has walruslike, whiskery setae that project forward to form a sparse fan or enclosure (cage). Head often somewhat retracted; has 8 or more gills and 2 large palps that sweep the ground for food particles.

5 genera, at least 8 species; mostly subtidal and easily overlooked. Species identification beyond what is given here requires microscopic study of setae. (1) *Pherusa* species fit the above description without further qualification; to $2\frac{3}{8}$ x $\frac{3}{16}$ in. (59 x 5 mm). *P. affinis* is shown. (2) *Brada* species are atypical in *lacking* a setal cage; to $1\frac{1}{2}$ x $\frac{3}{16}$ in. (38 x 5 mm). (3) *Piromis eruca* has fewer papillae than typical forms, arranged in *2 rows on back and belly* and more densely at sides around the parapodia; neuropodial hooks have a *tiny spur* at tip. To $2\frac{3}{8}$ x $\frac{3}{16}$ in. (59 x 5 mm). (4) *Flabelligera affinis* has a *thick mucous coating* and long club-tipped papillae. To $2\frac{3}{8}$ x $\frac{3}{8}$ in. (59 x 9 mm). (5) *Diplocirrus hirsutus* also has long papillae; neurosetae and notosetae similar, both long whiplike (capillary) types; neurosetae are hooks in all other genera except *Brada*. To 1 x $\frac{1}{16}$ in. (25 x 1.6 mm).

Where found: (1) *Pherusa* species, whole coast. *P. affinis,* Bay of Fundy to Chesapeake Bay; intertidal zone and estuaries. *P. plumosa,* Cape Cod to Arctic; lower intertidal to subtidal at shallow depths. *P. inflata,* Va. to Fla.; intertidal and in Eelgrass beds. (2) *Brada* species, New York Bight northward; mainly subtidal. (3) *Piromis eruca,* Maine to Va.; intertidal. (4) *Flabelligera affinis,* Boothbay Harbor south to N.J.; mainly subtidal but sometimes under rocks in tide pools. (5) *Diplocirrus hirsutus,* south shore of Cape Cod to Penobscot Bay; subtidal. Most of these species are mud dwellers.

Family: Flabelligeridae.

FAN WORMS *Sabella* and related genera　　　　　**Pl. 42**
  Identification: Tubes skinlike, soft to tough and leathery, coated with sand, mud, or other debris. Worm is stout, tapered, with a short thorax of about 8 setigers and a longer abdomen.

Head has *feathery tentacles* arising from a lobe on either side of mouth. These tentacles, or *radioles,* form a *branchial crown* and have both feeding and respiratory functions.

6 genera and at least 8 species in shallow water, others deeper or at edge of our range. (1) *Fabricia sabella* (not shown) is a tiny — $\frac{1}{8}$ in. (3 mm) — worm; atypical in that its body is *not* conspicuously divided into regions. It can leave its tube and move about freely; as an aid to this activity it has eyes at both ends of its body. (2) *Myxicola infundibulum* has radioles joined together by a membrane *almost to their tips.* Builds a thick mucous tube buried in substratum. To 8 in. (200 mm). (3) *Euchone elegans* and (4) *Chone infundibuliformis* (not shown) have branchial membrane *less* extensive; base of crown has a *collar.* (Remaining genera also have a collar but membrane unites *bases* of tentacles *only.*) In *E. elegans* end of abdomen has a *spoon-shaped cavity,* absent in *C. infundibuliformis;* 1st species to 1 in. (25 mm); 2nd to $4\frac{3}{4}$ in. (119 mm).

Most of the following species have *eyespots* along midrib of radioles. (5) *Sabella crassicornis* (not shown) has *2–6 pairs* of eyespots evenly spaced along midrib of each radiole. To 2 in. (50 mm). (6) *Sabella microphthalma* has *numerous* eyespots in 2 *irregular* rows (visible with a good hand lens although fading somewhat in pickled specimens). To $1\frac{3}{16}$ in. (30 mm). (7) *Potamilla reniformis* has *1–8 large* eyespots *randomly spaced* in a row on each filament. To 4 in. (100 mm). (8) *Potamilla neglecta* (not shown) has *no eyespots.* To $2\frac{3}{8}$ in. (59 mm).

Where found: (1) *Fabricia sabella,* whole coast (a related species south of Cape Hatteras); reported on Spider Crab shells in lower Chesapeake Bay. (2) *Myxicola infundibulum,* Arctic to New York Bight; in lower intertidal zone northward. (3) *Euchone elegans,* Boothbay Harbor to New York Bight; rare and mainly subtidal. (4) *Chone infundibuliformis,* also little known, Arctic–Boreal south at least to New York Bight, offshore. (5) *Sabella crassicornis,* Cape Cod north at least to Bay of Fundy, subtidal. (6) *Sabella microphthalma,* s. Maine to S.C., lower intertidal to subtidal at shallow depths; common on oyster beds in lower Chesapeake Bay. (7) *Potamilla reniformis,* whole coast, although not known in Chesapeake Bay; common on south shore of Cape Cod on shells. (8) *Potamilla neglecta,* Penobscot Bay south at least to Chesapeake Bay; subtidal.

Remarks: Fan worms feed on food particles suspended in the water; the radioles have a conveyor belt of cilia to carry entrapped items down to the mouth. They are common fouling animals on pilings, buoys, and the like, also in rock crevices and among other sessile animals.

Family: Sabellidae.

HARD TUBE WORMS *Spirorbis* and related genera **Pl. 42**
Identification: These worms are readily identified by their

hard, limy tubes. Head has 1 tentacle modified to form a plug or operculum.

3 genera, 6 species. (1) *Spirorbis* species have tiny tubes, in flat or partly raised *coils* $\frac{1}{8}$ in. (3 mm) across. *S. spirillum* and *S. violaceus* (not shown) have dextral or *right-handed* coils; *spirillum,* the more common species, is smooth; *violaceus* has 3 ridges running length of coil. *S. borealis* and *S. granulatus* (not shown) are sinistral or *left-handed; borealis,* also common, is smooth (not ridged); *granulatus* has 2–3 lengthwise ridges. (2) *Hydroides dianthus* tubes are *not* fascicled as in next species; may be twisted and coiled in part but *not tightly coiled* as in preceding genus. To 3 x $\frac{1}{8}$ in. (75 x 3 mm). (3) *Filograna implexa* tubes grow in tangled masses, *fascicled* (like bundles of spaghetti) and twisted together. Tubes less than $\frac{1}{16}$ in. (1.6 mm) in diameter though several inches long; worm to $\frac{1}{4}$ in. (6 mm). **Similar species:** Note flat, chambered coil of Spirula (Plate 35) and the Common Worm Shell (Fig. 28, p. 127).

Where found: (1) *Spirorbis* species, all 4 known to occur on south shore of Cape Cod; *S. spirillum* and *S. borealis* intertidal, other 2 in deep water — only collected by dredging. *Spirorbis* species are found on this coast from L.I. Sound to Arctic (also on Gulfweed). *S. borealis* is found attached to rockweeds and other seaweeds, seldom on stones; *S. violaceus,* on rocks and shells; *S. spirillum* and *S. granulatus,* on a wide variety of substrata. All may be cast ashore. (2) *Hydroides dianthus,* West Indies north to Cape Cod and locally at least to Bay of Fundy; a common worm from Cape Cod south, encrusting stones, shells, and other hard surfaces. (A 2nd species, *H. norvegica,* grows on flotsam or as a stowaway attached to ships; tubes indistinguishable from those of *H. dianthus.*) (3) *Filograna implexa,* whole coast; a common fouling species.

Remarks: The little coils of *Spirorbis,* attached to rockweeds and other bases, are as familiar north of Cape Cod as the larger snaky tubes of *Hydroides* are south of it. *Filograna implexa* forms its odd colonial bundles by asexual reproduction: the worm divides in its tube, the lower part forming a new worm that bores out through the tube wall to take up residence next door.

Family: Serpulidae.

Aquatic Earthworms: Class Oligochaeta

Most oligochaetes live on land or in fresh water. The garden earthworm is a familiar example. 3 families, however, are represented in marine habitats in our area, and some species range to abyssal depths. Members of Naididae are brackish-water worms found among bits of floating weed or swimming actively in spring-

Fig. 54.

MARINE OLIGOCHAETE

like coils; 1 species is an internal parasite in marsh snails. The Tubificidae also has many brackish-water species; most often they are found burrowing in sand or under rocks intertidally, especially in places with freshwater seepage. Some are highly tolerant of or even prefer foully polluted areas. A few subtidal species live in deep-water sediments. Enchytraeidae worms also extend into fairly deep water, down to about 230 ft. (69 m), but most live intertidally, often among decaying seaweeds and sea grasses in the upper intertidal zone.

Oligochaetes are distinctly segmented but have neither parapodia nor head appendages. Setae may occur singly but usually are in bundles of 2 or more (absent on head). Members of the 3 families discussed above are termed *microdriles;* they are thread-like — less than $\frac{1}{16}$ in. (1.6 mm) thick and up to $2\frac{3}{8}$ in. (59 mm) long. A microscope is needed to study these worms. Some details of internal anatomy can best be seen in live animals; most studies require stained specimens, and some need to be dissected to be identified. As usual, differences in setae are critical for many species determinations.

Interested readers should consult the work of Cook and Brinkhurst (see *Selected Bibliography;* these 2 authors have provided most of the modern information available on oligochaetes living along this coast. The publication cited gives identification keys, ecological and distributional information, has a detailed bibliography, and outlines techniques for study. Most of the work on our oligochaetes has been done within the past decade, and much remains to be done.

Sipunculan Worms:
Phylum Sipuncula

A small phylum of round, unsegmented worms with a 2-part body consisting of a slender retractile *introvert* followed by a thicker *trunk.* The mouth opens at the front of the introvert and is completely or partially ringed by lobes or tentacles; there are no other appendages. The inconspicuous anus opens on the upperside of the body near the front of the trunk. The complete contractibility of the introvert complicates indentification. If possible, specimens should be examined when they are relaxed and the introvert is fully extended. Sexes are separate but not distinctive externally; development is direct or through metamorphosis from a trochophore-like larva (see p. 61).

Most sipunculans are burrowers in a variety of substrata ranging from sandy mud to coral-rock; however, one of our common species shelters in snail shells and other refuges. Formerly allied with echiurid and priapulid worms (p. 109) in a catchall class, Gephyrea, of the phylum Annelida. Exclusively marine.

GOULD'S SIPUNCULID *Phascolopsis gouldii*   **Pl. 47**

Identification: *Skin silky smooth;* opaque whitish to cream, tan, pink, or gray. Introvert extended is $\frac{1}{3}$ trunk length. Trunk usually to 6 in. (150 mm) but reported to twice that; diameter $\frac{1}{4}-\frac{1}{2}$ in. (6–12 mm). Young — to $\frac{3}{4}$ in. (19 mm) — are transparent whitish to pink.

Similar species: Species of *Golfingia* (not shown) have body all or partly covered by papillae. (Name commemorates a golfing holiday enjoyed by the British naturalist Sir Edwin Ray Lankester and a Professor MacIntosh.) (1) *G. pellucida,* a southern species usually found in coral (*Oculina* species, p. 94) or in cemented shell rock, has well-developed tentacles. (2) *G. minuta* has only small *lobelike* tentacles. Both have trunks less than 1 in. (25 mm) long; introvert $\frac{1}{2}-\frac{3}{4}$ trunk length, extended. Both are subtidal and seldom collected. *G. pellucida,* rarely north to Cape Cod: *G. minuta,* Bay of Fundy to Cape Fear, N.C. Other species in deep water.

Where found: Bay of Fundy to Cape Hatteras along sandy or muddy shores from lower intertidal zone to subtidal at shallow depths.

Family: None established.

HERMIT SIPUNCULID   **Fig. 43 opp. Pl. 47**
Phascolion strombi

Identification: Lives in abandoned snail shells, worm tubes (*Hydroides, Pectinaria,* and *Hyalinoecia* species), in fragments of old bone, and such. Body form modified to fit shelter; color also varies — transparent to opaque, whitish to brown, tinted with yellow, pink, orange. Trunk with several *crossbands of hooks and papillae.* Introvert invariably *longer* than trunk. Usually to $\frac{1}{2}$ in. (12 mm), but sometimes to twice that.

Where found: Nova Scotia to Cape Fear, N.C.; subtidal in 30 ft. (9 m) or more.

Family: None established.

Fig. 55.

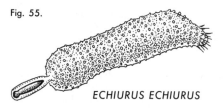

ECHIURUS ECHIURUS

Echiurid Worms: Phylum Echiurida

Like the preceding species, these are round, unsegmented worms with a 2-part body. However, the front part, termed a *proboscis,* is not retractile, although it can be shortened or extended. The proboscis has a trough or gutter on the underside. A short stout *trunk* follows.

Echiurids are an obscure little group hardly known on this coast. *Echiurus echiurus* (Fig. 55), reported by Roy Waldo Miner as occurring all along the eastern seaboard, does not appear in any of the local faunal lists. However, it was reported long ago in shallow water in Casco Bay; more recently it has been found on a shelly mud bottom just below the low tide line along the same coast. This worm is said to grow to 1 ft. (300 mm), so its apparent scarcity is not due to its being easily overlooked.

Several species of *Thalassema* are known: (1) *T. viridis,* a ¼-in. (6 mm) green worm, lives among blue clay nodules in deep water — 470 ft. (141 m) — in the Gulf of Maine. (2) *T. hartmani* is found in shallow water — 10 ft. (3 m) — in lower Chesapeake Bay, and (3) *T. mellita* occurs in tests of the Keyhole Urchin (Plate 62) from Va. southward. The last 2 species are reddish, to 1 in. (25 mm) and 1½ in. (38 mm), respectively; otherwise distinguished by internal anatomy. A white, presumably unnamed species of *Thalassema* has also been reported from lower Chesapeake Bay.

Echiurids, sipunculans, and priapulids (p. 109) once made up a polyphyletic class of Annelida, an arrangement now firmly rejected. Marine only.

Jointed-leg Animals: Phylum Arthropoda

Arthropoda has about twice as many species as Mollusca, the next largest phylum. It probably also leads in the number of individual animals, if protists and nematode worms are excluded. A few mostly microscopic forms are atypical, but the majority of arthropods can be readily identified by their jointed armorlike exoskeleton, which in some cases is actually soft and transparent; segmented appendages are also a highly characteristic trait.

Because there are so many species, the classification of arthropods is complicated by various sub- and supra-categories within the standard Linnaean series. 3 *subphyla* concern us. Sea spiders are the only members of the subphylum Pycnogonida. The Mandibulata, insects and crustaceans, contains arthropods with complex mouth parts including *mandibles* (jaws). They also have 1–2 pairs of *antennae,* and a body divisible into *head, thorax,* and *abdomen.* Members of the subphylum Chelicerata, horseshoe crabs and arachnids, *lack* mandibles and antennae; the body has only 2 clearly recognizable divisions, *prosoma* and *opisthosoma,* and even these are sometimes combined or one of them is reduced.

Within these 3 subphyla, 5 *classes* occur in marine habitats; the most important by far is Crustacea (p. 205). The others are Pantopoda, sea spiders (below); Merostomata, horseshoe crabs (p. 202); Arachnida, mites, true spiders, and pseudoscorpions; and Insecta, insects (both p. 203; arachnids and insects are grouped together as terrestrial arthropods).

Classification—Phylum Arthropoda

Subphylum Pycnogonida
    Class Pantopoda   Sea spiders
Subphylum Chelicerata
    Class Merostomata   Horseshoe crabs
    Class Arachnida   Mites, spiders,
                                     pseudoscorpions

Subphylum Mandibulata
    Class Crustacea   Crustaceans
    Class Insecta   Insects

Sea Spiders or Pycnogonids: Class Pantopoda

Sea spiders (Subphylum Pycnogonida) are only superficially spiderlike (see right back endpaper). The body of true spiders appears distinctly *2-parted,* with a *prosoma* carrying 4 pairs of legs and a pair of smaller leglike palpi in front; the rear part consists of the *abdomen* or *opisthosoma,* which is usually larger in size but without appendages except for fingerlike *spinnerets* at the rear. In sea spiders the opisthosoma is a mere nub; the prosoma consists of little more than a base for 4 pairs of legs. They do have a proboscis and (in some species) 1–3 pairs of appendages called (from front to back) *chelifores, palpi,* and *ovigers* (see Plate 48). Males, which are usually smaller than females, always have ovigers; females of certain species have them, others do not.

Some deep-water sea spiders have a 20-in. (500 mm) leg span; our shallow-water species are no more than a tenth this size, and most are smaller. Indeed, the common ones are so small that you must look carefully to find them at all. Not much is known about their habits, except that they are often found with hydroids and presumably feed on them. Sea spiders usually take on the color of their surroundings.

RINGED SEA SPIDER *Tanystylum orbiculare*   **Pl. 48**
  Identification: Prosoma compact, *round;* proboscis a broad truncated triangle in outline. Palpi a little longer than proboscis, chelifores are mere stubs. Leg span to $\frac{1}{4}$ in. (6 mm).
  Where found: Cape Cod to Brazil (locally north to Bay of Fundy). A very common little pycnogonid — if you look for it — on buoys and pilings among hydroids and other fouling organisms.
  Family: Tanystylidae.

LENTIL SEA SPIDER *Anoplodactylus lentus*   **Pl. 48**
  Identification: A common *southern* pycnogonid, slim-bodied and long-legged. Proboscis long, bulbous, with *slender chelifores* but no palpi. Body length to about $\frac{1}{4}$ in. (6 mm), leg span to $1\frac{1}{2}$ in. (38 mm).
  Similar species: Clawed Sea Spider, *Phoxichilidium femoratum* (Plate 48), a common species *north* of Cape Cod, is similar in body and chelifore proportions though less attenuated. Clawed Sea Spider has terminal claws with a *distinct auxiliary claw,* while that of Lentil Sea Spider is vestigial. Microscope needed for positive identification. Body length to $\frac{1}{8}$ in. (3 mm). Among hydroids and fine weeds from lower intertidal to subtidal in deep water. North to Arctic, reported in L.I. Sound but apparently rare south of Cape Cod.
  Where found: Reported north as far as Bay of Fundy, but chiefly Cape Cod south to Caribbean. Intertidal to subtidal in deep water, among hydroids and other fouling organisms.
  Family: Phoxichilidiidae, including *Phoxichilidium.*

LONG-NECKED SEA SPIDER   **Pl. 48**
Callipallene brevirostris
  Identification: A slender-bodied, long-legged pycnogonid with *short, thick chelifores*; no palpi. Front part of body drawn out in a *slender neck.* Body length to $\frac{1}{16}$ in. (1.6 mm).

Similar species: Compare with Lentil Sea Spider (Plate 48).
Where found: Cape Cod south at least to Fla. (locally north to Boothbay Harbor). A common *shallow-water* species on pilings among fouling organisms.
Family: Pallenidae.

ANEMONE SEA SPIDER   Pl. 48
Pycnogonum littorale

Identification: A broad-bodied pycnogonid; proboscis conical with *neither* palpi nor chelifores. Body length to $\frac{3}{16}$ in. (5 mm).
Similar species: Sargassum Sea Spider, *Endeis spinosa* (Plate 48) also lacks head appendages but is slender-bodied and long-limbed; females to $\frac{1}{4}$ in. (6 mm). On pelagic Gulfweed only. Family Endeidae.
Where found: Gulf of St. Lawrence to L.I. Sound; under stones in lower intertidal zone northward but subtidal at southern limit. It is described as clinging louselike to large anemones.
Family: Pycnogonidae.

Horseshoe Crabs: Class Merostomata

"Crab" is a misnomer, since this distinctive arthropod is more closely related to spiders and other arachnids (Subphylum Chelicerata) than to crustaceans. The horseshoe crab's appendages include a pair of *chelicerae* followed by 5 pairs of rather similar legs; the first, called *pedipalpi,* are modified as claspers in males; in both sexes the last pair have specially formed ends for digging. The mouth has no appendages of its own but opens at the base of the legs, which form a chewing mill. The only other appendages are 5 pairs of *book gills* on the underside of the abdomen. The lateral bumplike eyes are not stalked, and there is a 3rd median eye (quite inconspicuous) beneath the foremost spine on the horseshoe-shaped *prosoma.*

The horseshoe crab's only living relatives are found in the East Indies, China, and Japan. The genus *Limulus* dates back to the Triassic (the 1st period in the Age of Dinosaurs), but its earliest ancestors lived in Devonian seas more than 350 million years ago.

ATLANTIC HORSESHOE CRAB   Pl. 56
Limulus polyphemus

Identification: Unmistakable! Females reach 2 ft. (600 mm) including the tail spike; first 4 pairs of legs similar. Males smaller; 1st pair of legs heavier and different from other 3 pairs. Hatchlings lack tail spike; after 1st molt they resemble adults.
Where found: Bar Harbor, Maine, to Gulf of Mexico. Intertidal to subtidal down to about 75 ft. (22.5 m).
Remarks: Adults migrate into shallow water in late spring and

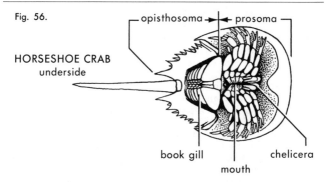

Fig. 56.

HORSESHOE CRAB
underside

opisthosoma → ← prosoma

book gill

mouth

chelicera

lay greenish eggs — ⅛ in. (3 mm) in diameter — in upper intertidal zone. Sand-colored young remain near shore, moving
gradually into deeper water as they grow older and darker.
Horseshoe crabs can swim, awkwardly and upside down, but
spend most of their time rummaging through bottom sand and
muck for the worms and mollusks that are their main food.
They were once harvested for fertilizer, and a few are still taken
to be chopped up for lobster bait. Despite their armament of
spines, tail spike, and wriggling, weakly clawed feet, horseshoe
crabs are harmless.
Family: Limulidae.

Arachnids and Insects:
Classes Arachnida and Insecta

Although they belong to different subphyla (see p. 200), the classes
Arachnida and Insecta are treated together as *terrestrial arthropods* (typical forms shown on **right back endpaper**).

The class Arachnida has 3 very distinct orders. (1) **Mites** (Order
Acari), the most numerous marine arachnids, are nearly microscopic — mostly less than $\frac{1}{32}$ in. (0.78 mm). Adults have a
rounded globular body without apparent segmentation and 4 pairs
of similar walking legs. Minute mouth parts (*chelicerae* and *pedipalpi*) are borne on a projecting *gnathosoma* or proboscis. There
are no other appendages. Some mites are herbivorous, others
carnivorous. Development is direct (without metamorphosis),
although hatchlings have only 6 legs.

(2) **Pseudoscorpions** (Order Pseudoscorpionida) resemble
miniature scorpions but have no sting; they are at most ⅛ in.
(3 mm) long. A few species of these otherwise strictly terrestrial
arthropods are common under debris just above the intertidal
zone.

(3) **True spiders** (Order Araneae) are also terrestrial, but occur at the edge of the sea. The most conspicuous are the wolf spiders often seen scurrying over rocks at the water line. Quite a variety of families and genera live in marshes, and some can stand submersion in salt water for several days. True spiders are easily distinguished from the strictly aquatic, exclusively marine sea spiders by their 2-part body with a distinctly separate abdomen; sea spiders (p. 200) have hardly any body at all.

Adult **insects** have a 3-part body, including a head with a pair of antennae, a thorax with 3 pairs of legs and usually 1–2 pairs of wings, and an abdomen without appendages. The class Insecta has more species than any other animal group but very few marine forms. Only 3 of the more than 2 dozen orders contain saltwater, aquatic adults; these are the beetles (Coleoptera), bugs (Hemiptera), and springtails (Collembola). *Anurida maritima* (Plate 48) is one of the common species of springtails. Individuals are only $\frac{1}{8}$ in. (3 mm) long, but rafts of them form dusty-looking blue-gray patches on the surface of rocky pools and marshy shores throughout New England. Springtails do not have a metamorphosis but hatch in adult form; they are wingless.

Several additional insect orders are aquatic in fresh water, and the number of species with fresh- and salt-water *larvae* is even larger. Some of these, the **biting flies** (Order Diptera), are renowned for making seashores almost uninhabitable at times. The culprits belong to 3 families: **mosquitoes** (Culicidae), **horse and deer flies** (Tabanidae), and **sand flies** or punkies — also called no-seeums and biting midges — (Ceratopogonidae); examples are shown on **Plate 48.** Members of the first 2 groups are familiar and obvious beach pests, but many shore visitors experience the persistently itchy bites of sand flies without being otherwise aware of their almost invisible attackers; these flies belong to several species of *Culicoides* whose larvae live in salt marshes and intertidal sands. They are found all along the coast. Mosquitoes are ubiquitous and can be as great a trial in Maine as in New Jersey or the Carolinas. The genera *Aedes, Anopheles,* and *Culex* contain species of saltwater mosquitoes that bite people. Members of the first genus (and possibly sand flies as well) have been implicated in the transmission of equine encephalitis, a very serious disease in humans that occurs sporadically (there have been outbreaks in New Jersey and Massachusetts within the past decade). Saltwater tabanids (deer and horse flies) belong to the genera *Chrysops* and *Tabanus;* none have been accused of carrying diseases, but as a daytime nuisance they have no equal.

The larvae of all these dipterans are aquatic, found chiefly in intertidal salt-marsh habitats. The 4th dipteran shown on Plate 48 is the **Stable Fly,** *Stomoxys calcitrans,* which looks like a House Fly (and also belongs to the family Muscidae) but bites. Its larvae develop in windrows of Eelgrass cast up on bay shores. The

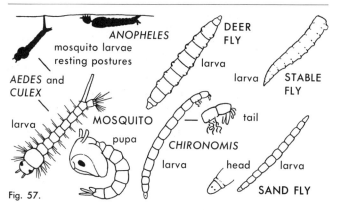

Fig. 57.

wormlike larvae of midges (nonbiting) belonging to another dipteran family, Chironomidae, are often found in shallow-water
dredge samples; their form is quite distinctive and easily recognized from the illustration for *Chironomis* (Fig. 57, above).

For a summary of noncrustacean arthropod groups and more
detailed coverage of the class Insecta, see *Field Guide to the
Insects.*

Crustaceans: Class Crustacea

This class includes animals such as crabs, shrimps, and lobsters,
plus other less familiar forms and a diversity of small relatives for
which microscopic study is necessary. The basic structural plan of
this class includes a segmented body divisible into *head, thorax,*
and *abdomen.* In higher crustaceans — all of the shrimp- and
crab-like forms, lobsters, and peracarids — there are 19 body segments or *somites,* each of which may have a pair of jointed appendages.

The head has 5 segments with 2 pairs of *antennae* (called antennae and antennules), and mouth parts composed of 1 pair of
mandibles and 2 pairs of *maxillae.* Usually the functional head
actually includes 1 or more thoracic somites and is properly
termed a *cephalothorax.* In many crustaceans the head and thorax are covered by a sort of hood or shell called the *carapace.*

The thorax has 8 segments with up to 8 pairs of undifferentiated
walking legs or *pereiopods;* often, however, 1 or more pairs are
specialized. The 1st pair in particular may be modified for feeding,
in which case they are known as *maxillipeds.* Decapods are so
called because they usually have 5 pairs of leglike pereiopods

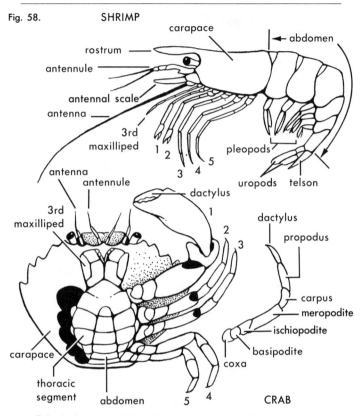

Fig. 58.   SHRIMP

CRAB

Principal body and limb divisions of a typical shrimp and crab.
Mouth parts — mandibles, maxillae (2 pairs), and 1st and 2nd
pairs of maxillipeds — are concealed beneath the 3rd pair of
maxillipeds in the crab and lie on the underside between the
bases of the antennae and 3rd maxilliped in the shrimp. The
crab's abdomen is tightly folded against the underside; the
pleopods are hidden under the abdomen, and there are no
uropods or telson. Thoracic limbs are numbered 1–5; enlarged,
claw-bearing legs of crabs are called chelipeds.

(some of which may be clawed) and 3 pairs of maxillipeds; the
latter frequently are not at all leglike, but they may be. The 2nd
and 3rd pairs of thoracic limbs of many peracarids are differentiated as *gnathopods;* essentially these are walking legs with claws
(see Plates 51 and 52).

The abdomen has 6 somites, and its appendages in higher crustaceans are 5 pairs of *pleopods* and a terminal pair of *uropods,* plus a flattened *telson* that is separate but not considered either an appendage or a somite. Lower crustaceans lack pleopods, uropods, and telson, and the abdomen typically ends in a pair of projections called *caudal rami.*

While many crustaceans conform to this structure, there are numerous exceptions. The most common modifications involve fusions of somites and loss of appendages.

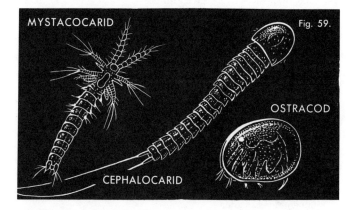

Most of the larger, more conspicuous crustaceans (with which this *Field Guide* is mainly concerned) belong to the subclass Malacostraca; see the classification table, p. 208. Members of the subclass Cirripedia containing the barnacles are also familiar. The remaining *lower* crustaceans are not as accessible to study and will be only briefly discussed here — most are very small, only a few measuring more than a fraction of an inch. Indeed, members of 2 of the subclasses, Mystacocarida and Cephalocarida (Fig. 59), are so obscure that they lived unnoticed at the very doorstep of generations of biologists near the Woods Hole laboratories on Cape Cod; they were first described in 1943 and 1955, respectively. Water fleas, p. 211 and Plate 34, are the only marine representatives of the largely freshwater subclass, Branchiopoda. Ostracods, of the subclass Ostracoda (Fig. 59), are also best known from fresh water; shallow-water marine species are mostly less than $\frac{1}{25}$ in. (1 mm) long and have received much less professional attention than their freshwater relatives. Copepods (Subclass Copepoda) are the most abundant marine crustaceans, but their small size excludes them from detailed study here. They are described briefly along with fish lice (Subclass Branchiura) on p. 211; see also Plate 34.

Simplified Classification: Crustacea

THE HIGHER CRUSTACEANS (SUBCLASS MALACOSTRACA): The discussion that follows should be read in close consultation with the **right back endpaper.**

Two important groups of small crustaceans *lack a carapace* and have a more or less regularly segmented body. Amphipods, p. 225, are usually *compressed* (flattened from side to side), and the abdomen has 3 pairs of swimming appendages and 3 pairs of uropods. Isopods, p. 220, are usually *depressed* (flattened from top to bottom), and the abdomen has 5 pairs of swimming appendages and 1 pair of uropods. A 3rd group, the tanaids, p. 220, are much like isopods, but the 1st pair of leglike appendages have small pincers. Caprellids, or skeleton shrimps, are an aberrant form of amphipods; see p. 229.

Two very different crustacean groups have a *short carapace* that leaves 4–5 thoracic segments exposed (when seen from above). Cumaceans, p. 219, have a headless look and may be mistaken for overgrown copepods. They either have no eyes, a fused median eye, or small unstalked ones. Mantis Shrimps, p. 218, are very distinctive with an unusual sequence of thoracic appendages including a pair of large, mantislike, predatory claws.

The remaining crustacean groups have a *full carapace,* and most can be described as either shrimp-, lobster-, or crab-like (see p. 232 for details). Mole Crabs, p. 244, are egg-shaped and otherwise unlike other larger crustaceans. True crabs, p. 244, have a pair of pincers and 4 pairs of walking legs with the last pair similar to the rest; anomuran crabs, p. 243, have the last pair greatly reduced. Hermit crabs, p. 240, are crablike in having a somewhat shortened body and large claws, but the abdomen is soft and is kept safely tucked into an abandoned snail shell; the last 2 pairs of walking legs are greatly reduced.

Lobsters, p. 239, even in the earliest hatchling stage, have pincers on 3 pairs of legs, with the 1st pair much larger than the rest. Typical penaeid shrimps, p. 233, which include the commercial shrimps of southern waters, also have claws on 3 pairs of legs, but all the claws are small. The remaining shrimp- or lobster-like crustaceans have no more than 2 pairs of legs with claws; the claws are very tiny in some. Mud shrimps, p. 240, and snapping shrimps, p. 236, are lobsterlike in that they have large pincers on the 1st legs; the pincers are usually very unequal in size. Typical caridean shrimps, p. 234, are a large shrimplike assemblage and include most of the more familiar species. They have 1–2 pairs of walking legs with small pincers.

Mysid and euphausiid shrimps, pp. 229 and 231, do not have claws on any of their walking legs, most of which are biramous — with 2 fairly equal-sized, filamentous branches. The mysid carapace is only attached at the front of the thorax and may be lifted free along most of its length. Also, the inner uropods of the mysid tail fan have an imbedded glassy bead (*statocyst*) near the base. Phyllocarid Shrimps, p. 217, are unique in lacking a tail fan; instead the last abdominal segment has a pair of caudal rami. Only 1 species occurs in our area.

CRUSTACEAN GROWTH AND DEVELOPMENT: The identification of crustaceans is complicated to some extent by the nature of their life histories. All of the orders of Peracarida (see classification table) produce young that resemble the adult at least in general body form, but in most of the other groups there is some degree of metamorphosis between hatchling and adult. In some cases this involves distinct developmental stages that do not resemble the final form.

A few groups shed their eggs in water to hatch at an early stage, but many crustaceans carry their eggs for a time and the hatchlings are more advanced in their development. In the first case the initial larva is usually a minute teardrop-shaped **nauplius** less than $\frac{1}{50}$ in. (0.5 mm) long with 3 pairs of appendages and a single eye (Plate 34). These are often abundant in the plankton, but perhaps the easiest way to see a typical nauplius is to hatch some brine shrimp eggs (sold in pet shops) and examine the first stages with a microscope or the strongest hand lens available.

The larvae of most of the lower crustaceans (first 7 subclasses of the classification table) are nauplii; those of barnacles are distinctive in having a pair of horns. Most of the nauplii found in the plankton belong to copepod species. Among higher crustaceans only euphausiid and penaeid shrimps hatch in this early stage; they then pass through a series of developmental forms or metamorphic stages.

The first, called a *copepodid,* is indeed copepodlike; subsequent *protozoea* and *mysis* phases are progressively more shrimplike. Other shrimp- and lobster-like crustaceans hatch in a protozoea stage without fully matured appendages, which makes some of them liable to confusion with mysid shrimps. Crablike crustaceans hatch as a very distinctive planktonic larva called a **zoea** (Plate 34); look for them in the summer plankton. Some are $\frac{1}{8}$ in. (3 mm) or more long. Metamorphosing crabs, called **megalopae** (Plate 34), have crablike limb formulae but a more conspicuous extended abdomen. Mantis Shrimps also have distinctive larvae (p. 218 and Plate 34), large enough to be seen with the naked eye; even at this stage they have mantislike claws.

Crustaceans grow by shedding their skins, and with each molt the larvae progress toward a more recognizable adult form. The number of preadult stages in different crustacean groups varies. Most copepods, for example, go through 6 naupliar and 6 copepodid molts before becoming adults.

Shedding is often a dangerous process, partly because the crustacean may have trouble getting free of its old skin. The process begins when the hard exoskeleton softens and a new skin forms underneath. Then the old skin splits, usually near the base of the carapace. The crustacean backs out to free itself and immediately begins to absorb water. This is the period of actual size increase. Lobsters gain up to 15% in length with each molt, and a Blue Crab with a $3\frac{1}{2}$ in. (88 mm) carapace swells to $4\frac{1}{2}$ in. (112 mm) within a few hours after shedding its skin. At this time the crustacean is almost defenseless. The normally pugnacious Blue Crab is docile and wants nothing more than a place to hide. And well it should, for at the "soft shell" stage the entire crab is deliciously edible. Lobsters remain soft for about 6 weeks, but are not considered a delicacy in this stage. As lime salts are deposited the new shell hardens, and there is no further growth until the next molt. The frequency of shedding varies. Some copepods have a lifespan of a month or less, molting about a dozen times between nauplius and adult. Young lobsters may molt 25 times in 4 or 5 years to reach a length of 10 in. (250 mm) or more, but older ones slow down to an annual shedding or perhaps only molt once in several years.

Water Fleas

These little animals make up a separate order, Cladocera, of the subclass Branchiopoda. Their near relatives, the fairy shrimps, live only in fresh water; most species of water fleas do, also. Marine cladocerans are nearly microscopic — less than $\frac{1}{16}$ in. (1.6 mm). They have a reduced carapace rather than the bivalve-like shell that encloses the body and abdomen of typical freshwater fleas. Plate 34 shows the 2 common marine genera, ***Podon*** and ***Evadne,*** identifiable with a hand lens despite their small size. The body segmentation is obscure; they have only 4 pairs of legs, 1 pair of large antennae for swimming and a minute 2nd pair, plus a single compound eye. Each genus has 3 species; microscope needed to distinguish between them. These are common plankters all along the coast, usually most abundant summer–fall.

Penilia avirostris (not shown) is marine but resembles the more familiar freshwater fleas; also occurs summer–fall, Cape Cod south. Several freshwater genera, including *Daphnia* (the water flea that serves as pet-fish food), also drift into estuaries. The highly atypical ***Leptodora kindti*** (Plate 34) is primarily a limnetic (lakes and ponds) species, but often extends into the brackish tributaries of Chesapeake Bay, in salinities as high as 6‰. It grows to $\frac{3}{4}$ in. (19 mm).

Copepods and Fish Lice

Almost any random scoop of saltwater will contain copepods (Plate 34) — tiny torpedo- or bottle-shaped bodies moving erratically through the water in short spurts. These are the most numerous marine crustaceans — both in number of individual animals and in number of species; 300–400 kinds occur in our area.

Most shallow-water copepods are $\frac{1}{16}$ in. (1.6 mm) or less; largest to $\frac{1}{2}$ in. (12 mm). Planktonic species belonging to the orders Calanoida and Cyclopoida have a thickened front end made up of a *cephalothorax* and 3–6 thoracic segments; the smaller, narrower tail (*urosome*) has 1–5 segments. The most conspicuous appendages are the long 1st pair of antennae. Sexes are sometimes quite different, and females may be found carrying packets of brightly colored eggs fixed to the base of the tail. The order Harpacticoida contains mostly benthic species less than $\frac{1}{32}$ in. (0.78 mm) long; many of these superficially resemble tiny isopods (p. 220).

Perhaps the most conspicuous copepods are those externally parasitic on fish. 2 copepod orders, Caligoida and Lernaeopodoida, and the fish lice, subclass Branchiura (formerly classified with copepods) contain such species. Many caligoids attain lengths of $\frac{1}{2}$-2 in. (12-50 mm), and species found on Swordfish and Ocean Sunfish may be 8-10 in. (200-250 mm) long, including a ribbon-like tail. Most caligoids and branchiurans retain some semblance of copepod form and may be found swimming free. Lernaeopodoida species and the caligoid ribbon lice (below), however, are highly modified, and once fixed in their host's flesh remain there.

BOOTED FISH LICE *Caligus*   Pl. 49
and other genera
  Identification: Copepodlike fish parasites; body regions usually well defined but varying greatly in proportions in different genera; somewhat flattened. 2nd antennae and 2 pairs of mouth appendages *prehensile,* with claws or pincers; swimming legs variously modified. Eyes small, not movable or compound. Urosome (tail) usually has a pair of caudal rami *at end.* Females often trail a pair of long stringlike egg sacs. Most species to more than $\frac{1}{4}$ in. (6 mm), some to 2 in. (50 mm) or more. 80 known species in numerous genera; typical male and female shown.
  Similar species: (1) Compare with Lazy Fish Lice (Plate 49). (2) At least 8 genera of copepods in the order Cyclopoida (not shown) are confirmed parasites; most are minute in size, typically copepodlike although 2nd antennae may be enlarged with a *prehensile claw.* On invertebrates and fishes.
  Where found: Whole coast on a wide variety of fishes or (males especially) swimming free.
  Family: Numerous families (Subclass Copepoda–Order Caligoida).

RIBBON LICE *Lernaeenicus* species   Pl. 49
  Identification: Females are so highly modified that they are unrecognizable as copepods; males unknown. Head and front of thorax *imbedded* in flesh of host; globular, with 2-10 rootlike horns, often branching, with 4 pairs of tiny legs. Rest of thorax and abdomen long, very slender — twisted in front, thicker behind. Egg sacs stringlike. To 2 in. (50 mm). Typical form shown.
  Similar species: (1) *Penella* species (not shown) are similar but rear end is tufted with furlike appendages. To 1 ft. (300 mm) or more. Parasitic on Swordfish and Ocean Sunfish. Family Penellidae. (2) Females of the order Lernaeopodoida (not shown) also become permanently attached to hosts. Body varies in shape; segmentation and appendages largely vestigial. Most

species less than $\frac{3}{8}$ in. (9 mm) long. At least 18 genera, whole coast.

Where found: Presumably whole coast since hosts are Bluefish, Menhaden, and other common fishes.

Family: Lernaeidae (Subclass Copepoda–Order Caligoida).

LAZY FISH LICE *Argulus* species   **Pl. 49**

Identification: Somewhat copepodlike fish parasites. Body flattened, with a *pair of suckers* below; 4 pairs of well-developed swimming legs. A pair of *movable compound eyes.* Urosome (tail) has 2 rounded or pointed lobes; caudal rami *inconspicuous,* located at *base* of tail. To $\frac{1}{2}$ in. (12 mm). Several species; typical form shown.

Similar species: Compare with Booted Fish Lice (Plate 49), which have *simple* eyes, lack ventral suckers, and usually have a pair of caudal rami at *end* of tail.

Where found: Whole coast, on a wide variety of fishes or swimming free.

Family: Argulidae (Subclass Branchiura).

Barnacles

The adult barnacle's shell of calcareous plates conceals an animal that does not look much like a crustacean. Segmentation is reduced, body organ systems are rearranged, and appendages diminished or missing. 6 pairs of jointed *cirri* are equated with the thoracic limbs of other crustaceans. There is a full complement of head appendages (see p. 205 for an account of crustacean appendages) but these, too, have undergone a radical metamorphosis. Abdominal appendages are lacking entirely.

Most barnacles are hermaphroditic but indulge in cross fetilization; the eggs are brooded in the mantle cavity. Hatchlings are typical *nauplii* (see p. 210), except for a pair of horns in front. At its next stage of development the barnacle is called a *cypris;* its bivalved carapace subsequently becomes a mantle and secretes the external shell of the mature animal. Our common acorn barnacles may reach full growth in a few months.

Barnacles form the subclass Cirripedia; acorn and goose barnacles belong to a single order, Thoracica. Additional cirripedian orders contain exclusively parasitic species; these are so grossly modified when mature that they are not recognizable as barnacles; the relationship is traced mainly through larval development. The bean- or sac-like form, *Sacculina* (Order Rhizocephala), is not known on this coast, but a relative, *Loxothylacus panopaei,* is found on crabs. Other parasitic barnacles bore into mollusk shells or live on cnidarians and echinoderms.

Acorn Barnacles

These are the familiar barnacles of intertidal rocks and boat bottoms; others live in deeper water, and some are crusty encumbrances on whales and sea turtles.

The shell consists of 6 calcareous plates; 2 are end plates (*carina* and *rostrum*), and 1 pair covers each side (*carinolaterals* and *rostrolaterals*). These interlock by an overlapping arrangement of flangelike extensions called (individually) *ala* and *radius*. The central opening is covered by a divided trapdoor composed of 2 pairs of plates (*terga* and *scuta*). The floor of this igloolike structure is termed the *basis* and is either calcified or membranous. The limy basis and plate walls are either solid or have hollow compartments.

The adult animal has been described as shrimplike and glued down by the top of its head. When covered with water, the barnacle rhythmically opens and closes its trapdoors to extend the 6 pairs of feathery *cirri* like a small hand, grasping blindly for any planktonic or detrital morsels adrift in the water.

Identifying barnacles is sometimes difficult because of individual variations, which are due in part to environmental influences during growth.

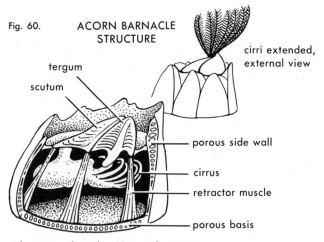

Fig. 60.　　**ACORN BARNACLE STRUCTURE**

cirri extended, external view

tergum

scutum

porous side wall

cirrus

retractor muscle

porous basis

side removed to show internal structure; diagrammatic, much simplified

LITTLE GRAY BARNACLE *Chthamalus fragilis*   **Pl. 18**
   Identification: A small, *dingy gray,* rather fragile, intertidal
   barnacle; basis *not* calcified. To ⅜ in. (9 mm).
   Similar species: The Little Gray and Northern Rock Barnacles (Plate 18) are the only species with a *membranous* basis —
   examine by prying barnacle off its substratum. Other barnacles
   have a *limy* basis. Little Gray Barnacle and Northern Rock
   Barnacle differ in plate arrangements; the former has *both* end
   plates overlapped by side plates, the latter only *one.*
   Where found: Abundant from Delaware and Chesapeake bays
   south to Caribbean; locally north to Cape Cod. *High* intertidal,
   often forming a zone above Northern Rock Barnacle or Ivory
   Barnacle when found with them. Penetrates slightly into estuaries.
   Family: Chthamalidae.

NORTHERN ROCK BARNACLE   **Pl. 18**
Balanus balanoides
   Identification: The common intertidal barnacle of northern
   shores in relatively *undiluted* seawater. Shell variable in shape,
   usually rough and folded; basis *not calcified.* White, unless
   overgrown with an algal coating or otherwise stained. Individuals in crowded colonies often columnar or twisted. To 1 in.
   (25 mm).
   Similar species: See Little Gray Barnacle (Plate 18).
   Where found: N. North Atlantic south on our coast to Del.
   Remarks: Extends subtidally into shallow water but most
   common intertidally, where it competes with Blue Mussel and
   rockweeds for space on rocks and pilings. Generally replaced in
   estuaries and southward by Ivory or Striped Barnacles.
   Family: Balanidae.

IVORY BARNACLE *Balanus eburneus*   **Pl. 18**
   Identification: Plates usually smooth and ivory white, *without*
   grayish or purplish lines; scuta *grooved* lengthwise (easily seen
   with hand lens); radii wide. Terga with a deeply *indented* spur.
   Basis calcified and hollow-chambered (tubiferous). To 1 in.
   (25 mm).
   Similar species: (1) Bay Barnacle, *B. improvisus* (Plate 18)
   has similar distribution south of Cape Cod but ranges north to
   Nova Scotia; lacks traits emphasized above; radii *narrow.* To
   ½ in. (12 mm). In brackish to almost fresh water, usually subtidal; a common fouling species. (2) Striped Barnacle, *B. amphitrite* (Plate 18) is distinguished by fine, gray to purple, vertical stripes; radii *wide,* scuta not grooved, and terga without
   indented spur. A subspecies, *B. a. niveus,* to ⅜ in. (9 mm); other
   subspecies larger. *B. a. niveus* is native in our range; chiefly
   subtidal to shallow depths and most likely to be found on

crustacean shells, mollusks, or rocks washed ashore; also in estuaries. Cape Cod to Caribbean and even more widely distributed as a fouling species. Other subspecies occur by accidental import.

Where found: E. Maine to South America, and elsewhere through accidental import. An *estuarine* form, where it often replaces Northern Rock Barnacle on rocks and jetties; also marine, subtidal in shallow water. Ranges into nearly fresh water together with Bay Barnacle. A common fouling species on boat bottoms.

Family: Balanidae.

CRENATE BARNACLE *Balanus crenatus*　　　**Pl. 18**

Identification: Basis calcified but *not* hollow-chambered (tubiferous); side plates are tubiferous, however. Radii narrow. To 1 in. (25 mm).

Similar species: (1) Bay Barnacle (Plate 18) has a tubiferous basis. (2) Northern Rock Barnacle (Plate 18) has a membranous basis. (3) Rough Barnacle, *B. balanus* (Plate 18) has wide radii; a strong craggy barnacle that adheres most tenaciously to rocks. To identify positively: break side plates and note (with hand lens) multiple grooves on inner walls. Crenate Barnacle has a simpler, more regular tube-groove arrangement in its side plates. To 2 in. (50 mm). A Boreal, chiefly subtidal species, ranging in deep water at least to N.Y.; in lower intertidal zone from e. Maine northward.

Where found: Arctic to Cape Cod; sparingly and only in deep water south to L.I. Sound. Chiefly subtidal to 100 ft. (30 m).

Family: Balanidae.

CRAB BARNACLE *Chelonibia patula*　　　**Pl. 18**

Identification: Found attached to crabs, particularly Blue and Horseshoe Crabs. Terga and scuta small and narrow, do not completely fill orifice. To $\frac{3}{4}$ in. (19 mm).

Similar species: Turtle barnacles, *C. testudinaria* (Plate 18) and *C. caretta* (not shown) are found on sea turtles. *C. testudinaria* has distinct radii, transversely notched or grooved; to 2 in. (50 mm) or more. *C. caretta* has barely perceptible radii. Sea turtles straggle northward from tropical or subtropical Atlantic to Cape Cod or beyond.

Where found: Practically worldwide in warm seas. Common from N.C. southward; reported in Chesapeake Bay but not much farther north.

Family: Balanidae.

Goose Barnacles

These unusual animals bear little resemblance to the more common acorn barnacles. Some species enter our coastal waters as wanderers attached to oceanic flotsam. Others live on the sea bottom in depths of 200 ft. (60 m) or more. Some of these have heavily scaled stalks; others conversely have greatly reduced plates.

STRIPED GOOSE BARNACLE   Pl. 17
Conchoderma virgatum
Identification: Body striped. Plates greatly reduced, vestigial. To 3 in. (75 mm) high.
Similar species: Eared Goose Barnacle, *C. auritum* (Plate 17) has a pair of earlike projections. To 6 in. (150 mm).
Where found: Oceanic; rarely seen inshore, but sometimes found on stranded whales and even on ship bottoms or sunken wrecks.
Family: Lepadidae.

PELAGIC GOOSE BARNACLES *Lepas* species   Pl. 17
Identification: Body compressed, enclosed by 5 limy plates, and mounted on a rubbery *stalk*. Handsomely colored in life with stalk dark purplish, plates snowy white or tinted pale bluish, edged with bright orange. Adults to $1\frac{3}{4}$ in. (44 mm) tall.
   5 species may occur on drifting planks, bottles, Gulfweed, and other flotsam. Only *L. anatifera* is shown. *L. fascicularis* has *paper-thin* plates; end plate (carina) sharply angled and ending in a flat disk below. *L. anatifera* and *L. hillii* have smooth or finely striated plates, while *L. anserifera* and *L. pectinata* are roughly furrowed or spiny. Positive identification requires dissection.
Where found: Virtually cosmopolitan. Mainly oceanic as fouling barnacles in deep water, but found ashore after storms or persistent onshore winds.
Family: Lepadidae.

Phyllocarid Shrimp

This little shrimp shares traits with both more and less highly evolved crustaceans, and fossil relatives extend its ancestry back to the Cambrian, the 1st geological period in which fossil-bearing rocks occur. Development from larva is direct, without metamorphosis. Superorder Phyllocarida.

NEBALIA SHRIMP *Nebalia bipes*   Pl. 53
Identification: Small and shrimplike, with a thin, flat, *bivalve-like* carapace. Abdomen ends in unsegmented *caudal rami.* Yellowish, tinted orange or green; carapace translucent; eyes red. To $\frac{1}{2}$ in. (12 mm).
Similar species: Higher shrimplike forms (Plates 53–56) have a fanlike tail (telson and uropods). Bivalved shell suggests an

ostracod (p. 207) or water flea (Plate 34) but abdomen and abdominal limbs are well developed and eyes are on short stalks. Cumacean shrimps (p. 219) have a short carapace, a pair of *segmented* uropods, and sometimes a telson; eyes *not* on stalks.

Where found: Maine to Labrador, also n. Europe and North Pacific. Little known in w. Atlantic but common in Britain, where it is found under stones in the lower intertidal zone. Reportedly attracted to such ripe fare as lobster bait.

Family: Nebaliidae.

Mantis Shrimps

A unique combination of traits sets the small order Stomatopoda apart from other crustaceans and justifies its classification as a distinct superorder, Hoplocarida; see table on p. 208.

MANTIS SHRIMP *Squilla empusa* **Pls. 34, 56**

Identification: Somewhat shrimplike but *flattened,* with a short carapace and unusual appendage structure: 3 pairs of weak walking legs; 3 pairs of subchelate maxillipeds; 1 pair of strong *mantislike* predatory claws; and another pair of weakly clawed maxillipeds. To 10 in. (250 mm).

Similar species: *Nannosquilla grayi* (not shown) has 10 teeth on predatory claws (6 in *Squilla*); smooth carapace and abdomen (ridged in *Squilla*). To $1\frac{1}{2}$ in. (38 mm). Secretive! Biologists had long identified 2 kinds of mantis shrimp larvae in the area of Woods Hole laboratories (Cape Cod) but did not find adult *N. grayi* until 1958. Family Lysiosquillidae.

Where found: Cape Cod to Gulf of Mexico; mud bottoms from lower intertidal to subtidal down to 500 ft. (150 m).

Remarks: Though common in our area, Mantis Shrimps escape detection by burrowing. They seldom wash ashore but may be taken in dredges or trawls. In *Stalking the Blue-eyed Scallop,* Euell Gibbons writes that Mantis Shrimps are delicious and describes a technique for noosing them in their burrows. However, burrows are complex, with more than one exit; watch out for the shrimp's claws! Larvae (Plate 34) are distinctive summer plankters.

Family: Squillidae.

Peracarids

The superorder Peracarida contains 5 orders of small crustaceans that are diverse in external appearance but united by similarities of internal anatomy. They are also alike in brooding habits, carrying their eggs in a pouch formed by 1 or more pairs of flaplike receptacles called *oostegites,* which are suspended quite conspicuously beneath the female thorax. The young develop directly, without metamorphosis.

The orders are (1) Cumacea, below, (2) Tanaidacea and (3) Isopoda (p. 220), (4) Amphipoda (p. 225), and (5) Mysidacea (p. 229).

Cumaceans

Very small peracarids with a short carapace that leaves 4–5 thoracic segments exposed. The lack of stalked eyes, or indeed of *any* eyes, in most cumaceans gives them a curiously headless appearance. Females are distinguishable from males by their *oostegites* (see above), the absence of abdominal appendages (except uropods), and their rudimentary 2nd antennae. Cumaceans are secretive little animals, mostly less than $\frac{5}{16}$ in. (8 mm) long, but may be found by carefully sorting through the small debris in dredge samples. Also, males of some species are part-time plankters and are attracted to lights. Order Cumacea.

Fig. 61.

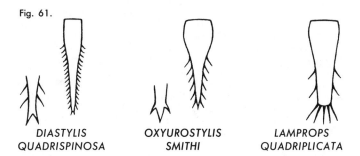

DIASTYLIS
QUADRISPINOSA

OXYUROSTYLIS
SMITHI

LAMPROPS
QUADRIPLICATA

SHARP-TAILED CUMACEAN *Oxyurostylis smithi*   **Pl. 51**
   Identification: This cumacean has a *telson* that is abruptly tapered and ends in a *sharp point.* To $\frac{5}{16}$ in. (8 mm).
   Similar species: (1) *Diastylis quadrispinosa* (Fig. 61, above) has a telson that tapers more gradually, with more marginal spines, and a *double point.* To $\frac{9}{16}$ in. (14 mm). 2 additional shallow-water *Diastylis* species, distinguished by fine details;

Nova Scotia south at least to Chesapeake Bay, not estuarine. Other species deeper, north to Arctic. (2) *Lamprops quadriplicata* (Fig. 61, p. 219) has telson *blunt-ended.* To $\frac{1}{2}$ in. (12 mm). Newfoundland to Cape Cod, subtidal at depths of 12 ft. (3.6 m) or more. Family Lampropidae. (3) Members of the families Bodotriidae, Leuconidae, and Nannastacidae (none shown) *do not* have a distinct telson. At least 10 species, largest only $\frac{5}{16}$ in. (8 mm) long; microscope is needed for positive identification. Whole coast.

Where found: Bay of Fundy south to Gulf of Mexico; a common estuarine to marine species in sand.

Family: Diastylidae, including *Diastylis.*

Tanaids and Isopods

The peracarid orders Tanaidacea and Isopoda are quite similar and were united in older classifications. Tanaids have 2 thoracic segments joined to the head, forming a short carapace; 6 thoracic segments are visible from above. Isopods have only 1 segment united to the head; like amphipods (p. 225), they lack a carapace and have 7 thoracic segments visible. Most isopods and tanaids are *depressed* (flattened from top to bottom); amphipods are usually *compressed* (flattened from side to side), and the abdomen has 3 pairs of swimming appendages and 3 pairs of uropods. Isopods have a telson and 1 pair of uropods; tanaids also have 1 pair of uropods but no telson. Both tanaids and isopods have 7 pairs of leglike thoracic appendages (only 5 in one isopod suborder); the 1st pair (gnathopods) in tanaids have subchelate claws, while many isopods have the first 3 pairs subchelate or prehensile. For a discussion of crustacean appendages see p. 205.

Sexes are distinguishable in many species by differences in the appendages, size of eyes, and other anatomical details, in addition to the female's brood pouch. Tanaids are small, adults to $\frac{3}{16}$ in. (5 mm), while adult isopods range from $\frac{1}{8}$–$1\frac{3}{8}$ in. (3–34 mm). There are numerous species of isopods, only a few of tanaids.

TANAIS CAVOLINII   Pl. 50

Identification: A slender, *cylindrical,* isopodlike crustacean with *spiky* uropods. Abdominal segments distinct, with *bundles of dense bristles* at each side. To $\frac{3}{16}$ in. (5 mm).

Similar species: (1) Other tanaids likely to be found in shallow water are tiny — $\frac{1}{16}$ in. (1.6 mm) or less; microscope required. Most likely to occur is *Leptochelia savignyi* (not shown), which is similar to *T. cavolinii* but *lacks* whiskery bristles; males have slender, clawed legs. Common from Cape Cod south at least to Chesapeake Bay; estuarine. Family Paratanaidae. (2) Compare with Slender Isopod (Plate 50).

Where found: Arctic to L.I. Sound; estuarine. Not rare but easily overlooked among fouling organisms and debris on pilings, Eelgrass bottoms, and the like, in shallow water.
Family: Tanaidae.

SLENDER ISOPOD *Cyathura polita*   **Pl. 50**

Identification: An elongate *cylindrical* isopod with telson and uropods forming a fan. To 1 in. (25 mm).
Similar species: (1) *C. burbancki* (not shown) is *very* similar but has less broadly rounded telson; 6th abdominal segment (very short) is separated from telson rather than fused with it as in *C. polita.* To ½ in. (12 mm). Chesapeake Bay to Ga.; prefers saltier water than *C. polita.* (2) *Ptilanthura tenuis* (not shown) is even more slender; has 1 pair of antennae 4–5 times longer than other pair. To ⅜ in. (9 mm). Bay of Fundy south at least to Chesapeake Bay on a variety of bottoms in estuaries and along shore. Not common. (3) *Tanais cavolinii* (Plate 50) is stouter; uropods spiky.
Where found: Maine to Gulf of Mexico, most common at upper limit of salt water, near freshwater seepages, outlets of tidal ponds and such, where it burrows in sandy mud. Often found in great abundance.
Family: Anthuridae, including *Ptilanthura.*

GREEDY ISOPODS *Cirolana* species   **Pl. 49**

Identification: Telson and uropods form a fan. First 3 pairs of legs have *prehensile claws;* last 4 pairs are unmodified.
    3 species. (1) *C. borealis* has rounded telson, rounded uropod blades; to ½ in. (12 mm). (2) *C. concharum* has *both* telson and inner blade of uropods notched; to 1 in. (25 mm). (3) *C. polita* has a rounded telson, inner blade of uropods notched; to ⅝ in. (16 mm).
Similar species: Compare with parasitic isopods (p. 224 and Plate 49). *Aega psora* has very large eyes. Cymothoids have *all* walking legs with similar, prehensile claws.
Where found: (1) *C. borealis,* whole coast but only in deep water. (2) *C. concharum,* Nova Scotia to S.C., but evidently only a winter species inshore south of Cape Cod. (3) *C. polita,* whole coast but inshore only from Cape Cod northward.
Remarks: Greedy isopods are scavengers on dead fish, crabs, and the like. Look for *C. concharum* around fish docks or try attracting it with appropriate bait. May bite if carelessly handled.
Family: Cirolanidae.

GRIBBLES *Limnoria* species   **Fig. 62**

Identification: Very small — to ³⁄₁₆ in. (5 mm) — *wood-boring*

Fig. 62.

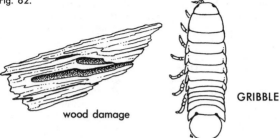

GRIBBLE

wood damage

isopods found in pilings and driftwood from lower intertidal zone to subtidal.

2 species. (1) Southern *L. tripunctata* has a row of tiny bumps (tubercles) along rear margin of telson. (2) Northern *L. lignorum* lacks these.

Similar species: A wood-boring amphipod, *Chelura terebrans* (Fig. 44 opp. Plate 51) sometimes found with gribbles, has well-developed uropods, the largest equal to about $\frac{1}{3}$ body length. To $\frac{3}{8}$ in. (9 mm). Family Cheluridae, Order Amphipoda (p. 225).

Where found: (1) *L. tripunctata,* Caribbean Sea north to R.I. (2) *L. lignorum,* R.I. north at least to Newfoundland.

Remarks: Surface of pilings infested with gribbles is peppered with holes $\frac{1}{16}$ in. (1.6 mm) or less in diameter; burrows penetrate about $\frac{1}{2}$ in. (12 mm) deep, usually running *with the grain;* reduce wood to a spongy consistency. As the rotten wood breaks away, new layers are exposed to attack; a soft-wood piling may thus lose up to 1 in. (25 mm) in diameter yearly. More destructive in some places than teredos (see p. 159). *Note:* Gribbles feed on a wood-dwelling fungus rather than the wood itself.

Family: Limnoridae.

SEA PILL BUG *Sphaeroma quadridentatum*   **Pl. 50**
Identification: This pretty little white-splotched isopod rolls into a ball when disturbed. To $\frac{3}{8}$ in. (9 mm).

Similar species: Other, less common members of same family (not shown) share the following traits: telson and uropods proportionately large, forming a fan; abdomen short, with only 2 segments. Shape of telson is distinctive for each species.

Where found: Cape Cod to Fla., intertidal zone among fouling organisms and weeds.

Family: Sphaeromidae.

IDOTEA **species**   **Pl. 50**
Identification: Uropods *fold* neatly against *underside* of

telson; eyes *at side* of head; the longer pair of antennae with multisegmented tips. 3 *Idotea* species in our area easily distinguished by shape of telson (as shown). To 1 in. (25 mm).

Similar species: 3 additional genera in our range have a similar telson–uropod arrangement (characteristic of the suborder Valvifera). All belong to the family Idoteidae, and typical forms are shown Plate 50. (1) *Chiridotea* species have a *broadly oval-shaped* body; abdominal segments separate (not fused); eyes *on top* of head. $\frac{1}{4}$–$\frac{3}{8}$ in. (6–9 mm). Several species, mostly north of L.I. Sound on sandy bottoms; *C. almyra,* a southern brackish-water form, Cape Cod to Ga. (2) *Edotea* species somewhat resemble preceding but head is narrow with eyes *at side;* abdominal segments fused. To $\frac{1}{4}$ in. (6 mm). 1 estuarine species, *E. triloba,* Nova Scotia south at least to Chesapeake Bay on Eelgrass; a 2nd similar species offshore. (3) *Erichsonella* species are *slender;* longer antennae are large-jointed *to tips.* To $\frac{1}{2}$ in. (12 mm). 2 species, mainly found in Eelgrass; *E. filiformis,* Cape Cod to Fla., with broader body than *E. attenuata,* L.I. Sound to N.C.

Where found: (1) *Idotea baltica,* Gulf of St. Lawrence to N.C. (2) *Idotea metallica,* whole coast. (3) *Idotea phosphorea,* Cape Cod to Gulf of St. Lawrence.

Remarks: *Idotea baltica* is likely to draw attention because of its abundance and its seemingly endless variation in color and pattern (see Fig. 63, below). Look for it swimming and crawling among weeds in pools and crevices in lower intertidal zone and Eelgrass beds. *Idotea metallica* is more often found on drifting weeds offshore. Related species require more diligent search. **Family:** Idoteidae, including *Chiridotea, Edotea,* and *Erichsonella.*

FRESHWATER ISOPODS *Asellus* species   **Fig. 64**
Identification: Uropods *broad-bladed* and *terminal.* Long-legged isopods, with legs progressively longer and stronger from front to rear. To $1\frac{1}{2}$ in. (38 mm).
Where found: Whole coast. Widespread in fresh water, sometimes straying into very low salinity water.
Family: Asellidae.

Fig. 63.

IDOTEA BALTICA
pattern variations

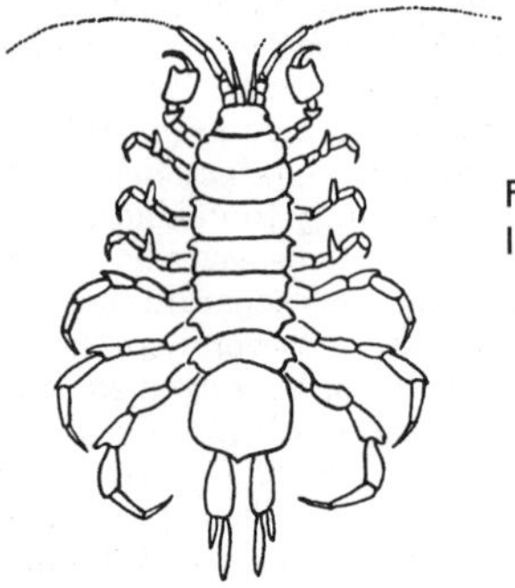

Fig. 64.

FRESHWATER
ISOPOD

LITTLE SHORE ISOPOD *Jaera marina*					**Pl. 50**
Identification: Uropods very short, *set in notch* at rear of broadly fan-shaped telson. To $\frac{1}{8}$ in. (3 mm).
Where found: Labrador south to Cape Cod and locally to s. N.J. A very common little isopod northward among fouling organisms and weeds on pilings and other intertidal objects.
Family: Janiridae.

SEA ROACH *Ligia exotica*					**Pl. 50**
Identification: These active, vaguely unpleasant isopods swarm over pilings and rocky riprap in upper intertidal zone on southern shores. If present at all, they are usually abundant and conspicuous. Note *terminal* position of uropods; telson much wider than long. To $1\frac{1}{4}$ in. (31 mm).
Similar species: (1) *L. oceanica* (not shown) is similar but smaller and has much shorter uropods; Massachusetts Bay northward. (2) Related, strictly terrestrial sowbugs (or pill bugs) are found under debris *above* intertidal zone. Both they and *Ligia* species belong to terrestrial suborder Oniscoidea.
Where found: Lower Chesapeake Bay south to Caribbean Sea.
Family: Ligiidae.

## Parasitic Isopods					**Pl. 49**
Bopyridae: Adult members of this family are grossly modified, permanently attached parasites on crabs and shrimps. Larval bopyrids resemble conventional isopods and swim free until they find a suitable host; the first arrival metamorphoses into an asymmetrically shaped female, whose only functions are feeding and breeding. Subsequent arrivals become male but remain as tiny — usually less than $\frac{1}{16}$ in. (1.6 mm) — parasites attached to the female. Example shown is *Probopyrus pandalicola,* $\frac{3}{8}$ in. (9 mm) long, found on shore shrimps, *Palaemonetes* species

p. 234); it lives under the shrimp's carapace, causing a noticeable bump.

Aegidae and **Cymothoidae:** Members of these families parasitize fish; they resemble ordinary isopods in form and may detach themselves and swim free. Some of the largest isopods belong to Cymothoidae. In Cymothoidae all 7 pairs of legs are prehensile (hooklike); in Aegidae only first 3 pairs are.

Aega psora is the only aegid likely to be found near the shore; it attacks commercially important fishes such as cod and halibut. Because of its large eyes it might be mistaken for a young cymothoid; note, however, its broader, more oval-shaped, pointed telson. It grows to 2 in. (50 mm). Juvenile cymothoids of different species are easily confused and have even been mistakenly placed in a separate genus, *Aegothoa*. Adults of 4 cymothoid species and 1 juvenile are shown on Plate 49. Telson and uropods *form a fan* in all species, but there are distinct differences in telson shape and body form. (1) *Olencira praegustator,* to $\frac{3}{8}$ in. (9 mm), is found on Menhaden; (2) *Cymothoa excisa,* to 1 in. (25 mm), on Scup; (3) *Lironeca ovalis,* to $\frac{7}{8}$ in. (22 mm), on Bluefish, Scup, and others; (4) *Nerocila acuminata,* to $\frac{7}{8}$ in. (22 mm), on dogfish. Parasites may be found on skin and fins, gills, or even in mouth cavity.

Amphipods

Amphipods, like isopods (p. 220), lack a carapace; 7 thoracic segments are visible from above and their appendages include 2 pairs of *gnathopods* with subchelate claws and 5 pairs of walking legs; the last 3 pairs are flexed back and outward, the first 2 pairs forward. (For a discussion of crustacean appendages see p. 205.)

While most amphipods are *compressed* — from side to side — the degree of flattening varies; some are nearly cylindrical and a few are *depressed* from top to bottom. The combination of *telson* and *3 pairs of uropods* at the tail end is unique.

Order Amphipoda contains 3 suborders: (1) Caprellidea (skeleton shrimps, p. 229) with several species of small, extremely aberrant amphipods; (2) Hyperiidea (following account), an equally small assemblage of planktonic and mostly oceanic species; (3) Gammaridea (pp. 226–228), a very large group with more than a hundred species representing the vast majority of amphipods likely to be found inshore. Though diverse in habits and habitat, they are difficult to distinguish without a microscope and often require meticulous dissection. Adults range in length from $\frac{1}{16}$–$1\frac{9}{16}$ in. (1.6–39 mm). Males are often distinctly larger and have more powerfully developed gnathopods.

Serious students will need E. L. Bousfield's *Shallow-water Gammaridean Amphipoda of New England* (see *Selected Bibliography,* p. 292).

BIG-EYED AMPHIPODS *Hyperia* species   **Pl. 51**
  Identification: Eyes *large* and *bulging.* Planktonic species either found swimming *free* or hiding on *underside* of umbrellas of large jellyfish. To $\frac{3}{4}$ in. (19 mm).

    2 species. (1) *H. medusarum* (not shown) has *very hairy gnathopods;* found on Lion's Mane (Plate 31). (2) *H. galba* has *sparsely haired* gnathopods; found on Moon Jelly (Plate 31).
  Similar species: See Planktonic Amphipod (Plate 51).
  Where found: Whole coast, with the jellyfish mentioned.
  Remarks: Additional hyperiids and members of several related families make up a separate amphipod suborder, the Hyperiidea. Most are only found offshore, where they are taken in plankton tows and on jellyfish and salps.
  Family: Hyperiidae.

PLANKTONIC AMPHIPOD *Calliopius laeviusculus*   **Pl. 51**
  Identification: A *large-eyed* amphipod often taken in plankton tows; telson *not* notched or split. Antennae have a somewhat brushlike appearance due to structures called *calceoli* (function unknown) and associated bristles. To $\frac{1}{2}$ in. (12 mm).
  Similar species: (1) *Pontogeneia inermis* (Plate 51), also frequently taken in plankton tows, has calceoli on large basal segments of male antennae only and telson is split. To $\frac{1}{2}$ in. (12 mm). Arctic south to L.I. Sound. Family Pontogeneiidae. (2) Note big-eyed amphipods (Plate 51).
  Where found: Arctic south at least to N.J.
  Family: Calliopidae.

BEACH FLEAS *Talorchestia* and *Orchestia* species   **Pl. 51**
  Identification: Semiterrestrial, living *at or above* upper limit of intertidal zone. *Leap erratically when disturbed.*

    2 genera, several species. (1) *Talorchestia* species are light, *sand-colored.* To $1\frac{3}{16}$ in. (30 mm). *T. longicornis,* the more common species, is larger, has longer 2nd antennae and smaller eyes than *T. megalophthalma.* (2) *Orchestia* species (not shown) are dark, *olive* to *reddish brown.* To $\frac{3}{4}$ in. (19 mm). 4 species differing in form of telson, antennae proportions, shape of male gnathopods, and other fine anatomical details. Note habitat differences between these 2 genera, under **Remarks.**
  Similar species: *Hyale* species (not shown) have a short, *deeply* notched or split telson; telson of above species *slightly* notched if at all. To $\frac{5}{16}$ in. (8 mm). Delaware Bay north at least to Nova Scotia; on *rocky* shores or pilings in upper intertidal zone. Family Hyalidae.
  Where found: (1) *Talorchestia longicornis* and *megalophthalma,* Cape Cod south at least to N.C. (2) *Orchestia* species, whole coast.
  Remarks: Common name comes from flealike jumping ability.

True fleas are insects (Order Siphonaptera) and suck blood; beach fleas are harmless scavengers. *Talorchestia* species dig burrows high up on sandy beaches and unless disturbed are not aboveground during the day; at night they are attracted to lights. *Orchestia* species are more often found *under* dead seaweeds and other wave-cast debris on salt marshes and beaches.
Family: Talitridae.

SCUDS *Gammarus* and related genera **Pl. 51**
Identification: Typical amphipods with a strongly compressed body. Telson usually distinctly *longer* than wide and *deeply* split; antennae about *equal* in length or *1st pair longer.* Largest species may be $1\frac{1}{4}$ in. (31 mm) on our coast, to almost 2 in. (50 mm) in Arctic.

Numerous species; microscope needed to distinguish between them. 2 common *Gammarus* species shown. (1) *G. mucronatus,* a brackish-water, Eelgrass form, has a distinctly *spiny* back. (2) *G. oceanicus* is a large, dark-colored, New England tide-pool amphipod.
Where found: Whole coast in a wide variety of habitats from fresh to salt water.
Remarks: Scuds, along with beach fleas (preceding account), are the most likely members of the order to draw the attention of casual beachcombers. Another name for them is "sideswimmers." Uncover a mass of rockweeds or turn an intertidal rock and you will often find teeming masses of scuds. They swarm in tide pools and crevices; beach fleas live higher on the shore. Unfortunately, scuds also typify a problem of amphipod identification: positive species determination usually requires meticulous dissection of appendages.
Family: Gammaridae.

FOUR-EYED AMPHIPODS **Pl. 52**
Ampelisca and *Byblis* species
Identification: *4 tiny, beadlike eyes* easily identify typical members of this family. Color pale with bright pink eyes. To $\frac{5}{8}$ in. (16 mm).

Ampelisca species have a split telson at least 2 times longer than wide. 5 species; typical form shown. In *Byblis* species (not shown) telson is only slightly longer than wide; 2 species.
Where found: Whole coast.
Remarks: Ampeliscids make parchmentlike tubes, but are perhaps most likely to be found in dredge hauls from Eelgrass bottoms or elsewhere in sand or mud.
Family: Ampeliscidae.

SEED AMPHIPODS *Stenothoe* and related genera **Pl. 52**
Identification: 1–3 coxal plates *exceptionally enlarged* even for

an amphipod; at a quick glance these small amphipods could be mistaken for ostracods (p. 207). 1 species to $\frac{1}{4}$ in. (6 mm); others $\frac{1}{12}-\frac{1}{6}$ in. (2-4 mm).

4 genera, several species. (1) *Stenothoe gallensis* (not shown) and (2) *Parametopella cypris* have only 1 coxal plate greatly enlarged; *S. gallensis* is a large Boreal species; *P. cypris* is southern and only $\frac{1}{16}$ in. (1.6 mm) long. Other stenothoids have 3 coxal plates enlarged.

Where found: Whole coast, often with colonial hydroids (Plates 13, 14).

Family: Stenothoidae.

DIGGER AMPHIPODS *Haustorius*   Pl. 51
and related genera

Identification: Legs modified for burrowing, the last 3 pairs especially wide and enlarged. Eyes small, weakly pigmented, or absent. To $\frac{3}{4}$ in. (19 mm).

A complex group with numerous species in several genera; *Haustorius canadensis,* which is shown, is a common example.

Where found: *H. canadensis* whole coast. Several others north to s. Maine, but most species live south of Cape Cod. *Lower intertidal zone* to subtidal on sandy beaches.

Family: Haustoriidae.

Tubicolous Amphipods   Pl. 52

Several dozen amphipod species in 5 families make tubular shelters of fine sand, mud, and other debris. Some of these are colonial and form *soft felty mats* on pilings, buoys, and such in lower intertidal zone and subtidally. Although a microscope is needed for positive species identification, some progress can be made with a hand lens.

Mottled Tube Maker, *Jassa falcata,* is distinguished by *powerful 2nd gnathopods* of male and conspicuous mottled coloration; 2nd antennae longer than 1st. To $\frac{3}{8}$ in. (9 mm). Whole coast. A related species found in deeper water. Family Ischyroceridae.

Slender Tube Makers have *very small coxal plates* and depressed body suggesting an isopod (Plates 49, 50). 2nd gnathopods usually stronger than 1st. 3rd uropods *unbranched. Corophium* species (typical form shown) are small — to $\frac{3}{16}$ in. (5 mm) — but form extensive mats replacing Mottled Tube Maker in brackish water. Whole coast. Species of a related genus, *Erichthonius* (typical form shown) have slender, about *equally long* antennae; grow to $\frac{3}{8}-\frac{1}{2}$ in. (9-12 mm). Boothbay Harbor south. Family Corophiidae (at least 20 species). Other slender, tube-making amphipods differ from corophiids in having *branched* 3rd uropods; 1st gnathopods much stronger than 2nd. *Microdeutopus gryllotalpa* is typical. To $\frac{5}{16}$ in. (8 mm). Cape Cod south. Family Aoridae.

Other tube makers, with *coxal plates well developed,* include the following amphipods. *Leptocheirus pinguis* is *banded;* has 1st gnathopods stronger than 2nd. 3rd uropods with *slender branches.* To $\frac{1}{2}$ in. (12 mm). Labrador south at least to L.I. Sound; related species to Chesapeake Bay. Family Aoridae. *Ampithoe* and related genera (typical form shown) are more uniformly colored, green to reddish brown; 3rd uropods have *short branches,* outer ones with microscopic hooks. Gnathopods are nearly *equal* in *Cymadusa compta* (not shown); 2nd pair somewhat stronger in *Ampithoe* species. $\frac{1}{2}$–$\frac{3}{4}$ in. (12–19 mm). Whole coast. Family Ampithoidae.

SKELETON SHRIMPS *Caprella*   Pl. 53
and related genera

Identification: Unlike any other amphipods; form and behavior suggest miniature praying mantises. Head and 1st thoracic segment more or less fused; 2nd segment bears mantislike claws; 3rd and 4th have paddle-shaped gills, oostegites, or rudimentary limbs; last 3 segments have prehensile legs. Abdomen a mere button. Often delicate and transparent but sometimes deeply colored, brown or reddish, to match their surroundings. Slow and methodical in movements. Commonly $\frac{1}{2}$–$\frac{3}{4}$ in. (12–19 mm); largest species more than 2 in. (50 mm).

Numerous species; microscope required to distinguish between them. Typical form shown.

Where found: Whole coast.

Remarks: These peculiar little amphipods are often abundant among bushy hydroids, bryozoans, fine weeds, and other fouling organisms on rocks, pilings, and buoys. Some are especially associated with sea stars, spider crabs, or sea turtles, and others prefer drifting flotsam.

Family: Caprellidae.

Mysid Shrimps

These are delicate little shrimps, translucent and lightly calcified; often fairly common but easily overlooked. The carapace is only attached *at the front;* none of the legs have pincers and most are *biramous* with a short basal branch (see Plate 53). Telson and uropods form a fan and each inner uropod has a glassy beadlike *statocyst,* detectable under a microscope with careful manipulation of the substage lighting. Compare with euphausiid shrimps, p. 231.

Though sometimes found in surface plankton tows, mysids are actually bottom-living animals and more likely to be taken in dredge samples. Like other peracarids (p. 218) these shrimps brood their young; even the youngest free-swimming individuals have a statocyst. Order Mysidacea.

BENT MYSID SHRIMP *Praunus flexuosus* **Pl. 53**
  Identification: A large mysid with *notched* telson and *blunt-ended* antennal scale. Pale yellowish or greenish, transparent, but with dark streaks and pinkish tail. To 1 in. (25 mm).
  Similar species: 2 *Mysis* species equal *Praunus* in size and have a notched telson, but antennal scale is *pointed;* details shown in Fig. 65. (1) *M. stenolepis* lives in shallow, grassy habitats from N.J. to Gulf of St. Lawrence. (2) *M. mixta,* a less frequently recorded species, is similar in appearance but prefers *weed-free* bottoms. South shore of Cape Cod northward. Microscope generally required for positive species identification: in *M. mixta* the *whole* outside edge of telson is bordered with spines, outer edge of antennal scale *straight; M. stenolepis* has outer tips of telson *without* spines, margin of antennal scale *curving* slightly.
  Where found: Since its first appearance on the north shore of Cape Cod in 1960, this mysid has spread northward at least as far as Nova Scotia and is common along the edges of many bays and sounds on the coast of Maine. An abundant species in n. Europe, where it penetrates brackish water.
  Family: Mysidae, including *Mysis.*

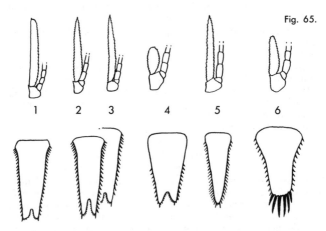

Fig. 65.

1 2 3 4 5 6

Mysid Shrimps: Top row, base of antennae and scales; bottom row, telsons. 1–4 have notched telsons. (1) *Praunus flexuosus,* scale blunt-ended. (2) *Mysis mixta,* outer edge of scale straight. (3) *Mysis stenolepis,* outer edge curved; outer tips of telson spineless. (4) *Heteromysis formosa,* scale broadly bladelike. (5) *Neomysis americana,* tip of telson narrowly tapered. (6) *Mysidopsis bigelowi,* tip of telson broadly rounded, strongly spined.

Additional Mysid Species Fig. 65

Most species of mysids found along this coast are so delicate and small — adults to $\frac{1}{2}$ in. (12 mm) — that a microscope is required to identify them; with magnification, however, they are easily distinguished by telson shape and spination, in combination with antennal scale differences. All belong to Family Mysidae.

Neomysis americana, one of the commonest shallow-water mysids between Va. and Gulf of St. Lawrence, has a gently tapered, blunt-ended telson edged with tiny spines. To $\frac{1}{2}$ in. (12 mm). In brackish as well as salt water. Swarms at surface Dec.–April in Woods Hole area.

Heteromysis formosa, like *Praunus* and *Mysis* species, has a *notched* telson but antennal scale is *broad* and *leaflike.* Females pinkish in part. To $\frac{3}{8}$ in. (9 mm). Often in dead Surf Clam shells, in shallow water from N.J. to Bay of Fundy.

Mysidopsis bigelowi is even smaller — adults to $\frac{5}{16}$ in. (8 mm) — with a broadly rounded telson tipped with 6 long spines. A southern species ranging north to Cape Cod; usually in deeper water — 30 ft. (9 m) or more — but sometimes in shallows.

Eucarids

The superorder Eucarida contains 2 orders. One of these, Euphausiacea (below), is composed of the krill shrimps, which are chiefly oceanic plankters. The other order, Decapoda (p. 232), has most of the crab-, shrimp-, and lobster-like crustaceans found near the shore.

Euphausiid Shrimps

Planktonic and chiefly oceanic, euphausiids are the krill shrimps familiar to whalers. They swarm in cold seas in numbers sufficient to color the water a pinkish hue. Euphausiids differ from higher shrimps in having at least 6 pairs of legs *biramous,* and none with pincers. They differ from mysid shrimps in that the carapace is attached *throughout* its length (rather than only at the front edge); inner uropods do *not* have a statocyst (see p. 229 and Plate 53). Young hatch as nauplii (see p. 210). Order Euphausiacea.

HORNED KRILL SHRIMP Pl. 53
Meganyctiphanes norvegica

Identification: Antennal peduncle (base or stalk) with an erect leaf; all legs including the 7th pair distinctly biramous. To $1\frac{1}{2}$ in. (38 mm).

Similar species: (1) *Euphausia* species (none shown) have 7th pair of legs nearly uniramous, with only a rudimentary branch.

Microscopic study required to distinguish between species. Adults $\frac{1}{2}$–$\frac{3}{4}$ in. (12–19 mm); usually offshore along whole coast. (2) *Thysanoessa* species (none shown) have biramous 7th legs but lack antennal leaf. *T. inermis* has dorsal spine on segment before tail fan; to $1\frac{3}{16}$ in. (30 mm). Sometimes common at surface in winter in Bay of Fundy; in summer offshore in 120–240 ft. (36–72 m). Other species rare inshore.

Where found: Along shore, summer–early fall in Bay of Fundy; strays south to latitude of Delaware Bay. Considered the most common euphausiid species in the Gulf of Maine.

Family: Euphausiidae, including *Euphausia* and *Thysanoessa*.

Decapods

Most higher crustaceans can be roughly classified as crab-, shrimp-, or lobster-like forms. The last 2 categories are not sharply differentiated. Both are characterized by a well-developed abdomen and tail fan composed of a *telson* and 2 pairs of *uropods*. The carapace covering the head and thorax is usually longer than wide. Typically, shrimplike forms are somewhat *compressed* from side to side rather than *depressed* from top to bottom. Most have rather weakly developed or *subchelate* pincers. Using the Northern Lobster as a model, snapping and mud shrimps (Plate 57) can be called lobsterlike because they have strongly developed claws on the front legs. (However, not all species of lobsters have this trait; the spiny or rock lobsters, for instance, do not have conspicuous claws on *any* of their feet.)

Decapods are so named because of their 5 pairs of walking legs which include the strongly clawed or *chelate* front limbs of crabs and Northern Lobsters; the other 3 pairs of thoracic appendages are usually specialized as auxiliary feeding tools and thus are functionally part of the head. (See p. 205 for a general discussion of crustacean appendages.) Other front-end details are used in identification, particularly the shape and spination of the *rostrum* and the location of spines on the *carapace*.

The type and arrangement of appendages is a useful diagnostic feature in identifying shrimplike forms (see right back endpaper). Count pairs of limbs *from the back forward* to avoid confusion with the 3rd maxillipeds, which may also be leglike.

Crablike crustaceans have the abdomen either weakly developed with appendages vestigial (as in hermit crabs) or pressed tightly against the underside (see p. 243). This definition covers the hippid crabs (p. 244 and Plate 55), otherwise atypical because they are rather elongate or egg-shaped and entirely clawless. Other crablike forms have claws on the 1st pair of legs.

Decapods are divided into 5 infraorders: Penaeidea (p. 233), Caridea (p. 234), Astacidea (p. 239), Anomura — including the mud shrimps (p. 240), hermit crabs (p. 240), and anomurans

(p. 243) — and Brachyura (p. 244). Order Decapoda.

Penaeid Shrimps

There are 2 quite different families of penaeids. The southern commercial shrimps of the family Penaeidae are typically shrimplike; members of the family Sergestidae are slender atypical forms. Both groups are readily distinguishable from other shrimplike crustaceans in that they have 3 pairs of legs with small pincers. They do not brood their eggs but shed them freely in the sea; the young hatch as nauplii (see p. 210). Infraorder Penaeidea.

SOUTHERN COMMERCIAL SHRIMPS   Pls. 55, 56
Penaeus species
Identification: First *3 pairs* of legs with small, nearly equal-sized claws; rostrum toothed above and below. To 8 in. (200 mm).

3 species; head end of typical form shown on Plate 55. (1) Pink Shrimp, *P. duorarum* (Plate 56) has groove running *full length* of carapace on each side of midline and usually a *dark abdominal spot.* (2) Brown Shrimp, *P. aztecus,* also has long grooves but no spot; juveniles have slightly turned-up rostrum, uropod with rust or brown near tips. (Positive separation of *duorarum* and *aztecus* may require study of genital apparatus.) (3) White Shrimp, *P. setiferus,* has short grooves, less than $\frac{1}{2}$ carapace length. The color differences implied by names are not entirely reliable, particularly for young estuarine specimens.
Similar species: (1) Several closely related genera *without* teeth on underside of rostrum occur southward, rarely as far north as N.C. (2) Rock shrimps, *Sicyonia* species (not shown) have hard, pitted and ridged shells, short upturned rostrum, and a toothed crest extending full length along middle of carapace; adults 2–6 in. (50–150 mm). Several species on Carolina coast but mainly south of Cape Hatteras. Excellent eating! (3) Caridean shrimps (Plate 55 and p. 234) *never* have claws on 3rd pair of legs. Several species, particularly shore shrimps (p. 234), may be dredged or seined with young *Penaeus* in brackish inlets from Chesapeake Bay southward.
Where found: All 3 species southward to Caribbean or South Atlantic, from shoreline down to about 200 ft. (60 m) or more. Northern limits are: (1) Pink Shrimp, Chesapeake Bay. (2) Brown Shrimp, Cape Cod. (3) White Shrimp, Fire Island, N.Y. None are common north of Virginia capes; Pink Shrimp is the predominant summer species in N.C.
Remarks: Adults appear in Cape Hatteras area in late spring and almost disappear from N.C. waters in winter. They are chiefly benthic, burrowers to some extent, but also known to swim upward, particularly at night. Eggs are laid on the bottom offshore; young drift in on bottom currents and grow to adult-

hood in grassy bays and sounds, returning to the sea when mature. Pamlico Sound is the northernmost shrimping ground; taken commercially in otter trawls.

Family: Penaeidae, including *Sicyonia*.

LUCIFER SHRIMP *Lucifer faxoni* Pl. 53
Identification: The long necklike carapace and slender compressed body identify this tiny and unusual penaeid. Transparent and colorless. To ½ in. (12 mm).
Similar species: *Acetes americanus* (Plate 53) is similar in body form but lacks the long neck. To 1 in. (25 mm). Lower Chesapeake Bay to Brazil. Planktonic, mostly oceanic but also in inlets (chiefly at night) and on flood tides.
Where found: A warm-water oceanic plankter but drifting north to Nova Scotia and w. Europe; practically cosmopolitan. Sometimes in estuaries.
Family: Sergestidae, including *Acetes*.

Caridean Shrimps

A large assemblage. Snapping shrimps (Family Alpheidae) somewhat resemble small lobsters; members of other families are typically shrimplike. Only the larger pandalids, such as Boreal Red Shrimps (p. 237), are used on this coast for food. Young hatch as shrimplike *protozoea,* pass through a *mysis* stage somewhat resembling mysid shrimps but lacking statocyst and with fully attached carapace; see p. 229. Infraorder Caridea.

Fig. 66.

teeth behind eye

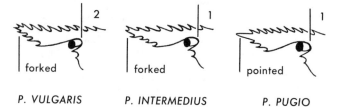

P. VULGARIS   P. INTERMEDIUS   P. PUGIO

PALAEMONETES species

SHORE SHRIMPS *Palaemonetes* species Pl. 55
Identification: Small shrimps with *distinct* claws on 1st and 2nd pairs of legs; 2nd pair strongest and longest (a family trait of the Palaemonidae). Rostrum extends beyond antennal scale

and is toothed for nearly its full length above and below. Color variable, usually pale and transparent with dark streaks. Adults 1½–2 in. (38–50 mm).

3 species. (1) Common Shore Shrimp, *P. vulgaris* (Plate 55 and Fig. 66) has 2 teeth on crest of carapace *behind* base of eyestalks. Movable finger of 2nd pair of claws has 2 small teeth at base (easily seen with hand lens in adult females, indistinct in males). (2) *P. intermedius* and (3) *P. pugio* (both Fig. 66) have only 1 tooth on crest behind eye (a 2nd tooth over or slightly in front of base of eyestalks). *P. intermedius* has rostrum toothed above *to tip;* female with 1 tooth at base of movable finger of 2nd claws, male none. *P. pugio* has tip of rostrum daggerlike with 1st tooth (above and below) *well back* from tip, finger of 2nd claw toothless.

Similar species: (1) *Leander tenuicornis* (not shown), one of 3 species of small shrimps found on floating Gulfweed (*Sargassum*), has fingers on 2nd claw much *longer* than palm (shorter in shore shrimps); olive with white spots. To 1⅞ in. (47 mm). For other *Sargassum* shrimps see Gulfweed Shrimp (p. 238). (2) *Palaemonetes paludosus* and (3) *Macrobrachium ohione* (neither shown) are *freshwater* species that stray into brackish water; both are rare in our range. *P. paludosus* has carpus (next joint above claw) of 2nd legs much *longer* than claw. To 1¾ in. (44 mm); N.J. to Fla. *M. ohione* has proportionately *much longer, hairy* 2nd legs. To 4 in. (100 mm); James R., Va., to Gulf of Mexico. (4) Veined Shrimp, *Hippolysmata wurdemanni* (Plate 55) has relatively weak 2nd pair of legs (with tiny claws), and carpus subdivided into about 30 joints. Rostrum fully toothed above and below, *shorter* than antennal scale. To 2⅛ in. (53 mm); lower Chesapeake Bay to Brazil, on pilings and jetties among hydroids. Family Hippolytidae. (5) Watch for young southern commercial shrimps (Plate 55), commonly found with shore shrimps from Chesapeake Bay southward.

Where found: Early studies did not accurately distinguish between the various species of shore shrimps; hence distributions and relative abundance are uncertain. Cape Cod to Gulf of Mexico; from nearly freshwater parts of tidal rivers to estuarine lagoons and inlets. Locally in warm bays north of Cape Cod. (1) *P. vulgaris,* north to Gaspé Peninsula; prefers saltier water than others. (2) *P. intermedius,* only to south shore of Cape Cod. (3) *P. pugio,* to Bay of Fundy.

Remarks: Shore shrimps are the most common shallow-water shrimps from Cape Cod Bay southward. Habitat preferences of individual species have not been established, but shore shrimps of one kind or another may be dredged in abundance from Eelgrass and other submerged plant beds, seined from open sandy shallows, or caught clinging to pilings. They even tolerate substantial pollution. Like most other shrimps they are more often found on a substratum than swimming free.

Family: Palaemonidae, including *Leander* and *Macrobrachium*.

SAND SHRIMP *Crangon septemspinosa*   **Pl. 54**
Identification: Easily identified by its *short* rostrum and *subchelate* claws on 1st pair of walking legs. Varies from almost colorless and transparent to opaque, mottled brownish or black. Body *depressed top to bottom* rather than compressed side to side. To $2\frac{3}{4}$ in. (69 mm), probably averaging smaller in South.
Similar species: (1) Red Sand Shrimp, *Sclerocrangon boreas* (Plate 54), a broad-bodied, rough-shelled relative, is red and has 3–4 teeth on midline of carapace (Sand Shrimp has only 1); to 5 in. (125 mm). Chiefly subtidal but occasionally at low tide line from Bay of Fundy to Arctic. (2) Several related genera of Boreal deepwater shrimps lack rostrum or have very short 2nd walking legs.
Where found: E. Fla. to Arctic; also North Pacific. From lower intertidal zone to subtidal down to 300 ft. (90 m) or more.
Remarks: An unusually wide-ranging little shrimp. It is the only *common* shallow-water species (except for mysids, p. 229) between Cape Ann and the Bay of Fundy, and is certainly not uncommon southward at least to Chesapeake Bay. South of Cape Hatteras it is only found inshore in the first half of the year. Chiefly on sandy bottoms but often in Eelgrass beds with shore shrimps; it is less widely distributed than they are south of Cape Cod and does not range as far into brackish water. A bottom dweller and more of a burrower than shore shrimps (p. 234). This, or a near relative, is the common edible shrimp of Britain, where large species are called prawns.
Family: Crangonidae, including *Sclerocrangon*.

LONG-EYED SHRIMP *Ogyrides alphaerostris*   **Pl. 53**
Identification: *Long slender eyestalks* immediately identify these small secretive burrowers. Transparent, with red and green flecks on appendages. To 1 in. (25 mm).
Similar species: *O. limicola* (not shown) is smaller — to $\frac{5}{8}$ in. (16 mm) — and has 8–14 tiny spines behind the short rostrum (*O. alphaerostris* has 1). In bottom mud of river mouths from lower Chesapeake Bay to Gulf of Mexico, in salinities as low as 9‰.
Where found: Cape Charles to Gulf of Mexico. In sand bars off ocean and inlet beaches. Locally common but seldom seen. Both species may occur in plankton.
Family: Ogyrididae.

BIG-CLAWED SNAPPING SHRIMP   **Pl. 57**
Alpheus heterochelis
Identification: A   small — to   2 in.   (50 mm) — *lobsterlike*

shrimp. Claws on 1st and 2nd legs; 1st pair *unequal* with one claw much larger; 2nd legs very weak, claws tiny, *carpus* ("wrist") divided into 5 joints. Greenish gray.

Similar species: Green Snapping Shrimp, *A. normanni* (not shown) is only half as large, and hood over each eye has a small *spine* (hoods rounded in *A. heterochelis*).

Where found: Lower Chesapeake Bay to Brazil, subtidal from tide line down to 100 ft. (30 m) or more. Burrows among stones and shells, especially on oyster reefs, often revealing its presence by loud popping sound made with specialized large claw.

Family: Alpheidae.

BOREAL RED SHRIMPS *Pandalus* species   **Pls. 54, 56**

Identification: Pink or reddish shrimps (young transparent with red stripes) with narrow rostrum *at least $1\frac{1}{4}$ times longer* than carapace. 2nd legs *unequal* and with small claws; 1st legs unclawed or claws microscopic. To 5 in. (125 mm).

3 species. (1) *P. borealis,* 3rd and 4th abdominal segments have *median spine.* (2) *P. propinquus* and (3) *P. montagui* (neither shown) *lack* median abdominal spine. *P. propinquus* has carpus of 2nd *right* leg with about 5 segments; *P. montagui* has about 20 segments.

Similar species: (1) *Dichelopandalus leptocerus* (not shown) is about equal in size but has a small, easily seen *branch* at base of leglike 3rd maxillipeds; *Pandalus* species do not. South to N.C. in deep water. (2) Small northern shrimps of the genera *Lebbeus, Eualus,* and *Spirontocaris* (all Plate 54) may have red markings; see Additional Caridean Species, p. 238.

Where found: Circumpolar; south along this coast as follows: (1) *P. borealis,* to Cape Cod; (2) *P. montagui,* to R.I.; (3) *P. propinquus,* to Del. Young sometimes at shallow depths in Bay of Fundy; adults usually in deep water to 100 ft. (30 m) or more.

Remarks: Boreal red shrimps, the edible Maine shrimps, are taken commercially by trawlers in winter; *P. borealis* is the most common one. These and related species are among the edible prawns of n. Europe.

Family: Pandalidae, including *Dichelopandalus.*

ARROW SHRIMP *Tozeuma carolinense*   **Pl. 55**

Identification: A long *slender* shrimp; *spiky* rostrum completely *toothless* above. Color variable, shades of green, brown to purple, or colorless. Behavior matches background of grass blades or sea whips: swims stiffly extended and in *vertical* position; often remains motionless even when disturbed. To 2 in. (50 mm).

Where found: Cape Cod to Caribbean, but rare north of Cape Hatteras. Shallow water.

Family: Hippolytidae.

GULFWEED SHRIMP *Latreutes fucorum*   **Pl. 55**
   Identification: A stray on our coast, found in drifting Gulfweed
   (*Sargassum*). Rostrum bladelike, blunt-ended, with spines at
   tip but otherwise toothless. Color highly variable, matching
   variations in the weed. To ³⁄₄ in. (19 mm).
   Similar species: 2 other species of shrimps, also with camouflaged coloring but with rostrum toothed above and below, are
   found on Gulfweed. (1) *Leander tenuicornis* (not shown) has leg
   pattern similar to related shore shrimps; see p. 234. (2) *Hip-*
   polyte coerulescens (not shown) has leg pattern similar to grass
   shrimps (see next account).
   Where found: Warmer Atlantic waters but drifting widely.
   Remarks: In a batch of Gulfweed collected off Chub Cay in the
   Bahamas, the author found 3 species in these proportions: 234
   Latreutes fucorum; 13 *Leander tenuicornis;* 1 *Hippolyte coeru-*
   lescens.
   Family: Hippolytidae.

GRASS SHRIMPS *Hippolyte* species   **Pl. 55**
   Identification: These shrimps have 2 color variations, bright
   green and dark or reddish brown. Abdomen sharply bent. 1st
   and 2nd legs with claws, the 1st stronger but *short,* the 2nd with
   carpus ("wrist") *divided* into 3 joints.
     2 species, doubtfully distinct; they *appear* to differ thus: (1)
   H. pleuracantha is larger, adult females almost ³⁄₄ in. (19 mm);
   rostrum much shorter than antennal scale, and basal segment of
   antennular peduncle (stalk) *without* spines at outer end (or not
   visible with hand lens). (2) *H. zostericola* has adult females only
   to ½ in. (12 mm); rostrum almost as long as antennal scale, and
   basal segment of antennular peduncle has 2 spines at outer end.
   Similar species: (1) *H. coerulescens* (not shown) is the rarest
   of 3 species found on floating Gulfweed. It *lacks hepatic spine*
   which above species have. See also under Gulfweed Shrimp
   (preceding account). (2) See Additional Caridean Species (Plate
   54 and next account); all are Boreal or deepwater forms with 7
   joints in carpus of 2nd legs.
   Where found: (1) *H. pleuracantha,* N.J. to Gulf of Mexico.
   (2) *H. zostericola,* Cape Cod to Caribbean. (Ranges subject to
   revision when taxonomic problems solved.) Grass shrimps live in
   beds of Eelgrass and submerged algae in shallow estuarine waters. Common but easily overlooked because of small size and
   camouflaged coloring.
   Family: Hippolytidae.

Additional Caridean Species   **Pl. 54**
From the cen. Maine coast northward a few additional caridean
shrimps may be found inshore; search for them in the lower intertidal zone in rocky pools and in puddles left behind on tide flats

and bay beaches. They are smallish — adults 1–3½ in. (25–88 mm) — and in life may be handsomely striped and mottled.

8 species, all members of the family Hippolytidae, are shown on Plate 54. Of these, *Eualus pusiolus* and *Lebbeus groenlandicus* appear to be most common intertidal species; *Eualus fabricii* and *Lebbeus zebra* have also been reported intertidally. The others are usually subtidal in depths of 30 ft. (9 m) or more. None are found south of Cape Cod except in deep water.

Lobsters

The Northern Lobster is our only species. Freshwater crayfish are lobsters in miniature but do not range into even brackish water. Both Northern Lobsters and crayfish are members of the infraorder Astacidea. Southern spiny lobsters, *Panuliris* and *Palinurus* species, and the less familiar Spanish lobsters, *Scyllarus* and *Scyllarides* species, range north to the offing of Cape Hatteras; all legs are clawless in males, and females have just the last pair of walking legs *subchelate* or minutely clawed. Infraorder Palinura for both southern spiny and Spanish lobsters.

NORTHERN LOBSTER *Homarus americanus*   **Pl. 56**
Identification: Unmistakable! Even 5/16-in. (8 mm) hatchlings have claws on *3 pairs* of legs. (So do penaeid shrimps, which are otherwise very different; see Plates 55 and 56.) To 3 ft. (900 mm) long, 45 lbs. (20 kg).
Where found: Labrador to Va.; subtidal from shallow water to edge of continental shelf; also ranging into slightly brackish water, to salinities of 20–25‰.
Remarks: Adults and young are found in shallow water north of Cape Cod. Southward, from N.Y. to Va., young lobsters — 1 ft. (300 mm) or less — wander within 10–15 ft. (3–4.5 m) of the shore in winter, but commercial lobstering is done in deeper water. The largest lobsters ("jumbos") come from the edge of the continental shelf.

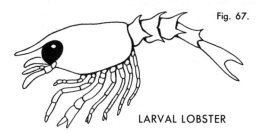

Fig. 67.

LARVAL LOBSTER

Females carry eggs 10–11 months. Hatchlings are spiny and planktonic; by their 5th molt, at lengths of about 1 in. (25 mm), they are proper bottom-dwelling lobsters. But growth is slow; 1½–2 lb. (680–906 g) sizes are about 4 years old. Lobsters are cannibals and scavengers, rejecting really putrid fare but not fastidious otherwise.

Family: Nephropsidae.

Mud Shrimps

Large claws on the front legs give these secretive burrowers a lobsterlike appearance. Some species have small claws on the 2nd pair of legs as well but never on the 3rd pair. The exoskeleton, weakly calcified, is almost parchmentlike in texture. Not likely to be found without a special effort; dig for them on sandy mud flats.

Mud shrimps hatch as shrimplike *protozoea* (p. 210) and remain planktonic until they are about ⅜ in. (9 mm) long. Several families make up a special group (Superfamily Thalassinoidea) within Infraorder Anomura.

SHORT-BROWED MUD SHRIMP   Pl. 57
Callianassa atlantica

Identification: Frontal part of carapace rounded above and *not* projecting over eyes, which appear as small dots on short, pointed stalks. 1st and 2nd legs clawed, the 1st pair much larger but unequal. To 2½ in. (62 mm).

Similar species: Naushon Mud Shrimp, *Naushonia crangonoides* (Plate 57) has frontal part of carapace rounded above and projecting *over* eyes. 1st legs with *subchelate* claws and no claws on 2nd legs. To 1⅜ in. (34 mm). South shore of Cape Cod; intertidal to subtidal at shallow depths in muddy sand. Family Laomediidae.

Where found: Nova Scotia to Fla.; sandy mud from lower intertidal zone to subtidal down to more than 100 ft. (30 m).

Family: Callianassidae.

FLAT-BROWED MUD SHRIMP *Upogebia affinus*   Pl. 57

Identification: Frontal part of carapace *flat* and covered with tufts of short *bristles*. 2nd pair of legs without claws. To 4 in. (100 mm).

Where found: Cape Cod to Brazil; estuarine mud flats in lower intertidal zone, and subtidal to about 90 ft. (27 m).

Family: Upogebiidae.

Hermit Crabs

These are familiar shore animals easily recognized by their habit of carrying about a snail shell in which the unarmored abdomen is

Fig. 68.

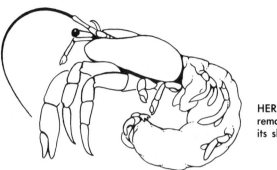

HERMIT CRAB
removed from
its shell

concealed. They have a pair of claws on the 1st legs. Only 2 pairs of walking legs are fully developed; the other 2 pairs are very small and highly modified. See Fig. 68.

Hermits can leave their shells at will, and captive individuals given an assortment of empty shells will sometimes make lightning-swift exchanges in search of an ideal fit. Rasps on the telson and uropods maintain a grip inside the shell that is often so tenacious the crab cannot be extracted without injury. A lighted match applied to the end of the shell is often an effective if not very sporting means of inducing the crab to vacate.

Hatchling hermit crab *zoea* (see p. 210) resemble those of mud shrimps. At metamorphosis the larvae have a segmented abdomen. Hermit crabs belong to Superfamily Paguroidea, Infraorder Anomura.

LONG-CLAWED HERMIT CRAB   Pl. 57
Pagurus longicarpus

Identification: Major claw narrow (width less than half of length), nearly cylindrical; palm nearly *hairless,* nearly *smooth* except for a weak row of spines down middle and along outer edge. Frequently with a dark, brownish or gray, median *stripe* on major claw. Carapace to $\frac{3}{8}$ in. (9 mm) long.

Similar species: (1) *P. annulipes* (not shown) is similar but smaller and major claw is *hairy*. Walking legs usually cross-banded in *annulipes,* striped in *longicarpus.* Carapace to $\frac{1}{4}$ in. (6 mm) long. Cape Cod to West Indies. *Subtidal* to 140 ft. (42 m). Usually occupying shells of Greedy Dove Shell (Plate 21). (2) Compare with Acadian Hermit Crab (Plate 57).

Where found: Massachusetts Bay to n. Fla. and Gulf of Mexico; locally in warm bays to Nova Scotia. Intertidal to subtidal down to 150 ft. (45 m). To minimum salinity of 18‰.

Remarks: This little hermit is ubiquitous in quiet shallows. Periwinkle, mud snail, and oyster drill shells are its preferred abodes; often these are fuzzy in appearance, pinkish or whitish, with incrustations of the hydroid Snail Fur (see Fig. 16, p. 78).
Family: Paguridae.

FLAT-CLAWED HERMIT CRAB *Pagurus pollicaris*   **Pl. 57**
Identification: Major claw *broad* and *flat;* covered with tubercles. Color pinkish. Carapace to $1\frac{1}{4}$ in. (31 mm) long.
Where found: Reported north to Penobscot Bay, but mainly Cape Cod to Texas. In shallow water along ocean beaches. Also in bays and estuaries to minimum salinity of 9‰.
Remarks: Our largest hermit; chiefly subtidal but may be cast ashore by storm tides. Occupies large moon shells and whelks. Latin name credits it with a thumb, perhaps an allusion to thumblike angle of movable finger on great claw.
Family: Paguridae.

HAIRY HERMIT CRAB *Pagurus arcuatus*   **Pl. 57**
Identification: A *very* hairy hermit. Major claw wide, heavily ridged with tubercles; dark brown, paling on fingers to orange. Minor claw *triangular* in cross section. Carapace to $1\frac{1}{4}$ in. (31 mm).
Similar species: *P. pubescens* (not shown) is *less* hairy. Details of *minor claw modeling* separate the 2 species: *P. arcuatus* has a central ridge of spines, doubled in part; outer face of palm *convex* and coarsely tubercled; *P. pubescens* has stronger central ridge of single spines; outer face *concave* and lightly tubercled. Ranges similar but *pubescens* only in deep water, 50 ft. (15 m) or more.
Where found: Boreal, south to latitude of Long Island. Occasionally in Maine tide pools but chiefly subtidal to more than 600 ft. (180 m).
Family: Paguridae.

ACADIAN HERMIT CRAB *Pagurus acadianus*   **Pl. 57**
Identification: Major claw moderately wide (width more than half the length), covered with tubercles; preceding joint with marginal spines. Minor claw a flattened *oval* in cross section; palm *rectangular* in outline. Major claw with bold *orange stripe.* Carapace to $1\frac{1}{4}$ in. (31 mm) long.
Similar species: Compare young with adult Long-clawed Hermit Crab (Plate 57); young Acadian Hermits have more strongly striped and *hairier* claws; Long-clawed Hermits are nearly hairless. The 2 species are not usually found together.
Where found: A Boreal species ranging south at least to Chesapeake Bay. Sometimes in tide pools northward but chiefly subtidal; only in deep water southward. Reported in as little as

12 ft. (3.6 m) in Vineyard Sound but probably in 80 ft. (24 m) or more off Sandy Hook.
Family: Paguridae.

STRIPED HERMIT CRAB *Clibanarius vittatus* **Pl. 57**
Identification: Claws nearly *equal* in size. Walking legs boldly striped, dark brown or greenish and white to pale orange. Carapace length to 1¼ in. (31 mm).
Similar species: *All* other shallow-water hermits in our area have claws *unequal* in size.
Where found: Rarely north of N.C. but straggling occasionally to Va.
Remarks: Look for this hermit in mud-flat pools, marsh borders, bay shores, and other protected places. Common around inlets, in large moon shells, whelks, and Scotch Bonnets.
Family: Diogenidae.

Anomuran Crabs

The infraorder Anomura contains a diverse group of animals. Besides the mud shrimps and hermit crabs dealt with above, there are several other superfamilies of more or less crablike forms. Porcellanids and lithodids are distinctly so; they differ most conspicuously from true crabs (Infraorder Brachyura) in that their last pair of legs is greatly reduced in size and usually carried closely pressed against the shell or hidden under it. Hippids are highly modified for a special habitat and hardly qualify as crabs at all.

The zoea larvae (p. 210) of *Lithodes* species resemble those of hermit crabs. Hippid and porcellanid zoea are more like those of true crabs (Plate 34) but lack a dorsal spine; also, the rostrum sweeps forward and down in a long curve, instead of pointing vertically downward.

LITHODES MAIA **Pl. 60**
Identification: Shell and legs of this large spidery crab are heavily armed with sharp *spines;* vestigial hind legs hidden beneath highly asymmetrical abdomen. To 4 in. (100 mm).
Where found: A Boreal deepwater crab, sometimes brought in by lobstermen because of its unusual appearance; normally at depths of more than 200 ft. (60 m).
Family: Lithodidae.

PARCHMENT WORM POLYONYX *Polyonyx gibbesi* **Pl. 60**
Identification: This small, grayish white crab with *oversized* flat claws is hardly ever found outside burrows of the Parchment Worm (p. 188). Females to ⅝ in. (16 mm), males less than ½ in. (12 mm).

Similar species: (1) *Pinnixa chaetopterana* (Plate 59) also lives in Parchment Worm tubes but has much smaller claws and shell is about twice as wide as long; the 2 crabs are seldom found in the same burrow. See also commensal crabs, p. 250. (2) Spotted Porcelain Crab, *Porcellana sayana* (Plate 60) is rust-colored with yellow- or blue-tinted whitish spots or stripes; adults $\frac{3}{8}$–$\frac{1}{2}$ in. (9–12 mm). Carolinas to Caribbean; not common in our area. Chiefly commensal with large hermit crabs but sometimes under stones or among oyster shells; from lower intertidal zone to subtidal down to 300 ft. (90 m) or more.

Where found: Cape Cod to Caribbean.

Family: Porcellanidae, including *Porcellana*.

MOLE CRAB *Emerita talpoida*   Pl. 55

Identification: Egg-shaped; sand-colored. Females to 1 in. (25 mm); males to less than $\frac{1}{2}$ in. (12 mm).

Similar species: Our only remotely similar species is *Euceramus praelongus* (not shown), a peculiar, more cylindrical anomuran crab, with sizable *claws* on front legs, 3 pairs of crablike walking legs, and a tiny 4th pair folded up behind. To $\frac{1}{2}$ in. (12 mm). Lower Chesapeake Bay to Gulf of Mexico; subtidal from tide line down to more than 100 ft. (30 m), on sand- or shell-bottoms. Family Porcellanidae.

Where found: On ocean beaches from Cape Cod Bay to Gulf of Mexico.

Remarks: Mole Crabs, like Wedge Clams, live in the turmoil of broken waves on sandy beaches, moving up and down the beach with the tide, constantly burrowing and being exhumed. They feed on organic debris caught by feathery antennae. Completely harmless, they cannot bite, pinch, or sting. Males are (at most) half the size of females and semiparasitic on them during much of year; free-living in winter when they and females move to deeper water.

Family: Hippidae.

True Crabs

Typical crabs, Infraorder Brachyura, have 4 well-developed pairs of walking legs. (Anomuran crabs, p. 243, though otherwise equally crablike, have only 3 such pairs, the 4th being vestigial.) The edge of the shell is often toothed and a distinction is made between *marginal teeth* (behind or lateral to the eyes) and *frontal teeth* (between the eyes). The eye socket (*orbit*) often is bounded by a tooth at each side; the outer orbital tooth is usually counted with the marginals, but a count of true frontal teeth does *not* include the inner orbitals (see Fig. 46 opp. Plate 61).

Crabs hatch in a *zoea* stage bearing no resemblance to the adult (Plate 34). Crab zoea are common summer plankters and for their size — about $\frac{1}{8}$ in. (3 mm) — are ferocious predators. In metamorphosis the zoea becomes a *megalopa,* which is more crablike but carries its small abdomen extended (Plate 34). With its next molt the megalopa becomes a tiny crab.

Most crabs are scavengers on dead animals, although they will take any live prey they can catch. Fiddlers tend toward a herbivorous diet; oyster crabs and their allies are parasitic or commensal.

DOLLY VARDEN *Hepatus epheliticus*   **Fig. 45 opp. Pl. 58**
  Identification: Clawed legs shaped to cover face; shell broad, abruptly tapered behind, *boldly spotted above.* To $2\frac{1}{2}$ in. (62 mm).
  Similar species: Shame-faced Crab, *Calappa flammea* (Fig. 45 opp. Plate 58) has shell strongly toothed behind, irregularly striped or mottled above. To 5 in. (125 mm). Less common than Dolly Varden. Additional *Calappa* species southward.
  Where found: A common shallow-water crab off southern beaches, often washed ashore; strays north of Cape Hatteras, the young rarely to Cape Cod.
  Family: Calappidae, including *Calappa.*

PURSE CRAB *Persephona punctata*   **Pl. 60**
  Identification: Shell *globular* with *3 sharp spines* behind. Pale gray or yellow with irregular dark markings. To 2 in. (50 mm).
  Where found: N.C. to Gulf of Mexico; reported north to N.J. but not common beyond the range given. Chiefly subtidal but sometimes washed ashore.
  Family: Leucosiidae.

TOAD CRAB *Hyas araneus*   **Pl. 60**
  Identification: Shell narrow, triangular; orbits with a *projecting postocular tooth;* tubercles in a row at sides and scattered above; rostrum nearly triangular, *slightly forked.* Reddish to olive, legs banded red-orange; young crabs brighter. To $3\frac{3}{4}$ in. (94 mm).
  Similar species: (1) *H. coarctatus* (Plate 60) is smaller — to $1\frac{1}{4}$ in. (31 mm). The rear portion of the large postocular tooth is more projecting in this species. Cape Hatteras to Arctic. (2) See Red-spotted Spider Crab (Plate 60).
  Where found: R.I. to Arctic. Usually subtidal in 25 ft. (7.5 m) or more on mud or pebbly bottoms, but sometimes in tide pools.
  Family: Majidae.

RED-SPOTTED SPIDER CRAB *Pelia mutica*   **Pl. 60**
  Identification: Shell narrow, triangular, *without* spines or tubercles; rostrum strong, *deeply forked.* Shell and legs spotted with bright red. To $\frac{1}{2}$ in. (12 mm). Often covered by sponge.

Similar species: Compare with Toad Crab (Plate 60) which has a shorter, nearly triangular rostrum.
Where found: Cape Cod to West Indies. Lower intertidal zone to subtidal down to 170 ft. (51 m).
Remarks: This small crab is easily overlooked among hydroids, sponges, and sea squirts on wharf pilings or among pebbles and shell fragments in bays and sounds.
Family: Majidae.

COMMON SPIDER CRAB *Libinia emarginata*   **Pl. 60**
Identification: A large spider crab — shell to 4 in. (100 mm), leg span to 1 ft. (300 mm). Shell strongly tubercled or spiny and covered with short hairs; about 9 spines along center of back. Rostrum broadly triangular, with a *shallow fork.* Brown to dull yellowish.
Similar species: *L. dubia* (Plate 60) is equal in size but only has 6 spines down the back; rostrum longer and *more deeply forked.* Reported north to Bay of Fundy but chiefly south of Cape Cod to Gulf of Mexico; said to be more abundant than Common Spider Crab in Chesapeake Bay but rarer elsewhere on our coast. Distinguish young with special care.
Where found: Nova Scotia to Gulf of Mexico. Common on all types of bottom; from shoreline in bays and inlets to subtidal at depths of 160 ft. (48 m) or more.
Remarks: Despite the formidable appearance of large individuals, this crab is slow-moving and completely innocuous. The short, hooked hairs are typical of spider crabs; shells are usually festooned with tangled debris and bits of live algae, hydroids, bryozoans, sponges, and even barnacles. Young have been found hitchhiking in bell of the jellyfish *Stomolophus meleagris* (see under Mushroom Cap, p. 89).
Family: Majidae.

CHIP CRAB *Heterocrypta granulata*   **Pl. 60**
Identification: Shell broadly triangular, divided above by raised ridges; margins irregular but not toothed. Clawed legs very large compared to walking legs. To $\frac{3}{4}$ in. (19 mm).
Similar species: Body–claw proportions somewhat suggest a porcellanid (Plate 60), but 4th pair of walking legs is not vestigial.
Where found: Cape Cod to Caribbean; subtidal at depths of 12 ft. (3.6 m) or more.
Remarks: This small crab so closely resembles the bits of shell and rock fragments among which it hides that it is difficult to know how common it might be.
Family: Parthenopidae.

ROCK CRAB *Cancer irroratus*   **Pl. 61**
Identification: Shell broadly oval, with 9 wide smooth- or

granulate-edged marginal teeth. Yellowish, freckled with reddish or purplish brown. To $5\frac{1}{4}$ in. (131 mm).

Similar species: Easily confused with Jonah Crab, *C. borealis* (Plate 61), but this species has *jagged* marginal teeth; to $6\frac{1}{4}$ in. (156 mm); Nova Scotia to Fla., usually in deeper water than Rock Crab.

Where found: Labrador to S.C. Intertidal north of Cape Cod; mostly subtidal and in progressively deeper water southward. Extends down to 2600 ft. (780 m) on all types of bottom. Mainly in salinities greater than 22‰, thus west in L.I. Sound only to Norwalk, Conn., and in Chesapeake Bay to Mobjack Bay.

Remarks: One of the commonest shallow-water crabs in New England. Look for them, along with Green Crabs, under rocks and in crevices in jetties and tide pools. Rock and Jonah Crabs are caught in lobster pots and marketed either as whole crabs or as disjointed large claws. These crabs pinch if provoked but have a more stolid disposition than Blue and Lady Crabs. Dungeness Crab of Pacific coast is related.

Family: Cancridae.

GREEN CRAB *Carcinus maenas*   Pl. 61

Identification: Shell *somewhat* broader than long with 5 marginal and 3 *frontal teeth* (very weak in young crabs); last pair of legs flattened but not paddle-shaped. Males and juveniles chiefly greenish above, yellowish below, adult females *red-orange* below. To 3 in. (75 mm).

Similar species: (1) Young might be confused with White-fingered Mud Crab (Plate 59) which has only 4 marginal teeth (first 2 fused) and *notched* frontal margin. (2) Red Crab, *Geryon quinquedens* (not shown) is a reddish, deep-water species with 4–5 marginal and 2 frontal teeth; to 6 in. (150 mm). Taken in pots and trawls in Gulf of Maine. Family Geryonidae.

Where found: N.J. to Nova Scotia. Unknown north of Cape Cod in the 19th century; now probably the most common New England shore crab at least as far north as Bay of Fundy. South in N.J. at least to Manasquan Inlet but absent from Delaware Bay. Intertidal to subtidal at shallow depths.

Remarks: A common British and n. European crab, also reported from Brazil, Panama, Suez Canal, Australia, and Hawaii, presumably by accidental transport. Tolerates salinities as low as 6‰. Found under stones and in pools intertidally, also in crevices in sea walls and jetties.

Family: Portunidae.

BLUE CRAB *Callinectes sapidus*   Pl. 61

Identification: Last pair of legs paddle-shaped; shell more than *twice as wide* as long with 9 marginal teeth (9th a strong spine). Usually olive or bluish-green above, claws bright *blue* below; young paler. Male abdomen abruptly tapered, female's broadly

rounded. To 9 in. (225 mm) wide between tips of longest spines.
Similar species: (1) *C. similis* (Fig. 46 opp. Plate 61) is easily
mistaken for *C. sapidus,* which, however, has 2 large frontal
teeth while *similis* has 4 (not counting the inner orbital teeth).
C. similis is smaller than *sapidus,* reaching at most 5 in.
(125 mm) across. A common estuarine crab south of Cape Hatteras, ranging into fresh water; reported from Cape May southward, usually in depths of 30 ft. (9 m) or more and salinities of
about 15‰. (2) Speckled Crab, *Arenaeus cribrarius* (Plate 61)
has shell similar in shape but brown above with small, rounded,
whitish spots. To 4½ in. (112 mm). A southern species, regularly
north to N.C. and occasionally to Cape Cod; off ocean beaches
in moderately shallow water. (3) Several *Portunus* species (Fig.
46 opp. Plate 61) stray north to Cape Cod: *P. sayi* on Gulfweed,
which it matches in color; *P. gibbesii, spinimanus,* and *spinicarpus,* from shrimp grounds south of Cape Hatteras, are
marked with red and brown, lack blue. 2–3½ in. (50–88 mm).
Where found: Cape Cod to Uruguay, sometimes north to Massachusetts Bay (questionably reported in Nova Scotia). Offshore to at least 120 ft. (36 m), but especially common in estuaries, where it ranges into fresh water.
Remarks: An important commercial species with the annual
catch ranging from 20–80 million lbs. (9–36 million kg) plus an
untold quantity taken by weekend crabbers. Soft-shelled Blue
Crabs are obtained commercially by keeping so-called peelers in
water boxes until they shed. Except when soft, Blue Crabs are
quick and aggressive, snapping viciously when caught; even
half-grown young can inflict painful pinches. Migrate to deep
water in winter, salt water for breeding. Barnacles commonly
attach themselves to Blue Crabs, particularly in southern regions. Striped Barnacle and Turtle Barnacle (both Plate 18) are
found externally; a small goose barnacle, *Octolasmus lowei* (not
shown) in gill chamber, and the bean-shaped sacculinid, *Loxothylacus texanus* (not shown) under abdomen. A parasitic
nemertean worm, *Carcinonemertes carcinophila* (not shown), is
found on gills of female crabs; worm is pinkish on virgin crabs,
red on breeders.
Family: Portunidae, including *Arenaeus* and *Portunus.*

LADY CRAB *Ovalipes ocellatus*   **Pl. 61**
  Identification: Last pair of legs paddle-shaped; shell *slightly*
  broader than long, with 5 marginal teeth. Pale grayish with
  minute purple specks in clusters. To 3 in. (75 mm).
  Similar species: *O. guadulpensis* (not shown) is very similar in
  form and habits but is gray above *without* dark spots. Cape
  Hatteras southward.
  Where found: Common in summer, Cape Cod to Gulf of Mexico; also Prince Edward I. (probably an isolated population). In

shallow water, mainly subtidal on sandy bottoms but to water-line when tide is in; also in bays and sounds including L.I. Sound and in Chesapeake Bay as far north as mouth of Potomac R.
Remarks: This handsome crab is as quick and ill-tempered as the Blue Crab; handle with care. Like the Blue Crab it often buries itself in sand with only eyestalks exposed. In North migrates to deeper water in winter.
Family: Portunidae.

BLACK-FINGERED MUD CRABS *Panopeus*   Pl. 59
and related genera

Identification: Shell much wider than long with 5 marginal teeth (first 2 more or less fused); frontal margin straight or curving with a *central notch.* Claws distinctly unequal; fingers black, palms paler. Mud-colored.

4 species. (1) *Panopeus herbstii,* dark color extends somewhat on palm; major claw with a *large tooth* near base of movable finger *visible* with fingers closed; wrist ungrooved; 3rd maxil-liped with a small red spot in males and some females; to $1\frac{1}{2}$ in. (38 mm). (2) *Hexapanopeus angustifrons,* only fingers dark; basal tooth on movable finger of major claw *hidden* when fingers shut; wrist *grooved;* 3rd maxilliped unmarked; to $1\frac{1}{8}$ in. (28 mm). (3) *Neopanopeus sayi,* dark color on finger of major claw extends broadly on palm; fingers of minor claw edged like *cutting pliers;* inner face of 3rd maxilliped unmarked or with a red dot; to $\frac{7}{8}$ in. (22 mm). (4) *Eurypanopeus depressus,* similar to preceding species but fingers of minor claw *spooned;* inner face of 3rd maxilliped with a large red spot; to $\frac{3}{4}$ in. (19 mm).
Similar species: White-fingered Mud Crab (Plate 59) is similar in form but has *pale* fingers and the frontal margin appears *doubled.*
Where found: (1) *P. herbstii,* Massachusetts Bay to Brazil, local north of Delaware Bay; in salinities of 10‰ or more. (2) *H. angustifrons,* Cape Cod to Gulf of Mexico, the least common species; usually subtidal at depths of *20 ft.* (*6 m*) *or more.* (3) *N. sayi,* Prince Edward I. to e. Fla., the most common mud crab north of Delaware Bay; in salinities of 15‰ or more. (4) *E. depressus,* Massachusetts Bay to Gulf of Mexico, the chief Chesapeake Bay species; in salinities of 4–20‰.
Remarks: Mud crabs are important predators on young oysters and clams; their powerful claws can crush $\frac{1}{2}$-in. (12 mm) Quahogs (Hard Clams); also attack barnacles and larger clams by chipping their shells. Mud crabs are often abundant in sponge colonies, among bushy bryozoans and hydroids on pilings, and intertidally under rocks or other debris on protected shores. The edible Stone Crab (*Menippe mercenaria*) of the southern Atlantic and Gulf coasts is a member of the same family.
Family: Xanthidae.

WHITE-FINGERED MUD CRAB   Pl. 59
Rhithropanopeus harrisii

Identification: A nondescript little mud crab, with *fingers lighter than palm.* To ¾ in. (19 mm).

Similar species: (1) See black-fingered mud crabs (Plate 59 and preceding account). (2) See Green Crab (Plate 61).

Where found: Cape Cod to Brazil, and locally north to Gulf of St. Lawrence (Miramichi Bay). Accidentally transported with oysters and now a pest on Pacific Coast and in North Sea. In brackish (25‰ salinity) to fresh water; under stones and debris intertidally, on oyster beds, and among hydroids and seaweeds on buoys and pilings. Probably more common than the spotty records suggest.

Family: Xanthidae.

COMMENSAL CRABS *Pinnotheres*   Pl. 59
and related genera

Identification: Shell often thin and paperlike, round to oval, *without* marginal teeth. Very small crabs, ¼ in.–¾ in. (6–19 mm). *Commensal with or parasitic in* bivalves, tube worms, colonial tunicates, or echinoderms.

7 species. (1) Oyster Crab, *Pinnotheres ostreum,* shell round, unmarked, and nearly hairless; females to ⅝ in. (16 mm), males to ³⁄₁₆ in. (5 mm). (2) Mussel Crab, *Pinnotheres maculatus* (not shown), shell round; males darkly furred, with pale bald spots; females sometimes have a dull brownish fur that may be shed or rubbed off; claws stronger than female Oyster Crab. Females to ⅝ in. (16 mm), males to ⅜ in. (9 mm). (3) Urchin Crab, *Dissodactylus mellitae* (not shown), shell somewhat wider than long, squared behind; tips of walking legs *forked;* less than ¼ in. (6 mm). (4) *Pinnixa* species, shell about twice as wide as long. 4 species, differentiated by proportions of claws and walking legs; ½–¾ in. (12–19 mm).

Where found: (1) Oyster Crab, Massachusetts Bay to Brazil; chiefly in oysters, sometimes in scallops, mussels, or Parchment Worm tubes. (2) Mussel Crab, Cape Cod to Argentina; in mussels, scallops, Parchment Worm tubes, or colonial tunicates. (3) Urchin Crab, Cape Cod to S.C.; on underside of Keyhole Urchins and Sand Dollars. (4) *Pinnixa* species, Cape Cod to Gulf of Mexico: *P. chaetopterana* in Parchment Worm tubes; *P. sayana* and *P. cylindrica* with Lugworms; *P. retinens* with mud shrimps.

Remarks: The Oyster Crab, most familiar of these little crustaceans, is no longer considered a harmless guest, since it damages the host's gills and robs it of food. More than 200 crabs have been found in a single oyster, and in Delaware Bay the infection rate may exceed 75%. Young crabs enter the water-conducting system of oysters in late summer. Within a year both sexes pass through a hard, flat-shelled phase; males leave on a free-swimming nuptial "flight" to females in other oysters and then die; females become soft-shelled and plump, live 2–3 more years. The fancy for Oyster Crabs as a gourmet item appears to have passed along with that for hummingbirds' tongues.

Both male and female Mussel Crabs are polymorphic and may be found swimming free; males survive the breeding period. Not as much is known about *Pinnixa* species, but their life histories presumably are less complex than those of Oyster and Mussel Crabs; they are sometimes found living free in mud. Infection rates of Lugworm burrows by *Pinnixa cylindrica* may exceed 75%.

Family: Pinnotheridae.

GULFWEED CRAB *Planes minutus*   Pl. 58

Identification: Shell truncated at the front and about as long as it is broad, with marginal notch. Yellow-olive or reddish brown with white spots and brown flecks, perfectly matching the Gulfweed on which it lives. Usually ½ in. (12 mm) or less, occasionally to ¾ in. (19 mm).

Where found: On drifting Gulfweed (*Sargassum*) or other oceanic flotsam.

Remarks: The scientific name means "little wanderer." Columbus saw them in mid-Atlantic.

Family: Grapsidae.

MARSH CRAB *Sesarma reticulatum*   Pl. 58

Identification: Shell squarish, with a small marginal *notch;* space between eyes much *greater* than eyestalk length; terminal joints on first 3 walking legs furry. Dark olive to blackish or purple. To 1⅛ in. (28 mm).

Similar species: (1) Wharf Crab, *S, cinereum* (Plate 58) does not have marginal notch. Brown to olive; to 1 in. (25 mm). Chesapeake Bay (Arundel on the Bay) to Gulf of Mexico and Caribbean, fresh to salt water; intertidally on wharves and under debris on muddy shores; a frequent shipboard stowaway. (2) Ghost Crab and female fiddler crabs (both Plate 58) have space between eyes much *shorter* than eyestalks.

Where found: Local, from Cape Cod to Texas; intertidal.

Remarks: Marsh Crabs dig burrows with multiple openings in salt marshes together with fiddler crabs. They prey on fiddlers to some extent but are chiefly herbivorous.

Family: Grapsidae.

GHOST CRAB *Ocypode quadrata*   Pl. 58

Identification: Shell squarish, somewhat wider behind, margins finely beaded but toothless; space between eyes much *shorter* than eyestalks. Pale *sand color,* claws white. To 2 in. (50 mm).

Similar species: (1) See Marsh Crab (Plate 58). (2) Female fiddler crabs (Plate 58) have shell *tapered* behind, are dark-colored.

Where found: Adults regularly from Cape Henlopen, Del., south through Caribbean and Gulf of Mexico to Brazil, above intertidal zone on ocean beaches. Adults and young occasionally reported to e. Long Island and R.I., but not common north of Va.

Remarks: These active, inquisitive crabs and their burrows are a familiar sight on southern beaches. Crabs often rush into the wash of broken surf to wet their gills or forage for bits of refuse but drown if kept submerged. Young burrow just above intertidal zone, adults at higher levels and even behind front dunes. Burrows have only 1 opening and go down 2–4 ft. (0.6–1.2 m) at a 45° angle. Often abroad during the day but most active at night. *Ocypode* means "swift-footed."

Family: Ocypodidae.

FIDDLER CRABS *Uca* species Pl. 58

Identification: Shell squarish, tapered behind, without marginal notch; space between eyes much *shorter* than eyestalks. Males with 1 claw (either right or left) *enormously enlarged.* Females with claws about equally small; identified chiefly by associated males.

3 species. (1) Sand Fiddler, *U. pugilator,* inner palm of major claw smooth. Carapace width to 1 in. (25 mm), major claw to 1⅝ in. (41 mm); in salinities similar to next species. (2) Mud Fiddler, *U. pugnax,* male's major claw with oblique row of turbercles on inner palm. Carapace width to ⅞ in. (22 mm), major claw to 1½ in. (38 mm); in strongly brackish to saltwater marshes. (3) Brackish-water Fiddler, *U. minax,* similar to Mud Fiddler but larger; shell with a distinct *groove* behind each eye. Joints of major claw red (color persists after death). Carapace width to 1½ in. (38 mm), major claw to 2 in. (50 mm) or more; in freshwater to mildly brackish marshes.

Similar species: See Marsh Crab and Ghost Crab (both Plate 58).

Where found: All 3 species range from Cape Cod to Texas; Mud Fiddler absent from Fla. south of St. Augustine. Habitat preferences of Mud and Sand Fiddlers overlap, but Mud Fiddler more common on mud flats, while Sand Fiddler is found in sandier situations and often higher up on the beach.

Remarks: Fiddlers burrow in flats and banks in or near coastal marshes. Burrow openings of Brackish-water Fiddler are often above water; those of the other 2 species chiefly intertidal. Burrows have only 1 opening and may be up to 2 ft. (600 mm) deep. Fiddlers are colonial, active by day. Their ritualized courtship behavior involves posturing by the male with the whole body, semaphorelike signals made with the great claw, and audible stridulations. Although occasionally cannibalistic, fiddlers feed mainly on bacteria, minute algae, and fermenting marsh plants gleaned from the soil. Despite the size of the male's great claw, fiddlers are not particularly dangerous to handle. Pin them quickly with the flat of your hand and hold the big claw shut as you pick them up. Take care — the claws break off easily if roughly handled.

Family: Ocypodidae.

Spiny-skinned Animals:
Phylum Echinodermata

Echinoderms are a unique group of exclusively marine animals with rather obscure relationships to other phyla.

Body form varies but is usually based on a 5-part, radial pattern. Calcareous skeletal elements and surface spines also vary in different classes. Most echinoderms have contractile *tube feet* for locomotion or feeding; these are operated by an internal plumbing arrangement called the *water-vascular system.* Sexes are separate but usually not distinguishable externally. A few species brood eggs that develop without distinctive larval forms; others shed sperm and eggs in water and the young pass through a complex metamorphosis (see p. 61 for a discussion of larval types). Most species have considerable ability to regenerate lost or damaged parts.

Several classes have been totally extinct since before the Age of Dinosaurs. All of the remaining ones occur in shallow water except Sea Lilies and Feather Stars, Class Crinoidea, which are not found in our range in less than 100 ft. (30 m). Typical crinoids have a crown of 10 feathery arms and are either attached to the bottom by a slender stalk or are stalkless and free-moving. 3 classes covered in this *Field Guide:* Holothuroidea (below), Echinoidea (p. 257), and Stelleroidea (p. 258).

Sea Cucumbers: Class Holothuroidea

Body cucumber- or worm-like; highly changeable in shape but with definite front and rear ends. Front sometimes with a collar-like *introvert;* mouth surrounded by a ring of contractile tentacles. Anus at rear. Tube feet may or may not be present, highly contractile to very little so. Skin smooth or warty; imbedded calcareous *deposits* (sometimes scarce or absent) visible with lower powers of compound microscope (see Fig. 42 opp. Plate 46). To prepare a sample, snip out a $\frac{1}{8}$-in. (3 mm) block of skin, place on microscope slide, dissolve soft parts with Clorox, add a drop of water and a cover slip; then examine.

Synaptas and their relatives ingest bottom material, absorb digestible parts as they pass through body. Other sea cucumbers trap plankters or sweep up detritus with their tentacles. Roughly handled cucumbers may eject their "innards"; new ones will be regenerated.

SCARLET PSOLUS *Psolus fabricii*   **Pl. 46**
   Identification: Bright red, anus ringed with 5–6 granular *scales*. Top and bottom sharply defined. Bottom is like the sole of a tennis shoe, flat, rimmed with marginal band of tube feet and a weaker row down the middle. Top domed, with a short tail on a mound at one end, introvert at other. To 8 in. (200 mm).
   Similar species: (1) *P. phantapus* (not shown) is similar in form but has smaller, more numerous scales and longer tail. North of Cape Cod in deep water, 60 ft. (18 m) or more. When contracted these cucumbers look like sea squirts; see Plate 17.
   Where found: Cape Cod to Arctic from lower intertidal zone to subtidal down to more than 300 ft. (90 m) on hard bottoms.
   Family: Psolidae.

HAIRY CUCUMBER *Sclerodactyla briareus*   **Pl. 46**
   Identification: Body saclike, tapered behind, and *nearly covered* with slender tube feet. Color olive, brown, or black to purplish. To 6 in. (150 mm) or more. Skin smooth with few or no calcareous deposits except at ends. *Note:* Deposits in this species are *tables;* see Fig. 42 opp. Plate 46 for visual key to shapes.
   Similar species: *Havelockia scabra* (not shown) is similar but has a more distinct tail, is paler — whitish brown — and has a rough skin with numerous deposits. To 3 in. (75 mm). A rare Boreal species, south in deep water to Delaware Bay. Family Phyllophoridae.
   Where found: Cape Cod to Gulf of Mexico; subtidal from shallow water down to 60 ft. (18 m); locally abundant in soft mud.
   Family: Sclerodactylidae.

ORANGE-FOOTED CUCUMBER   **Pl. 46**
Cucumaria frondosa
   Identification: Distinctly cucumber-shaped; skin opaque, leathery. Tube feet in 5 *bands*; 10 densely bushy tentacles. Young are 1–2 in. (25–50 mm); translucent, pale orange to deep brown at front end. Adults dark purplish or reddish brown, paler below; tube feet often bright orange-tipped. To 10 in.

(250 mm) in shallow water; almost twice as long in deep water. Deposits mostly roundish *plates,* scarce except in young.

Similar species: Additional species with *tube feet in bands* include the following species (none shown but see **deposits,** Fig. 42 opp. Plate 46). (1) *Duasmodactyla commune* has *20 tentacles* (others have 9–11, usually 10); tube feet contractile in 8 broad bands, a few scattered in between. To 6 in. (150 mm). Deposits scarce, *tables.* In gravel or under stones, Gulf of Maine to Newfoundland; erratic but perhaps more common northward. (2) *Stereoderma unisemita* is covered with tube feet above, has a double row *below* with a bare strip on each side. To about 2 in. (50 mm). Deposits numerous, *buttons* or *plates.* Offshore on sandy bottoms, Long Island to Newfoundland; not common. (3) *Pentamera pulcherrima,* a southern sand-colored species, has 5 rows of noncontractile feet; to 2 in. (50 mm). Deposits numerous, *plates* and *tables.* Lives in U-shaped tubes in mud; also reported from old oyster beds. Cape Cod to Caribbean, but erratic north of Cape Hatteras; washes ashore. Family Phyllophoridae. (4) *Thyonella gemmata,* also southern, even rarer, has 5 rows of tube feet, a few scattered in between. To 6 in. (150 mm). Deposits are *cups* and *buttons,* no plates. Mainly south of Cape Hatteras.

Where found: Cape Cod north to Arctic, from lower intertidal zone and cold tide pools to subtidal down to more than 1000 ft. (300 m).

Remarks: This is probably the commonest, certainly the most conspicuous, sea cucumber on the New England coast; abundant in rock crevices where it adheres strongly with its tube feet. Though normally rather firm-bodied, it becomes flaccid out of water and is as changeable in shape as most sea cucumbers. Said to be delicious boiled but its appearance offers little culinary inducement.

Family: Cucumariidae, including *Duasmodactyla, Stereoderma,* and *Thyonella.*

SYNAPTAS *Leptosynapta* species   **Pl. 46**

Identification: Wormlike; fragile and transparent, *without* tube feet. 12 *pinnate* tentacles, each with 2–8 pairs of opposing branches. Deposits are *anchors* and *anchor plates* (see Fig. 42 opp. Plate 46).

2 species. (1) Pink Synapta, *L. roseola,* is rosy pink to deep red and tentacles have 2–3 (sometimes 4) pairs of branches. To 4 in. long by $\frac{1}{4}$ in. in diameter (100 x 6 mm). (2) White Synapta, *L. tenuis* (not shown) is white to pink; tentacles usually have 5–8 pairs of branches but may have as few as 3. To 6 x $\frac{3}{8}$ in. (150 x 9 mm). Positive identification requires dissection: radial plate of esophageal ring (an internal circle of ossicles around the gullet) has a hole in *tenuis,* a notch in *roseola;* see Fig. 69.

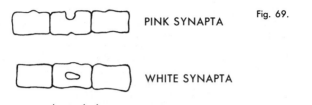

PINK SYNAPTA   Fig. 69.

WHITE SYNAPTA

esophageal plates

Similar species: (1) Silky Cucumber (Plate 46) has *peltate* tentacles. (2) Compare with burrowing sea anemones (Plate 47).
Where found: (1) Pink Synapta, Bay of Fundy to L.I. Sound; locally common in coarse sand or gravel or under stones. (2) White Synapta, whole coast, also Pacific coast and Europe; usually in sand but habitat varies from soft mud to coarse gravel and stones. Lower intertidal to subtidal down to more than 600 ft. (180 m).
Remarks: Synaptas live in depressions under rocks and in holes. Look for a mound with about a $\frac{1}{4}$-in. (6 mm) hole; you may find synaptas with their tentacles extended, vacuuming the surface for fragments of edible debris. When handled, the anchorlike skin deposits snag on fingers and are pulled free of the body wall. Like many "worms," synaptas have the distressing habit of breaking into pieces when disturbed; probably only front ends regenerate.
Family: Synaptidae.

SILKY CUCUMBER *Chiridota laevis*   **Pl. 46**
Identification: Wormlike, finger-shaped; *without* tube feet. 12 *peltate* tentacles — palmlike with 10 radiating digits. Smooth, translucent, pinkish to pale peach-colored. To 6 in. (150 mm). Deposits are 6-spoked *wheels,* localized in papillae.
Similar species: Synaptas (Plate 46) have *pinnately* branching tentacles.
Where found: Cape Cod to Arctic; under stones and in rocky pools, subtidal from shallow water down to 200 ft. (60 m).
Family: Chiridotidae.

RAT-TAILED CUCUMBER *Caudina arenata*   **Pl. 46**
Identification: Body short, plump, with a *tail* about $\frac{1}{3}$ body length. No tube feet; 15 tentacles, each with 4 short digits. Pinkish to purplish. To 7 in. (175 mm) or more.
Similar species: *Molpadia oolitica* (not shown) is *blackish* due to special deposits called *phosphate bodies.* Found in the Gulf of Maine and southward in deep water — usually more than 200 ft. (60 m). Family Molpadiidae.

Where found: Gulf of St. Lawrence to R.I.; lower intertidal northward, and subtidal down to 50 ft. (15 m).
Remarks: Most cucumbers "breathe" through their rear ends; this species, a burrower in sand or mud, leaves the end of its tail exposed for this purpose.
Family: Caudinidae.

Sea Urchins and Sand Dollars:
Class Echinoidea

Skeleton consists of close-fitting calcareous plates forming a rigid *test;* body globular to disklike, covered with fine to coarse, movable spines. Typical 5-part plan sometimes modified towards bilateral symmetry with obvious front–rear, left–right organization. Tube feet in bands, protruding through tiny pores; pore pattern useful in identification (see Plate 62). Sea urchin tests have a large central opening above for the anus (*periproct*) and another below for the mouth (*peristome*). In Sand Dollars the peristome is at center below, periproct at disk margin. Peristome and periproct are at front and rear respectively in bilateral echinoids.

PURPLE SEA URCHIN *Arbacia punctulata*   **Pl. 62**
  Identification: Spine length equals about $\frac{1}{2}$ test width, those on underside *spatulate-tipped;* periproct with 4 (rarely 3 or 5) plates. Purplish to rusty brown. To 2 in. (50 mm) test diameter.
  Similar species: Green Sea Urchin (Plate 62) has shorter spines, periproct with many small plates; shoreline ranges do not overlap. To distinguish tests see Fig. 47 opp. Plate 62.
  Where found: Cape Cod to West Indies. Erratically and locally abundant north of Cape Hatteras, appearing and disappearing unpredictably. Near jetties or pilings in lower intertidal zone, and on sandy to cobbly bottoms or oyster beds subtidally down to almost 700 ft. (210 m).
  Remarks: An omnivorous feeder on seaweeds, sedentary invertebrates, and dead animals of any kind.
  Family: Arbaciidae.

GREEN SEA URCHIN   **Pl. 62**
Strongylocentrotus droebachiensis
  Identification: Spine length equals *no more than* $\frac{1}{3}$ test width; periproct with many *small plates* (or 1 large and several small plates in young). Mostly greenish. To 3 in. (75 mm) test diameter.
  Similar species: See Purple Sea Urchin (Plate 62).
  Where found: The most common tide-pool sea urchin of the

New England coast. Arctic south to Cape Cod and in deeper water to N.J. To more than $\frac{1}{2}$ mile (792 m) deep.

Remarks: Despite their prickly coverings, sea urchins are eaten by cod and other fishes, sea stars, and along the shore by foxes, sea birds, and people. Sea otters eat this species on the Pacific Coast.

Family: Strongylocentrotidae.

SAND DOLLAR *Echinarachnius parma*   **Pl. 62**
Identification: A *flat* echinoid; test almost round with a 5-petaled pattern of tiny holes; bleaches white. In life with a feltlike coating of fine spines; brownish, tinted purple to red; sometimes distinctly patterned with darker petals and large marginal spots. To 3 in. (75 mm) diameter.

Similar species: Keyhole Urchin, *Mellita quinquiesperforata* (Plate 62) has 5 slitlike *holes;* in life light- to golden-brown tinged with green; tests bleach whitish. To 3 in. (75 mm) or more. A southern species; test common on ocean beaches south of Cape Hatteras, locally north to eastern shore of Va.; old records show Keyhole Urchins north to L.I. Sound and Cape Cod. Family Mellitidae.

Where found: Labrador to N.J. Mostly subtidal to more than $\frac{1}{2}$ mile (792 m) deep on sand bottoms, but also in lower intertidal zone (especially northward) in bays and on ocean beaches.

Remarks: Sand Dollars shuffle through loose sand, feeding on diatoms and other microorganisms. Flounders and other bottom fishes, in turn, feed on them. Color highly soluble, stains indelibly.

Family: Echinarachnidae.

HEART URCHIN *Moira atropos*   **Pl. 62**
Identification: Egg- or heart-shaped; test very fragile, with 5 *deep* grooves. In life with a furry covering of fine spines, gray to brownish. To 2 in. (50 mm).

Where found: Mainly south of Cape Hatteras to the tropics, subtidal in shallow water buried in mud or sandy mud. Reported north to Chesapeake Bay offshore.

Family: Schizasteridae.

Sea Stars and Brittle Stars:
Class Stelleroidea

These 2 subclasses are easily distinguished. Tube feet of sea stars are in 2 or 4 rows in an *open groove* along underside of arms; those of brittle stars emerge from *tiny pores* in pairs on underside of each arm joint. In sea stars, base of arms and central disk merge, with the junction almost indistinguishable; sharply differentiated in brittle stars. Both subclasses have obvious radial symmetry and a skeleton of deeply imbedded limy plates (*ossicles*) usually obscured by surface spines, bumps, plates, or other ornamentation.

Sea Stars

Special descriptive terms include: *paxillae* — erect, columnar spines topped with granules or smaller spines and appearing as a mosaic of rosettes or blocks on top of disk and arms; *pedicellariae* — tiny pincerlike projections on upper surface; *madreporite* — a small plate near center of disk sometimes mistaken for an eye; it is perforated and connects with the water-vascular system. See Fig. 70.

Sea stars have no relation to fish — hence this name is preferable to starfish. All are predators; some have special tastes, others not. Measurements are given in terms of the radius (R), calculating from center of oral disk to tip of any full-grown arm. Subclass Asteroidea.

ASTERIID SEA STARS

Fig. 70.

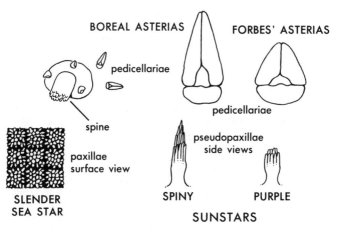

BOREAL ASTERIAS

FORBES' ASTERIAS

pedicellariae

pedicellariae

spine

pseudopaxillae
side views

paxillae
surface view

SLENDER
SEA STAR

SPINY

PURPLE

SUNSTARS

SLENDER SEA STAR *Luidia clathrata*   **Pl. 63**
  Identification: Arms slender; upperside with small blocklike *paxillae* in about a dozen fairly regular rows. Gray, blue-gray, or (less often) salmon to light brown; frequently with a fine, dark midline on each arm. R 3–4 in. (75–100 mm).

Where found: Cape Hatteras to Brazil. A common species off southern beaches, subtidal but often washed ashore. Occasionally northward to Va. and rarely to N.J.

Remarks: Lives buried in sand; feeds on other echinoderms, especially brittle stars.

Family: Luidiidae.

MARGINED SEA STARS *Astropecten* species   **Pl. 63**

Identification: These are handsome sea stars with distinct *upper* and *lower marginal plates.* Upper plates *without* conspicuous spines; lower plates with a fringe of spines. Upperside covered with paxillae. R 3-5 in. (75-125 mm).

2 species. (1) *A. americanus* (not shown), common north of Cape Hatteras, is confined to *deep water.* (2) *A. articulatus* occurs in shallow water but is uncommon northward. *A. americanus* is relatively stouter and has fewer large upper marginal plates; specimens with 3-in. (75 mm) radius have about 35 plates along edge of each arm; *A. articulatus* about 45. Additional species occur southward but are rare north of Cape Hatteras.

Similar species: (1) Other sea stars with distinct marginal plates occur in deep water. (2) See Mud Star (Plate 63).

Where found: (1) *A. americanus,* N.J. to Cape Hatteras. Subtidal in 150 ft. (50 m) or more; sometimes brought in by trawlers. (2) *A. articulatus,* Cape Hatteras to Uruguay, rarely north to N.J. This is a common *Astropecten* off southern beaches and sometimes washes ashore.

Family: Astropectinidae.

MUD STAR *Ctenodiscus crispatus*   **Pl. 63**

Identification: This northern sea star has distinct upper and lower marginal plates, *each with a flattened spine;* upperside otherwise covered with paxillae. Stiff; almost pentagonal in shape. Brownish yellow. R to 2 in. (50 mm).

Similar species: *Hippasteria phrygiana* (not shown) is somewhat similar in form but marginal plates have erect *beadlike* spines; upperside with beadlike spines surrounded by much smaller spines. Also with scattered, bivalved *pedicellariae* that look like little clam shells, easily seen with naked eye in larger stars or with a hand lens in smaller ones. Red with golden margin. R to 8 in. (200 mm). Arctic to N.Y., subtidal in 60 ft. (18 m) or more; often picked up by trawlers north of Cape Cod. Family Goniasteridae.

Where found: Arctic to Cape Cod and less commonly to N.C.; subtidal on mud bottoms at depths of 20 ft. (6 m) or more northward; deeper southward, to more than ½ mile (792 m).

Family: Goniopectinidae.

SUNSTARS *Solaster* and *Crossaster* species   **Pl. 63**

Identification: Commonly with 7 or more arms (usually 9-12 but up to 14). Surface bristles or prickles consist of bundles of fine spines on short stumps (pseudopaxillae).

2 species. (1) Spiny Sunstar, *Crossaster papposus,* has fewer and larger pseudopaxillae than next species and is *coarsely bristly;* usually 10–12 arms. Boldly marked in concentric bands of red, pink, whitish. R to 7 in. (175 mm). (2) Purple Sunstar, *Solaster endeca,* has upperside covered with *short, prickly* pseudopaxillae; usually 9–10 arms. Yellowish red to purple. R to 8 in. (200 mm).

Where found: Arctic or subarctic south to Gulf of Maine, and Purple Sunstar in deep water to Cape Cod — in about 120 ft. (36 m) at Chatham — or somewhat beyond. Common at scuba-diving depths in e. Maine; often found in lower intertidal zone from Eastport area northward.

Family: Solasteridae.

BLOOD STARS *Henricia* species   **Pl. 63**

Identification: These brightly colored little 5-armed sea stars have a fine granular covering of small, equal-sized spines; 2 rows of tube feet. Usually red or orange, sometimes yellowish to purple, or mottled. R usually 2 in. (50 mm) or less, but up to twice that northward.

The taxonomic status of the several Atlantic species has not been clearly defined; typical form shown.

Where found: Circumpolar; south on our coast to Cape Hatteras. Fairly common in tide pools and rocky shallows from Maine northward; subtidal southward in cold, deep water — 15 ft. (4.5 m) or more at R.I., 80 ft. (24 m) or more at N.J.

Remarks: Said to feed exclusively on sponges. Females brood their eggs and there is no free-swimming larval stage.

Family: Echinasteridae.

ASTERIID SEA STARS   **Pl. 63**
Asterias and *Leptasterias* species

Identification: 2 traits distinguish asteriid sea stars from others: Tube feet in 4 rows (2 rows in other sea stars); also, skin has tiny pincerlike pedicellariae (see Fig. 70, p. 259), scattered or in clusters, visible with a good 20X hand lens. Asteriids are rough-skinned with varisized spines; no distinct marginal plates or paxillae.

Genera differ in breeding habits but are not otherwise easily distinguished. *Leptasterias* broods its eggs, and there is no pelagic larval stage. *Asterias* has free-floating eggs and complexly metamorphosing young (see p. 61).

Species identification problematic. Forbes' Asterias, *A. forbesi,* the common species *south* of Cape Cod, has a bright orange madreporite; R to 5 in. (125 mm). Boreal Asterias, *A. vulgaris,* the common species *north* of Cape Cod, has a pale yellowish madreporite; R to 8 in. (200 mm). Both *Asterias* species vary in color through shades of olive, brown, yellow, orange, red, or purple, with paler spines; young may be almost white. Boreal Asterias is sometimes handsomely striped. Both species typically 5-armed, but abnormalities common.

Several *Leptasterias* species are listed for this coast, but only the following are likely to occur in shallow water. Slender Asteriid, *L. tenera* (not shown), 5-armed, more slender than the above *Asterias* species, with a whitish madreporite; R to 1½ in. (38 mm). Polar Sea Star, *L. polaris,* normally *6-armed,* greenish tan; R to 5 in. (125 mm).

Where found: Forbes' Asterias, Penobscot Bay to Gulf of Mexico, intertidal to subtidal down to 150 ft. (45 m). Generally replaced north of Cape Cod by Boreal Asterias, Labrador to Cape Hatteras; intertidal northward; south of Cape Cod subtidal in progressively deeper water to 2000 ft. (600 m). Slender Asteriid, Newfoundland to Va., intertidal from e. Maine northward; strictly subtidal southward, to 800 ft. (240 m). Polar Sea Star, Arctic south to New England, intertidal on north shore of Gulf of St. Lawrence but subtidal southward to 350 ft. (105 m).

Remarks: Species identification problems aside, these are the most familiar sea stars on this coast. *Asterias* species tolerate brackish water to salinities of 15–20‰. They are common in rocky tide pools and near jetties and pilings but also occur on sandy or stony bottoms. Though normally benthic, they can float free and drift on strong currents.

In L.I. Sound especially they are a menace on oyster beds; sea stars breed slightly before oysters and infant sea stars await oyster spat, quite literally, with open arms. They grow rapidly and arms may be 3 in. (75 mm) long by age 4 months. The oyster is opened after a tug of war and devoured by the sea star's everted stomach. Sea stars also eat other mollusks, barnacles, or almost any animal they can catch. Bottom-feeding fishes, in turn, eat them. Sea stars migrate to deeper water in winter. An active individual *could* travel a mile in about a week.

Family: Asteriidae.

Brittle Stars

The name is appropriate. Handle these fragile, secretive animals gently or they will be in pieces. They are faster crawlers than sea stars, and when uncovered, quickly begin moving their arms about, almost independently of one another, seeking a hiding place. Snaky movements justify an alternate name, "serpent stars." Look for them beneath rocks or other bottom debris, among seaweed holdfasts, or burrowing in sand or mud. Food consists of minute detrital particles and larger prey such as polychaete worms and small crustaceans. Subclass Ophiuroidea.

BASKET STAR *Gorgonocephalus arcticus*   **Pl. 64**
Identification: Arms *branching* repeatedly, outer parts forming a dense tangle. Disk naked with spines on 5 pairs of *radial
ridges* and scattered in between. Yellowish to brown. Disk to
$1\frac{1}{2}$ in. (38 mm) across, much larger in Arctic.
Where found: Cape Cod to Arctic; subtidal to more than
4000 ft. (1200 m). In our area at scuba-diving depths — 18 ft.
(5.4 m) or more — Bay of Fundy north. On a variety of bottoms,
often with Sea Whips.
Family: Gorgonocephalidae.

DAISY BRITTLE STAR *Ophiopholis aculeata*   **Pl. 64**
Identification: Each upper arm plate is *ringed* by a dozen or
more small scales, readily visible with the naked eye in large
individuals, with a hand lens in young. 5–6 arm spines, about as
long as arm width. Disk covered with fine, blunt spines and
large oval plates. Colors and markings extremely variable. Disk
to $\frac{3}{4}$ in. (19 mm), arms about $4\frac{1}{2}$ times longer.
Where found: Arctic south to Cape Cod and rarely to e. L.I.
Sound.
Remarks: This pretty species is our commonest brittle star.
Look for it exposed or hidden under rocks in tide pools in lower
intertidal zone. Ranges subtidally to almost 5000 ft. (1500 m)
deep.
Family: Ophiactidae.

SPINY BRITTLE STAR *Ophiothrix angulata*   **Pl. 64**
Identification: Spines 2–6 per arm segment, *glassy,* edged with
fine teeth, and longer than arm width. Disk has similar spines
on upperside. Colors and markings variable, but frequently with
light stripe lengthwise on top of each arm. Disk to $\frac{1}{2}$ in.
(12 mm), arms about 5 times longer.
Where found: Lower Chesapeake Bay (Tangier Sound) to
Brazil; subtidal at depths of 14 ft. (4.2 m) or more.
Family: Ophiothricidae.

SHORT-SPINED BRITTLE STAR   **Pl. 64**
Ophioderma brevispina
Identification: Easily recognized by the *7–8 short spines*
pressed to the side of each arm segment, projecting outward
somewhat more in young. Disk covered by fine granules. Mot-
tled or nearly uniform dull green, olive, or brownish to black.
Disk to $\frac{5}{8}$ in. (16 mm), arms about 4 times longer.
Where found: Cape Cod to Brazil in shallow water, typically
on muddy Eelgrass bottoms. Common on south shore of Cape
Cod and in L.I. Sound but apparently not elsewhere in our
range.
Family: Ophiodermatidae.

DWARF BRITTLE STAR *Axiognathus squamatus* **Pl. 64**
Identification: A small species, disk typically $\frac{3}{16}$ in. (5 mm), arms about 5 times longer — to almost 1 in. (25 mm). Use hand lens to see *scaly covering* of disk, and pairs of larger plates (radial shields) at base of each arm. 3 arm spines, fairly long and projecting. Gray or brownish with lighter spots; young have orange disk.

Similar species: Additional species with *scaly disk*: (1) *Ophiura robusta* (not shown) has *very small* radial shields, but is similar in other details; disk to $\frac{3}{8}$ in. (9 mm), arms about 3 times longer — to $1\frac{1}{4}$ in. (31 mm). Arctic to Cape Cod, mainly subtidal but also in lower intertidal zone from Bay of Fundy northward. A related Boreal species, *Ophiura sarsi* (not shown) is much larger, *red* in color, with big radial shields; subtidal at depths of 30 ft. (9 m) or more from Gulf of Maine northward. Family Ophiuridae. (2) Burrowing Brittle Star, *Amphioplus abditus* (Plate 64) has disk to $\frac{1}{2}$ in. (12 mm); arms *very long and slender,* 12–16 times disk length — 6–8 in. (150–200 mm). Radial shields *separated* by a narrow row of scales; brownish. Cape Cod south at least to mouth of Chesapeake Bay; burrows several inches in mud with 1 or more arms extending to surface. (3) *Micropholis* species (not shown) are also burrowers, reported from lower Chesapeake Bay southward; disk to $\frac{3}{8}$ in. (9 mm), with arms about 10 times longer — to $3\frac{3}{4}$ in. (94 mm). Disk scales very small with a *distinct bordering row;* radial shields may be *partly* separated by a wedge of scales. (4) Short-spined Brittle Star (Plate 64), not otherwise similar, may reveal scaly disk if covering granules are rubbed off.

Where found: Arctic to L.I. Sound and reported to N.J. Common (but easily overlooked) among stones and debris in large tide pools; subtidal on gravelly bottoms from shallow water down to more than 1000 ft. (300 m).

Remarks: The only brittle star in our range that broods its young; these emerge from brood pouches as tiny brittle stars.
Family: Amphiuridae, including *Amphioplus* and *Micropholis*.

Acorn Worms: Phylum Hemichordata

These wormlike animals are of great scientific interest because they may serve to link invertebrate and vertebrate phyla. Acorn worms have larvae very similar to a type found in the invertebrate phylum Echinodermata (see p. 253), but structural features, mainly in gill apparatus, also connect them to fishlike lancelets (*Branchiostoma*); lancelets are not actually bony but have a notochord which links *them* to bony fishes — and ultimately to man. The one common species of acorn worms in our range is atypical in that the larvae develop directly, without metamorphosis.

KOWALEWSKY'S ACORN WORM   Pl. 37
Saccoglossus kowalewskii

Identification: Soft-bodied, *easily fragmented.* Body 3-parted but not segmented and without appendages. Parts are: slender whitish *proboscis,* short orange *collar,* and a long, brownish, tapered *trunk.* To 6 in. (150 mm).

Similar species: Other little-known acorn worms (not shown) have a short proboscis and trunk with modified subregions. Occurrence of distinctive larvae in plankton indicates presence (possibly in deeper water) of other species both north and south of Cape Cod.

Where found: S. Maine south at least to Beaufort, N.C. Intertidal to subtidal at shallow depths; salinity as low as 19‰.

Remarks: Look for ½ -in. (12 mm) piles of *stringlike mud castings* at burrow openings on sand-mud flats. The worms are almost impossible to collect unbroken. U-shaped burrow has 2 openings; it may extend 8–14 in. (200–350 mm) underground. Worms often smell of iodine.

Family: Harrimaniidae.

Tunicates: Phylum Chordata

Invertebrate chordates, called tunicates, are classified in the same phylum as fish, mammals, and other bony animals but occupy a separate subphylum, Urochordata. The relationship is established by the presence of a supporting rod, the *notochord,* which is found in the tail of larvacean tunicates, the tadpole-like larvae of other tunicates, and the embryos of vertebrate chordates. Members of these groups also have a *dorsal nerve cord* and *gill slits* at some stage of development.

The name "tunicate" derives from the external covering, called a *test* or *tunic,* that encloses the animal. Usually the test has 2 openings, an incurrent mouth or *branchial siphon* and an excurrent *atrial siphon.* Inside, the body has 2 chambers separated by a partition pierced with rows of *stigmata* — the gill slits. Tunicates are filter-feeders. Plankters and detritus are collected on a mucus-producing *endostyle* in the branchial chamber, or *pharynx,* and conveyed into a digestive tract. Tunicates have a circulatory system and a rather simple nervous apparatus. Practically all are hermaphrodites, but self-fertilization is blocked in most cases by physiological obstacles. A few tunicates live in brackish water, but none in fresh water.

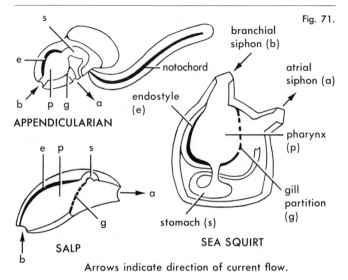

Fig. 71.

APPENDICULARIAN

s, e, b, p, g, a, notochord, branchial siphon (b), atrial siphon (a), endostyle (e)

SALP

e, p, s, a, g, b

SEA SQUIRT

pharynx (p), gill partition (g), stomach (s)

Arrows indicate direction of current flow.

Urochordata has 3 distinct classes: Ascidiacea (below), Thaliacea (p. 273), and Larvacea (p. 274).

Ascidians: Class Ascidiacea

Another name for this group is "sessile tunicates." Many of them live permanently attached to a substratum; others are free but immobile. Larvae are vaguely tadpole-like and planktonic. The class includes solitary and colonial forms.

Compound Ascidians

At first glance it may be hard to determine what colonial tunicates are. Their taxonomic status and even their animal nature are not immediately obvious. The individual animals (*zooids*) are quite small, to a maximum of $\frac{3}{16}$ in. (5 mm). Creeping Ascidian zooids (p. 269) resemble miniature sea squirts but are joined together by slender branches (*stolons*) and short stalks. Other species form colonies in which the zooids are imbedded in a common matrix; this varies from a thin film or crust to a thick rubbery mass. The zooids are often arranged in circular or oval groups or starlike *systems,* with individual incurrent siphons and a single, shared excurrent opening. Some ascidians have a matrix with imbedded,

calcareous *spicules* that differ from one species to another
(Plate 10); these are small, a few thousandths of an inch. Species
identification may require microscopic study of spicules and individual zooids, which must be carefully extracted from the matrix
with dissecting needles.

WHITE CRUSTS *Didemnum* species **Pl. 10**
  Identification: Colonies are *tough crusts* densely infiltrated
  with microscopic calcareous spicules. Zooid arrangement and
  apertures often obscure. White, less often yellow to reddish.
  Colonies extend 3–4 in. (75–100 mm); to $\frac{3}{16}$ in. (5 mm) thick.
  Sometimes encrusting and taking the form of bushy bryozoans
  or other supports.
    2 species, distinguishable by spicule sizes (microscope re-
  quired) and geographic ranges (below). *D. candidum* has spicules less than 0.02 mm; *D. albidum* 0.05 mm or larger.
  Similar species: (1) *Lissoclinum aureum* (not shown) is usually translucent gray or brownish but sometimes whitish due to
  greater concentration of spicules — 0.03–0.05 mm. Colony to
  $1\frac{1}{8}$ in. wide by $\frac{1}{4}$ in. thick (28 x 6 mm). Arctic south to Cape
  Cod but generally in deep water except at extreme northern
  limit of our range. (2) Note encrusting algae (p. 48), some of
  which produce calcareous crusts; also encrusting bryozoans
  (Plate 16), which have cell-like structure easily visible with hand
  lens.
  Where found: (1) *D. candidum,* Bay of Fundy south to Brazil
  (some uncertainty as to whether tropical and northern forms are
  the same species). Abundant on pilings and other substrata in
  lower intertidal zone on south shore of Cape Cod; evidently
  scarce elsewhere on our coast. (2) *D. albidum,* Arctic south to
  Cape Cod, but in shallow water only near northern limit of our
  range.
  Family: Didemnidae, including *Lissoclinum.*

GOLDEN STAR TUNICATE *Botryllus schlosseri* **Pl. 10**
  Identification: These tunicates begin life as *soft flat patches.*
  When mature, they may form *loose bloblike rolls and lobes.*
  Zooids tiny — $\frac{1}{16}$ in. (1.6 mm) — growing in rounded or lobed
  groups, or in the case of small colonies, somewhat starlike systems of 5–20 zooids. Color *extremely variable* even in same
  locality; often quite handsome with contrasting golds and
  purples or dark browns. Colonies to 3–4 in. (75–100 mm). No
  spicules.
  Where found: Boston (or less regularly, Bay of Fundy) south
  at least to Chesapeake Bay. Lower intertidal zone to subtidal at
  shallow depths and in estuaries to salinities of 18‰ or less.
  Sporadically south to Gulf of Mexico. Also in Europe, where our
  species may have come from on ship bottoms. Related species in

deep water north to Arctic and in shallow water in the Caribbean.

Remarks: This is our most conspicuous compound ascidian, common and often abundant *in summer* along most of the coast in bays and lagoons. Adheres to pilings, boat bottoms, Eelgrass, seaweeds, or almost any other reasonably firm substratum.

Technical details of zooid structure and development ally this species more closely with solitary styelid sea squirts (p. 271) than with other compound ascidians.

Family: Styelidae.

SANDY-LOBED AMAROUCIUM   Pl. 10
Amaroucium pellucidum

Identification: 2 traits ordinarily distinguish this species: Colony is usually coated and infiltrated with sand; also, it is composed of closely packed, cauliflowerlike lobes — $\frac{3}{16}$-$\frac{3}{8}$ in. (5–9 mm) long — radiating from a base. Lobes actually are zooid systems with common exit pore at top. Sand-colored, though zooids are partly orange-red. Colonies to 8 in. (200 mm) wide, $3\frac{1}{2}$ in. (88 mm) high.

Similar species: (1) *A. pellucidum* may easily be confused with *A. constellatum* (not shown). Colonies of *constellatum* sometimes form *coarse* lobes and may be crowded together, *usually without sand coating. A. pellucidum,* however, may also have some lobes enlarged and without sand coating. Zooids are similar but larvae are distinct. (2) See Sea Pork (Plate 10 and next account).

Where found: Cape Cod to Gulf of Mexico, but local and chiefly subtidal; reported north to Boothbay Harbor.

Family: Polyclinidae.

SEA PORK *Amaroucium stellatum*   Pl. 10

Identification: Colonies are *rounded, hard, rubbery lumps or slabs,* pinkish to white in color with brighter red or orange zooids in circular systems of 6–20. Spreading to 1 ft. (300 mm) or more; to 1 in. (25 mm) thick. No spicules.

Similar species: Additional *Amaroucium* species may sometimes require dissection and microscopic study, but often they can be identified in the field. (1) *A. constellatum* (not shown) is similar in color but *softer,* cushion- or turban-shaped, attached by a narrow base; sometimes in large crowded lobes (see preceding account). Usually the zooids are *irregularly* arranged rather than in neat circular or starlike systems; typically to 1 in. wide by $\frac{3}{8}$ in. thick (25 x 9 mm), in exceptional cases up to 3 times that size. Subtidal in shallow water from Isles of Shoals to lower Chesapeake Bay and at greater depths south to Gulf of Mexico. (2) *A. glabrum* (not shown), the common *Amaroucium* in e. Maine and northward, is *cap-shaped* with narrow base, well-separated zooids, and usually *gray* or *bluish*. Colonies to 1 in. (25 mm). In deep water off R.I. and Cape Cod, but in lower intertidal zone in Bay of Fundy and northward. (3) *A. pallidum* (not shown) is low and cushionlike compared to *A. glabrum;* usually *coated or infiltrated with sand*. Colonies to 1 in. (25 mm). Subarctic south to R.I., in deep water southward.

Where found: Reported north to Bay of Fundy but chiefly from Cape Cod to Gulf of Mexico; subtidal in 25 ft. (7.5 m) or more. Local, but commonly washed ashore where it does occur.

Remarks: It is hard to believe that the pink blubbery chunks of Sea Pork found on beaches are live animals; they are, and sharks, skates, and other bottom-feeding fishes eat them. Common on south shore of Cape Cod and nearby islands, evidently rare or absent southward, but abundant again on some Carolina beaches. *A. constellatum* is a more common *Amaroucium* on the intervening coast.

Family: Polyclinidae.

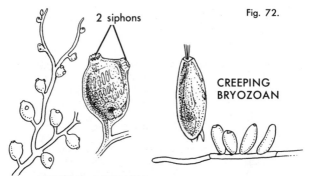

Fig. 72.

2 siphons

CREEPING BRYOZOAN

CREEPING ASCIDIAN
a colonial tunicate

CREEPING ASCIDIAN   Fig. 72
Perophora viridis

Identification: *Colonies* have zooids up to ⅛ in. (3 mm) *on short stalks* branching from a *creeping stolon*. Nearly transparent to greenish. May extend several inches over rocks, pilings, or other firm substratum.

Similar species: Do not confuse with hydroids or bryozoans (Plates 13, 14, 15) which have tentacles; Creeping Ascidian has 2 short siphons visible with hand lens.

Where found: Cape Cod to Fla.; lower intertidal zone to sub-

tidal at shallow depths, mainly in estuarine waters.
Family: Perophoridae.

Sea Squirts

Sooner or later most shore visitors will encounter sea squirts. These animals have grape-, walnut-, or vase-shaped bodies with 2 short projecting spouts. Prodding them usually provokes the ejection of a short spurt of water — hence the name. The siphons can be partially retracted, but for species identification should be observed when they are extended. Most of the shallow-water sea squirts are fairly distinctive *except* the various molgulids (p. 272), which must be dissected and studied with a microscope.

SEA VASE *Ciona intestinalis*   **Pl. 17**
  Identification: Test *tall* and *slender; transparent* whitish or yellow with 5–7 conspicuous muscle bands on each side. Siphons dissimilar, one 8-lobed, other 6-lobed. To 2½ in. (62 mm) or more. One of our most elegant sea squirts.
  Where found: Arctic south to Cape Cod, rarely to R.I., but worldwide in colder water due to accidental transport. In shallow water on pilings and the like.
  Family: Cionidae.

CALLUSED SEA SQUIRT *Ascidia callosa*   **Not shown**
  Identification: Test *tough, smooth* except in older, encrusted individuals; commonly attached by its left side. Siphons dissimilar, one 8-lobed, other 6-lobed; not very prominent and widely separated — one near one end, the other well down on the side. Translucent and colorless to opaque brown. To 3½ in. (88 mm) in Arctic; only half that size at its southern limit.
  Similar species: (1) *A. prunum* (not shown) is confined to deep water; can only be distinguished by dissection. (2) Compare with Sea Grapes (Plate 17) which have one siphon 6-lobed, other 4-lobed, or Blood Drop Sea Squirt (Plate 17) which has both siphons 4-lobed and is bright red.
  Where found: Arctic south to Cape Cod; lower intertidal zone in n. Bay of Fundy, subtidal southward.
  Family: Ascidiidae.

BLOOD DROP SEA SQUIRT *Dendrodoa carnea*   **Pl. 17**
  Identification: In color and form this small ascidian does indeed resemble a drop of blood; both siphons low, squarish (4-lobed). To ⅜ in. (9 mm).
  Similar species: *D. grossularia* (not shown), only distinguishable by microscopic dissection, replaces *D. carnea* from Gulf of St. Lawrence northward.
  Where found: L.I. Sound to Newfoundland. From lower inter-

tidal zone to subtidal down to more than 200 ft. (60 m) on stones and shells.

Family: Styelidae.

ROUGH SEA SQUIRT *Styela partita* **Pl. 17**
Identification: An unprepossessing sea squirt, rough and gristly; often growing in untidy crowded clumps. *Both* siphons squarish or *4-lobed* but obscure when contracted amid lumps and wrinkles of test; siphons sometimes *striped*. To $1\frac{1}{8}$ in. (28 mm).
Similar species: Compare with Sea Grapes (Plate 17) which have siphons *dissimilar,* and, though often encrusted with sand or debris, are relatively smooth when cleaned off.
Where found: Bay of Fundy to Caribbean. Distribution puzzling; it is common on pilings on south shore of Cape Cod and into L.I. Sound but not elsewhere in our range. Not reported from Delaware or Chesapeake bays. South of Cape Hatteras (at Beaufort, N.C.) *S. plicata,* a larger relative with boldly striped siphons, is common on jetties.
Family: Styelidae.

CACTUS SEA SQUIRT *Boltenia echinata* **Pl. 17**
Identification: Easily recognized by its covering of short bristly columns; resembles a cactuslike cushion. General color may be dull, earthy, but siphons bright red. To $1\frac{3}{8}$ in. (34 mm) in Arctic, $\frac{1}{4}$–$\frac{1}{2}$ in. (6–12 mm) on our coast.
Where found: Arctic south to Cape Cod, rarely beyond. From lower intertidal zone to subtidal at shallow depths.
Family: Pyuridae.

STALKED SEA SQUIRT *Boltenia ovifera* **Pl. 17**
Identification: A very distinctive sea squirt with a *stalk* 2–4 times longer than body. Yellowish to bright pinkish or orangered. Body may be 3 in. (75 mm) or more long, usually much smaller near shore.
Where found: Arctic south to Cape Cod and rarely to R.I. Usually subtidal to great depths but sometimes in lower intertidal zone or washed ashore.
Family: Pyuridae.

SEA PEACH *Halocynthia pyriformis* **Pl. 17**
Identification: Yellowish-white to peach or orange-red color and *clean granular surface* distinguish this large northern sea squirt. Barrel-shaped; both siphons 4-lobed, but lower one smaller and often has lobes partly fused to form a cleft-shaped opening. To $2\frac{1}{2}$ in. (62 mm), but often only half that size, and in far North to 5 in. (125 mm).
Where found: Subarctic to Massachusetts Bay, uncommon

south of e. Maine. Usually subtidal in 20 ft. (6 m) or more but sometimes in shallow water.

Family: Pyuridae.

SEA GRAPES   Pl. 17
Molgula and *Bostrichobranchus* species

Identification: Test globular, *grapelike;* often so encrusted with debris as to obscure the animal's form. Siphons *dissimilar,* one 4-lobed, other 6-lobed.

2 *unattached* species (neither shown) *subtidal* in or on sand or mud. (1) *Bostrichobranchus pilularis* has longish, *closely-spaced* siphons; usually mud-covered but base of siphons encircled by a narrow, naked band; commonly $\frac{5}{16}$ in. (8 mm), exceptionally to 1 in. (25 mm) or more. (2) *Molgula arenata* has short, *widely separated* siphons; test flattened; to $\frac{3}{4}$ in. (19 mm).

Several *attached Molgula* species, mostly smaller than $\frac{5}{16}$ in. (8 mm) and subtidal; positive identification may require dissection. Most common are the following: (3) *M. manhattensis,* the only large species south of Cape Cod, to $1\frac{3}{8}$ in. (34 mm). (4) *M. provisionalis* (not shown) is similar but smaller, to $\frac{1}{2}$ in. (12 mm), has more *widely separated* siphons, and is unknown south of Casco Bay. (5) *M. citrina* ranges south to R.I.; also has more widely separated siphons than *manhattensis;* positive identification requires dissection. To $\frac{5}{16}$ in. (8 mm), rarely twice that. Less common and also requiring dissection are (6) *M. siphonalis* and (7) *M. retortiformis* (neither shown), both Arctic species found in shallow water only as far south as upper Bay of Fundy; *siphonalis* up to 1 in. (25 mm), *retortiformis* commonly reaches $1\frac{1}{2}$ in. (38 mm) and in Arctic 3–4 in. (75–100 mm).

Similar species: Other sea squirts either have both siphons alike or have one 8-lobed, the other 6-lobed.

Where found: (1) *B. pilularis,* whole coast but scarce south of Cape Cod; subtidal in 6–700 ft. (1.8–210 m) or more. (2) *M. arenata,* Bay of Fundy to Cape May; subtidal in 15–75 ft. (4.5–22.5 m). (3) *M. manhattensis,* Bay of Fundy to Gulf of Mexico; intertidal to subtidal in shallow water and to minimum salinity of 15‰. (4) *M. provisionalis,* Maine (Portland northward); shallow water, on Eelgrass beds. (5) *M. citrina,* Gulf of St. Lawrence south to Cape Cod, rarely to R.I. (6) *M. siphonalis,* Arctic south to Casco Bay; usually subtidal. (7) *M. retortiformis,* Arctic to Cape Cod; in deep water south of Bay of Fundy.

Remarks: *M. manhattensis* is the common sea squirt south of Cape Cod, growing on almost any firm substratum, and tolerant even of the foul water in New York Harbor. One of the few ascidians that lives in brackish water.

Family: Molgulidae.

Salps and Doliolids: Class Thaliacea

These are barrel-shaped, transparent, planktonic animals some-times joined in chains or clusters; hooplike muscle bands are conspicuous. Identification is complicated by extreme variability in some species. Solitary and aggregate forms may be quite different in body proportions, number and arrangement of muscle bands, and other details. Variations involve complex life histories, including alternation of sexual and asexual generations.

Asexual generations of salps produce chains of individuals, sometimes hundreds in one chain. These mature, separate first into groups, then divide into solitary sexual individuals (hermaphroditic but not self-fertilizing). Young develop within mother and are born as the 1st individuals of new chains. Doliolid life histories are even more complicated. Individuals in a salp chain are all alike, but colonial doliolids have individuals specialized in appearance and function: some are food gatherers; some (called "nurses") look after budding chains whose members eventually mature as sexual individuals. *Their* offspring are free, tadpole-like larvae from which new colonies are budded.

There are perhaps 10 species of doliolids and 12 of salps, some poorly known or of dubious validity. They are mainly oceanic plankters. Because of these factors, it is not practical to do more than sample the group. As with other tunicates, the outer covering is called a *test;* see p. 265.

SALPS *Salpa* and *Thalia* species   **Pl. 33**

Identification: Test a *single chamber* with an oblique *gill bar.* 4–20 muscle bands, frequently grouped and converging in X's above. Mature salps range from less than $\frac{1}{16}$ in. (1.6 mm) to more than 8 in. (200 mm).

2 common species inshore. (1) *Thalia democratica,* solitary form has 2 strong hornlike projections at rear; 6–7 muscle bands. To 1 in. (25 mm). Aggregate form (not shown) lacks horns, has 5 muscle bands in 2 groups, the first 3 and second 2 converging above. (2) *Salpa fusiformis* (not shown), solitary form lacks horns, has 9–10 muscle bands, the last 2 forming an X above and first 3 also converging above; to 3 in. (75 mm). Aggregate form is spindle-shaped; has 7 muscle bands in 2 groups, first 4 and last 2 converging above.

Where found: Salps are chiefly warm-water, offshore plankters; rare north of Cape Cod and then usually in aggregate form. Though infrequent visitors inshore, salps may sometimes be found in abundance; more than a *bushel* of *T. democratica* was once collected in a 10-minute plankton tow in Delaware Bay. **Family:** Salpidae.

DOLIOLIDS *Doliolum* and related genera   **Not shown**
   Identification: Test chamber *divided* by a partition with many gill slits; 8–9 muscle bands, the 2nd through the 8th sometimes fused in 1 sheet. To $\frac{5}{8}$ in. (16 mm). 3 genera in our range.
   Where found: As with salps, these are chiefly warm-water Gulf Stream plankters. Occasionally driven inshore by wind and currents during the summer and fall.
   Family: Doliolidae.

Appendicularians: Class Larvacea

These minute plankters somewhat resemble the larvae of other tunicates in that they have a tail with that chordate trademark, the *notochord* (see p. 265). One end of the appendicularian body is a swollen mass containing the gonads; the tail emerges from *midbody*. Other tunicate larvae are more typically tadpole-like. The appendicularian drifts among plankton, ensconced within a fragile bubblelike "house" which the animal secretes and inflates around itself. The house has a pair of grid-covered windows, and water currents stirred by the animal's tail flow through them. Inside, the currents are directed through ultrafine cone-shaped nets that collect food items — mostly bits of detritus and flagellate algal cells smaller than 0.02 mm; the very existence of some of these cells or *nannoplankton* was unknown until studies were made of appendicularian feeding habits.

OIKOPLEURA *Oikopleura* species   **Pl. 33**
   Identification: Appendicularians with oval body and *pointed or rounded* tail. Body length of northern species is $\frac{1}{8}$–$\frac{3}{8}$ in. (3–9 mm) or more, southern species to $\frac{1}{16}$ in. (1.6 mm); tail $3\frac{1}{2}$–4 times longer.
   At least 5 species; identified by distribution of *subnotochordal* cells in tail musculature; microscope needed to distinguish between them. Typical form shown.
   Similar species: (1) *Fritillaria* species (not shown) have a more elongate *tripartite* body, *fork-tipped* tail; body to $\frac{1}{16}$ in. (1.6 mm); North Atlantic south at least to Delaware Bay. (2) *Appendicularia* species (not shown) also have forked tail but body is more oval-shaped; to $\frac{1}{32}$ in. (0.78 mm). Gulf Stream drifters. Both genera are in Family Fritillariidae.
   Where found: Whole coast. *O. labradoriensis* (and possibly *O. vanhoeffeni*) are mainly Boreal but south to Delaware Bay in winter–spring. *O. longicauda* and *O. fusiformis* are Gulf Stream plankters. *O. dioica* is the most common species south of Cape Cod in late summer–fall; in salinities as low as 11.4‰.
   Remarks: It's a pity these incredible little plankters cannot be more easily studied; often they are quite common. 270,000

Fritillaria borealis have been caught in a single 10-minute tow off Delaware Bay, and *O. dioica* is a regular visitor (3000–5000 per cubic meter) in early fall. Netted appendicularians are rather tadpole-like. Handling usually destroys their houses. To see them intact, first make certain appendicularians are present in fair numbers by plankton net tows; then search for them by scooping up a jar of water and examining it with a bright, glancing light. The house may be the size of a cherry, or even larger, with a wiggling appendicularian within.

Family: Oikopleuridae.

Glossary
Selected Bibliography
Index

Glossary

THE TERMS included here are defined only as they are used in this book. Cross-references indicate drawings (figures and plates) or expanded definitions in the text. All terms are given in the singular form unless they are always used in plural.

Abdomen: In arthropods and some polychaete worms — the hindmost of 2 or 3 distinct body divisions.

Aciculum: In polychaete worms — a stiff internal bristle supporting a bundle of fine setae in the base of each foot, or parapodium (see Fig. 48, p. 165).

Acontia: In some sea anemones — threadlike internal structures protruded through small pores when the animal is severely disturbed (see Fig. 21, p. 95).

Annulated: Having ringlike segments, constrictions, or markings.

Antennal scale: In many shrimplike crustaceans — a scale, or spinelike projection, at the base of each antenna (see Fig. 58, p. 206).

Anterior canal: In many gastropods — a grooved or tubular projection of the shell aperture (see Fig. 27, p. 125).

Apex: Tip or projecting summit of any structure.

Avicularium: In some bryozoans — a small pincer- or beak-like structure used to prevent fouling organisms from attaching themselves to the colony (see Fig. 24, p. 111).

Axis: The main stem or center line of any structure.

Beak (or umbo): In bivalves — a projection near the hinge (see Fig. 31, p. 143).

Benthic: Living on the sea bottom, including all plants and animals that creep, crawl, burrow, or attach themselves to the bottom and to structures such as ships, buoys, and wharf pilings. Compare with **sessile.**

Biramous: Having 2 branches (see Plate 53).

Calcareous: Limy; made of calcium carbonate.

Carapace: In many crustaceans — a hood- or shield-like covering of head and thorax (see p. 205).

Carpus: In crustaceans — 3rd from last segment of a leg; a wristlike joint (see Fig. 58, p. 206).

Caudal rami: In some crustaceans — a pair of projections at the tail end (see Plate 53).

Cerata: In shell-less gastropods — leaf-, club-, or finger-like projections on the back (see Plates 44 and 45).

Chelate: Clawlike or having claws.

Chelifores: In some sea spiders — the first pair of appendages (see Plate 48).

Chitin: Skeletal substance of the shell or skin of arthropods; *chitinous* — made of such material.

Chondrophore: In bivalves — a spoonlike pit in the shell hinge (see Fig. 31, p. 143).

Cilia: Minute, movable, hairlike projections on internal and external body surfaces; present in most phyla, with arthropods a notable exception.

Cirrus: A finger-, tentacle-, or hair-like projection; cirri vary widely in different phyla (see Fig. 48, p. 165, Fig. 60, p. 214, and Plate 37).

Colonial: A collection of individuals *of the same species* living together and usually structurally joined; compare with **commensal.**

Columella: In gastropods — the central pillar or axis of the shell (see Fig. 27, p. 125).

Commensal: Organisms *of different species* living together and sharing benefits; compare with **colonial.**

Coxa: In arthropods — the basal segment of a leg (see Fig. 58, p. 206).

Crenulated: With a notched or scalloped margin.

Degenerate: A structure that has lost its original or main function as compared with the same structure in related animals.

Detritus: Fragments of dead plants or animals (of various sizes down to microscopic); a major food source for many animals.

Dextral: Right-handed, referring mainly to the common pattern of gastropod shell symmetry; opposite of **sinistral.**

Ephyra: The tiny 8-armed stage of young jellyfish (see Plate 34).

Epiphyte: A plant that lives on or attached to the surface of another; compare with **parasite.**

Epitoke: In some polychaete worms — a modified sexual swimming phase (see p. 174).

Eversible: Capable of being turned inside out or retracted.

Eyespot: A simple light-sensitive area or structure; see also **ocellus.**

Fascicled: In hydroids — stems bound or attached in bundles (see Fig. 14, p. 72).

Filiform: Threadlike.

Fouling: Growing on the surface of man-made structures or on other organisms; usually considered a nuisance.

Frond: In seaweeds — a leaflike form but lacking the complex internal structure of a true leaf.

Frontal teeth: In crabs — projections along the front of the carapace *between* the eyes.

Gnathopod: A crustacean appendage or leg modified for grasping (see Plates 51 and 52).

Gonophore: In hydroids — a sexual bud (see Fig. 14, p. 72).

Gonotheca: In some hydroids — a protective sac or capsule encasing a gonophore (see Fig. 14, p. 72; Plates 13 and 14).

Hydranth: In hydroids — the structure bearing the mouth and tentacles (see Fig. 14, p. 72).

Hydrotheca: In some hydroids — a protective cup or capsule encasing the hydranth (see Fig. 14, p. 72).

Holdfast: In seaweeds — an attachment at the base of the plant (see Fig. 6, p. 26).

Introvert: A structure that is capable of being either withdrawn or extended (see pp. 197 and 253 for examples in sipunculid worms and sea cucumbers).

Lappet: In jellyfish — an individual lobe on the scalloped margin of the bell or umbrella.

Ligament: In bivalves — the tough, rubbery, usually dark-colored part of the hinge that joins the 2 shells (see Fig. 31, p. 143).

Madreporite: In echinoderms — a porous plate through which the internal water-vascular system opens to the exterior. Often conspicuous in sea stars and mistaken for an eye (see Plate 63).

Manubrium: In some hydromedusae — a pendulous, clapperlike projection beneath the umbrella containing part of the stomach (see Fig. 15, p. 73).

Marginal teeth: In crabs — projections along the edge of the carapace *behind* the eye.

Midrib: In some seaweeds — a thickened central rib within the frond.

Nematocyst: In cnidarians — complex microscopic structures developed for injecting poison or snaring prey; the "sting cells" of jellyfish (see Fig. 13, p. 71).

Neuropodium: In polychaete worms — the main lower branch of each parapodium or foot (see Fig. 48, p. 165).

Neurosetae: In polychaete worms — bristles on the neuropodium; see preceding.

Notopodium: In polychaete worms — the main upper branch of each parapodium or foot (see Fig. 48, p. 165).

Notosetae: In polychaete worms — bristles on the notopodium; see preceding.

Ocellus: A simple eye or eyespot.

Octant: In jellyfish — one of the 8 segments that form the bell or umbrella.

Operculum: A lid or flap such as the horny or limy plate attached to the foot of many gastropods, used to seal the shell opening (see Fig. 27, p. 125).

Oral disk: In sea anemones — the top disklike structure with the mouth at center and a ring or rings of tentacles near the edge (see Fig. 21, p. 95).

Orbit: The cavity in which the eye is located.

Osculum: In sponges — an exit pore for water currents; usually larger than the ostium.

Ostium: In sponges — an entrance pore for water currents.

Oxea: In sponges — a type of spicule that is pointed at both ends (see Fig. 11, p. 64).

Pallial line: In bivalves — a scar on the inner shell surface marking the attachment of the shell-secreting mantle (see Fig. 31, p. 143).

Pallial sinus: In bivalves — an indentation in the pallial line (see Fig. 31, p. 143).

Palp: In polychaete worms — one of several types of sensory appendages on the head (see p. 165).

Papilla: A small bump or projection.

Parapodium: In polychaete worms — one of the lateral footlike appendages (see Fig. 48, p. 165). In sea butterflies — a winglike extension of the foot.

Parasite: An organism that lives on or within the body of another and is dependent on its host for food and shelter without giving any benefit in return; compare with **commensal.**

Paxilla: In sea stars — a columnar projection on the skin, usually somewhat flat-topped and covered with tiny granules or spines (see Fig. 70, p. 259).

Pedal disk: In sea anemones — the adherent foot of the columnar body, at the opposite end from the **oral disk** (see Fig. 21, p. 95).

Pedicellariae: In some sea stars — tiny pincers on the surface of the skin (see Fig. 70, p. 259).

Pelagic: Plants and animals that are free-floating and drift passively as part of the *plankton,* or are strong active swimmers called *nekton;* opposite of **benthic** (see p. 19).

Peduncle: In hydromedusae — the stalk attaching the stomach to the underside of the bell or umbrella; see also **manubrium.**

Periostracum: In shelled mollusks — a skinlike outer covering on the shell.

Plankton: Pelagic organisms, free-floating and carried by waves and currents.

Prehensile: Adapted for grasping.

Proboscis: A snout or trunk, with distinct structural peculiarities in different phyla (see especially the various worms: nemerteans, p. 103; priapulids, p. 109; annelids, p. 165; echiurids, p. 199; and acorn worms, p. 264).

Prostomium: In polychaete worms — the front part of the head (see p. 165).

Radial canal: In hydromedusae — a fine spokelike tube radiating from the stomach to the ring canal which encircles the margin of the umbrella (see Fig. 15, p. 73).

Radial ribs: In bivalves — ridges on the outer surface of the shell radiating from the beak (see Plate 26).

Radial symmetry: Spokelike arrangement of parts around a central axis as in jellyfish, sea stars, and so forth.

Rhinophore: In shell-less gastropods — the hindmost pair of tentacles on the head (see Plates 14 and 15).

Rostrum: In shrimps — the bladelike projection between the eyes (see Fig. 58, p. 206).

Seine: (n.) A type of fish net (such as a bait seine or purse seine). (v.) To use this type of net.

Sessile: Attached or stationary; compare with **benthic.**

Setae: Bristles, especially of annelid worms (see for example **notosetae** and **neurosetae**).

Sinistral: Left-handed, referring mainly to the less common pattern of gastropod shell symmetry; opposite of **dextral** (see p. 124; also, compare the position of the shell opening in Black Triphora, Plate 21, with other shells on the plate).

Siphon: A tube. Bivalves usually have an *incurrent* siphon and an *excurrent* siphon for carrying water in and out of the body (see Fig. 31, p. 143). In tunicates these are called *branchial* and *atrial* siphons, respectively (see Fig. 71, p. 266).

Spicule: Needlelike or granular, usually microscopic structures buried within the skin of octocorals and some colonial tunicates (see Plate 10) or forming the skeleton of sponges (see Fig. 11, p. 64). Similar structures in the skin of sea cucumbers are called *deposits.*

Style: In sponges — a type of spicule that is pointed at one end, rounded at the other (see Fig. 11, p. 64, which includes 2 subtypes: *tylostyle* with one end knobbed, and *acanthostyle* with spines).

Stipe: In seaweeds — the stalk or stem (see Fig. 6, p. 26).

Stolon: In colonial animals — a creeping vinelike structure along which individual zooids develop (see Plates 13 and 14).

Subchelate: In crustaceans — a weak or somewhat imperfectly formed claw (see Plate 54).

Suture: A line of union along which 2 immovable parts meet.

Telson: In crustaceans — the last abdominal segment (see Fig. 58, p. 206, and Plate 53).

Test: A hardened outer shell or covering (see Plate 62).

Thallus: In seaweeds—the whole plant (see Fig. 6, p. 26).

Thorax: In arthropods — one of 3 body divisions (see p. 205).

Trawl: (n.) A large conical fishing net, commonly towed across the sea bottom. (v.) To use a trawl.

Trochophore: A microscopic larval stage common to many invertebrates (see Fig. 10, p. 61).

Tubercle: A small bump, slightly larger than a papilla.

Tube feet (podia): In echinoderms — tiny, tubular, suction-cup-tipped extensions of the internal water-vascular system; used for locomotion and feeding.

Tylote: In sponges — a type of spicule with a similar knob at both ends (see Fig. 11, p. 64).

Umbilicus: In shelled gastropods — a sometimes conspicuous dent or hollow at the base of the columella (see Fig. 27, p. 125).

Uniramous: Having a single branch.

Uropods: In crustaceans — the terminal pair of abdominal appendages (see p. 206).

Valve: In mollusks — one of the parts of the shell: bivalves have 2 (hinged together); gastropods have 1; chitons have 8.

Velum: A veil-like membrane. In hydromedusae — the curtain-like ring on the underside of the umbrella (see Fig. 15, p. 73).

Veliger: A molluscan larval stage roughly equivalent to the trochophore stage of other phyla, characterized by one or more veil-like swimming lobes (see Fig. 10, p. 61).

Vesicle: A small cavity or sac.

Whorl: A circular arrangement of parts. In gastropods — one turn of the shell; the *body whorl* houses the snail; additional whorls make up the shell's spire (see Fig. 27, p. 125).

Zoea: A crustacean larval stage, especially of crabs or crablike forms (see Plate 34).

Zooecium: In bryozoans — the sac- or box-like chamber in which the animal (zooid) lives.

Zooid: In colonial animals — one of the individuals of the colony.

Selected Bibliography

THERE ARE only a few "popular" summaries of the vast (and continually growing) store of information that is available about seashore plants and animals. The most useful references consist of taxonomic monographs and technical papers, faunal and floral checklists, and ecological reports. This literature is both voluminous and scattered, much of it in specialized journals and other publications with limited circulation. Some of the material is, of course, quite technical, but a lot of it is not beyond the understanding of anyone with a strong interest. A more difficult problem is gaining access to publications that may only be available in large university or museum libraries. The persistent student can solve this problem with the help of interlibrary loans or photocopies of needed publications.

In my *Guide to Identification of Marine and Estuarine Invertebrates,* fairly extensive bibliographies are given for the different animal groups, but even these lists are necessarily selective and were intended partly to provide access to still more books and papers. The list that follows is much more severely restricted; I have included what seem to be the broadest treatments available, with special emphasis on publications that postdate the *Guide* cited above.

General References

Arnold, Augusta F. 1968. The sea-beach at ebb-tide. New York: Dover.

Carson, Rachel. 1955. The edge of the sea. Boston: Houghton Mifflin.

Gibbons, Euell. 1964. Stalking the blue-eyed scallop. New York: David McKay.

Gosner, Kenneth L. 1971. Guide to identification of marine and estuarine invertebrates. New York: Wiley.

Hardy, Alister. 1971. The open sea: its natural history. Boston: Houghton Mifflin.

Jaeger, Edmund C. 1972. A source-book of biological names and terms. 3rd ed. Springfield, Ill.: Charles C. Thomas.

Knudsen, Jens W. 1966. Biological techniques: collecting, preserving, and illustrating plants and animals. New York: Harper and Row.

MacGinitie, G. E., and Nettie MacGinitie. 1968. Natural history of marine animals. 2nd ed. New York: McGraw-Hill.

Miner, Roy W. 1950. Field book of seashore life. New York: Putnam.

Richards, Horace G. 1938. Animals of the seashore. Boston: Bruce Humphries.

Robbins, Sarah F., and Clarice M. Yentsch. 1973. The sea is all about us. Salem, Mass.: Peabody Mus. of Salem and Cape Ann Soc. of Mar. Sci.

Southward, Alan J. 1967. Life on the sea-shore. Cambridge, Mass.: Harvard University Press.

Yonge, C. M. 1963. The sea shore. London: Collins–World.

Regional Lists

Anderson, J. M., et al. 1972–3. Checklist of the marine flora and fauna of the Isles of Shoals. Isles of Shoals, N.H.: Shoals Mar. Lab. Mimeographed.

Kirby-Smith, W. W., and I. E. Gray. 1973. A checklist of common marine animals of Beaufort, North Carolina. Beaufort, N.C.: Duke Univ. Lab. Ref. Mus.

Knowlton, Robert E. 1971. Preliminary checklist of Maine marine invertebrates. Res. Inst. Gulf of Maine, 1:1–11.

Saila, Saul B., ed. 1973. Coastal and offshore environmental inventory Cape Hatteras to Nantucket Shoals. Mar. Publ. Ser., Univ. Rhode Island, Nos. 2, 3.

Smith, Ralph I., ed. 1964. Keys to marine invertebrates of the Woods Hole region. Woods Hole, Mass.: Mar. Biol. Lab., No. 11.

Sumner, Francis B., Raymond C. Osburn, Leon J. Cole, and Bradley M. Davis. A biological survey of the waters of Woods Hole and vicinity. Bull. U.S. Bur. Fish. 31.

Wass, Marvin L., ed. 1972. A checklist of the biota of lower Chesapeake Bay. Va. Inst. Mar. Sci., Spec. Sci. Rept. 65.

Watling, Les, and Don Maurer. 1973. Guide to the macroscopic estuarine and marine invertebrates of the Delaware Bay region. Newark, Del.: College of Mar. Studies, Univ. Delaware.

Specific Groups

PLANTS

Dawson, E. Yale. 1966. Marine botany: an introduction. New York: Holt, Rinehart, and Winston.

————. 1956. How to know the seaweeds. Dubuque, Ia.: Wm. C. Brown.

Kingsbury, John M. 1969. Seaweeds of Cape Cod and the islands. Chatham, Mass.: Chatham Press.

Newton, Lily. 1931. A handbook of the British seaweeds. London: British Mus.

Petry, Loren C. 1975. A beachcomber's botany. Chatham, Mass.: Chatham Press.

Taylor, William Randolph. 1957. Marine algae of the northeastern coast of North America. Ann Arbor, Mich.: Univ. Michigan Press.

ANIMALS

PORIFERA

deLaubenfels, M. W. 1936. A discussion of the sponge fauna of the Dry Tortugas in particular and the West Indies in general, with material for a revision of the families and orders of the Porifera. Pap. Tortugas Lab. 30.

Hartman, W. D. 1958. Natural history of the marine sponges of southern New England. Bull. Peabody Mus. Nat. Hist., 12:x + 1–144.

Wells, H. W., M. J. Wells, and I. E. Gray. 1960. Marine sponges of North Carolina. Jour. Elisha Mitchell Sci. Soc., 76:200–245.

CNIDARIA

Calder, Dale R. 1971. Hydroids and hydromedusae of southern Chesapeake Bay. Va. Inst. Mar. Sci., Spec. Pap. Mar. Sci., 1.

Carlgren, O. 1949. A survey of the Ptychodactiaria, Corallimorpharia, and Actiniaria. K. Svenska Vetensk-Akad. Handl., vol. 1, no. 1.

Deichmann, Elizabeth. 1936. The Alcyonaria of the western part of the Atlantic Ocean. Mem. Mus. Comp. Zool., Harvard Univ. 53.

Field, L. R. 1949. Sea anemones and corals of Beaufort, North Carolina. Bull. Duke Univ. Mar. Stn. 5.

Fraser, C. M. 1944. Hydroids of the Atlantic coast of North America. Toronto, Ontario: Univ. Toronto Press.

————. 1946. Distribution and relationship in American hydroids. Toronto, Ontario: Univ. Toronto Press.

Hargitt, C. W. 1914. The Anthozoa of the Woods Hole region. Bull. U.S. Bur. Fish. Wash. (for 1912), 32:223–254.

Kramp, P. L. 1959. The hydromedusae of the Atlantic Ocean and adjacent waters. Dana Rept. 46.

————. 1961. Synopsis of the medusae of the world. Jour. Mar. Biol. Assn. U.K. 40.

Mayer, A. G. 1910. Medusae of the world. Hydromedusae. Vols. 1 and 2. Carnegie Inst. Wash., Publ. 109.

————. 1912. Ctenophores of the Atlantic coast of North America. Carnegie Inst. Wash., Publ. 162.

Parker, G. H. 1900. Synopses of North American invertebrates: the Actiniaria. Amer. Nat., 34:747–758.

Totton, A. K., and H. E. Bargmann. 1965. A synopsis of the Siphonophora. London: British Mus.

PLATYHELMINTHES

Hyman, Libbie H. 1940. The polyclad flatworms of the Atlantic coast of the United States and Canada. Proc. U.S. Natl. Mus., 89:449–493.

RHYNCHOCOELA

Coe, W. R. 1943. Biology of the nemerteans of the Atlantic coast of North America. Trans. Conn. Acad. Arts Sci., 35:129–328.

McCaul, W. E. 1963. Rhynchocoela: nemerteans from marine and estuarine waters of Virginia. Jour. Elisha Mitchell Sci. Soc., 79(2):111–124.

ENTOPROCTA AND BRYOZOA

Maturo, F. 1957. Bryozoa of Beaufort, North Carolina. J. Elisha Mitchell Sci. Soc., 73(1):11–68.

Osburn, R. C. 1912. The Bryozoa of the Woods Hole region. Bull. U.S. Bur. Fish. Wash. (for 1910), 30:205–266.

————. 1933. Bryozoa of the Mount Desert region. Biol. Surv. Mt. Desert Reg., 291–385.

————. 1944. Bryozoa of Chesapeake Bay. Chesapeake Biol. Lab. Publ., 63:3–55.

BRACHIOPODA

Dall, W. H. 1920. Annotated list of the recent brachiopods in the collection of the United States National Museum. Proc. U.S. Natl. Mus., 57:261–377.

MOLLUSCA

Abbott, R. Tucker. 1974. American Seashells. 2nd ed. New York: Van Nostrand Reinhold.

Morris, Percy A. 1973. A field guide to the shells of the Atlantic and Gulf coasts and the West Indies. 3rd ed. Boston: Houghton Mifflin.

ANNELIDA

Day, J. H. 1973. New Polychaeta from Beaufort, with a key to all species recorded from North Carolina. NOAA Tech. Rept. NMFS Circ-375.

———. 1967. A monograph on the Polychaeta of Southern Africa. London: British Mus.

Cook, David G., and Ralph O. Brinkhurst. 1973. Marine flora and fauna of the northeastern United States. Annelida: Oligochaeta. NOAA Tech. Rept. NMFS Circ-374.

Pettibone, Marian H. 1963. Marine polychaete worms of the New England region. Bull. U.S. Natl. Mus. 227(1).

SIPUNCULA

Cutler, E. B. 1973. Sipuncula of the western North Atlantic. Bull. Amer. Mus. Nat. Hist. 152(3).

ARTHROPODA

Pycnogonida

McCloskey, Lawrence R. 1973. Marine flora and fauna of the northeastern United States. Pycnogonida. NOAA Tech. Rept. NMFS Circ-386.

Cirripedia

Pilsbry, H. A. 1907. The barnacles contained in the collections of the U.S. National Museum. Bull. U.S. Natl. Mus. 60.

———. 1916. The sessile barnacles (Cirripedia) contained in the collections of the United States National Museum. Bull. U.S. Natl. Mus. 93.

Zullo, V. A. 1963. A preliminary report on systematics and distribution of barnacles (Cirripedia) of the Cape Cod region. Woods Hole, Mass.; Mar. Biol. Lab.

Cumacea

Calman, W. T. 1912. The Crustacea of the order Cumacea in the collection of the United States National Museum. Proc. U.S. Natl. Mus., 41:603–676.

Tanaidacea and Isopoda

Richardson, Harriet. 1905. Isopods of North America. Bull. U.S. Natl. Mus., 54:3–54.

Schultz, George A. 1970. How to know the marine isopod crustaceans. Dubuque, Ia: Wm. C. Brown.

Amphipoda

Bousfield, E. L. 1973. Shallow-water gammaridean Amphipoda of New England. Ithaca, N.Y.: Cornell Univ. Press.

McCain, J. C. 1968. The Caprellidae (Crustacea: Amphipoda) of the western North Atlantic. Bull. U.S. Natl. Mus. 278.

Mysidacea

Tattersall, W. M. 1951. A review of the Mysidacea of the United States National Museum. Bull. U.S. Natl. Mus. 201.

Euphausiacea

Hansen, H. J. 1915. The Crustacea Euphausiacea of the United States National Museum. Proc. U.S. Natl. Mus., 48:59–114.

Decapoda

Holthuis, L. B. 1955. The recent genera of Caridean and Stenopodidean shrimps (class Crustacea, order Decapoda, supersection Natantia) with keys for their determination. Zool. Verh. Leiden., 26:1–157.

Rathbun, Mary J. 1918. The grapsoid crabs of America. Bull. U.S. Natl. Mus. 97.

———. 1925. The spider crabs of America. Bull. U.S. Natl. Mus. 129.

———. 1930. The cancroid crabs of America. Bull. U.S. Natl. Mus. 152.

———. 1937. The oxystomatous and allied crabs of America. Bull. U.S. Natl. Mus. 166.

Schmitt, W. C. 1935. Mud shrimps of the Atlantic coast of North America. Smith. Inst. Misc. Colls. 93(2).

Williams, A. B. 1965. Marine decapod crustaceans of the Carolinas. Fishery Bull., U.S. Fish Wildl. Serv. 65(1).

ECHINODERMATA

Coe, W. R. 1912. Echinoderms of Connecticut. Bull. St. Geol. Nat. Hist. Surv., Conn., 19.

Clark, H. L. 1915. Catalogue of recent ophiurans based on the collections of the Museum of Comparative Zoology. Mem. Mus. Comp. Zool., Harvard Univ., 25:163–376.

Deichmann, Elizabeth. 1930. The holothurians of the western part of the Atlantic Ocean. Bull. Mus. Comp. Zool., Harvard Univ., 71(3):43–226.

Grainger, E. H. 1966. Sea stars (Echinodermata: Asteroidea) of Arctic North America. Bull. Fish. Res. Bd. Can. 152.

Gray, I. E., Maureen E. Downey, and M. J. Cerame-Vivas. 1968. Sea stars of North Carolina. Fishery Bull., U.S. Fish Wildl. Serv. 67(1):127–163.

CHORDATA

Van Name, W. G. 1945. The North and South American ascidians. Bull. Amer. Mus. Nat. Hist. 84.

Fraser, J. H. 1947. Thaliacea I–II. Family Salpidae and family Doliolidae. Sheets 9, 10:1–4. Fiches d'identification du Zooplancton. Conseil International pour l'Exploration de la Mer.

Index

THIS INDEX lists the scientific and common names of all the species discussed in this *Field Guide*. Numbers in **boldface** refer to illustrations. Obsolete and alternate names are also given; an *equals* sign directs the reader to the current or preferred name. The *see* cross references indicate species that are treated as "similar species" within a diagnostic text account and are not described separately anywhere in the guide. See *How to Use this Book,* p. 2, for a more detailed explanation of this system.

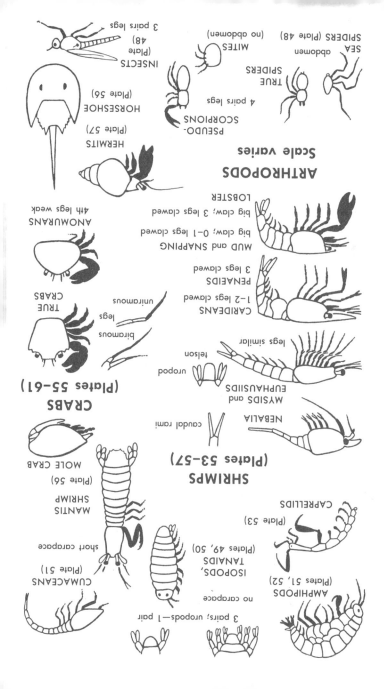

ARTHROPODS Scale varies

SEA SPIDERS (Plate 48)
abdomen

MITES (no abdomen)

TRUE SPIDERS

PSEUDO-SCORPIONS
4 pairs legs

INSECTS (Plate 48)
3 pairs legs

HORSESHOE (Plate 56)

HERMITS (Plate 57)

CRABS (Plates 55–61)

ANOMURANS
4th legs weak

TRUE CRABS

legs
biramous
uniramous

MOLE CRAB (Plate 56)

MANTIS SHRIMP
short carapace

CUMACEANS (Plate 51)

SHRIMPS (Plates 53–57)

LOBSTER
big claw; 3 legs clawed

MUD and SNAPPING
big claw; 0–1 legs clawed

PENAEIDS
3 legs clawed

CARIDEANS
1–2 legs clawed

legs similar

EUPHAUSIIDS
uropod
telson

MYSIDS and NEBALIA
caudal rami

CAPRELLIDS (Plate 53)

AMPHIPODS (Plates 51, 52)

ISOPODS, TANAIDS (Plates 49, 50)
no carapace

3 pairs; uropods—1 pair

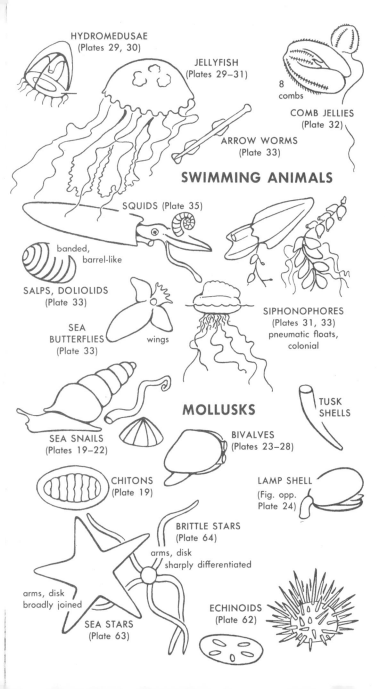

HYDROMEDUSAE
(Plates 29, 30)

JELLYFISH
(Plates 29–31)

COMB JELLIES
(Plate 32)

8 combs

ARROW WORMS
(Plate 33)

SWIMMING ANIMALS

SQUIDS (Plate 35)

banded, barrel-like

SALPS, DOLIOLIDS
(Plate 33)

SEA
BUTTERFLIES
(Plate 33)

wings

SIPHONOPHORES
(Plates 31, 33)
pneumatic floats,
colonial

MOLLUSKS

TUSK
SHELLS

SEA SNAILS
(Plates 19–22)

BIVALVES
(Plates 23–28)

CHITONS
(Plate 19)

LAMP SHELL
(Fig. opp.
Plate 24)

BRITTLE STARS
(Plate 64)

arms, disk
sharply differentiated

arms, disk
broadly joined

SEA STARS
(Plate 63)

ECHINOIDS
(Plate 62)